'Conceiving the post-Ottoman space less through hard borders than porous borderlands, and highlighting the interests of both local and colonial actors, Tejel and Öztan develop "regimes of mobility" into a percipient rubric for the mandate period. Framed by an astute introduction and afterword, eleven case studies trace how traders, nomads, priests and refugees negotiated customs controls, quarantine regulations and national churches amid competing notions and uses of territory. This is a timely study of both the disconnections and redirections that define eras of deglobalisation.'

**Nile Green, author of *Global Islam: A Very Short Introduction***
**Professor of History and Ibn Khaldun Endowed Chair in**
**World History, UCLA**

'*Regimes of Mobility* offers a much-needed historical perspective on the current crisis in the eastern Arab world, where states have collapsed and societies have shattered, and where the world's largest concentration of permanent refugees grows ever larger. Contrary to previous state-centred histories, these cutting-edge essays engage the bottom-up story of how Syria, Lebanon, Palestine, Transjordan and Iraq emerged as states, created by the League of Nations after World War I. Unlike older histories that assumed Europeans' unilateral power to define state borders, the scholars here demonstrate the agency of the ordinary people who occupied the many new borderlands. As they contested borders to demand Ottoman pensions, sell cars, stop the spread of germs, reorganise their churches and maintain tribal migration routes, civilians negotiated new "regimes of mobility" that defined limits to state sovereignty and the meanings of nation and citizenship. Out of these negotiations arose new social orders: winners who won privileges in the new states and losers who became vulnerable to displacement and violent oppression in future decades. This volume is an important contribution to multiple historical literatures on World War I, the interwar era in the Middle East, and the general study of refugees, forced displacement and borderlands.'

**Elizabeth F. Thompson, author of *How the West Stole***
***Democracy from the Arabs***
**Mohamed S. Farsi Chair of Islamic Peace, American**
**University in Washington, DC**

'This volume brings together a fantastic group of scholars whose top-notch articles, based on multilingual and transnational research, provide nuanced accounts of the emergence of Middle Eastern states and their boundary regimes. The articles skilfully incorporate the theoretical literature of global borderland studies with the emerging field of Middle Eastern borderland studies. Analysing striking episodes in global, regional and local contexts with an environmental lens, the brilliantly interlinked chapters in this volume present a complex analysis of how post-Ottoman states, boundaries, identities and ideas of belonging were built from the ground up and the outside in. Tejel and Öztan's volume is a must-read for those interested in the history of subaltern groups, territoriality, mobility, nationalism, and state and identity formation in the post-Ottoman and inter-war Middle East.'

**Sabri Ateş, author of** *The Ottoman-Iranian Borderlands:*
*Making a Boundary, 1843–1914*
**Associate Professor of History, Southern Methodist University**

'Departing from the premise that borders move as well as people and that regimes come and go, *Regimes of Mobility* is an outstanding contribution to what Europeans designated "Middle Eastern" historical studies. This highly readable volume also provides invaluable insights into processes of bordering, multiscalar networking, state-making, mobility, individual agency, and imperial hard and soft power.'

**Nina Glick Schiller, co-author of** *Migrants and City Making*
**Emeritus Professor of Social Anthropology, University of Manchester**

# REGIMES OF MOBILITY

*Borders and State Formation in the
Middle East, 1918–1946*

**Edited by Jordi Tejel and
Ramazan Hakkı Öztan**

EDINBURGH
University Press

Edinburgh University Press is one of the leading university presses in the UK. We publish academic books and journals in our selected subject areas across the humanities and social sciences, combining cutting-edge scholarship with high editorial and production values to produce academic works of lasting importance. For more information visit our website: edinburghuniversitypress.com

Edinburgh University Press Ltd
The Tun – Holyrood Road
12 (2f) Jackson's Entry
Edinburgh EH8 8PJ

Typeset in 11/15 Adobe Garamond by
IDSUK (DataConnection) Ltd, and
printed and bound by CPI Group (UK) Ltd, Croydon, CR0 4YY

A CIP record for this book is available from the British Library

ISBN  978 1 4744 8796 2 (hardback)
ISBN  978 1 4744 8798 6 (webready PDF)
ISBN  978 1 4744 8799 3 (epub)

European Research Council
Established by the European Commission

# CONTENTS

# FIGURES

# NOTES ON CONTRIBUTORS

**Alexander E. Balistreri** studied politics and Middle Eastern history in Wisconsin, Istanbul and Princeton. He currently serves as research associate (*wissenschaftlicher Assistent*) at the University of Basel's Programme in Near and Middle Eastern Studies, where he teaches on the modern history of Turkey, the Caucasus and the Middle East. His dissertation, defended at Princeton University in the summer of 2021, examines the governance of the contested borderlands around Kars. He has published on the political history of the Turkish Republic, the historiography of the Caucasus, and the Russian Revolution in *Die Welt des Islams*, *Kritika* and other venues.

**Lauren Banko** is research associate in the Department of History at the University of Manchester. She is an historian of the modern Arab Middle East and pre-1948 Palestine. Her first book, *The Invention of Palestinian Citizenship, 1918–1947*, was published in 2016 by Edinburgh University Press. Lauren received her PhD in Near and Middle East History from SOAS, University of London. She has held research and teaching positions at SOAS, the University of Manchester and Yale. Her current monograph project focuses on illicit mobility along Palestine's frontiers by refugees, displaced persons, labour migrants, orphans and other marginalised groups.

**Samuel Dolbee** is an environmental historian of the modern Middle East and a lecturer on History and Literature at Harvard University. He completed his MA in Arab Studies at Georgetown University and his PhD in History and Middle Eastern & Islamic Studies at New York University. His published work includes 'The Desert at the End of Empire: An Environmental History of the Armenian Genocide' in *Past & Present* and '"Impossible is Not Otto-man": Menashe Meirovitch, 'Isa al-'Isa, and Imperial Citizenship in Palestine' in *International Journal of Middle East Studies*. He is also the editor-in-chief of the Ottoman History Podcast.

**Robert S. G. Fletcher** is Professor of History and Kinder Professor of British History at the University of Missouri. He grew up in East Anglia and read Modern History at Magdalen College, University of Oxford. Before joining Missouri, he held positions as the Postdoctoral Research Fellow in Global History at Oxford, Lecturer in Imperial and Global History at the University of Exeter, and Reader in the History of Britain and Empire at the University of Warwick. Much of Robert's work has focused on the interwar Middle East; his first book, *British Imperialism and 'The Tribal Question': Desert Administration and Nomadic Societies in the Middle East, 1919–1936*, was published in 2015. Robert has been the Principal Investigator on several research projects supported by the UK Arts and Humanities Research Council, including *Science in Culture* awards on the international campaign against the desert locust in the twentieth century.

**Simon Jackson** teaches the global and colonial history of the modern Middle East and Mediterranean at the University of Birmingham (UK), where he is an Assistant Professor. His research, which focuses on France and its colonial empire in the Middle East and the Mediterranean, has been published in journals including *Humanity, Comparative Studies of South Asia, Africa and the Middle East* and *Contemporary European History*. His book, *Mandatory Development: French Colonial Empire, Global Capitalism and the Politics of the Economy after World War One*, is under contract with Cornell University Press.

**César Jaquier** is a PhD candidate at the University of Neuchâtel and the Université Lumière Lyon 2. Before starting his PhD, he studied at the University of Geneva and Saint Joseph's University. He has also worked in several research and archiving centres in Switzerland and Lebanon. His dissertation focuses on mobility, state formation and border-making in the interwar Middle East. It articulates a social, economic and political history of the so-called 'transdesert routes' that opened up between the nascent states of Lebanon, Syria and Iraq in the 1920s and 1930s with the expansion of motor transport.

**Reşat Kasaba** is Anne H. H. and Kenneth B. Pyle Professor at the Henry M. Jackson School of International Studies at the University of Washington, Seattle. His publications include volume four of the *Cambridge History of Modern Turkey* (ed.) and *A Moveable Empire: Ottoman Empire, Migrants and Refugees*. Reşat Kasaba was born in Turkey and completed his early education in that country. He received his PhD in Sociology from the State University of New York at Binghamton.

**Katharina Lange** is a social anthropologist who has done fieldwork in Syria and Iraq's Kurdistan region. In 2001 she received her doctorate and in 2018 her Venia Legendi (Habilitation) in anthropology, both from Leipzig University, where she also teaches. Lange has worked on Arabic anthropology, oral history, tribal belonging, the politics of resources and land use. She is a senior research fellow at Leibniz-Zentrum Moderner Orient, Berlin (ZMO) where she heads the interdisciplinary research unit *Environment and Justice*, as well as a research group investigating experiences of 'normality' and 'crisis' among Syrian immigrants to Germany. She is currently beginning a project on agrarian history in Syria.

**Norig Neveu** is a research fellow at CNRS and a member of the Institute of Research and Study on the Arab and Muslim Worlds (IREMAM). Her research first focused on social dynamics around holy sites in southern Jordan from the late Ottoman period. She is currently approaching a connected history of Christian and Muslim religious authorities in Jordan, Palestine and Iraq between the nineteenth and twenty-first centuries. She contributes to several research programmes on migration dynamics such as the Lajeh ANR and MAGYC (H2020). She has published several articles on sacred topographies, religious tourism and faith-based NGOs and charities in Jordan and Palestine. She co-authored with Philippe Bourmaud and Chantal Verdeil *Experts et expertise dans les mandats de la Société Nations: figures, champs, outils* (2020).

**Orçun Can Okan** is a junior postdoctoral research fellow in the area of Global History and Governance at the Scuola Superiore Meridionale (SSM) of the University of Naples Federico II. He received his PhD in History from Columbia University in 2020. Prior to his doctoral studies, Okan completed an MA in History (2013), a BA in History (2010) and a BA in Turkish Language and Literature (2010) at Boğaziçi University. His current work focuses on nationality and citizenship, imperial collapse and state succession in the aftermath of the First World War.

**Ramazan Hakkı Öztan** is Assistant Professor of History at the Atatürk Institute for Modern Turkish History at Boğaziçi University, Istanbul. He completed his PhD in May 2016 at the University of Utah and was a post-doctoral researcher at the University of Neuchâtel, where he worked in an ERC project on the borders of the interwar Middle East. He has published articles in *Past and Present, International Journal of Middle East Studies, Journal of Contemporary History* and *Journal of Migration History*. He has also co-edited with Alp Yenen *Age of Rogues: Rebels, Revolutionaries, and Racketeers at the Frontiers of Empires* (2021).

**Cyrus Schayegh** is Professor of International History at the Graduate Institute for International and Development Studies in Geneva, Switzerland; before this he was Associate Professor at Princeton University and Assistant Professor at the American University of Beirut. He has authored *Who Is Knowledgeable, Is Strong: Science, Class, and the Formation of Modern Iranian Society, 1900–1950* (2009) and *The Middle East and the Making of the Modern World* (2017); published articles in *The American Historical Review, Comparative Studies in Society and History* and *International Journal of Middle East Studies*, among other journals; co-edited *A Global Middle East: Mobility, Materiality and Culture in the Modern Age, 1880–1940* (2014) and *The Routledge History Handbook of the Middle East Mandates* (2015); and edited *Globalizing the U.S. Presidency: Postcolonial Views of John F. Kennedy* (2020).

**Laura Stocker** is a PhD candidate in the Department of History at the University of Neuchâtel. She works for a European Research Council funded research project titled 'Towards a Decentred History of the Middle East:

Transborder Space, Circulations, Frontier Effects and State Formation, 1920–1946' (BORDER), led by Professor Jordi Tejel. She has a BA in History and Near & Middle Eastern Studies from the University of Basel and an MA in Islamic and Middle Eastern Studies from the University of Bern. In her dissertation she examines Bedouin tribes, pastoral economy and modern practices of territorial governance in the Syrian-Iraqi borderlands in the period from 1920 to 1945.

**Jordi Tejel** is a Research Professor in contemporary history at the University of Neuchâtel. His main research interests are nationalism, minorities, borders and state formation processes in the Middle East. Since 2017 he is leading a ERC research project on the borderlands of the interwar Middle East. His books and edited volumes include *Syria's Kurds. History, Politics and Society* (2009), *Writing the History of Iraq: Historiographical and Political Challenges* (2012), *La question kurde: passé et présent* (2014) and *Les Kurdes en 100 questions* (2018). He has published in journals such as *Journal of Borderlands Studies, Iranian Studies, British Journal of Middle East Studies, Middle East Studies, European Journal of Turkish Studies* and *Ethnic and Racial Studies*. He is currently preparing a monograph on the Turkish–Syrian–Iraqi borderlands in the interwar period.

# ACKNOWLEDGEMENTS

This volume is the result of a two-day workshop held on 10–11 October 2019 at the University of Neuchâtel which brought together several scholars working on borders and mobilities in interwar Middle East. The workshop is part of a larger research project at the University of Neuchâtel, titled 'Towards a Decentered History of the Middle East: Transborder Spaces, Circulations, Frontier Effects and State Formation, 1920–1946' (BORDER). This project, as well as the publication of this volume on open access, is supported by the European Research Council (ERC) under the European Union's Horizon 2020 research and innovation approval Grant Agreement (No 725269). For more information, please visit https://www.unine.ch/border/home.html.

We would like to take this opportunity and thank our contributors who have made this volume possible; it has truly been a pleasure to work with them. We also thank the two anonymous reviewers whose feedback helped shape this volume. Maurus Reinkowski, Aline Schlaepfer, Mehdi Sakatni, Carl Shook, Adrien Zakar, Nadav Solomonovich, Nina Studer, Magnus Halsnes, Ellen Hertz and Jérémie Forney had participated in the original workshop and enriched the discussions, and Victoria Abrahamyan and Ramon Wiederkehr extended logistical support. Jasmine Soliman helped us secure the rights to the cover image and César Jaquier prepared the index.

We finally thank Nicola Ramsey and Emma Rees from Edinburgh University Press for their support from start to finish.

*April 2021*
*Jordi Tejel, Neuchâtel*
*Ramazan Hakkı Öztan, Istanbul*

# FOREWORD

## *Reşat Kasaba*

'A nation has borders, but the edges of an empire are frayed'.[1]

The articles in this collection have a precise historical focus. They explain the forces that shaped and sustained the borders that came to define the modern Middle East in the 1920s and the 1930s. But these essays are also relevant to our contemporary period because the early twentieth and early twenty-first centuries have some striking similarities. As such, learning about what went on in the 1920s and 1930s can help us understand what is happening today and perhaps even give us clues as to how we might avoid some of the pitfalls and move forward from our current predicament.

Like our own period now, the world had just come out of an era of intense globalization in the early twentieth century. The unprecedented increases in the movement of goods, money, people and information across continents in the nineteenth century had generated wealth on a scale not seen before. This wealth was concentrated in the hands of certain groups, which led to growing tensions that pit different regions and people against each other. At the same time, the world was experiencing major shifts in international relations marked with the relative decline of the British Empire and the increasing assertiveness of other European and Asian powers who were trying to expand their own regional and global influence, in competition with each other and with Britain.

---

[1] Jill Lepore, *These Truths: A History of the United States* (New York: Norton, 2018), 241.

These domestic and international tensions directly led to the First World War that killed and maimed millions and caused massive destruction across Europe and Asia. The First World War also unleashed the forces that led to the collapse of the Russian, Austria-Hungarian and the Ottoman Empires. Just as the war was ending, the world was shaken further by the global pandemic of influenza that killed millions of people. For all intents and purposes, what historians described as the long nineteenth century came to an end in the 1920s. Its replacement with a new order would take a global economic depression and another world war, both of which were yet to come.

In the Middle East, the 1920s witnessed the formal end of the Ottoman Empire and its replacement with nineteen states, most of whom were placed under the control of European powers. These borders would be further refined and consolidated during the interwar years and most of the states would gain their independence after the end of the Second World War, more or less within the borders that were drawn in the 1920s.

There is some truth to the often-repeated claim that the borders that came to define the modern Middle East reflected primarily the interests of Britain and France, the victorious powers of World War I. As soon as they were established, however, these borders became part of a wide array of social, economic and political relationships on the ground. Tribal leaders, merchants, Kurdish rebels, Armenian refugees, political leaders, landlords, peasants, nomads and workers had to position themselves in relation to both the global changes and the new fragmented reality of the post-Ottoman space. Depending on the circumstances, these groups ignored, avoided, resisted or adjusted to the new borders. As the articles in this collection show, the ultimate shape of the borders was determined to a large extent through these multifarious interactions among the many actors that were involved in this transition.

We know that ultimately those who adjusted their activities and priorities to the new borders subscribed to the ideologies of national homogeneity, and the political leaders who became champions of these new arrangements prevailed in the Middle East, as they did in other parts of the world. Damascus and Aleppo were cut off from their outlets on the Mediterranean; Kurdish tribes across Turkey's borders with Syria and Iraq were divided and separated from their kin; and port cities such as Izmir lost their commandeering place in the regional and global networks of trade. Those who tried to maintain their long-distance movements and connections, such as local merchants or the Kurdish and Bedouin tribes, did so at the risk of being targeted as smugglers, illegals or rebels by the newly empowered state authorities.

The transformation of multi-ethnic and multi-religious land-based empires into states with compact borders, each containing supposedly homogeneous peoples, was so prevalent that an influential body of literature asserts that nations are an inevitable step in the global march to modernity; *sine qua non* of success for all communities in the world. The articles in this book show, however, that this was a contingent transformation; shaped by several distinct processes.

While their consolidation took place in the twentieth century, the foundations for the new political structures in the Middle East were laid much earlier. Starting as early as in the eighteenth century, partly in response to the changes in the world, the Ottoman Empire took steps to shore up its institutions, settle its large nomadic populations and protect its borderlands. The Ottoman Empire and its successors continued these policies through the nineteenth and into the twentieth century. In addition to reform and reorganisation they also resorted to force, including campaigns of violence, genocide and compulsory relocation of millions of people to undo the relationships, networks and patterns of living that had characterised the region for centuries. The move towards well-defined national communities with clearly demarcated boundaries gained strength also with the spread of ideologies that extolled ethnic purity and solidarity while propagating fear of the 'other' who was deemed to be different from and incompatible with one's kin.

The long-term transformation of the economic and political relations in the world, the policies of the Ottoman state and its successors, the increasingly exclusive ideologies of nationalism and the particular conjuncture of the interwar years were all important in the emergence of the modern Middle East. However, each one of these factors had their distinct origins and it was their convergence in the 1920s that shaped the complex history that is presented in this collection. There was nothing predestined about this outcome. Furthermore, actual decisions made by real people, political leaders as well as ordinary individuals, ended up determining the path and shape of these changes.

Today we are faced with circumstances that resemble the 1920s in many ways. The economic expansion of the 1990s and early 2000s and the new industries and technologies of communication of the last twenty years have generated immense amount of wealth while transforming our lives in fundamental ways. Once again, this period of expansion has created deep inequalities and tensions, fuelling protest movements and creating demands for redistribution and political participation across the world. On a global level, the United States is being challenged by the rising power of China and the Covid pandemic has radically upended how we live, work and relate to each other. Finally, we are, once again, witnessing the growing prevalence of ideologies that emphasise the desirability of staying close to one's own and encourage indifference if not outright enmity to the fate of migrants, refugees, the poor and homeless; in short, anybody that is defined as being 'different'. Being able to look back at the early decades of the twentieth century with the hindsight of knowing what happened in the rest of that century gives us a unique advantage. In addition to learning the rich history that these contributions or chapters present, we can also use them as a guide as we try to make sense of and navigate our own uncertain world.

# INTRODUCTION: REGIMES OF MOBILITY IN MIDDLE EASTERN BORDERLANDS, 1918–46

## Jordi Tejel and Ramazan Hakkı Öztan

The First World War brought an end to what scholars have called the first wave of globalisation.[1] Since the 1850s the world had turned into a more connected place, as breakthroughs in transportation and communication technology compressed time and space in unparalleled ways, enabling faster travel and more condensed experiences of temporality.[2] In this age of steam and print, not only did ideas and diseases spread more easily across the world,[3] but also goods, capital and labour – all in all circuits of capital – penetrated

---

[1] For two prominent surveys on globalisation, see C.A. Bayly, *The Birth of the Modern World, 1780–1914* (Malden, MA: Blackwell, 2004); Jürgen Osterhammel, *The Transformation of the World: A Global History of the Nineteenth Century* (Princeton: Princeton University Press, 2014). For an analysis of the historical dynamics that shaped the first wave of globalisation during the long nineteenth century, see Kevin H. O'Rourke and Jeffrey G. Williamson, *Globalisation and History: The Evolution of a Nineteenth-Century Atlantic Economy* (Cambridge, MA: The MIT Press, 1999).

[2] David Harvey, *The Condition of Postmodernity: An Enquiry into the Origins of Cultural Change* (Cambridge: Blackwell, 1989), p. 240. See also David Edgerton, 'Creole Technologies and Global Histories: Rethinking how Things Travel in Space and Time', *Journal of History of Science Technology*, Vol. 1, No.1 (2007), pp. 75–112.

[3] Ilham Khuri-Makdisi, *The Eastern Mediterranean and the Making of Global Radicalism, 1860–1914* (Berkeley: University of California Press, 2010); Stacy Fahrenthold, 'Transnational Modes and Media: The Syrian Press in the Mahjar and Emigrant Activism during

well beyond coastal zones, reaching into interior markets and hence expanding chains of supply and demand.[4] What the Great War ultimately disrupted was this greater inter-dependence and connectedness – a shared reality that had increasingly defined the human condition since the second half of the nineteenth century.

This process of disruption was particularly contentious in the Middle East, where the First World War brought an end to the Ottoman rule and led to the partition of an empire that had been deeply entangled within various global circuits of mobility and capital.[5] As Britain and France sought to establish their own spheres of influence across this post-Ottoman space, the mandates of Syria and Lebanon, Iraq, Palestine and Transjordan were created,[6] while

World War I', *Mashriq & Mahjar*, Vol. 1, No. 1, (2013), pp. 30–54; James L. Gelvin, Nile Green (eds), *Global Muslims in the Age of Steam and Print* (Berkeley: University of California Press, 2014); Roland Wenzlhuemer, *Connecting the Nineteenth-Century World: The Telegraph and Globalisation* (Cambridge: Cambridge University Press, 2015); Liat Kozma, Cyrus Schayegh and Avner Wishnitzer (eds), *A Global Middle East: Mobility, Materiality and Culture in the Modern Age, 1880–1940* (London: I. B. Tauris, 2015); Houri Berberian, *Roving Revolutionaries: Armenians and the Connected Revolutions in the Russian, Iranian, and Ottoman Worlds* (Berkeley: University of California Press, 2019).

[4] Jacob Norris, *Land of Progress: Palestine in the Age of Colonial Development, 1905–1948* (Oxford: Oxford University Press, 2013); Uri M. Kupferschmidt, 'On the diffusion of "small" western technologies and consumer goods in the Middle East during the era of the first modern globalization', in *A Global Middle East: Mobility, Materiality and Culture in the Modern Age, 1880–1940*, Liat Kozma, Cyrus Schayegh and Avner Wishnitzer (London: I. B. Tauris, 2014), pp. 243–44.

[5] Eugene L. Rogan, *The Fall of the Ottomans: The Great War in the Middle East* (New York: Basic Books, 2015); Mustafa Aksakal, 'The Ottoman Empire', in Robert Gerath and Erez Manela (eds), *Empires at War, 1911–1923* (Oxford: Oxford University Press, 2014), pp. 17–33.

[6] Nadine Méouchy (ed.), *France, Syrie et Liban, 1918–1946: Les ambiguïtés et les dynamiques de la relation mandataire* (Damas: IFEAD, 2002); Nadine Méouchy and Peter Sluglett (eds), *The British and French Mandates in Comparative Perspectives* (Leiden: Brill, 2004); Susan Pedersen, *The Guardians. The League of Nation and the Crisis of Empire* (Oxford: Oxford University Press, 2015); Cyrus Schayegh and Andrew Arsan (eds), *The Routledge Handbook of the History of the Middle East Mandates* (London: Routledge, 2015); Idir Ouahes, *Syria and Lebanon under the French Mandate* (I. B. Tauris, 2018).

local resistance to these efforts resulted in the emergence of an independent Turkey.[7] The introduction of international borders not only delineated these novel zones of sovereignty, but they also began to order gradually what was once an imperial geography of mobilities and interconnections into a distinctly national one.

As the title of this volume suggests, we frame the introduction of national borders to the Middle East as a radical re-ordering of the region's existing *regimes of mobility*. This term was first used by Ronen Shamir who argued that globalisation was as much characterised by mobility as it was by systemic practices of closure and containment.[8] Nina Glick Schiller and Noel B. Salazar developed the concept further in their critical appraisal of mobility and migration studies. Departing from the field's traditional tendency to prioritise the study of flows, migration and itinerancy, Schiller and Salazar proposed 'regimes of mobility' as an alternative to the analytic categories that otherwise attribute fixed relationships between people and territory. For them, the term 'regime' underscores 'the role both of individual states and of shifting international regulatory and surveillance administrations that have an impact upon individual mobility', while certainly echoing notions of governmentality and hegemony.[9]

As historians of empires, nationalisms and borderlands, we deploy 'regimes of mobility' in a similar but narrower sense, seeing it as a particularly useful framework to rethink the transition from a *borderless* empire to a *bordered* Middle East in the aftermath of the First World War. In a bid to do so, our concern is first and foremost methodological. Despite the important advances of the field over the past few decades, nationalism continues to territorialise our social science imaginaries, while also attributing fixed

---

[7] For a transregional appraisal of local resistance movements against European imperialism in the Middle East in the early 1920s, see Michael Provence, *The Last Ottoman Generation and the Making of the Modern Middle East* (Cambridge: Cambridge University Press, 2017).

[8] Ronen Shamir, 'Without Borders? Notes on Globalisation as a Mobility Regime', *Sociological Theory* Vol. 23, No. 2 (2005), pp. 197–217.

[9] Nina Glick Schiller and Noel B. Salazar, 'Regimes of Mobility across the Globe', *Journal of Ethnic and Migration Studies*, Vol. 39, No. 2 (2013), pp. 188–89.

functions to historical actors and processes we study.[10] In this sense, 'regimes of mobility' provides a process-centred approach that is neither premised on a particular historical outcome – most notably, the collapse of an empire – nor remains in denial of it.[11] Second, 'regimes of mobility' is useful on an empirical level too, for it opens up a productive field of analysis for historians. Accordingly, the chapters that follow not only explore the continued relevance of Ottoman mobilities in a post-imperial space, but also examine the contentious ways in which the post-Ottoman bureaucracies sought to establish their own regime of mobilities.

Our focus is as much global as it is regional, however, for we see the radical re-ordering of the existing regimes of mobility as part of an entangled global history during which the first wave of globalisation also came to an end. As the contributions to this volume show, none of these historical processes unfolded neatly. For one, Ottoman modes of mobility that had consolidated for generations did not disappear overnight,[12] as imperial networks remained

[10] For some insightful interventions on methodological nationalism, see Andreas Wimmer and Nina Glick Schiller, 'Methodological Nationalism and Beyond: Nation-State Building, Migration, and the Social Sciences', *Global Networks*, Vol. 2, No. 4 (2002), pp. 301–34; Ellen Comisso, 'Empires as Prisons of Nations versus Empires as Political Opportunity Structures: An Exploration of the Role of Nationalism in Imperial Dissolutions in Europe', in Joseph Esherick, Hasan Kayali, and Eric Van Young (eds), *Empire to Nation: Historical Perspectives on the Making of the Modern World* (Lanham: Rowman & Littlefield, 2006), pp. 138–66; Daniel Chernilo, 'Methodological Nationalism and the Domestic Analogy: Classical Resources for their Critique', in *Cambridge Review of International Affairs*, Vol. 23, No. 1 (March 2010), pp. 87–106.

[11] For interventions in the late Ottoman Studies, see Ramazan Hakkı Öztan, 'Nationalism in Function: "Rebellions" in the Ottoman Empire and Narratives in Its Absence', in Hakan Yavuz and Feroz Ahmad (eds), *War and Collapse: World War I and the Ottoman State* (Salt Lake City: University of Utah Press, 2016), pp. 161–202; Ramazan Hakkı Öztan, 'Point of No Return? Prospects of Empire after the Ottoman Defeat in the Balkan Wars (1912–1913)', *International Journal of Middle East Studies*, Vol. 50, No. 1 (2018), pp. 65–84; Alp Yenen, 'Envisioning Turkish-Arab Co-Existence between Empire and Nationalism', *Die Welt des Islams* (Apr 2020), pp. 1–41.

[12] For internal forms of mobility in the late Ottoman period, see Mehmet Genç, 'Osmanlı Devleti'nde İç Gümrük Rejimi,' in *Tanzimat'tan Cumhuriyet'e Türkiye Ansiklopedisi*, Vol.3 (İstanbul: İletişim Yayınları, 1985); Norman Lewis, *Nomads and Settlers in Syria and Jordan, 1800–1980* (Cambridge: Cambridge University Press, 1987); Faruk Tabak, 'Local Merchants

resilient in many ways well into the early 1930s.[13] To be sure, international boundaries introduced new political realities, but 'older geographies continued to make their presence known, even when reformulated in the presence of borders and states'.[14] The Middle East did not get disaggregated neatly from the world markets, either. After all, colonial rule was extended into the Middle East in order to serve the imperatives of British and French political economy in the first place.[15] Finally, the institution of borders did not solely seek to curtail movement in the region. Borders not only created their own local mobilities, but also helped regulate, channel and, at times, facilitate movement that was cross-regional, if not global.[16]

*Regimes of Mobility* ultimately sees border zones as privileged sites to observe how globalising processes interact with more exclusivist agendas. By

---

in Peripheral Areas of the Empire: The Fertile Crescent during the Long Nineteenth Century', *Review (Fernand Braudel Center)*, Vol. 11, No. 2 (Spring 1988), pp. 190–93; Charles Issawi, *The Fertile Crescent 1800–1914: A Documentary Economic History* (New York/Oxford: Oxford University Press, 1988); Hala Fattah, *The Politics of Regional Trade in Iraq, Arabia and the Gulf, 1745–1900* (Albany: State University of New York, 1997); Reşat Kasaba, *A Moveable Empire: Ottoman Nomads, Migrants, and Refugees* (Seattle: University of Washington Press, 2009); Philippe Pétriat, 'Caravan Trade in the Late Ottoman Empire: the 'Aqīl Network and the Institutionalization of Overland Trade', *Journal of the Economic and Social History of the Orient*, Vol. 63, Nos. 1–2 (2019), pp. 38–72.

[13] Cyrus Schayegh, *The Middle East and the Making of the Modern World* (Cambridge, MA: Harvard University Press, 2017).

[14] Toufoul Abou-Hodeib, 'Involuntary History: Writing Levantines into the Nation', *Contemporary Levant* (January 2020), pp. 44–53.

[15] Geoffrey Schad, 'Colonialists, Industrialists, and Politicians: the Political Economy of Industrialization in Syria, 1920–1954' (PhD diss., University of Pennsylvania, 2001); Frank Peter, *Les entrepreneurs de Damas: nation, imperialism et industrialization* (Paris: L'Harmattan, 2010); Andrew Arsan, *Interlopers of Empire: The Lebanese Diaspora in Colonial French West Africa* (New York: Hurst & Co Publishers Ltd, 2014); Sherene Seikaly, *Men of Capital: Scarcity and Economy in Mandate Palestine* (Stanford, CA: Stanford University Press, 2016); Joseph Bohling, 'Colonial or Continental Power? The Debate over Economic Expansion in Interwar France, 1925–1932', *Contemporary European History*, Vol. 26, No. 2 (2017), pp. 217–41.

[16] Robert S. G. Fletcher, 'Running the Corridor: Nomadic Societies and Imperial Rule in the Inter-War Syrian Desert', *Past and Present*, Vol. 220, No. 1 (2013), pp. 185–215; Valeska Huber, *Channelling Mobilities: Migration and Globalisation in the Suez Canal Region and Beyond, 1869–1914* (Cambridge: Cambridge University Press, 2013).

taking its cue from scholarship that suggests interpreting the 'centre' through the lens of the 'periphery',[17] this volume proposes to examine the connected politics of borderlands across the region by focusing on the period from the institution of borders in the early 1920s until the start of decolonisation in the mid-1940s. Contrary to popular and traditional depictions of borders as areas where national sovereignty comes to an end, *Regimes of Mobility* seeks to illustrate how border areas and borderlanders become the very centres of influence, movements and tensions that transformed sovereignties into new forms, in tandem with the global and regional processes.[18]

*Regimes of Mobility* is thus a response to the growing interest in Middle Eastern borders, seeking to provide an informed historical discussion about the ways in which borderlanders, travellers, refugees, diseases, commodities, nomads and bureaucrats, among others, interacted in refashioning the borderlands across the Middle East. In reconstructing these episodes, we hope to trace the 'lived experiences of territoriality' and 'capture the dynamic interaction between state and local actors in the forging of modern bordered political identities'.[19] The volume's novelty lies in its attempt to go beyond singular case studies and instead reconstruct a connected history of borders and mobilities that could shed light on shared historical trajectories in the Middle East. While our approach decidedly remains local, the contributions that follow are receptive to the transregional and global dynamics that were at play. After all, borderlands are zones of incessant flows, with a multiplicity of origins and destinations; their history should be equally multipolar as well.

## Mapping Out the Field

Contemporary developments over the past decade have renewed interest in the study of borders, borderlanders and cross-border mobility in the Middle East. While it is certainly true that the ongoing Arab-Israeli conflict always

---

[17] Joel S. Migdal, *State in Society: Studying How States and Societies Transform and Constitute One Another* (Cambridge: Cambridge University Press, 2001).

[18] Oscar J. Martínez, 'The Dynamics of Border Interaction: New Approaches to Border Analysis', in Clive H. Schofield (ed.), *Global Boundaries, World Boundaries, Vol. I* (London and New York: Routledge, 1994), p. 14.

[19] Matthew H. Ellis, *Desert Borderland: The Making of Modern Egypt and Libya* (Stanford, CA: Stanford University Press, 2018), p. 8.

garnered scholarly attention,[20] the rise of ISIS in general and the latter's symbolic acts at defying the Sykes-Picot borders in particular have sparked greater public curiosity in the borders of the Middle East.[21] The outpouring of millions of refugees away from these conflict zones too, especially from Syria, has also brought to the fore issues central to these struggles, such as the rapid fragmentation of the territorial state systems in the region and the roles international borders play in perpetuating humanitarian crises.[22] As part and parcel of these contentious political developments, the construction of border walls has gained a particular sense of urgency. The Turkish–Syrian border, for example, which was once a site of visa-free travel back in the early 2000s, now features a well-surveilled wall which, as a trend, parallels similar developments elsewhere in the region (for example, the border walls between Egypt and Gaza, or Saudi Arabia and Yemen) as well as across the globe.[23]

Contemporary resonance of borders should not make one assume the novelty of the topic, however. Much to the contrary, neither the debates about the evolution of borders across the world, nor the analyses on crises of territoriality are completely new to scholarship. In fact, no serious scholar sees

---

[20] S. Latte Abdallah and C. Parizot (eds), *À l'ombre du mur. Israéliens et palestiniens entre séparation et occupation* (Arles: Actes Sud/MMSH, 2011); Asher Kaufman, *Contested Frontiers in the Syria-Lebanon-Israel Region: Cartography, Sovereignty, and Conflict* (Washington, DC: Woodrow Wilson Center Press, 2014); Daniel Meier, *Shaping Lebanon's Borderlands* (London: I. B. Tauris, 2016); Laura Robson, *States of Separation: Transfer, Partition, and the Making of the Modern Middle East* (Oakland: University of California Press, 2017).

[21] Michael D. Berdine, *Redrawing the Middle East: Sir Mark Sykes, Imperialism and the Sykes-Picot Agreement* (London: I. B. Tauris, 2018); Ariel I. Ahram, *Break all the Borders: Separatism and the Reshaping of the Middle East* (Oxford: Oxford University Press, 2020).

[22] Inga Brandell (ed.), *State Frontiers. Borders and Boundaries in the Middle East* (London and New York: I. B. Tauris, 2006); Leïla Vignal, *The Transnational Middle East: Peoples, Places, Borders* (London: Routledge, 2016); Paul Drew, *Israel/Palestine: Border Representations in Literature and Film* (Edinburgh: Edinburgh University Press, 2020); Matthieu Cimino (ed.), *Syria: Borders, Boundaries, and the State* (New York: Palgrave Macmillan, 2020).

[23] While nineteen walls and barriers were built between 1945 and 1991, only seven walls were added during the 1990s to the thirteen that survived the Cold War. Within a decade after the events of '9/11', however, twenty-eight walls were already completed or planned. See Élisabeth Vallet and Charles-Philippe David, 'Introduction: The (Re)Building of the Wall in International Relations', *Journal of Borderlands Studies*, Vol. 27, No. 2 (2012), pp. 111–19.

borders today as a mere historical consequence or a neat closure to the contentious episodes that had transpired in a distant past. Instead, borders and borderlands are framed central to the making of history and seen as charged sites, where identities are forged, policies take shape and interests clash on a continual basis.[24] This point perhaps comes across more forcefully today than any other time before, as we witness, in the words of Charles Maier, how 'inclusion and exclusion have become or re-emerged as the underlying stakes of contemporary politics precisely as, and because, the spatial definitions of insiders and outsiders weaken'.[25] This contemporary paradox was rooted in the collapse of the Soviet Union, which not only led to the multiplication of national borders in post-Soviet spaces in the early 1990s but also led to the triumph of the idea of a borderless and supranational world – embodied in the spirit of the fall of Berlin Wall.[26]

These transformative developments have helped shape the field of borderlands studies for the past three decades.[27] Traditionally, borders had been analysed in terms of their geopolitical dimension, namely as physical limits between two contiguous sovereign territorial systems.[28] By the same token,

[24] Thomas M. Wilson and Hastings Donnan (eds), *Border Identities: Nation and State at International Frontiers* (Cambridge: Cambridge University Press, 1998); Henk van Houtum and Ton van Naerssen, 'Bordering, Ordering, and Othering', *Tijdschrift voor Economische en Sociale Geografie*, Vol. 93, No. 2 (2002), pp. 125–36; David Newman, 'Borders and bordering: Towards an interdisciplinary dialogue', *European Journal of Social Theory*, Vol. 9, No. 2 (2006), pp. 171–86; Seda Altuğ, 'The Turkish–Syrian Border and Politics of Difference in Turkey and Syria (1921–1939)', in Matthieu Cimino, (ed), *Syria: Borders, Boundaries*, pp. 47–73.

[25] Charles S. Maier, 'Transformations of Territoriality, 1600–2000', in Gunilla Budde, Sebastian Conrad and Oliver Janz (eds), *Transnationale Geschichte: Themen, Tendenzen und Theorien* (Göttingen: Vandenhoeck & Ruprecht, 2006), p. 36.

[26] Lester Russell Brown, *World without Borders* (New York: Vintage, 1973); Kenichi Ohmae, *The Borderless World: Power and Strategy in the Interlinked Economy* (New York: Harper Business, 1990); Kenichi Ohmae, *The End of the Nation State: The Rise of Regional Economies* (New York: Simon & Schuster, 1995); Michael Shapiro and Hayward Alker (eds), *Challenging Boundaries: Global Flows, Territorial Identities* (Minneapolis: University of Minnesota Press, 1996).

[27] James Anderson, Liam O'Dowd and Thomas M. Wilson, 'Introduction: Why Study Borders Now?', *Regional & Federal Studies*, Vol. 12, No. 4 (2002), pp. 1–12.

[28] Michel Foucher, *Fronts et frontières: Un tour du monde géopolitique* (Paris: Fayard, 1991); Daniel Nordman, *Frontières de France. De l'espace au territoire XVI<sup>e</sup>–XIX<sup>e</sup> siècles* (Paris: Gallimard, 1999).

Michiel Baud and Willem Van Schendel conceived *borders* as 'the political divides that were the result of state building',[29] whilst *boundaries* would refer to 'lines' on a political map.[30] From the 1990s onwards, however, the study of borders became less about political centres and the conditions that inform these outer lines of sovereignty than about the zones that form on both sides of a border and the continued effects of borders. Anthropologists, political scientists and geographers have accordingly begun to examine border regions in order to observe the impact of international borders upon local populations.[31] Starting from the premise that the border is a social construct – that is, not a rigid and immutable material reality – many studies have sought to understand the ways in which border zones are subjectively experienced by 'border populations' not only as an area of instability and risk but also as a potential resource for those living in its proximity.[32]

The emergence of these approaches that study borders 'from below' was concomitant with the broader shift among historians to prioritise the study of 'margins' and 'peripheries' to that of 'centres'.[33] In particular, the increasing importance attached to develop competency, and carry out research in, local languages helped scholars capture the perspectives of borderlanders. While this took many forms, scholars have, by and large, highlighted the strategies and daily activities of individuals and/or groups seeking to transgress the border, such as cross-border marriages, smuggling and trafficking, as well as criminal circuits and secessionist movements that thrived in border

---

[29] Michiel Baud and Willem van Schendel, 'Toward a Comparative History of Borderlands', *Journal of World History*, Vol. 8, No. 2 (1997), pp. 214–15.

[30] J. Prescott, *The Geography of Frontiers and Boundaries* (Chicago, Aldine Publishing Company, 1965), pp. 35–36.

[31] Hastings Donnan and Thomas M. Wilson (eds), *Borderlands. Ethnographic Approaches to Security, Power, and Identity* (London and New York: University Press of America, 2010).

[32] Janet Roitman, 'The Garrison-Entrepôt: A Mode of Governing in the Chad Bassin', in Aihwa Ong and Stephen J. Collier (eds), *Global Assemblages. Technology, Politics and Ethics as Anthropological Problems* (London: Blackwell, 2005); Judith Schelle, *Smugglers and Saints of the Sahara. Regional Connectivity in the Twentieth Century* (Cambridge: Cambridge University Press, 2012).

[33] Kate Brown, *A Biography of No Place: From Ethnic Borderland to Soviet Heartland* (Cambridge, MA: Harvard University Press, 2004); Firoozeh Kashani-Sabet, *Frontier Fictions: Shaping the Iranian Nation, 1804–1946* (Princeton: Princeton University Press, 1999).

regions.[34] As a result of such practices that may appear strange to citizens living in the 'centre' of the nation states, border regions would constitute a world apart;[35] a place of traffickers and, at times, even a zone of refuge for groups and individuals seeking to avoid the control of the modern state.[36]

Framing borders as zones that are in some ways independent of national heartlands also led to the rehabilitation of the concept 'borderland'. The term was originally applied by American historians such as Herbert Bolton and David J. Weber to North America's 'colonial frontier', but the concept gradually gained new epistemological implication from the 1990s onwards, when it also became increasingly applied to broader geographies from Asia to Europe and Africa.[37] In its most basic sense, a borderland can be defined

[34] Homi Bhabha, *The Location of Culture* (London and New York: Routledge, 1994); Katharyne Mitchell, 'Transnational discourse: Bringing geography back in', *Antipode*, Vol. 29, No. 2 (1997), pp. 101–14; Jean-David Mizrahi, 'Un "nationalisme de la frontière": Bandes armées et sociabilités politiques sur la frontière turco-syrienne au début des années 1920', *Vingtième Siècle Revue d'histoire*, Vol. 78 (Apr–Jun 2003), pp. 19–34; Alison Blunt, 'Cultural Geographies of Migration: Mobility, Transnationalism and Diaspora', *Progress in Human Geography*, Vol. 31, No. 5 (2007), pp. 684–94; Isa Blumi, 'Illicit Trade and the Emergence of Albania and Yemen', in I. William Zartman (ed), *Understanding Life in the Borderland: Boundaries in Depth and in Motion* (Athens, GA: University of Georgia Press, 2010), pp. 73–100; Cyrus Schayegh, 'The Many Worlds of 'Abud Yasin; or, What Narcotics Trafficking in the Interwar Middle East Can Tell us about Territorialization', *The American Historical Review*, Vol. 116, No. 2 (2011), pp. 273–306; Liat Kozma, 'White Drugs in Interwar Egypt: Decadent Pleasures, Emaciated Fellahin, and the Campaign against Drugs', *Comparative Studies of South Asia, Africa and the Middle East*, Vol. 33, No. 1 (2013), pp. 89–101; Samuel Dolbee, 'The Locust and the Starling: People, Insects, and Disease in the Ottoman Jazira and After, 1860–1940' (PhD diss., New York University, 2017); Metin Atmaca, 'Fragile Frontiers: Sayyid Taha II and the Role of Kurdish Religio-Political Leadership in the Ottoman East during the First World War', *Middle Eastern Studies*, Vol. 54, No. 3 (2018), pp. 361–81; Jordi Tejel, 'States of Rumors: Politics of Information along the Turkish–Syrian Border, 1925–1945', *Journal of Borderlands Studies* (first online) (2020): https://doi.org/10.1080/08865655.2020.1719866

[35] Clive H. Schofield (ed.), *Global Boundaries. World Boundaries, Vol. I* (London and New York: Routledge, 1994).

[36] James C. Scott, *The Art of Not Being Governed. An Anarchist History of Upland Southeast Asia* (New Haven and London: Yale University Press, 2009).

[37] For a general overview of this concept and the historiography related to it, see Pekka Hämäläinen and Samuel Truett, 'On Borderlands', *The Journal of American History*, Vol. 98, No. 2 (2011), pp. 338–61.

as an area that flanks an internationally recognised border. It is therefore an area in the form of strip that is of 'indefinite extent and thus cannot be measured in so many meters or miles',[38] but one 'whose centers are physically and socially distant from that border'.[39] Rather than a definite geographical territory, however, borderlands are sites where state structures are less fully articulated, and where the image of the state loses its clarity, developing more fluid forms. Because the two sides of the border constitute an organic whole that 'naturally' differs from the rest of a given national territory,[40] borderlands are marginal zones that are unique in their geopolitical, socioeconomic, political and cultural environments.[41]

Although there is no single definition of borderlands, many scholars readily acknowledge the concept's analytic potential to rethink the processes of state-making and identity formation, because it privileges the local. As historians have shown time and again, local dynamics and agencies are essential to understanding the formation of modern international borders and that the regulation of inter-imperial affairs in borderlands are not merely top-down affairs.[42] To the contrary, these encounters between state and non-state actors could at times take contentious, if not violent turns, so much so that Jeremy Adelman and Stephen Aron defined borderlands as 'contested boundaries

---

[38] Edward S. Casey, 'Border versus Boundary at la Frontera', *Environment and Planning D: Society and Space*, Vol. 29 (2011), p. 389.

[39] James Anderson and Liam O'Dowd, 'Borders, Border Regions and Territoriality: Contradictory Meanings, Changing Significance', *Regional Studies*, Vol. 33, No. 7 (1999), p. 595.

[40] Michiel Baud and Willem van Schendel, 'Toward a Comparative History of Borderlands', *Journal of World History*, Vol. 8, No. 2 (1997), p216.

[41] Pınar Şenoğuz, *Community, Change and Border Towns* (London: Routledge, 2018), p. 24.

[42] For a seminal work on these dynamics, see Peter Sahlins, *Boundaries: The Making of France and Spain in the Pyrenees* (Berkeley: University of California Press, 1989). See also Sabine Dullin, 'L'invention d'une frontière de guerre froide à l'ouest de l'Union soviétique (1945–1949)', *Vingtième Siècle Revue d'histoire*, Vol. 102 (2009), pp. 49–61; Isa Blumi, 'Agents of Post-Ottoman States: The Precariousness of the Berlin Congress Boundaries of Montenegro and how to Define/Confine People', in Hakan Yavuz and Peter Sluglett (eds), *War and Diplomacy: Russo-Turkish War and Berlin Treaty* (Salt Lake City: University of Utah Press, 2011); Sabri Ateş, *The Ottoman-Iranian Borderlands. Making a Boundary, 1843–1914* (Cambridge: Cambridge University Press, 2013).

between colonial domains'.[43] From the early 2000s onwards, this influential perspective informed a number of studies that framed borderlands as productive zones of competition, violence and resistance.[44]

Borderlands were the theatres of contentious interactions in more subtle ways as well. The cultural turn, for instance, has inspired scholars to frame borderlands as a site inextricably embedded within various power relations, whether of macro or micro scales. On a macro level, borderlands are seen as areas of multiple sovereignties and legal regimes that require renegotiations of power among a myriad of local, national and transnational actors.[45] On a micro level, border zones are important sites to observe the contradictions and dynamics at work in a given society whose power relations took their most explicit forms along its borders. In this sense, the state and society relations around borderlands offer an excellent opportunity to study the territorialisation of modern nation states, providing insights into the specific configurations of identity politics in zones that are otherwise characterised by fluid identities, shifting allegiances and cross-cultural exchanges.[46]

[43] Jeremy Adelman and Stephen Aron, 'From Borderlands to Borders: Empires, Nation-States, and the Peoples in between in North American History', *The American Historical Review*, Vol. 104, No. 3 (1999), p. 816.

[44] Michael Reynolds, *Shattering Empires: The Clash and Collapse of the Ottoman and Russian Empires, 1908–1918* (Cambridge: Cambridge University Press, 2011); Mark Levene, 'The Tragedy of the Rimlands, Nation-State Formation and the Destruction of Imperial Peoples, 1912–48', in Panikos Panayi and Pippa Virdee (eds), *Refugees and the End of Empire*, pp. 51–78 (London: Palgrave Macmillan, 2011); Omer Bartov and Eric D. Weitz (eds), *Shatterzone of Empires: Coexistence and Violence in the German, Hapsburg, Russian, and Ottoman Borderlands* (Bloomington: Indiana University Press, 2013); Alfred J. Rieber, *The Struggle for the Eurasian Borderlands: From the Rise of Early Modern Empires to the End of the First World War* (Cambridge: Cambridge University Press, 2014); Ramazan Hakkı Öztan, 'Tools of Revolution: Global Military Surplus, Arms Dealers and Smugglers in the Late Ottoman Balkans, 1878–1908', *Past & Present*, Vol. 237, No. 1 (2017), pp. 167–95; Ramazan Hakkı Öztan and Alp Yenen (eds), *Age of Rogues: Rebels, Revolutionaries and Racketeers at the Frontiers of Empires* (Edinburgh: Edinburgh University Press, 2021).

[45] Bradley Miller, *Borderline Crime: Fugitive Criminals and the Challenge of the Border, 1819–1914* (Toronto: Toronto University Press, 2016); Will Smiley, *From Slaves to Prisoners of War: The Ottoman Empire, Russia, and International Law* (Oxford: Oxford University Press, 2018).

[46] Joel S. Migdal (ed.), *Boundaries and Belonging. States and Societies in the Struggle to Shape Identities and Local Practices* (Cambridge: Cambridge University Press, 2004); Paolo Novak, 'The Flexible Territoriality of Borders', *Geopolitics*, Vol. 16, No. 4 (2011), pp. 741–67.

Finally, borderlands are not just zones where actors compete and resist, locals negotiate, cultures intermingle and identities transform, but also where individuals cross, commodities are exchanged, and diseases are spread. 'The essence of a border is . . . to act as a barrier,' as David Newman noted, 'but borders are equally there to be crossed.'[47] In this sense, borderlands are not where mobilities come to an end, but rather places where they are 'channelled' – i.e. prevented, promoted, re-directed, as states seek to derive revenues, legitimacy and power.[48] As such, borderlands are where 'regimes of mobility' are re-cast and re-shuffled, just as it began to happen in the Middle East from the early 1920s onwards.

## The Making of the Modern Middle East

The emergence of the modern Middle East is the result of three complementary historical developments: the disintegration of the Ottoman Empire; the institution of British and French control in its stead; and the nationalist challenges to this colonial scramble. The introduction of international borders that accompanied this process is popularly portrayed as the drawing of lines in the sand,[49] an artificial partitioning that brought diplomatic closure to an otherwise contested historical space. For the past two decades, however, insights gained from the burgeoning field of borderlands studies have not only enabled a newer generation of scholars to challenge such prevalent depictions, but also help them go beyond the well-established paradigms of studying centre-periphery relations.[50] For them, the region's borderlands

---

[47] David Newman, 'On Borders and Power: A Theoretical Framework', *Journal of Borderlands Studies*, Vol. 18, No. 1 (2003), p. 14.

[48] Joel Quirk and Darshan Vigneswaran (eds), 'Mobility Makes States', in *Mobility Makes States: Migration and Power in Africa* (Philadelphia: University of Pennsylvania Press, 2015), pp. 6–8.

[49] James Barr, *A Line in the Sand: Britain, France and the Struggle that Shaped the Middle East* (London: Simon & Schuster, 2011).

[50] Matthew H. Ellis, 'Over the Borderline? Rethinking Territoriality at the Margins of Empire and Nation in the Modern Middle East (Part II)', *History Compas*, Vol. 13, No. 8 (2015), pp. 411–22. For a paradigm-setting article in the field on centre-periphery relations, see Şerif Mardin, 'Center-Periphery: A Key to Turkish Politics', *Daedalus*, Vol. 102 (1973), pp. 169–90. For a particularly successful critique that also provides an alternative framework of analysis, see Cem Emrence, *Remapping the Ottoman Middle East: Modernity, Imperial Bureaucracy and the Islamic State* (London: I. B. Tauris, 2011).

were not just mere sites of peripheral activity, but rather zones of interaction, contention and influence central to state- and nation-formation across the Middle East.[51]

Our story begins in the early 1920s, when Middle Eastern states began to transform the physical and social landscape of border areas by establishing border posts and engaging in shared bureaucratic practices that involved authorities from both sides of borders. These bordering processes in these initial years were, however, less about establishing physical barriers – i.e. demarcating the border – than about settling and delimiting the actual site of the boundary, around which a new regime of movement can be constructed. The meaning of these new boundaries certainly varied for the local populations. While some borderlanders opted for stasis, and worked, socialised and married as if the new boundaries did not present new opportunities, many locals quickly came to terms with the emerging 'regimes of mobility' and began to use passports and border crossing cards in daily life, thereby interacting with the symbolic as well as material tools of mobility in ways they have never experienced before.[52] Other borderlanders, meanwhile, viewed the international border for what it was – that is, the realm of separate sovereignties and

---

[51] Eugene L. Rogan, *Frontiers of the State in the Late Ottoman Empire: Transjordan, 1850–1921* (Cambridge: Cambridge University Press, 1999); Anthony B. Toth, 'Tribes and tribulations: Bedouin losses in the Saudi and Iraqi struggles over Kuwait's frontiers, 1921–1943', *British Journal of Middle Eastern Studies*, Vol. 32. No. 2 (2005), pp. 145–67; A. C. S. Peacock (ed), *The Frontiers of the Ottoman World* (Oxford: Oxford University Press, 2009); Seda Altuğ and Benjamin T. White, 'Frontières et pouvoirs d'État: La frontière turco-syrienne dans les années 1920 et 1930', *Vingtième Siècle Revue d'histoire*, Vol. 103, No. 3 (2009), pp. 91–104; Robert S. G. Fletcher, 'Running the Corridor: Nomadic Societies and Imperial Rule in the Inter-War Syrian Desert', *Past & Present*, Vol. 220, No. 1 (Aug 2013), pp. 185–215; Sabri Ateş, *The Ottoman-Iranian Borderlands*; Matthew H. Ellis, *Desert Borderland: The Making of Modern Egypt and Libya* (Stanford: Stanford University Press, 2018); Jordi Tejel, 'Making Borders from Below: the Emergence of the Turkish-Iraqi Frontier, 1918–1925', *Middle Eastern Studies*, Vol. 54, No. 5 (May 2018), pp. 811–26; Ramazan Hakkı Öztan, 'The Great Depression and the Making of Turkish–Syrian Border, 1921–1939', *International Journal of Middle East Studies*, Vol. 52, No. 2 (2020), pp. 311–26.

[52] To be sure, the documentation of status, together with mobility control, was not completely new in the region, as passports and internal travel documents became increasingly widespread in the late Ottoman period when more individuals got in motion. David Gutman,

hence an opportunity to benefit from disconnected jurisdictions. Borders accordingly became a resource as much for smugglers as they did for deserters, émigrés and fugitives.[53] As such, borderlanders became both connectors of, and active participants in, new mobility strategies that emerged from the early 1920s onwards.

Just as borders created their own traffic, so too did they lead to increased bureaucratisation. The attempts to introduce anti-smuggling measures, extradite criminals, keep diseases at bay, or remove the politically undesirable away from border zones gradually turned borders into social institutions, with concrete frontier effects, as power relations began to unfold between state agents and borderlanders.[54] Obviously, these interactions were context-specific and very complex.[55] Not all individuals were treated equally by state authorities; the ability to cross a border relatively freely depended on many factors such as social status and the identity of the crosser, while instances of violence and refugee crossings could at times strain those relations. Notwithstanding this, cooperation and the exchange of information constituted alternate ways for states to interact among themselves or with locals along the newly established

'Travel documents, mobility control, and the Ottoman State in an age of global migration, 1880–1915', *Journal of the Ottoman and Turkish Studies Association*, Vol. 3, No. 2 (2016), pp. 347–68; İlkay Yılmaz, 'Governing the Armenian Question through Passports in the Late Ottoman Empire (1876–1908)', *Journal of Historical Sociology*, Vol. 32, No. 4 (2019) pp. 388–403. Yet, bureaucratic records show that most people did not collect the identification documents available to them at that time. See Will Hanley, *Identifying with Nationality: Europeans, Ottomans, and Egyptians in Alexandria* (New York: Columbia University Press, 2017), pp. 70–74. See also John Torpey, *The Invention of the Passport. Surveillance, Citizenship, and the State* (Cambridge: Cambridge University Press, 2000).

53  Jordi Tejel, 'Des femmes contre des moutons: franchissements féminins de la frontière turco-syrienne (1929–1944)', *20 & 21. Revue d'histoire*, Vol. 145 (2020), pp. 35–47; Ramazan Hakkı Öztan, 'Republic of Conspiracies: Cross-Border Plots and the Making of Modern Turkey', *Journal of Contemporary History*, Vol. 56, No. 1 (January 2021), pp. 55–76.

54  Toufoul Abou-Hodeib, 'Sanctity across the Border: Pilgrimage Routes and State Control in Mandate Lebanon and Palestine', in Cyrus Schayegh and Andrew Arsan (eds), *The Routledge Handbook of the History of the Middle East Mandates* (London: Routledge, 2015), p. 383.

55  Timothy Mitchell, *Rule of Experts: Egypt, Techno-Politics, Modernity* (Berkeley: University of California Press, 2002).

borders, too.[56] Therefore, borders not only produced their own mobilities on a local scale, but also served as the charged site of confrontations and identity politics on a national level.

The refugee issue was a case in point. As we have argued elsewhere,[57] by the early 1920s the post-war settlement introduced a precise territorial order to the region with a new set of international boundaries. The introduction of sovereign territoriality was accompanied by the efforts of the emerging ruling elites in the region to re-define who belonged to the nation and thereby what determined the criteria of citizenship. These terms of inclusion, however, also specified the terms of exclusion, as some groups were defined out of state, leading to their categorisation as refugees and aliens. Both the League of Nations and local elites perceived refugeedom not only as an opportunity to minimise the prospects of ethno-religious conflict but also as a means of consolidating the nation state. As such, creating refugees and welcoming them was a mutually constitutive process that reproduced discourses of governmentality and justified modern territorial states, while redefining the limits of belonging.[58]

In pursuing these inquiries further, *Regimes of Mobility* is engaged in conversation with three specific historiographies. First is with the historiography of the late Ottoman Empire, where scholars have developed increasingly critical approaches to methodological nationalism and the ways in which nationalist teleology continues to order scholarship on the end of empires and emergence of nation states. In this sense, the study of borderlands offers a means of writing history free from the teleology of the nation state. To be sure, we do not dismiss the centrality of diplomacy and high-level geostrategic dynamics in the resolution of international conflicts, the promotion and prevention of movement, and the shaping of economic policies. In this sense, scholars cannot 'consign the state to a dustbin marked error', as states were central to building crucial institutions in many borderland

---

[56] Robert S. G. Fletcher, *British Imperialism and the Tribal Question* (Oxford: Oxford University Press, 2015).

[57] Jordi Tejel and Ramazan Hakkı Öztan, 'Towards Connected Histories of Refugeedom in the Middle East', *Journal of Migration History*, Vol. 6, No. 1 (2020), p. 2.

[58] Mark Mazower, *No Enchanted Palace: The End of Empire and the Ideological Origins of the United Nations* (Princeton, NJ: Princeton University Press), pp. 104–48.

contexts.[59] Yet, we argue for the necessity of not assigning interpretative priority to states. Instead, borderland and mobility histories should seek to link different scales of analysis to one another,[60] while also appreciating the roles played by non-state actors in those processes in order to better understand the emergence of the modern Middle East in the interwar years. By embracing cross-border mobilities as our point of departure, *Regimes of Mobility* moves beyond the analytic categories of the national and instead highlights the potential of studying the cross-regional.

*Regimes of Mobility* is also informed by the fields of global and transnational history as well as entangled histories (*histoires croisées*) that have centred the historiographical debate on the significance of flows, connections, networks and itinerancy.[61] Yet, as critical approaches to mobility studies have recently shown, the impact of globalisation was neither even nor equal, and mobility could very well co-exist with stasis.[62] In that sense, by changing the scale of analysis as well as by examining particular subjects that speak to wider questions, the collection of chapters in this volume confirms Valeska Huber's characterisation of the first wave of globalisation as the interplay between the acceleration and deceleration of movement, between old and new forms of mobility, between movement and stasis, between integration and exclusion of a multiplicity of actors, and finally between the local and the global.[63] Indeed, local knowledge and practices – legal and illicit commercial networks, transport routes, religious circuits, Bedouin transhumance – deeply informed the emerging mobility strategies across the region after the introduction of new

[59] Paul Readman, Cynthia Radding and Chad Bryant, 'Introduction: Borderlands in a Global Perspective', in *Borderlands in World History, 1700–1914* (London: Palgrave Macmillan, 2014), p. 12.

[60] Jacques Revel (ed.), *Jeux d'échelles. La micro-analyse à l'expérience* (Paris: Gallimard/Seuil, 1996), pp. 15–36.

[61] 'AHR Conversation: On Transnational History', *American Historical Review*, Vol. 111 (2006), pp. 1,441–64; M. Werner and B. Zimmermann, 'Beyond comparison: Histoire Croisée and the Challenge of Reflexivity', *History and Theory*, Vol. 45 (2006), pp. 30–50; Richard Drayton and David Motadel, 'Discussion: the Futures of Global History', *Journal of Global History*, Vol. 13 (2018), pp. 1–21.

[62] Kevin Hannam, Mimi Sheller, John Urry, 'Editorial: Mobilities, Immobilities and Mooring', *Mobilities*, Vol. 1, No. 1 (2006), pp. 1–22.

[63] Valeska Huber, *Channelling Mobilities*, pp. 6–8.

borders. As our contributors will also illustrate, cross-border movement of goods, diseases, individuals, capital and travellers reflect a more refined understanding of globalisation, with a willingness to explore the seemingly contradictory ways in which the compression of time and place came to unfold.[64] In so doing, not only does this volume reject framing globalisation in linear and celebratory terms,[65] it also refuses to see borders as lines of enclosure that solely deny movement once consolidated. By placing 'regimes of mobility' at the centre of our analysis, we seek to rethink the transition from empires to nation states from an angle of mobility studies. In doing so, the volume highlights the significance of global, regional and national contexts in determining the contours of regimes of mobility.

Finally, *Regimes of Mobility* is in conversation with environmental history.[66] After all, many of the borders that were introduced to the Middle East crossed through vast arid landscapes that stretched across Syria, Iraq, Transjordan and Saudi Arabia. Well before the creation of these countries, however, these desert zones were populated by myriad nomadic groups that

---

[64] Simon Jackson, 'Introduction: The Global Middle East in the Age of Speed: From Joyriding to Jamming, and from Racing to Raiding', *Comparative Studies of South Asia, Africa and the Middle East*, Vol. 9, No. 1 (May 2019), pp. 112–13; Mikiya Koyagi, *Iran in Motion: Mobility, Space, and the Trans-Iranian Railway* (Stanford: Stanford University Press, 2021); Nile Green, 'New Histories for the Age of Speed: The Archaeological-Architectural Past in Interwar Afghanistan and Iran', *Iranian Studies*, Vol. 54, No. 3–4 (2021), pp. 349–97.

[65] For a similar argument, see Nile Green, 'Fordist Connections: The Automotive Integration of the United States and Iran', *Comparative Studies in Society and History*, Vol. 58, No. 2 (2016), p. 292.

[66] For few important studies in the field, see Diana Davis, *Resurrecting the Granary of Rome. Environmental History and French Colonial Expansion in North Africa* (Athens, OH: Ohio University Press, 2007); Sam White, *The Climate of Rebellion in the Early Modern Ottoman Empire* (Cambridge: Cambridge University Press, 2011); Diana Davis and Edmund Burke III (eds), *Environmental Imaginaries of the Middle East and North Africa* (Athens, OH: Ohio University Press, 2011); Alan Mikhail (ed.), *Water on Sand. Environmental Histories of the Middle East and North Africa* (New York: Oxford University Press, 2013); Alan Mikhail, *Under Osman's Tree. The Ottoman Empire, Egypt, and Environmental history* (Chicago: University of Chicago Press, 2017); Onur İnal and Yavuz Köse (eds), *Seeds of Power: Explorations in Ottoman Environmental History* (Cambridgeshire: The White Horse Press, 2019).

traditionally criss-crossed the region in search of winter and summer pastures. Even though the Ottoman Empire had already begun to introduce
various practices of territorial governance to the region,[67] these interventions
remained largely episodic, constrained by the realities of the late nineteenth-
century Ottoman state capacity. The introduction of borders in the early 1920s
therefore presented immediate challenges to the tribes, with a potential to
reshuffle the tribal regimes of mobility that had otherwise reflected a delicate
balance of power across the desert.[68] In examining the interactions between
modern practices of territorial governance, environmental crises and Bedouin
pastoral economies, *Regimes of Mobility* underscores the dialectic – albeit not
deterministic – relationship between humans and nature in the desert borderlands in order to explore how non-human factors can also become the driving forces of mobility regimes, border-making processes and, ultimately, the
emergence of the modern nation states in the Middle East.

### In This Volume

Reşat Kasaba frames the contemporary relevance of studying the politics of
borders in the Middle East. The subsequent contributions will have a tem-
poral range from the early 1920s to the 1940s, while covering a geography
from Transjordan to the Caucasus, and Turkey to Syria, Iraq and Palestine.
In the first chapter, Alexander Balistreri provides a critical example from new
diplomatic history that has moved away from singular state-centred accounts
of foreign relations to an appreciation of the interconnected nature of diplomacy, where domestic and foreign relations interact and the regional and the
local exert influence and agency. In particular, Balistreri makes a case for the
necessity to approach the post First World War diplomacy of border-making
from a comparative perspective. Focusing on the year 1921 his contribution
traces how Turkey's borders with the Soviet Union in the northeast and with
French Syria in the south were simultaneously defined through a range of
bilateral treaties. Trying to bring the nation state back into the narrative, the

---

[67] Norman Lewis, *Nomads and Settlers in Syria and Jordan, 1800–1980* (Cambridge: Cambridge
University Press, 1987).

[68] Martha Mundy and Basim Musallam (eds), *The Transformation of Nomadic Society in the
Arab East* (Cambridge: Cambridge University Press, 2000).

chapter remains wary of methodological nationalism, approaching the making of these two borders as the outcomes of particular historical processes that were not inevitable. Balistreri argues that both borders were in fact results of 'highly personal diplomacy set against a backdrop of armed struggle', which illustrated the divide between national ideas and the realities of geopolitics.

Orçun Can Okan likewise emphasises the importance of situating borders in particular historical contexts for gaining insights into their functions and impacts. He contextualises the borders between Turkey and the League of Nations Mandates in the Middle East in terms of their role in the dismantling of the Ottoman Empire. Noting that borders did not immediately lead to a neat division of the empire into distinct units, Okan instead highlights borders' role in ongoing processes of state succession and changes in administrative and legal regimes. The chapter emphasises that borders necessitated new paths of official correspondence for reference to Ottoman administrative records and new contexts of legal interaction among former Ottoman subjects. Borders' role in bringing about these new paths and contexts was crucial, the chapter argues, in establishing new state-subject relations in the former domains of a recently partitioned empire. Okan's close attention to claims and disputes over retirement pensions, maintenance support and land ownership illustrates how borders had consequences for a wide range of social actors living near and far beyond the envisioned borderlines.

Ramazan Hakkı Öztan in turn explores the contentious ways in which the institution of borders came to re-order what was once a connected Ottoman economy. With a case study on Aleppo, the important centre of commerce that connected southern Anatolia and Mosul to the world beyond, Öztan shows how the introduction of a Turkish–Syrian border threatened to separate the city from its traditional hinterland through a customs barrier. The chapter carefully traces the contentious and prolonged customs negotiations between Turkey and French Syria that took place against a background of violence along the border. Unfolding at a time when the British and French administered mandates sought to introduce open-door policies in the modern Middle East, the negotiations over the commercial future of Aleppo showcased their broader ambitions to maintain the continuity of interregional economic ties inherited from the Ottoman times and Ankara's insistence on economic independence at the expense of Aleppo. 'The Ottoman Empire did not "collapse" like a house of cards,' as Öztan argues, 'but rather got disentangled, particularly in places like Aleppo where imperial rule was less of an imagined affair than a connected one.'

In Chapter Four, Simon Jackson examines the ways in which a variety of actors challenged, negotiated and ultimately transformed the parameters of post-Ottoman territoriality on the ground. By zooming in on the example of Charles Corm, a Beirut-based Ford car dealer, he traces how Corm's global and cross-regional connections transitioned to the commercial realities of the post-Ottoman space. Corm was active in the region from 1920 to 1934, distributing tractors, automobiles and spare parts across the newly emerging borders, an operation that was embedded within a global network of Ford's commercial empire. By taking Corm/Ford branches and their commercial undertakings across borders as his unit of analysis, the chapter helps us rethink the centre-periphery dynamics implicit in studies of borderlands, and points to the significance of studying business networks as dynamic sites to observe not only the flows of cars and their spare parts across newly established state borders, but also the borders among individuals – aka emotions of capitalism. In so doing, Jackson offers to reconceptualise borders and mobility regimes less in terms of centre-periphery spatial hierarchies and 'more in terms of a rhizomic cartography of dynamically networked nodes.'

Next, in Chapter Five, Norig Neveu examines how the institution of new borders in the Middle East turned what were once imperial ecclesiastical institutions into entities whose jurisdictions began to spread over a number of countries and the corresponding debates on the emergence of 'national' churches. Building upon a burgeoning strand of literature that has thus far approached religious mobilities from the angle of pilgrim crossings, Neveu frames her discussion from a more institutional perspective and focuses on how the Greek Orthodox and Melkite Churches transitioned to a new territorial order in the emirate of Transjordan. The latter was an emerging space that not only offered opportunities for expansion for both churches, but also a bounded territorial unit that challenged the existing administrative boundaries of both churches. Neveu accordingly charts how the Melkite Church also gradually became a national Transjordanian church by tapping into Arab nationalism. For the Greek Orthodox Church, on the other hand, the interplay between territorialisation and transnational religious networks unfolded through debates on the degree of the Arabisation of the clerical hierarchy and if the church should adjust to the new territorial order, or not.

Katharina Lange in turn focuses on the politics of violence along the Turkish–Syrian border by providing case studies on two cross-border rebellions that took place two decades apart. With a focus on the Kurd Dagh region to the west of Aleppo, Lange frames this space as a terrain contested as much in history as in memory. In the first rebellion, which rocked the region in 1920, the French authorities failed to identify the complex networks of insurgents that mounted this anti-colonial struggle, which leads Lange to chart carefully the heterogeneous nature of the groups that were active in the insurgency. The context had shifted radically in Kurd Dagh, however, by the second rebellion in 1939, a time when Ankara was busy making strides to annex the neighbouring Sanjak of Alexandretta. The rank and file of the rebels in Kurd Dagh enjoyed close ties to Turkey, while those who participated in the 1920 insurgency now sided with the French, which reflected the emerging fault lines within the Kurd Dagh society. In reconstructing these two contentious episodes that unfolded next to the Syrian–Turkish border, Lange skilfully weaves together an account by engaging in local historiography and memory.

Part II has a thematic focus of cross-border mobilities. Samuel Dolbee starts off by examining the cross-border spread of diseases, particularly looking at the ways in which cattle plague and malaria occasioned state intervention and border consolidation in Syria's borderlands with Turkey and Iraq. Despite the advances in germ theory and the discovery of parasites and viruses since the late nineteenth century, as Dolbee notes, diseases continued to be associated with space and seen peculiar to certain environments, a spatial understanding of disease that was further strengthened by the quarantine regimes established along the borders and the settlement programmes that negotiated the cross-border arrival of refugees. Building upon the late Ottoman practices of territorial control, the interwar bureaucrats on both sides of the border developed measures to contain cattle plague, which not only curtailed patterns of nomadic migrations but also consolidated state sovereignty in border zones. Malaria fulfilled a similar function, too, informing the contours of the debate on the resettlement of Assyrians to Syria. As the chapter illustrates, 'the border between Syria and Turkey and the territorial meaning of Syria emerged in dialogue with disease.'

In Chapter Eight, César Jaquier discusses the introduction of motor transport between Damascus and Baghdad, examining the ways in which crossing the desert shaped relations between mandatory authorities and expanded state capacity to the borderlands. The introduction of the trans-desert routes was crucial for the British and French who saw this burgeoning business as a way of upholding their political and economic interests across the Middle East. They encouraged companies to form by giving subsidies and awarding contracts. The mandatory authorities certainly regulated the trans-desert traffic as well, encouraging the types of mobilities that served their interests, while restricting many others. But the coming of motorised transport to the desert presented many opportunities to those willing to exploit them. Particularly in times of political uncertainty and unrest, the actions of tribes, rebels and bandits led to further state intervention and informed more elaborate security measures across the desert. The chapter shows that while the motorised transport was informed by earlier Ottoman precedents of mobility, it certainly resulted in 'a change in the speed, scale and type of movement', reshaping patterns of mobility in the Syrian and Iraqi borderland.

Lauren Banko focuses on Palestine's northern border with Syria, Lebanon and Transjordan, where she reconstructs illicit crossings as a backdrop of the British attempts to consolidate the border as a site of infrastructural power – providing a case study that holds relevance for contemporary times. Palestine's northern frontier remained fluid throughout the 1920s, as the border continued to be adjusted on the ground as part of the negotiations between the British and French authorities. Because the border was not fully delimited, however, bureaucratic tensions continued to emerge over the regulation of the border crossings of individuals, with or without papers. While the existing literature has tended to examine Jewish migration into Palestine from Europe and the Americas, Banko chooses to study non-Zionist groups of migrants and mobile residents who illicitly crossed Palestine's northern border for a variety of reasons. The development of the border infrastructure, she notes, went hand in hand with the growing ambition to bring illicit border crossings under control, as the border walls, checkpoints, fencing and barbed wire increasingly began to dot Palestine's northern border throughout the 1930s.

In Chapter Ten, Robert S. G. Fletcher turns the focus to the desert and the Bedouin communities that populated it by reconstructing three episodes of Bedouin flight that took place within a decade after the disintegration of the Ottoman Empire. While the existing literature has largely studied the displacement of sedentarised groups in the borderlands between Turkey, Syria and Iraq, the deprivations faced by the nomadic communities in the south across the Syrian, Iraqi and Arabian deserts have not received due attention. In seeking to bring refugee studies into conversation with the studies on nomadic groups, Fletcher examines how the bureaucratic difficulty to categorise nomads as refugees – after all, nomads were by definition on the move – reflected, and was informed by, the broader distinctions in the interwar period between Christian refugees who were stateless and non-violent and displaced Muslims who belonged to a lesser category of the displaced. The nomads fared worse, as they were armed and not even settled, falling into a category where the interdependence between interwar internationalism and imperialism was far sharper. Ultimately, the three episodes that Fletcher reconstructs illustrate the ways in which Bedouin displacement, while justifying British attempts to extend further state control to the desert, also included the possibility of its own undoing.

Finally, Laura Stocker zooms in on the geography of the Northern Badiya, that is, the arid zones home to large Bedouin coalitions whose seasonal migratory circuits criss-crossed the projected borders delineating the new states of Iraq, Syria, Transjordan and Saudi Arabia. The chapter seeks to rethink the changing contours of state-tribal relations between 1929 and 1934 by reconstructing an important episode of livestock raiding known as 'the camel dispute', which had pitted two rival coalitions of the 'Anaza tribe to one another, while also leading to the direct involvement of the British and French mandatory authorities in the resolution of the conflict. By paying attention to the trans-border dynamics at play, Stocker charts how the attempts of states to extend influence and control over the arid zones in fact created various opportunities for tribes to assert their own historical agencies. As such, the chapter illustrates two competing tendencies that emerged in the late 1920s: while cross-border tribal mobility required interstate competition along the borderlands, the consolidation of borders put a premium on 'the competition for resources and sovereignty over people and territory in the Northern Badiya'.

In the Afterword, Cyrus Schayegh provides an assessment of the broader questions the volume raises on territoriality, borders and mobility, while also delineating the outlines of a research agenda for the future. As the contributions to this volume make it clear, borders are where global flows meet the regional and local, and the personal criss-crosses the institutional. As zones characterised by such a variety of networks, actors and interests, borderlands are home to multiple narratives and historicities. 'Regimes of mobility' therefore provides a useful tool to analyse similarities and differences across different border zones, even when borders that define these relationships may differ in their materiality and nature. As such, this volume seeks to move away from the tendency to study state-formation and border-making in singular case studies and instead highlights the interconnectedness of these processes across the region. This certainly does not mean that there is a single type of Middle Eastern border. Nor do we suggest that there is a preconfigured path of historical development, devoid of local variation.

The discussions in this volume instead help us flesh out two broad conclusions on borders, mobilities and state formation in the Middle East. First, the transition to nation states in the post-imperial spaces required the renegotiation of legal, commercial, personal and religious networks and legacies. Older geographies of mobilities and well-trodden networks inherited from the Ottoman Empire certainly proved difficult to dismantle, but the developments throughout the interwar period also helped transform them. In this process, states not only sought to prevent mobilities but also to re-channel them in ways serving their own interests. Second, tracing individual trajectories, such as those of merchants and sheikhs, or institutional networks, such as those of churches and businesses, is a productive way through which we can uncover the agencies of borderlanders and illustrate the ways in which they came to interact with the authorities on both sides of borders. As such, borders transformed mobilities, while mobilities made borders; states, on the other hand, drew their authority from the regimes of mobility they had sought to implement.

# PART I

POST-OTTOMAN TERRITORIALITY

# 1

## REVISITING *MILLÎ*: BORDERS AND THE MAKING OF THE TURKISH NATION STATE

### Alexander E. Balistreri

Nineteen twenty-one was Turkey's year of the border. A flurry of diplomatic activity on the part of the nationalist government in Ankara that year defined two long segments of the post-war country's territory: its northeastern border with the Caucasus, running from the Black Sea to Nakhichevan, and its southern border with Syria, running between the Mediterranean and the Tigris. The northeastern border was settled in two 1921 treaties, the Treaty of Moscow in March and the Treaty of Kars in October. The southern border was delineated in two 1921 agreements, the London Agreement in March and the Ankara Agreement in October. Though the subsequent Treaty of Lausanne (1923) has overshadowed discussion of these agreements, it would hardly be an exaggeration to point to 1921 as the year the Turkish nation state took concrete shape. Articles, speeches and parliamentary debates that year refer incessantly to the inviolability of its 'national border' (*hudud-ı milliye* or *millî hudut*). Yet in reality, these 'inviolable borders' were both pragmatic and open to change. Referring to the region around Aleppo, Mustafa Kemal Paşa (Atatürk) spoke of his '*active* determination of the border which we *today* call the national border' at the end of the war.[1] In other words, Turkey's national borders could be actively determined and their

---

[1] '*Bugün hudûd-ı milliye dediğimiz hududu fiilen tespit*'. Gazi Mustafa Kemal, *Nutuk* (İstanbul: Yapı Kredi Yayınları, 2011) [hereafter: *Nutuk*], p. 620. Emphasis mine.

definition could change throughout history. The mismatch between the supposed inviolability of national borders and their actual flexibility was both a product of conflicts over how to define the nation state as well as the inherent challenge of defining a nation on the basis of political borders.

## Bringing the Nation State Back In

By examining the border-making processes of 1921 here, I propose two arguments, one empirical and one methodological. Empirically, I highlight the simultaneity of border-making on both sides of the country. The chronological coincidence of these processes, for example, is striking: the London Agreement and Moscow Treaty were discussed on the same day in the Turkish parliament (17 March 1921), and the final international agreements that formed the basis for Turkey's northeastern and southern borders were also introduced to deputies on the same day (24 October 1921). Moreover, the negotiations surrounding these two borders, conducted bilaterally with separate countries who were themselves in a state of hostility toward one another, were closely interrelated: not only did Turkish negotiators hope to play off sides to gain more territorial concessions, but the techniques of compromise and pressure used during border discussions helped the slapdash diplomatic corps of the new government in Ankara learn for future negotiations.

The second, methodological argument of this chapter relates to the way historians approach borders in the modern era. When analysing the transition between the Ottoman Empire and the Turkish nation state, many historians have attempted to avoid the excesses of methodological nationalism and, in so doing, implicitly downplayed the actual establishment of the nation state between 1920 and 1923. This happens in various ways: Ottoman historians focusing on the early modern era tend to locate the transition to modern statehood far *before* the 1920s, while historians of twentieth-century Turkey and the Middle East find strong continuities across the first decades of the century and locate the break to true nation statehood many years *after* the 1920s. In both cases, the borders drawn around Turkey between 1918 and 1923 are often disregarded as arbitrary, artificial or altogether porous. Keith David Watenpaugh, for example, argues that historians' focus on the First World War as a turning point potentially 'reifies the Franklin-Bouillon Line between Republican Turkey and French Mandate Syria – the path of which merely traces a ceasefire line determined by a railroad bed – into a relevant cultural and ideological boundary'.[2]

In light of a dominant historiographical paradigm that shuns the nation state, this chapter's focus on nation state boundaries demands justification. It is possible to study a nation state border without reifying it – to highlight the importance of nation state borders as 'ideological boundaries' without resorting to methodological nationalism. Historians can view nation state borders not as an inevitable or desirable historical outcome, but rather examine each border as the product of its own historical context and of human agency. The drawing of Turkish 'national borders' in 1921 was not a 'mere tracing of a ceasefire line' without any effect; rather, the actual process of negotiating national borders had the immediate effect of forcing Turkish officials and lawmakers to define the nation itself and, by extension, the entire scope of their political activity horizon. New borders swept officials up in diplomacy and compelled new borderlanders to consider loyalties and identities.[3] Studying nation state borders is valuable because it helps us understand the worldview of Turkish nationalist leaders, the way they imagined and internalised the map of their country as well as their role in it. In other words, it helps us understand territory, in Charles S. Maier's words, as both 'decision space' and 'identity space', while highlighting the accelerated effort to join the two in the nineteenth and twentieth centuries.[4] At the same time, detailed scrutiny of the nation-state border process reveals the incompleteness of these efforts. Nation state borders remained the rough fringes of imagined territories. This chapter thus highlights the awkwardness of nation state borders – awkward in the sense that their very existence was trumpeted as a triumph of nationalism even as they were the result of significant concessions of territory claimed by nationalists.

---

[2] Keith David Watenpaugh, *Being Modern in the Middle East: Revolution, Nationalism, Colonialism, and the Arab Middle Class* (Princeton, NJ: Princeton University Press, 2006), p. 182.

[3] On the political effects of border-drawing in the early 1920s, see Chapter Two of this volume, by Orçun Can Okan. For the longer term cultural and symbolic effects of drawing these borders, see Mathijs Pelkmans, *Defending the Border: Identity, Religion, and Modernity in the Republic of Georgia* (Ithaca, NY: Cornell University Press, 2006), pp. 5, 14.

[4] Charles S. Maier, *Once Within Borders: Territories of Power, Wealth, and Belonging since 1500* (Cambridge, MA: The Belknap Press, 2016), p. 3.

Scholars of Turkey widely share the view that early 'Kemalist nationalism was above all territorial' in nature – that is, that it eschewed irredentism among Turkic groups outside of the Ottoman core and that it defined the Turkish nation as those Muslims living within Turkey's borders.[5] 'The indivisibility of the Turkish state and its nation and the irreversibility of its borders,' writes Ayşe Kadıoğlu, 'constitute the cornerstone of Turkish national identity.'[6] This strong association of borders with identity differentiates nation state territoriality from imperial territoriality. Nevertheless, policies like irredentism and assimilation blur the difference between late-imperial and nation state boundaries. As was the case in other 'rump states' whittled down from the polyethnic empires, Turkish nationalism tended at first to be civic and assimilationist rather than ethnic and exclusionary,[7] though it did not rule out irredentism either. In this respect, the vague characterisation of Turkey's new borders as *millî* (national) served nationalist leaders well. In the early 1920s, the definition of *millet* (nation) was in flux – its definition encompassed religious, ethnic, political and territorial elements whose emphasis could be adjusted as the situation called for.[8] The strong territorial

---

[5] Ali Kazancıgil, 'The Ottoman-Turkish state and Kemalism', in Ali Kazancıgil and Ergun Özbudun (eds), *Atatürk: Founder of a Modern State* (London: C. Hurst, 1981), p. 51. See also Bernard Lewis, *The Emergence of Modern Turkey*, 3rd. ed. (Oxford: Oxford University Press, 2002), p. 352; Behlül Özkan, *From the Abode of Islam to the Turkish Vatan: The Making of a National Homeland in Turkey* (New Haven: Yale University Press, 2012), pp. 60, 90; Frank Tachau, 'The Search for National Identity among the Turks', *Die Welt des Islams*, N.S. Vol. 3 (1962–63), pp. 165–76.

[6] Ayşe Kadıoğlu, 'The Twin Motives of Turkish Nationalism', in Ayşe Kadıoğlu and E. Fuat Keyman (eds), *Symbiotic Antagonisms: Competing Nationalisms in Turkey* (Salt Lake City: University of Utah Press, 2011), p. 48.

[7] Karen Barkey, 'Thinking About Consequences of Empire', in Karen Barkey and Mark von Hagen (eds), *After Empire: Multiethnic Societies and Nation-Building* (Boulder, CO: Westview Press, 1997), p. 107.

[8] M. Asım Karaömerlioğlu, 'The Role of Religion and Geography in Turkish Nationalism: The Case of Nurettin Topçu', in P. Nikiforos Diamandouros, Thalia Dragonas, and Çağlar Keyder (eds), *Spatial Conceptions of the Nation: Modernizing Geographies in Greece and Turkey* (London: I. B. Tauris, 2010), pp. 98–100; Erik Jan Zürcher, 'The vocabulary of Muslim nationalism', *International Journal of the Sociology of Language*, Vol. 137 (January 1999), pp. 81–92.

element introduced after the war added instability to the concept of *millet*; to ask whether the nation defined the borders or the borders defined the nation led only down the road of infinite regression. One thing was clear: in 1920 and 1921 the definition of the nation was for most nationalists not a strictly ethnic one. Mustafa Kemal, in speeches to parliament in 1920, defined the national borders as encompassing either one *millet* or 'sibling *millets*' composed of multiple Muslim elements, including Turks, Kurds and Circassians.[9] The Turkish nationalist leader was even more explicit in a speech to parliament in 1921:

> What is our national border [*hudud-ı millimiz (sic)*]? Is it strictly necessary that places inhabited by Turks and by Kurds, struggling alongside us [to determine] our fate, be included in our national border? No, no. That would be too broad . . . Our national border is that national border which enables us to live happily and independently, and whichever border we can draw to best optimise our interests will be our national border. [There is] after all [no] clearly delineated boundary.[10]

The fact that nationalist leaders did not use 'national borders' as the equivalent of ethnic borders is further demonstrated by the contemporary translation of the French term *frontière éthnographique* not as *hudud-ı milliye* but rather as *hudud-ı ırkiye*. Nationalist leaders' preference for ethno-national, rather than strictly ethnographic, borders would have far-reaching consequences.

One central element of the Turkish nationalist narrative that can be more properly understood by focusing on the specifics of the border-making process of the early 1920s is the *Misak-ı Millî*, or National Pact. The *Misak-ı Millî*, adopted by the nationalists of the last Ottoman chamber of deputies in 1920, is a statement of the aims of the nationalist movement. It pledges to defend the core territories of the Ottoman Empire, protect the rights of Muslims and followers of other religions, and develop the country through economic independence. As a declaration in line with contemporary global

---

[9] *Türkiye Büyük Millet Meclisi Zabıt Ceridesi* [hereafter: TBMMZC] (24 April 1920), pp. 16–17; TBMMZC (1 May 1920), p. 165.

[10] *Türkiye Büyük Millet Meclisi Gizli Celse Zabıtları* [hereafter: TBMMGCZ] (16 October 1921), p. 355.

calls to self-determination, the pact defends the right of Muslims living around the borders of the country to conduct plebiscites on whether to join the Ottoman-Turkish state. Since its passage, the *Misak-ı Millî* has been invoked as the quintessential founding document of modern Turkey. The treaties and agreements of 1921 examined in this chapter mention or quote it explicitly. In the Turkish popular mind, the *Misak-ı Millî* is understood to be a definitive statement of borders for the coming nation state. These '*Misak-ı Millî* borders' are thought to reflect maximalist, irredentist claims and thus thought to unequivocally include, for example, Mosul, Aleppo or Western Thrace within the boundaries of modern Turkey. Criticising such widespread assumption of clear borders, some scholars have questioned the extent to which the *Misak-ı Millî* defines a border at all; one leftist historian infamously called the idea of the *Misak-ı Millî*, as used in Turkish state discourse, as 'not much more than a legend'.[11] Others have defended it, meanwhile, as 'a charter carefully prepared through the meticulous efforts of several ministries, the general staff, and commissions of the Ottoman Empire'.[12]

In fact, the *Misak-ı Millî* represents not a self-evident, uncontested manifesto but the negotiated outcome of fundamental discussions between the pragmatically orientated leadership of the nationalist movement, which preferred an ethno-national basis for the nation state and a clear statement of borders, and other Turkish-Muslim nationalists, some of whom pursued more utopian goals of retaining extensive imperial territory. Nationalist factions serving on the *Misak-ı Millî* commission, debated, for example, whether greater Syria should be envisioned as part of a future, possibly federated, state together with Anatolia.[13] While the commission rejected this as an explicit aim, the text of the *Misak-ı Millî* appeased the more imperially minded nationalists by remaining deliberately vague about where the border of the

---

[11] Mete Tunçay, '*Misak-ı Millî*'nin 1. Maddesi Üstüne', *Birikim*, Vols. 18–19 (Ağustos-Eylül 1976), p. 16.

[12] Enes Demir, *Yeni Belgeler Işığında Vazgeçilmeyen Topraklar: Mîsâk-ı Millî* (İstanbul: Post Yayın Dağıtım, 2017), p. 143.

[13] Rıżā Nūr, *Türk Tārīḥi*, Cild 1 (İstanbul: Maṭba'a-i 'āmire, 1924), p. 196. On the history of this idea in the last years of the Ottoman Empire, see: Alp Yenen, 'Envisioning Turco-Arab Co-Existence between Empire and Nationalism', *Die Welt des Islams*, Vol. 61, No. 1 (January 2021), pp. 72–112.

future nation state would be. The pact's first article refers to the ceasefire line of 30 October 1918 as if it were a kind of potential border, but continues by claiming that

> all of the territories, *whether inside or outside this ceasefire line*, which are inhabited by a majority of Ottoman Muslims united in religion, culture, and aim, [and] filled with a feeling of mutual respect and solidarity . . . constitute a *de facto* and *de jure* whole whose division is unacceptable for any reason.[14]

The phrase 'inside or outside this ceasefire line' has caused consternation in Turkish historiography, since many subsequently published versions of the *Misak-ı Millî* omit the words 'or outside'.[15] Indeed, it was Mustafa Kemal himself who opposed including this defence of territory beyond the ceasefire line in the *Misak-ı Millî*, arguing that its inclusion was a 'fundamental deviation from our principles on the border'.[16] The Turkish nationalist leader argued that the priority should be a clearly articulated, defensible border; territory could then be expanded beyond this border in the future as conditions allowed. There is also a contradiction between the pledge to defend all Ottoman territory outside the ceasefire line as indivisible and the promise to provide populations living on such territories with the possibility of a plebiscite; this unresolved contradiction in the text of the *Misak-ı Millî* is arguably the result of the same dispute between pragmatic and utopian nationalist factions. As this chapter demonstrates, the heated debates over 'compromises' on Turkey's northeastern and southern borders that took place in 1921 can thus be understood as an extension of the original discussion of the *Misak-ı Millî*, itself revolving around the central question of how Turkey's future territory should be conceived: as a new country, or as a way of rescuing the Ottoman Empire.

---

[14] The text of the *Misak-ı Millî* as made public by the Ottoman parliament is in *Meclis-i Mebusan Zabıt Ceridesi* (17 February 1920), pp. 144–45. The italics are mine.

[15] Tevfik Bıyıklıoğlu, *Atatürk Anadolu'da (1919–1921)* (İstanbul: Yeni Gün Haber Ajansı Basın ve Yayıncılık, 2000), pp. 136–37; Nejat Kaymaz, 'Mîsâk-ı Milli Üzerinde Yapılan Tartışmalar Hakkında', *VIII. Türk Tarih Kongresi*, III. Cilt (Ankara: Türk Tarih Kurumu, 1977), 1957; Özkan, p. 87.

[16] '. . . *sınır hakkındaki prensiplerimizle esaslı bir fark* . . .' Telegram of Mustafa Kemal to Rauf Bey [Orbay] (7 February 1920), in *Atatürk'ün Bütün Eserleri*, Cilt 6 (28 Aralık 1919–1 Mart 1920) (İstanbul: Kaynak Yayınları, 2015), p. 171.

## Moscow, Kars and the Enemies of One's Enemies

One of the regions which was promised a plebiscite in the *Misak-ı Millî* was the *Elviye-i Selâse*, or the 'Three Districts' of Kars, Ardahan and Batum (Batumi). In fact, it was the recent history of this region that likely inspired nationalists' call for plebiscites around the entire empire: as early as 1918 the Treaty of Brest-Litovsk had allowed the Ottoman government to arrange a plebiscite for the *Elviye-i Selâse* on the issue of joining the Ottoman Empire. Even as it did so, however, the Ottoman government simultaneously waged war against Georgia and Armenia, forcing both to give up even more territory in the Treaty of Batum. That treaty's border – including the territories of Akhaltsikhe (Ahıska), Iğdır, Borchalo and Nakhichevan – represented the outermost extent of concrete Ottoman claims after the First World War but remained a mostly theoretical one, since the territories it encompassed were never incorporated into Ottoman civilian rule. The ceasefire conditions and British occupation in late 1918 forced the Ottoman government and army back behind the empire's pre-war borders, giving up its gains from both the Treaties of Brest-Litovsk and Batum.

By the spring of 1920, conditions re-emerged for a new Turkish advance into the Caucasus. Compared to 1918, however, the geopolitical situation had changed considerably – and Turkish officials' view of the border along with it. The *Misak-ı Millî* of January that year was a watered-down version of Ottoman claims at the end of the war; it recognised only Kars, Ardahan and Batum as regions potentially within a national border and avoided mention of Akhaltsikhe, Iğdır and other 'Turkish-majority' areas in the southwest Caucasus that had been occupied in 1918. Turkish leaders were aware of the pending Bolshevisation of the South Caucasus. While they opposed an outright Bolshevik annexation of the region, they welcomed Bolshevik influence there and had no intention of alienating the Bolsheviks by occupying extensive territories in the Caucasus. At the same time, Kâzım Karabekir Paşa, commander of Turkish forces in the east, developed a strategy for the advancing Turkish army: take territory up to the Brest-Litovsk border and see how far the Red Army and Georgian Menshevik Army had come before deciding whether to advance beyond this boundary, especially into Armenia.[17] At the

---

[17] Kâzım Karabekir, *İstiklâl Harbimiz* (İstanbul: Yapı Kredi Yayınları, 2008), p. 745.

same time, Karabekir began describing this strategic border, drawn arbitrarily in the nineteenth century, as a national one. He wrote:

> Our borders should follow the basic principle of ethnicity and religion – and this is an utmost necessity. From this perspective, the borders of the military operation on our eastern front . . . are to terminate at the borders of Georgia, thereby ending the enslavement of the fellow members of our ethnicity and replacing it with peace and security.[18]

In the late summer of 1920 the Ankara government began negotiations with Soviet Russia in Moscow regarding the recognition of Turkey and the acquisition of Russian aid. Turkey's delegation to Moscow led by Foreign Minister Bekir Sami Bey (Kunduh) aimed to have Soviet Russia recognise the borders it had described in the *Misak-ı Millî*. Russia's foreign minister Georgiy Chicherin, negotiating for the Russians, rejected the *Misak-ı Millî*'s conjunctural definition of Turkey's borders and said that the Bolsheviks' interpretation of self-determination meant they would only recognise a Turkey within its ethnographic boundaries (*hudud-ı ırkiye*). This posed a problem for Turkey, because while Chicherin and Karabekir's standard for tracing boundaries around ethnicities was seemingly the same, each promoted different ethnicities and defined them differently. At issue were provinces such as Van and Bitlis, areas that had been occupied by Russia during the war and which the Russians now believed should belong to an Armenian state.[19] On the topic of Turkish sovereignty in Kars, Ardahan and the hinterland of Batum, the Turkish delegation was not willing to negotiate. On other borderland territories, however, the delegation was open to discussion; they would accept Russian mediation regarding the territories of the Armenian Republic disputed between Turkey and Armenia, and they would negotiate with the South Caucasian governments regarding the status of the city and port of Batum.[20] Russia budged somewhat, claiming in a letter to Mustafa Kemal that they

---

[18] Ibid., pp. 697, 801–2.

[19] TBMMGCZ (16 October 1920), p. 170; Kâmuran Gürün, *Türk-Sovyet İlişkileri (1920–1953)* (Ankara: Türk Tarih Kurumu, 1991), p. 37; Yusuf Kemal Tengirşe[n]k, *Vatan Hizmetinde* (İstanbul: Bahar Matbaası, 1967) [hereafter: Tengirşenk], pp. 167–70.

[20] TBMMGCZ (16 October 1920), pp. 170–71; Tengirşenk, pp. 188–89.

would respect the *Misak-ı Millî*, but deliberately ignored the scope of the territory that it claimed could be subject to referendum. In line with the Russian interpretation of ethnographic boundaries, self-determination was to be implemented in any areas that were not 'indisputably Turkish', including (in the geographic terms used by Chicherin) Armenia, Kurdistan, Lazistan, the hinterland of Batum, Eastern Thrace and any areas in which Turks and Arabs lived together. Syria and the Arab lands to the south were to be completely independent, without recourse to a plebiscite.[21]

While discussions between Turkey and Russia continued in 1920 and 1921, all observers expected that the Caucasus would be divided between the Bolsheviks and the nationalist Turks. Yet when the Sovietisation of the Caucasus stalled, the Ankara government had to take its neighbours into consideration: the Republics of Georgia and Armenia. War broke out between the Republic of Armenia and the Ankara government in the late summer of 1920, with Armenia seeking to secure the borders it had been promised at Sèvres and Turkey attempting to regain Kars, which it had lost with the British occupation. Turkish forces advanced easily, even seizing territory beyond the Brest-Litovsk border when it took Aleksandropol' (Gyumri, Gümrü) in November.[22] Throughout 1920 Turkish leaders pursued their advance into Kars and Armenian territory with a cautious eye on Soviet Russia, which also claimed influence in the region and with whom the Ankara government sought good relations. So when the Armenian Republic sued for peace in November, Turkey aimed to definitively debilitate the Armenian army but advanced mild political conditions, including plebiscites in disputed border regions, free commerce across borders and a return of all displaced persons to their homes.[23] The resulting Treaty of Aleksandropol' between Turkey and Armenia in December 1920 traced a border very similar to today's. Although the Sovietisation of Armenia prevented the treaty from coming into force, the latter did serve as a basis for discussion on the border between Turkey and

---

[21] Gürün, pp. 51–52.

[22] A detailed account of the Turkish–Armenian war of 1920 and its geopolitical context is given in Richard G. Hovannisian, *The Republic of Armenia, Vol. IV: Between Crescent and Sickle: Partition and Sovietization* (Berkeley: University of California Press, 1996), Chapters 5–6.

[23] Ibid., pp. 275–78.

Russia.[24] Less intensive diplomatic relations were initiated with Georgia in September 1920.[25] Here, Turkey and Georgia were able to secure non-intervention in each other's disputes with Armenia and Russia. Georgia did not resist when Turkish troops in early 1921 pushed into Ardahan and Batum.[26]

In late February 1921 Turkish and Russian diplomats began meeting for a second round of talks in Moscow. Turkish diplomats, who had complained to the Russian government about Chicherin's intransigence on the issue of the Turkish border, were now given assurances that Soviet Russia's commissar of nationalities, Iosif Stalin, would take matters into his own hands to ensure a speedy resolution. Delegation member Ali Fuat Paşa (Cebesoy), believing that Turkey's military successes and its impending rapprochement with France made the Russians pursue a more pro-Turkish policy, argued that 'the official news that Stalin would actively participate in the Moscow conference could be nothing other than a subtle hint that . . . Chicherin's incompetent policy against Turkey was going to be corrected'.[27] Turkish delegates to the conference considered Stalin, an ethnic Georgian, to be fiercely anti-Armenian.[28] Indeed, Stalin's entry into the discussion meant the issue of the border could be resolved at lightning speed, and without Chicherin's idealism. Stalin dispensed with diplomatic formalities, meeting personally with Turkish negotiators behind closed doors. In less than two weeks, they had agreed on the allocation of territories as they stand today. The border that emerged was the one proposed personally by Stalin.[29] The district of Batum,

[24] For the text of the Treaty of Aleksandropol' and an analysis, see Gotthard Jaeschke, 'Der türkisch-armenische Friedensvertrag von Gümrü (Alexandropol)', *Die Welt des Islams*, Vol. 2 (1953), pp. 25–47.

[25] Karabekir, p. 983; Tengirşenk, pp. 185–86; Serpil Sürmeli, *Türk-Gürcü İlişkileri (1918–1921)* (Ankara: Atatürk Araştırma Merkezi, 2001), p. 569.

[26] Karabekir, pp. 1,024, 1,028, G.İ. Kvinitadze, *Moi vospominaniya v godı nezavisimosti Gruzii, 1917–1921* (Paris: YMCA-Press, 1985), pp. 330–31; Sürmeli, pp. 644–48, 664–65.

[27] Ali Fuat Cebesoy, *Moskova Hatıraları* (İstanbul: Vatan Neşriyatı, 1955), pp. 114–22, quotation from p. 121; Gürün, pp. 65–66; Tengirşenk, pp. 221–24, 238–39.

[28] Rıza Nur, *Hayat ve Hatıratım*, Vol. 3 (İstanbul: İşaret Yayınları, 1992), p. 151; Karabekir, pp. 1,060–61.

[29] Memoirs of Saffet Arıkan as related to Knox Helm, counsellor at the British embassy in Ankara, in: TNA, FO 371/59241 (23 March 1946). For a version of how Lenin and Stalin decided on this border in local Adjaran lore, see: Pelkmans, p. 20.

along with the city and its port, would go to Georgia, while Iğdır would go to Turkey. Turkish negotiators told Stalin they would be willing to cede Batum if Soviet Russia recognised the *Misak-ı Millî*.[30] Smaller territorial adjustments were carried out in the districts of Artvin and Kars. A final treaty was signed a week after that, on 16 March 1921.[31] Article 1 was a victory for Turkey, with Russia recognising Turkey's definition as 'those territories included in the National Pact of 28 January 1920'.[32]

The Treaty of Moscow is highly unusual in at least one major respect: Russia and Turkey defined the northeastern Turkish border without the involvement of those states (Georgia, Armenia and Azerbaijan) actually sharing this border. That Soviet Russia already exerted de facto hegemony in the South Caucasus is made clear, however, by the Treaty of Moscow's Article XV, which compelled Turkey to sign similar agreements with the Caucasian republics and Russia to mediate if necessary to obtain this result. Turkish officials met with delegates from Soviet Russia and the newly Sovietised South Caucasian Republics in the fall of 1921 to carry out this task. Though the Ankara government feared that the South Caucasian republics would use the opportunity to demand changes to the border delimited at Moscow – for example with the Georgians demanding Artvin – the presence of a Soviet Russian delegation imposed a general silence on the Soviet Caucasian delegates, and the border that had been foreseen in Moscow was duly approved in the Treaty of Kars (13 October 1921).[33] The discussions of the border at the Kars

---

[30] Tengirşenk, p. 221.

[31] In fact, the treaty was signed on 18 March, while the official date was given as 16 March in order to coincide with the one-year anniversary of Istanbul's occupation by the Allies. Tengirşenk, p. 230.

[32] For the full text of the treaty in Russian and Turkish, see: Ministerstvo Inostrannıkh Del SSSR, *Dokumentı Vneshney Politiki SSSR*, Tom 3 (Moskva: Gosudarstvennoe izdatel'stvo politicheskoy literaturı, 1959), pp. 597–604; Tengirşenk, pp. 293–302. On Russia's acceptance of the *Misak-ı Millî*, see Tengirşenk, pp. 238–39.

[33] For the Turkish assessment of negotations at Kars, and for the treaty text in Turkish, see: Karabekir, pp. 1,110–32. For the text of the treaty in Russian, see: Ministerstvo Inostrannıkh Del SSSR, *Dokumentı Vneshney Politiki SSSR*, Tom 4 (Moskva: Gosudarstvennoe izdatel'stvo politicheskoy literaturı, 1960), pp. 420–29. For a Soviet assessment of the negotiations, see: S.V. Kharmandaryan, 'Karskaya [*sic*] Konferenstiya 1921 g. i eë predıstoriya', *Banber Hayastani Arkhivneri* 3 (1963), pp. 177–208.

Conference merely revolved around a few disputed sites, including the ruins of the ancient Armenian capital of Ani, which the Turkish delegation briefly considered handing to Armenia as a gesture of goodwill.

## London, Ankara, and the Arbitrariness of the Border

In theory, the *Misak-ı Millî* had also promised Arab-majority areas to the south of Anatolia the possibility of plebiscites on joining a future Turkish state. Nevertheless, it is hard to imagine that Turkish nationalist deputies, resigned to the loss of the Arab-majority lands, had much real interest in pressing for such a referendum. 'We have no aim other than to live freely and independently within our national borders,' Mustafa Kemal told deputies in the Turkish parliament in 1921.

> We have already paid the price we owed for the defeat suffered by the alliance to which we belonged during the World War; we paid it by handing over the administration and right of self-determination over our expansive territory, including Syria and Iraq, to the people who live there, thereby foregoing our sovereign rights.[34]

The determination of Turkey's border with France's mandate in Syria was a result – just like in the country's northeast – of highly personal diplomacy set against a backdrop of armed struggle. The initial definition of the border by both sides varied widely. The Treaty of Sèvres, signed by the Allies and the Ottoman government in August 1920, included much of present-day southern Turkey, including the cities of Antep, Maraş and Urfa, as well as the Gulf of Alexandretta (İskenderun) within the French mandate. Turkish nationalists, meanwhile, insisted on retaining all territories held by the Ottoman army upon the signing of the ceasefire on 30 October 1918. Turkish nationalists defined this ceasefire line as the country's legitimate political border throughout 1919, with Mustafa Kemal explicitly describing it as starting south of the Gulf of Alexandretta near Antakya and passing north of Aleppo to Jarablus on the Euphrates. From there, the border would curve sharply southward to include Deyr-i Zor and the regions of Mosul, Kirkuk and Sulaymaniyah. Like Karabekir in the north, Mustafa Kemal also equated this strategic border

---

[34] TBMMZC (19 September 1921), 261.

with an ethno-national one: 'Just as this is the border being defended in arms by our army, it simultaneously delineates the areas of our homeland that are populated by Turkish and Kurdish elements. In the area to its south are our fellow Muslims who speak Arabic'.[35]

As Turkish national forces battled French troops and their Armenian allies for control of the region, high-level members of the French government expressed their willingness to reach a compromise with the Turkish nationalists on the border issue. French High Commissioner François Georges-Picot had suggested to Mustafa Kemal as early as December 1919 that France would be willing to withdraw from Cilicia, Antep, Urfa and Maraş in exchange for economic concessions from Turkey.[36] After repeated, unsuccessful attempts to sit down at the negotiating table, the first concrete results on Turkey's southern border came at the Conference of London in February and March 1921.[37] While the official agenda did not include a revision of Turkey's southern border, Foreign Minister Bekir Sami, as Ankara's representative, did declare Turkey's 'minimum' demand for territory in the *Misak-ı Millî* and demanded a border separating Turkey from an 'Arab majority' in the south as well as a border 'on the basis of the principles of nationality' in the northeast.[38] Bekir Sami also met secretly with French Prime Minister Aristide Briand and signed a bilateral agreement to regulate political, military and economic matters and to determine the Turkish–Syrian border. This agreement, which Bekir Sami apparently signed on his own initiative,[39] resembled Picot's proposal. It gave significant economic

---

[35] Speech of 28 December 1919, in *Atatürk'ün Bütün Eserleri*, Cilt 6, p. 30.

[36] Bige Yavuz, '1921 Tarihli Türk-Fransız Anlaşması'nın Hazırlık Aşamaları', *Atatürk Araştırma Merkezi Dergisi* 8:23 (Mart 1992), p. 275; Stanford J. Shaw, *From Empire to Republic: The Turkish War of National Liberation*, Vol. 3, Part 2 (Ankara: Türk Tarih Kurumu, 2000), pp. 1,386–87; Karabekir, pp. 438–39.

[37] Summaries of the proceedings at the London Conference can be found in Shaw, III:1, pp. 1,223–47 and, from the Ottoman perspective, Erkin Akan, 'Osmanlı Arşiv Belgelerine Göre Londra Konferansı (21 Şubat 1921–12 Mart 1921)', *Çanakkale Araştırmaları Türk Yıllığı* 16:24 (Bahar 2018), pp. 245–67.

[38] Shaw, III:1, p. 1,230.

[39] This was admitted by Bekir Sami in front of Turkish parliament. TBMMGCZ (12 May 1921), p. 74.

concessions to France but revised the border in Turkey's favour. The new border, a line between the Gulf of Alexandretta and Cizre, would include Cilicia, Antep, Urfa and Maraş in Turkey but exclude Antakya, which would receive special administrative status to protect Turkish cultural rights there.[40]

The London Agreement caused an uproar when the Turkish parliament first heard of it on 17 March 1921. All who spoke that day denounced the agreement as a violation of the Turkish national cause. Deputies did not comment on the specifics of the agreement, though it was likely the broad economic concessions in Article G that caused the most consternation. Deputies were also angered that the delegation led by Bekir Sami had made these concessions in the form of an international agreement without prior authorisation and without the approval of parliament. One deputy spouted: 'I don't care if it's a ceasefire agreement, or a treaty, or whatever – to my mind it's a sheet of paper without a shred of value, and those of us with a conscience must use that paper to slap the faces of the delegates we sent [to London]'.[41] The mood in parliament was extremely anti-West. Some deputies questioned the backbone and political skill of the Turkish nationalist delegates in London, angered that they would concede anything to the 'devils at the green table' when their task had been a simple one: to just insist on the *Misak-ı Millî*. 'It seems that our colleagues were swept up by all the tall buildings and feasts of London,' quipped one.[42]

It remains to be explained why Bekir Sami, who had insisted so doggedly on the *Misak-ı Millî* against the Russians in the summer of 1920 would supposedly fail to defend it against the French in early 1921, or why someone who was hesitant to come to an agreement with the Russians and Britain on controversial topics without consulting the parliament[43] would now

---

[40] A reproduction of the London Agreement is found in Yavuz, pp. 294–96. A translation of the London Agreement into Turkish can be found in: BCA, 930.2, 1.7.1 (9 March 1921); I thank Ramazan Hakkı Öztan for this reference.

[41] TBMMGCZ (17 March 1921), p. 5. For their part, critics of Briand's policy also lambasted the outcome at London as 'humiliating' and 'rash', a 'border considered unacceptable by everyone'. Roger de Gontaut-Biron and L. Le Révérend, *D'Angora à Lausanne: Les étapes d'une déchéance* (Paris: Plon-Nourrit, 1924), pp. 14–15, 31, 69.

[42] TBMMGCZ (17 March 1921), pp. 7–8.

[43] Tengirşenk, 164; Shaw, III:1, p. 1,240.

sign significant secret agreements with France (and Italy) of his own accord. Mustafa Kemal would himself later call Bekir Sami's behaviour 'inexplicable', only pointing out that Bekir Sami sought peace 'at all costs' and believed the entente could be convinced to come to an agreement with Turkey without requiring a compromise of principles.[44] Yet in the spring of 1921, Mustafa Kemal seemed to take a different approach. When Bekir Sami returned from London, he and Mustafa Kemal remained on strikingly cordial terms. Rather than excoriate Bekir Sami for his 'failure' to defend Turkish independence in Europe, Mustafa Kemal praised his 'important work in London, Paris and Italy' in front of the parliament. And while Mustafa Kemal quietly asked him to resign as foreign minister, he continued to believe that Bekir Sami could serve as a means of drawing certain elements in the West into an agreement with the Turkish nationalists.[45] This adds to the impression that Mustafa Kemal and his immediate circle were more willing to compromise with Western governments on the border than most deputies, who continued to vociferously denounce the agreement when its details were revealed in May.[46]

After the Turkish parliament and Ankara government rejected the London Agreement, Prime Minister Fevzi Paşa (Çakmak) made it known to France that it considered the border traced in the agreement an 'unjustified attack' on the *Misak-ı Millî* and on 'the principle of nationality'. Ankara considered, but refrained from, sending a delegation headed by the interior minister to Beirut to demand İskenderun and Antakya for Turkey.[47] Instead, the government's new proposal for the border – which Fevzi argued was designed 'in order to approximate as closely as possible the ethnographic and geographic border and to balance the interests of the two parties, while simultaneously taking

---

[44] *Nutuk*, pp. 515–18.

[45] TBMMGCZ (12 May 1921), 73; telegram of Mustafa Kemal to Bekir Sami (19 May 1921), in *Nutuk*, 516; Shaw, III:1, p. 1,251.

[46] This interpretation runs counter to that of Stanford J. Shaw, who, copying the later interpretation of the *Nutuk* describes Bekir Sami as a quitter, even as Mustafa Kemal sought to push on militarily at all costs. Shaw, III:1, pp. 1,249, 1,252. Rıza Nur, however, suspected – as I do – that Mustafa Kemal may have personally authorised Bekir Sami's moves in London; Rıza Nur, p. 171. Solitary voices of support for Bekir Sami and for a compromise for peace came from Vehbi Efendi (Çelik) and Zekâi Bey (Apaydın).

[47] Gontaut-Biron and Le Révérend, p. 40.

historical considerations into account' – included the railway and much of present-day northeastern Syria in Turkey but left İskenderun, Antakya and Aleppo in the French mandate.[48]

Economy Minister Yusuf Kemal Bey (Tengirşenk), on his way back to Ankara from leading negotiations in Moscow, was informed that he had been elected on 16 May 1921 to replace Bekir Sami as foreign minister. By coincidence, in İnebolu, he encountered Henry Franklin-Bouillon, a Turkophilic plenipotentiary sent by the French government, en route to Ankara as well. The Ankara government informed Yusuf Kemal that, as the new foreign minister, he was to help Mustafa Kemal and Fevzi negotiate an agreement with Franklin-Bouillon to end the war underway between Turkey and France in the south.[49] Negotiations now took place privately, not at a conference – i.e. outside of the oversight of parliament. Yusuf Kemal merely reported to the Turkish parliament in June 1921 that he, 'together with an esteemed French gentleman who had come to Ankara, were in private talks to look for solutions to end the state of war between the two nations'.[50]

Discussions in June 1921 revolved around establishing the principles of an agreement. After Franklin-Bouillon returned from a trip to consult with his superiors in Adana, official negotiations continued in earnest in mid-September. On the Turkish side, Yusuf Kemal and Fethi Bey (Okyar) both noted that the question of the border – and the related question of minority rights – threatened to upend talks in early October.[51] As in Moscow, the Turkish delegation insisted on not diverging from the *Misak-ı Millî*. While the French demanded special recognition of minority rights in the areas evacuated by the French army, Yusuf Kemal insisted that Article 5 of the *Misak-ı Millî*, which guaranteed the rights of minorities in Turkey if the rights of

---

[48] Letter of Fevzi to Briand (no date [mid-May 1921]), reproduced in Yavuz, p. 298; counter proposal in ibid., p. 303.

[49] Tengirşenk, pp. 246–47. Franklin-Bouillon was the target of criticism by hardline French observers, who accused him of being 'a novice in the psychology of the Oriental' and for kowtowing to the Turks. Gontaut-Biron and Le Révérend, pp. 17, 51.

[50] TBMMZC (27 June 1921), p. 61.

[51] Ali Fethi Okyar and Kansu Şarman (eds), *Büyük Günlerin Adamı: Fethi Okyar'ın Hayatından Kareler (İstanbul: Türkiye İş Bankası Kültür Yayınları, 2016)*, p. 52; Tengirşenk, pp. 251–52; TBMMGCZ (16 October 1921), pp. 352–53.

Muslims be equally protected in neighbouring countries, should be taken as the basis for an agreement with the French. Here, as in Moscow, Turkish insistence on the *Misak-ı Millî* won the day. The exact wording of the Pact's Article 5, minus the stipulation that neighbouring Muslims' right be guaranteed, was repeated in Article 6 of the final Turkish-French agreement.[52]

The issue of the border would be more difficult to resolve to the benefit of Ankara, particularly as, unlike in the case of Turkey's northeast border, the *Misak-ı Millî* did not clearly specify what boundary the Turkish nationalists claimed. The French had assumed that the platform of the Baghdad Railway would be taken as the basis for a new border, since this was the proposal that had been discussed since the London Conference in March 1921. This, after all, was already seen as a concession by the French, who had for years assumed the 'natural border' of Turkey would follow the Taurus mountain range to the north.[53] Turkish claims that Briand had promised in a newspaper interview the establishment of a commission to determine a border based on nationality (*hududun milliyetler esası üzerine çizilmesi*) were emphatically rejected by Franklin-Bouillon.[54] But in the absence of a clear national border, Fethi and Yusuf Kemal made one final maximalist claim, arguing that Turkey's natural border stretched from the Mediterranean along the Orontes (Asi) River to its southward bend. From there, it would follow a straight line – hardly the hallmark of a 'natural border'! – to the Euphrates, and along the latter river until the old province of Mosul, which would likewise belong to Turkey.[55] In the end, it was the French interpretation that won out – while the Turkish delegation was able to pry economic concessions from the French, the border in the Ankara Agreement remained the same as that defined in London.

---

[52] For the text of the Ankara Agreement, see: *League of Nations Treaty Series*, Vol. 54, No. 1284 (1926–27), pp. 177–93.

[53] Stefanos Yerasimos, *Milliyetler ve Sınırlar: Balkanlar, Kafkasya ve Ortadoğu*, trans. Şirin Tekeli (İstanbul: İletişim, 2009 [1994]), pp. 139–40; Gontaut-Biron and Le Révérend, pp. 68–69.

[54] TBMMGCZ 91 (12 Ekim 1337), p. 295. French hardliners argued that an ethnographic boundary would have included Antep, Maraş and Urfa in the mandate, as a majority of the population there was 'Syrian'; see: Gontaut-Biron and Le Révérend, pp. 52, 67–68.

[55] Tengirşenk, p. 253.

## Batum, İskenderun and the Awkwardness of Nationalism

The border drawn in 1921, both in the north and the south, thus represented a significant compromise on the principles outlined in the *Misak-ı Millî*. In the north, the Treaty of Moscow ceded Batum without offering the population of the region the possibility of a plebiscite; in the south, the Ankara Agreement ceded İskenderun, which was considered by Turkish nationalists to be Turkish in character and which had been held by Turkish forces at the end of the war. How could these borders be justified, when nationalist leaders, just months earlier, had associated territorial compromises with the death of the Turkish nation state? 'There is no doubt', Mustafa Kemal had written Bekir Sami in November 1920

> that . . . to give up even a tiny part of the territory contained in the border established in the *Misak-ı Millî*, the border being avidly defended . . . by the nation, would mean the demise of the sacred cause that we are resolutely defending against an entire world of enemies, and thus the very dissolution of the national resistance . . .[56]

The nationalists charged with drawing the borders of their nation state, constrained by state capacity and geopolitics, thus faced the awkward situation of justifying the compromises of Moscow and Ankara. In both cases, reactions to the border emerged in similar ways, with the parliament vociferously decrying the agreements' violations of the *Misak-ı Millî* and the government defending concessions on the border as a matter of national necessity.

The Treaty of Moscow, for example, came as a major disappointment to deputies when it was introduced to them on 17 March 1921.[57] As late as 21 February of that year the government had assured parliament that it could not fathom 'even approaching' an agreement which ceded Batum to Georgia and continued insisting on a plebiscite for the region.[58] When the treaty came in March, because the Turkish parliament was so convinced of Turkey's resolve and ability to carry out the principles of the *Misak-ı Millî*,

---

[56] Telegram of Mustafa Kemal to Bekir Sami (8 November 1920), in Tengirşenk, p. 192.
[57] Karabekir, p. 1,047
[58] TBMMGCZ (21 February 1921), p. 450.

some deputies could not comprehend the treaty and reassured themselves vocally that Batum had been included in the new border. This was the impression that the government itself, nervous about deputies' reactions to the new border, tried to foster by, for example, emphasising that Turkish troops had occupied ethnically Turkish parts of Georgian territory, even though this occupation had no bearing on the border whatsoever. Several deputies blamed the government for a grave error in allowing Batum to be handed over, while others called it a violation of the *Misak-ı Millî* and threatened not to ratify the final treaty.[59] When the Treaty of Moscow was presented for ratification in July, the five deputies from Batum lodged a fervent protest against their district being severed from the 'motherland'. Nevertheless, most deputies accepted the importance of establishing relations with Russia, even at this cost. The final vote was 201 deputies in favour, one abstention and five in opposition.[60]

The Ankara Agreement, too, triggered a week of serious and almost daily criticism from deputies when it was discussed in mid-October 1921. Questioning the efficacy of tracing the border along a railway bed, one deputy exclaimed, 'This border is no border!' (*Bu hudut, hudut değildir*),[61] a phrase which became a kind of refrain through the rest of the week. Already angered by having to cede Batum, nationalist deputies now directed their criticism against the very leader of the nationalist movement, Mustafa Kemal. One exchange in parliament on 16 October 1921 is remarkable in this regard. İsmail Safa Bey, deputy from Adana, told him that if there was a Turkish majority in İskenderun, the district must be included within the national boundary. 'That is a different issue,' replied Mustafa Kemal. The border delineated in the Ankara Agreement 'does not contradict our *Misak-ı Millî*. Our *Misak-ı Millî* does not include a definite, clearly determined boundary. Whatever boundary we determine with our strength and our power will be the country's border. It has no [other] meaning'. İsmail Safa responded with incredulity, saying deputies understood the *Misak-ı Millî* to be a promise that Turkish-majority districts adjacent to the homeland would be included in it,

---

[59] TBMMZC (24 March 1921), pp. 205–10.
[60] TBMMZC (21 July 1921), pp. 325–33.
[61] Hulusi Bey [Kutluoğlu], TBMMGCZ (12 October 1921), p. 291.

while ambiguous cases were to be resolved by plebiscite. This was the obvious, and correct, interpretation of the *Misak-ı Millî*, of course, but İsmail Safa could not offer a practical alternative. Implicitly recognising the awkwardness of nationalism, İsmail Safa said there was 'no ceasefire line that does not constitute a violation [of the *Misak-ı Millî*], and will never be'. After a terse exchange with other deputies, Mustafa Kemal continued. 'It is quite unfortunate, isn't it, that having a Turkish majority in places like [İskenderun] is not a sufficient condition for them to be included in the *Misak-ı Millî*. The border in the Ankara Agreement, Mustafa Kemal argued, was the best that Turkey could achieve. 'I don't find it that important that one line in an agreement has left [this region] south of the border,' he admitted. 'Greater success in securing autonomy or independence could not be obtained.'[62]

To defend against maximalist demands, Yusuf Kemal drew on other arguments from the government's arsenal. The border, he reassured deputies, was drawn out of necessity, not to 'please the French'. Still, it had the benefit of ensuring Turkey's independence. He argued:

> Thus if we examine the issue from the perspective of the basic principle of the *Misak-ı Millî*, that is to say, our independence and freedom within our national borders, then we are not acting in violation of our *Misak-ı Millî*. But from the perspective of territory, we are unable to achieve our aims in their entirety.[63]

Because it was classified as an agreement, and not a treaty, the text hammered out in Ankara did not require ratification by parliament, as the Treaty of Moscow had. Nevertheless, the government did ask deputies for authorisation to sign the agreement, which they gave, to much commotion, on 18 October.

For both the northeastern and southern borders, the government always justified the compromises on the *Misak-ı Millî* with appeals to the immediate national security needs of the day. One example was the case of Batum,

---

[62] TBMMGCZ (16 October 1921), pp. 355–56. Mustafa Kemal had already made similar arguments about defending Eastern Thrace while dealing with Western Thrace pragmatically; see: Özkan, p. 86.

[63] TBMMGCZ (15 October 1921), p. 328.

whose cession was explained in loops by the deputy foreign minister Muhtar Bey. On 10 March 1921, Muhtar announced that Turkey would not carry out plebiscites in Ardahan and Artvin because Georgia had been 'convinced that there was no need to implement this method of realising our national claims'. Yet he continued to promise a plebiscite in Batum, then occupied by the Turkish army: 'We are going to secure – or rather, in a manner of speaking – to legitimise our occupation there by appealing to a referendum'.[64] Two weeks later, when confronted about the cession of Batum in the Treaty of Moscow, a cornered Muhtar could only say, 'The *Misak-ı Millî* was accepted as the basis [for discussion]. But there are a few modifications that the *Misak-ı Millî* underwent due to the political situation'.[65] This 'political situation' was the threat of the loss of Russian material support for the nationalist cause, which depended on coming to a speedy agreement. The fear of having to station significant numbers of troops to defend a contested Batum against the Russians may have also played a role.[66] The government pleaded equal urgency in reaching a deal with the French.[67] Turkey, Yusuf Kemal argued, needed to come to terms with the French to focus on the war against the Greeks in western Anatolia. Any border would have been a disappointment, he and the government argued; the loss of territory in the Ankara Agreement was bitter but not the worst possible outcome. Mustafa Kemal detailed to deputies how he and the Turkish delegation had earnestly demanded more territory, but that the French, willing to pull back the economic clauses of the London Agreement, would not budge on the border issue. Finally, since the Ankara Agreement was not technically a peace treaty, reassured the government, its stipulations remained open to later modification.[68]

For the northeastern and southern borders of Turkey, the first years after delimitation were a critical period in which the borders drawn on paper

---

[64] Deputy Foreign Minister Muhtar Bey (10 March 1921). At the same time, Bekir Sami continued to tout a plebiscite for the northeast border region at negotiations in London. Akan, p. 257.

[65] TBMMZC (24 March 1921), pp. 205–10.

[66] Rıza Nur, pp. 164–65.

[67] TBMMGCZ (12 May 1921), p. 73.

[68] TBMMGCZ (12 October 1921), pp. 294–95; TBMMGCZ (18 October 1921), pp. 363–64.

became border regimes on the ground, and in which the more fluid borders of empires crystalised into nation state borders. In this respect, while nationalists' initial reactions to the border were similar, the years immediately following their establishment saw a divergence in trajectories in two ways. The first revolved around the undefined status of the line defined by the Ankara Agreement. The 1921 Ankara Agreement had been vague about defining the line dividing French and Turkish troops as the border between two sovereign entities, so the negotiations in the years following the agreement were carried out with a sense of gravity: more than a demarcation line between two armies, the negotiations after 1921 were to establish state boundaries. The Treaties of Moscow and Kars in 1921, meanwhile, had been treaties of friendship, not only delimiting the border but also providing for mutual border protections and specific provisions for borderlanders' mobility. In the case of the Syrian–Turkish border, the two countries had to wait until 1926 for a friendship treaty that would specify the same level of detail on border practices and until 1929 for the entire border between them to be delimited. As Turkey and France's relative strength vacillated, so did each side's willingness to concede on various aspects of delimitation, and each segment of the border, agreed upon in different agreements and protocols, represents the relative balance of power at that particular moment.[69]

The two borders also differed in their stability following delimitation. After some tension surrounding the timetable of Turkish troop withdrawal from Aleksandropol' and Batum,[70] the northeast border remained unchanged. Discussions between Turkey and the Soviet Union generally revolved around the regulation of everyday cross-border mobility. Here, the Soviet Union was more

[69] Seda Altuğ and Benjamin Thomas White, 'Frontières et pouvoir d'État: La frontière turco-syrienne dans les années 1920 et 1930', *Vingtième siècle, revue d'histoire*, Vol. 103 (Juillet–Septembre 2009), pp. 91–104. On the negotiations over delimiting the Turkish–Syrian border, see: Shoeila Mameli-Ghaderi, 'Le tracé de la frontière entre la Syrie et la Turquie (1921–1929)', *Guerres mondiales et conflits contemporain*, Vol. 207 (Juillet–Septembre 2002), pp. 125–38; Yücel Güçlü, 'The Controversy over the Delimitation of the Turco-Syrian Frontier in the Period between the Two World Wars', *Middle Eastern Studies*, Vol. 42, No. 4 (July 2006), pp. 641–57.

[70] Paul Dumont, 'L'axe Moscou-Ankara: Les relations turco-soviétiques de 1919 à 1922', *Cahiers du Monde russe et soviétiqu*, Vol. 18, No. 3 (Juillet–Septembre 1977), pp. 180–81.

dissatisfied with the border, seriously restricting border crossings in the 1930s as well as intimating that it would demand the territories of Kars and Ardahan after the Second World War.[71] Turkey's southern border with Syria, meanwhile, continued to be the subject of negotiation and revision for decades. Both sides complained about the border. French observers wrote in 1924 that 'the Syrian border remains precarious, subject to all sorts of challenges, poorly defended, and poorly surveilled'.[72] Even in 1931, years after Turkish and French negotiators had hammered out a border, the Turkish interior minister continued to call the country's southern border 'complex and unnatural'.[73] Dissatisfaction fuelled irredentism. French hardliners called for renewed French 'adventures' north of the border to extend French territory and defend its mandate in Syria.[74] For Turkey, the issue of İskenderun and Antakya remained open; the Turkish government was able to take advantage of a change in status of the Syrian mandate to successfully press for the cession of this region – now known as Hatay province – into Turkey between 1936 and 1939.[75]

## Conclusion

The process of delineating Turkey's northeastern and southern borders in 1921, although they appear to be separate, were closely interconnected.

---

[71] On cross-border mobility in this region during the 1920s and 1930s, see Étienne Forestier-Peyrat, '"Dans les forêts d'Adjarie . . .": Franchir la frontière turco-soviétique, 1922–1937', *Diasporas*, Vols. 23–24 (2014), pp. 164–84; Pelkmans, pp. 22–29.

[72] Gontaut-Biron and Le Révérend, p. 34. In 1925, one observer defined the delineation of the Syrian–Turkish border as the major issue continuing to plague French administration of the mandate; see: H. Charles Woods, 'The French in Syria', *Fortnightly Review*, Vol. 118, No. 706 (October 1925), p. 498.

[73] Quoted in Ramazan Hakkı Öztan, 'The Great Depression and the Making of Turkish–Syrian Border, 1921–1939', *International Journal of Middle Eastern Studie*, Vol. 52, No. 2 (May 2020), p. 311.

[74] Gontaut-Biron and Le Révérend, pp. 193–94.

[75] A diplomatic history of Turkey's annexation of Hatay is Sarah D. Shields, *Fezzes in the River: Identity Politics and European Diplomacy in the Middle East on the Eve of World War II* (Oxford: Oxford University Press, 2011). For a Turkish state perspective on the Hatay question, see Yücel Güçlü, *The Question of the Sanak of Alexandretta: A Study in Turkish-French-Syrian Relations* (Ankara: Turkish Historical Society, 2001); for the Syrian perspective, see Emma Lundgren Jörum, *Beyond Syria's Border: A History of Territorial Disputes in the Middle East* (London: I. B. Tauris, 2014), pp. 89–111.

One argument I have advanced in this chapter posits the simultaneity of these border-making processes. These borders were not simply two distinct 'fronts' of the National Struggle (*Millî Mücadele*), as they have sometimes been portrayed. Instead, their courses were negotiated and debated by the same actors, with developments on one border acting reciprocally on developments on the other.

One way this becomes particularly obvious is at the level of biography. Turkey's two primary negotiators in 1921, Bekir Sami and Yusuf Kemal, were the central figures in both borders. Bekir Sami, as foreign minister of the Ankara government, had led its first official delegation to Moscow in the summer of 1920, intending to hammer out a preliminary treaty with Soviet Russia. Perhaps inspired by his family's background of antagonism towards Russia,[76] Bekir Sami was skeptical of the direction of negotiations with the Soviets, finding their demands in 1920 to be akin to those of the (Western) 'imperialists'.[77] The Soviets, for their part, viewed Bekir Sami as a 'reactionary' and were happy to see his replacement as foreign minister by Yusuf Kemal in 1921.[78] Bekir Sami was decidedly more predisposed towards the French. He had made the acquaintance of Picot in Beirut and convinced the latter to travel to Sivas to meet with the Turkish nationalists in late 1919 – the meeting in which Picot had offered concessions on the border.[79] Meanwhile, Yusuf Kemal, as minister of economics, had taken the long journey to Moscow together with Bekir Sami in the summer of 1920, later leading his own delegation there in order to finalise the Treaty of Moscow. This success in 1921 cemented Yusuf Kemal's credentials as anti-imperialist, a reputation that must have encouraged the Ankara government to use him to stand up to the French after the apparent debacle with Bekir Sami in London.

---

[76] Bekir Sami was born in Ossetia as the son of the general Musa Kundukhov, who organised a mass emigration of Muslims from the region and fought against the Russian Empire in 1877–78.

[77] Gürün, p. 37; Dumont, p. 179.

[78] Report of İbrahim Əbilov to Narkomindel ASSR (3 February 1922), in Azərbaycan Respublikasının Dövlət Arxivi, f. 28 op. 1-s d. 68, l. 101. Rıza Nur's portrayal of Yusuf Kemal suggests the latter was Bekir Sami's complete opposite: allegedly a 'proud communist', Yusuf Kemal also 'did not know how to write French'. Rıza Nur, pp. 92–93, 267.

[79] Sina Akşin, 'Franco-Turkish Relations at the End of 1919', in Sina Akşin (ed.), *Essays in Ottoman Turkish Political History* (Istanbul: The Isis Press, 2000), pp. 60–61.

A second way in which the border processes can be viewed as simultaneous is through the lens of geopolitics. Negotiations over the two borders were not conducted in hermetically sealed conditions. France and Soviet Russia were mutually hostile, and both shared the concern that Turkey would switch decisively to one side or the other. In early 1921, 'intense propaganda' surrounding the Turco-French agreement in London swirled around Moscow and gave the Soviets cause to doubt Turkish sincerity about their anti-imperialist intentions.[80] Rıza Nur Bey, one of Turkey's negotiators in Moscow, observed Russian reactions to Bekir Sami's rapprochement with the French in March 1921 and criticised the latter for jeopardising aid from the Russians, whom he called 'Turkey's sole hope'.[81] But Russian worries continued even after the Turkish government rejected the London agreement and Bekir Sami resigned. As the Turkish government prepared to sign an agreement with the French in October 1921, the Soviet ambassador asked for an audience with Mustafa Kemal and asked about rumours that the agreement required Turkey to break off its alliance with Russia and support a return of the Caucasus to the imperialist West. These were rumours that Mustafa Kemal categorically denied.[82] The French, too, were eager not to push Turkey into the arms of the Soviets and followed negotiations between the two keenly.[83] At home, French hardliners shrieked about the need to extend Syrian territory northwards to prevent Turkey from becoming a tool of the Bolsheviks and interfering in French and British interests in the Middle East.[84] Franklin-Bouillon, in the first day of negotiations with Yusuf Kemal, demanded to see a copy of the Moscow Treaty and asked whether there were any 'secret amendments' that would fix the Turks against the West. A proud Yusuf Kemal assured him that it was an open treaty and could point to specific concessions Turkey had won from the Soviets as an example of what they might achieve with France.[85]

---

[80] Tengirşenk, pp. 151, 227.

[81] Rıza Nur, p. 94.

[82] TBMMGCZ (16 October 1337), p. 356. On Russian fears about Turkish rapprochement with the French after the Moscow Treaty, see also Dumont, p. 181.

[83] Shaw, III:1, p. 1,250.

[84] Gontaut-Biron and Le Révérend, pp. 195–96. For documentation of similar concerns on the part of the British in 1921, see Shaw, III:1, p. 1,204.

[85] Tengirşenk, p. 250.

Ankara, too, was well aware of the rivalry between Russia and France and attempted to use this geopolitical situation to its advantage when pushing for territorial concessions. Though Turkish foreign policy and public opinion were predisposed to cooperation with Russia and frowned upon cooperation with Western European powers, Turkish officials' ultimate goal was nevertheless not to get pinned down to one side or the other.[86] Turkey's first priority in 1921 was simply to secure military and financial aid from Soviet Russia. The Ankara government's rejection of the London Agreement, signed just a week before the Moscow Treaty, was inspired by the fear that it would put such aid in jeopardy.[87] The signing of the Moscow Treaty then enabled the government to quickly refocus on its goal of establishing suitable relations with western Allies. This timing explains why the government was suddenly enthusiastic about coming to a border agreement with the French in the summer of 1921 – an agreement very similar to the one it had just rejected. Fevzi, the Turkish prime minister, reminded a disgruntled parliament in May of the 'necessity to come to an agreement with the French as soon as possible, an agreement which carries urgency for us'.[88] The urgency of coming to an agreement with at least one Western European power after the Moscow Treaty explains in part the Turkish government's willingness to compromise to a considerable degree on issues like the national border. Yusuf Kemal writes: 'After the treaty with the Soviets, we desperately needed to open up towards Europe by means of France, so we were forced to accept [the border] by necessity'.[89] At the same time, as Turkish officials were well aware, the war-fatigued and Soviet-phobic French administration was in a position in 1921 particularly susceptible to territorial concessions.[90]

The other argument I have advanced in this chapter is that we can arrive at a better understanding of the nature of the early Turkish nation state, in

---

[86] TBMMZC (19 September 1921), p. 262; TBMMGCZ (12 May 1921), p. 72. On Ankara's use of Russia to achieve its diplomatic goals in the West, see Samuel J. Hirst, 'Transnational Anti-Imperialism and the National Forces: Soviet Diplomacy and Turkey, 1920–23', *Comparative Studies of South Asia, Africa and the Middle East*, Vol. 33, No. 2 (2013), pp. 223–24.

[87] Shaw, III:1, p. 1,249.

[88] TBMMGCZ (12 May 1921), p. 72.

[89] Tengirşenk, p. 253.

[90] Mameli-Ghaderi, pp. 126, 137; Gontaut-Biron and Le Révérend, p. 14.

particular its concept of 'the national' (*millî*), through an analysis of its border-making process. Based on the discussion in this chapter, this argument can be expanded in three ways.

First, the process of delineating nation state borders can pose a serious threat to the legitimacy of nascent nation state governments. This arises from the inevitable contradiction between the maximalist territorial demands put forward by nationalists and the necessity of compromise when drawing a border in an ethnically mixed and geographically open space without resorting to endless war. In the case of the Turkish borders, the more pragmatically orientated cabinet, particularly Mustafa Kemal, faced serious difficulties presenting its border policy to an ebullient parliament, threatening a breach between the branches of government at a time when Turkish fortunes vacillated in their war against the Greeks. Discontent with the government's handling of the London Agreement even led to the resignation of Bekir Sami as foreign minister, the resignation of the parliament president and a reshuffling of the cabinet in May 1921.[91] Parliament used the topic of border concessions to assert their authority by painting themselves as 'truer' nationalists than the government, which was seeking greater powers at the time. Deputies challenged the nationalist credentials of cabinet members during discussions of the border, rhetorically asking them: 'Isn't your signature on the *Misak-ı Millî?*'.[92] As government officials attempted, sometimes awkwardly, to justify territorial concessions, deputies threatened to reject agreements and responded with machismo, opposing giving up 'even an inch' of the territory of the *Misak-ı Millî* and claiming that 'death is preferable to living in servitude'.[93]

Second, this tension between nationalist discourse and the necessity of pragmatism on the border can force nation state founders to debate the new state's fundamental mission or ideological foundations. In the case of nationalist Turkey, this meant wrangling over the meaning of the *Misak-ı Millî*, taken by nationalists as the 'mission statement' of their movement. The Ankara government was partially successful in imposing its interpretation of the *Misak-ı Millî* in the Moscow and Kars Treaties (Article 1) and

---

[91] Shaw III:2, p. 1,406
[92] TBMMGCZ (16 October 1921), p. 342.
[93] Ibid., p. 338; see also TBMMGCZ (12 May 1921), p. 75.

the Ankara Agreement (Article 6). Nevertheless, the vagueness of the border in the *Misak-ı Millî* allowed for continued discussion in Ankara on what the bounds of the nation should be. While the government interpreted the *Misak-ı Millî* as a policy aim, several parliamentarians saw the *Misak-ı Millî* as a policy minimum. For many who thought about Turkey's border in 1921, the 'national border' was essentially an Ottoman border without religious minorities; others rejected the establishment of national borders altogether as an unconscionable division of the Islamic *ümmet*. Similar logic continued to undergird decades of conservative criticism of the Lausanne Treaty of 1923, which eventually resulted in British control over Mosul Province.

Finally, far from being a disadvantage for nationalists, ambiguity or insecurity surrounding national borders can serve as a means for a nation state to consolidate power. In both Turkey's northeastern and southern borders, the ambiguities of the border, unregulated mobility and acts of violence justified continued state action and the strengthening of the state apparatus. Seda Altuğ and Benjamin Thomas White have fittingly called the Turkish–Syrian border 'above all, an ideal that motivated the intensification of state authority'.[94] Inherent in the principle of national borders was the idea of their flexibility. Thus, nationalists like Mustafa Kemal or Yusuf Kemal, who in 1921 pushed pragmatic compromises on border delineation, did not believe that such compromises would necessarily constrain state action. Ankara could, for example, provoke national liberation movements in neighbouring countries if it was in the interest of the nation state, as Mustafa Kemal wrote to Karabekir as the *Misak-ı Millî* was being discussed in early 1920:

> Like in Syria or Iraq, in Azerbaijan and the Caucasus, too, there are nations striving to bring about their own national existence and independence. To

---

[94] Altuğ and White, p. 103. Altuğ and White in this article contrast France's imperial approach to the Turkish–Syrian border with Turkey's nationalist approach. This distinction is highly relevant when it comes to each state's policy towards borderland demographics. Nevertheless, as I argue here, this difference in perspective should not be understood as a Turkish preference for a fixed boundary and a French acceptance of an ever-expanding 'frontier'. As I have tried to show, even though the identity of borderlanders became more relevant for nation states, ambiguity in the definition of national borders also allowed nation states like Turkey to demand border expansion, just as imperial states could.

direct their forces against the enemies who are plaguing Turkey would never be a violation of the nation's decision to liberate [*tahlis*] our interests within our national borders. On the contrary, [such activity] would be part of the efforts to carry out this national resolution.[95]

Aside from the fact that a perceived disconnect between the nation and national borders could legitimise intervention across the border, the ambiguity of the border also left open the possibility of outright irredentism, seen in the case of Hatay in the 1930s or Soviet claims in the northeast after the Second World War. Ambiguity meant that such action could be legitimised in perpetuity. The 'sentiments' of borderlanders 'left out' by a national border were a never-ending source of rumours that could be generated or harnessed to direct diplomatic negotiations or state-building policies.[96] Mustafa Kemal attempted to mollify angry deputies in 1921 in this way, arguing that the border being decided then could easily be changed in the future if the military strength of the Turkish nation state increased.[97] This was understood by Yusuf Kemal, too, as he negotiated with the French in mid-1921. He wrote:

I did not hold back from repeatedly telling Franklin-Bouillon that the border drawn by the Agreement was considered by Turkey to be one imposed by force, that we will never forget the Turkish territories and people left south of the border, that these were hallowed lands bound to return to Turkey one day, and that Turkish children would consider this to be their sacred duty.[98]

[95] Karabekir, pp. 528–29.
[96] Jordi Tejel, 'States of Rumors: Politics of Information Along the Turkish–Syrian Border, 1925–1945', *Journal of Borderlands Studies* (Feb 2020), DOI: 10.1080/08865655.2020.1719866.
[97] TBMMGCZ (18 October 1921), p. 366.
[98] Tengirşenk, p. 253.

# 2

# BORDERS OF STATE SUCCESSION AND REGIME CHANGE IN THE POST-OTTOMAN MIDDLE EAST

*Orçun Can Okan[1]*

A particular historical context shaped the functions and impacts of borders between Turkey and the League of Nations Mandates in present-day Syria, Lebanon and Iraq. These borders were instituted amidst efforts to dismantle the Ottoman Empire and manage state succession in its former lands. With an emphasis on this context in the 1920s, this chapter highlights two key functions borders served as implementers of state succession and

[1] This chapter draws largely from the ideas and cases I discuss in my dissertation; 'Coping with Transitions: The Connected Construction of Turkey, Syria, Lebanon and Iraq, 1918–1928', (PhD thesis, Columbia University, 2020). For cordial conversations that helped me think about my work in more direct relation to borders and borderlands, I am grateful to the participants of the conference 'Borders, Mobilities, and State Formation in the Middle East, 1920–1945' at the University of Neuchâtel in October 2019. I would like to express my gratitude to the conveners Jordi Tejel, Ramazan Hakkı Öztan, Victoria Abrahamyan, César Jaquier and Laura Stocker for bringing us together in an inspiring setting. Special thanks to Tejel and Öztan, as well as the anonymous reviewer of the volume, for highly valuable comments on early versions of the chapter. The archival research informing this study was supported by the Social Science Research Council's International Dissertation Research Fellowship with funds provided by the Andrew W. Mellon Foundation and Koç University's Center for Anatolian Civilizations (ANAMED) in Istanbul.

regime change.[2] In the first place, the chapter highlights that the new borders rendered diplomacy necessary for coping with administrative and legal hardships in territories formerly subject to a single state authority. With the new borders in place, recourse to diplomacy became necessary to address some of the most basic needs and concerns of the day. Secondly, by causing exposure to new paths of administrative, legal and diplomatic correspondence, the new borders helped entrench the terms of new, unfamiliar political relationships in former imperial domains. This contributed to the establishment of new state-subject relations in the former domains of a recently partitioned empire. The new borders did not bring about an immediate division of former Ottoman territories into completely separate units with hermetically sealed domestic spheres. They served, rather, key purposes in implementing state succession and regime change in lands previously subject to Ottoman imperial rule.

There are compelling reasons to qualify the particularity of these borders with an emphasis on their role in the dismantling of the Ottoman Empire. Situating borders in historical context is an essential endeavour in each chapter of this volume. This represents a highly useful approach that is distinct from thinking in terms of 'regional' traits of borders in the Middle East.[3]

---

[2]   I use the phrase 'regime change' in the sense of broad political change (such as the transition from dynastic rule to republican and mandate regimes) as well as changes in particular administrative and legal regimes (i.e. frameworks, norms and mechanisms) in the construction of new state-subject relations in former Ottoman domains.

[3]   In the seminal study published by Baud and Van Schendel in 1997 it was underlined that 'there are broad regional differences in state formation and the imposition of national borders', and that analyses of borders and borderlands would benefit from attention to 'different historical experiences'. Michiel Baud and Willem Van Schendel, 'Toward a Comparative History of Borderlands', *Journal of World History*, Vol. 8, No. 2 (1997), p. 240. Although critical engagement with particularities of borders and borderlands is indeed crucial, undertaking this engagement in terms of regional types (such as Eurasian, African, American), as suggested in the work of Baud and Van Schendel, may not be the most promising path for offering nuanced analyses of these particularities. For useful overviews of a large and growing body of literature on borders in the modern Middle East, see Daniel Meier, 'Introduction to the Special Issue: Bordering the Middle East', *Geopolitics*, Vol. 23, No. 3 (2017), pp. 495–504; Matthew H. Ellis, 'Over the Borderline? Rethinking Territoriality at the Margins of Empire and Nation in the Modern Middle East (Part I)', *History Compass*, Vol. 13, No. 8 (2015), pp. 411–22 (as well as Part II in the same volume, pp. 423–34); Inga Brandell (ed.), *State Frontiers: Borders and Boundaries in the Middle East* (London; New York: I. B. Tauris, 2006), esp. pp. 1–33 ; 199–215.

This chapter employs the term 'post-Ottoman Middle East' as part of its emphasis on the role borders between Turkey and the Mandates played in the dismantling of the Ottoman Empire.[4] The borders between Turkey and the Mandates were instituted on the lands of an empire where the existing state structures and practices proved highly resilient even after defeat in the First World War. This resilience was especially influential in the making of post-Ottoman Turkey, but the 'relatively strong, relatively modern' Ottoman state also presented the Mandate regimes in the Middle East with an inheritance that was 'unusual' for colonial regimes.[5] By the time of the Ottoman demise following the First World War, Ottoman bureaucratic and military presence in its 'Arab provinces' had become more extensive than it had ever been.[6] The war years 'constituted the peak of the modern Ottoman state's exercise

[4] The state authorities in these neighbouring polities were the main signatories of the Treaty of Lausanne (signed in July 1923) – Turkey, France and Britain. This treaty served as the key diplomatic and legal instrument in the dismantling of the Ottoman Empire. Historians can, of course, fruitfully discuss and emphasise a wide range of factors, events and processes when contextualising new borders in former Ottoman domains. Comparing the following studies, for example, will convey a good sense of the multiplicity of alternative approaches and emphases: Eliezer Tauber, 'The Struggle for Dayr al-Zur: The Determination of Borders between Syria and Iraq', *International Journal of Middle East Studies*, Vol. 23, No. 3 (1991), pp. 361–85 ; Reem Bailony, 'From Mandate Borders to the Diaspora: Rashaya's Transnational Suffering and the Making of Lebanon in 1925', *Arab Studies Journal*, Vol. 26, No. 2 (2018), pp. 45–74 ; Jordi Tejel Gorgas, 'Making Borders from Below: The Emergence of the Turkish–Iraqi Frontier, 1918–1925', *Middle Eastern Studies*, Vol. 54, No. 5 (2018), pp. 811–26; Ramazan Hakkı Öztan, 'The Great Depression and the Making of Turkish–Syrian Border, 1921–1939', *International Journal of Middle East Studies*, Vol. 52, No. 2 (2020), pp. 1–16.

[5] Regarding the point made here about Turkey, see, for instance, Erik J. Zürcher, *The Young Turk Legacy and Nation Building: From the Ottoman Empire to Ataturk's Turkey* (London; New York: I. B. Tauris, 2010), esp. p. 141. With regard to the Mandates; as pointed out by Rashid Khalidi, 'the mandate regimes in the Middle East had the specific characteristic, one unusual for a colonial regime, that they took over from a relatively strong, relatively modern state – the late Ottoman Empire'. See Rashid Khalidi, 'Concluding Remarks' in Nadine Méouchy and Peter Sluglett (eds), *The British and French Mandates in Comparative Perspectives* (Leiden; Boston: Brill, 2004), pp. 696–97.

[6] See in this regard, for example, Hasan Kayalı, *Arabs and Young Turks: Ottomanism, Arabism, and Islamism in the Ottoman Empire, 1908–1918* (Berkeley: University of California Press, 1997) and M. Talha Çiçek, *War and State Formation in Syria: Cemal Pasha's Governorate during World War I, 1914–17* (New York: Routledge, 2014); for more on the end of

of territoriality'.[7] Once the Empire collapsed after this 'peak', managing the links people still had to the Ottoman past often required combined efforts across the new borders between Turkey and the Mandates. Analyses of Ottoman legacy or heritage within the confines of particular successor states tend to overlook the reasons for, and the impacts of, these crucial cross-border interactions. By contrast, contextualising borders in terms of their role in the dismantling of an empire enhances the scholarly understanding of these borders as well as of the wider political transformations they served to implement in former Ottoman lands in the 1920s.

As contributions in especially the second part of this edited volume demonstrate, historians of the Middle East have paid, and continue to pay, useful attention to the cross-border movement/mobility of goods, ideas, services, diseases and peoples. However, the cross-border movement/mobility of some other things are yet to receive the attention they deserve. These include the records produced by the defunct Ottoman state. This is what the first part of the discussion below highlights. States and their subjects in former Ottoman territories needed to reach beyond the new borders for reference to Ottoman records for a variety of purposes. These included certification of biographical information, evidencing professional background and proving ownership of land and property. Recourse to diplomacy for these and similar purposes became a necessity because former imperial subjects still had links to the Ottoman past through their relation to the former state. The first part of the chapter elaborates on this, taking as its starting point the pension claim raised in Damascus under French mandate rule by the family of a deceased Ottoman official, in return for services rendered to the Ottoman state.

The second part shifts the focus to relations among former Ottoman subjects and relations to land. Highlighted in this part first is the claim by

Ottoman rule in the Arab Middle East and beyond, see Leila Fawaz, *A Land of Aching Hearts: the Middle East in the Great War* (Cambridge, MA: Harvard University Press, 2014); Eugene Rogan, *The Fall of the Ottomans: the Great War in the Middle East* (New York: Basic Books, 2015); Ryan Gingeras, *Fall of the Sultanate: the Great War and the End of the Ottoman Empire, 1908–1922* (Oxford: Oxford University Press, 2016); Yiğit Akın, *When the War Came Home: the Ottomans' Great War and the Devastation of an Empire* (Stanford: Stanford University Press, 2018); Melanie Tanielian, *The Charity of War: Famine, Humanitarian Aid, and World War I in the Middle East* (Stanford: Stanford University Press, 2018).

[7] Cyrus Schayegh, *The Middle East and the Making of the Modern World* (Cambridge, MA; London: Harvard University Press, 2017), p. 116.

a woman in Istanbul to maintenance support from her former husband in Baghdad, who was also a former Ottoman official. Attention is then drawn to the claim by a landowner sheikh and his expectation of legal support from French mandate authorities in defending his lands against 'his' peasants near the present-day border between Turkey and Syria. Combined attention to these cases underscores the role borders played in constituting new administrative and legal regimes in former Ottoman domains. They also highlight a crucial, related consequence of borders as ultimate symbols of a new political status quo.[8] Borders played an important role in reinforcing the significance of difference in terms of nationality in former imperial domains. Especially in claims and disputes that transcended the confines of particular successor states, the new borders reinforced former Ottoman subjects' 'identification with' nationality in post-Ottoman circumstances.[9] Advancing these points through the cases outlined above facilitates moving beyond binaries of imposition by states versus resistance by 'local' 'non-state' actors when contextualising borders and their impacts. Borders shaped lives near and far beyond envisioned borderlines.[10] They factored into a wide range of social relations and networks involving also those who straddled the categories of state and non-state actors. Attention to state succession and regime change helps us grasp the true extent of borders' consequences in former imperial

---

[8] On borders as political divides resulting from processes of state-building and ultimate symbols of a political status quo, see Baud and Van Schendel, 'Toward a Comparative History of Borderlands', esp. pp. 211, 214.

[9] The term nationality is discussed in this chapter primarily in the sense of an essential legal link between states and those subject to their authority. My approach in this regard and use of the term 'identification with nationality' are informed by the work of scholars such as Will Hanley, whose analyses of the emergence of nationality as a social and legal category is part of a growing body of literature on nationality in late Ottoman contexts and beyond. See Will Hanley, *Identifying with Nationality: Europeans, Ottomans, and Egyptians in Alexandria* (New York: Columbia University Press, 2017), as well as, for example, contributions in Lâle Can, Michael Christopher Low, Kent F. Schull and Robert Zens (eds), *The Subjects of Ottoman International Law* (Bloomington: Indiana University Press, 2020).

[10] Modern borders, as noted by Seda Altuğ and Benjamin White, are 'part of the efforts made by states to impose their authority on the national territory and its populations: not only as a result but also as a tool; not only in the border regions but also throughout the country'. Seda Altuğ and Benjamin T. White, 'Frontières et pouvoir d'État: La Frontière Turco-Syrienne dans les Annés 1920 et 1930', *Vingtième Siècle, Revue d'Histoire*, Vol. 103 (2009/3), p. 92.

domains where state and society had become deeply integrated. The new borders' administrative and legal consequences were integral components of the ways in which they transformed social networks and relations across former Ottoman domains in the 1920s.[11]

## A New Necessity in Managing the Past and Present: Recourse to Diplomacy

Even though they did not live anywhere near the border that came to separate Turkey and Syria in the 1920s the new border had direct consequences for the family of the deceased ex-Ottoman military doctor Ahmed Akif Effendi. Halide Hanum and her four children were residing in Damascus as she repeatedly sought the help of French mandate authorities in receiving the retirement pension Ahmed Akif had earned in return for his services to the Ottoman state. The changes in the state authority in Damascus following 1918 meant new challenges for the family in concrete, tangible terms. Although the family's situation was not unique, their claim to the retirement pension is worthy of particular attention because it generated a particularly large body of cross-border correspondence from mid-1923 all the way into the 1930s. In more than fifty instances during this period, state officials in Damascus, Beirut, Istanbul and Ankara corresponded with the aim of locating and utilising Ottoman records to establish factual grounds in dealing with the retirement pension of Ahmed Akif's family.[12]

---

[11] When analysing how borders impacted social networks and the 'transnationalisation' of these networks in former Ottoman domains, historians would benefit from a greater degree of attention to problems of state succession. A good reference point in this regard is especially the third chapter in the useful recent monograph by Cyrus Schayegh, *The Middle East and the Making of the Modern World* (Cambridge, MA; London: Harvard University Press, 2017). Cross-border interactions geared towards managing state succession during the dismantling of the Ottoman Empire, a long and arduous process in which the Ankara government played a key role, are worthy of attention when contextualising 'transnationalised late-Ottoman ties' and the 'cross-border communication, even coordination' Schayegh points out in his analyses pivoting on Bilad al-Sham in the 1920s. See in this connection esp. pp. 181–82.

[12] At least fifty, on the basis of files in the following archival records: *Centre des Archives Diplomatiques de Nantes* (CADN) : 1SL/1V/2531; CADN: 1SL/5/203; CADN: 1SL/1V/2526; and State Archives of the Presidency of the Republic of Turkey (*T.C. Cumhurbaşkanlığı Devlet Arşivleri*, former Prime Ministerial Archives of the Ottoman Empire (*Başbakanlık*

Upon the military doctor Ahmed Akif's death in the First World War the Ottoman government had allocated a provisional pension to his wife Halide Hanum, their daughter and three sons. The family began receiving this temporary pension from the Treasury of Damascus during the war and were expecting a certificate from Istanbul for the definitive allocation. Before that certificate reached them, however, Damascus fell to Allied occupation in October 1918. As of mid-1923, in the absence of a certificate for the definitive allocation, the Director of Finances in the State of Damascus did not know the real amount of the permanent pension the family was entitled to.[13] Since their temporary pension was only a proportion of what the permanent pension would be (about one third), this presented a major problem for the family. As correspondence between states lingered over the years, officials of the State of Damascus had to remind the French High Commissioner's delegate in the city that the family 'kept asking about the matter'.[14]

Although the paperwork concerning this case became exceptionally extensive the problems necessitating it were not uncommon. As it was the case in dozens of similar situations, officials in Syria and Lebanon needed certain Ottoman records to carry out their duties, and these records were located in former Ottoman lands beyond their administrative reach. By September 1923 the Governor of the State of Damascus had already identified the official documents necessary for settling the family's case.[15] However, the diplomatic

---

*Osmanlı Arşivi*)), (BOA): HR.İM.: 95–33; BOA: HR.İM.: 10–4; BOA: HR.İM.: 118–10; BOA: HR.İM.: 150–42; BOA: HR.İM.: 177–64.

[13] For the information in this paragraph up to this point, see the report the Director of Finances in the State of Damascus submitted to the Governor of the State of Damascus, which was forwarded to the French High Commissioner in Beirut by the High Commissioner's Delegate to the States of Damascus and Djebel Druze on 2 July 1923, in CADN – 1SL/1V/2531 – *Pensions* (subfile 30:2).

[14] See the information submitted in this regard to the French High Commissioner's Delegate in Damascus on 10 January 1928, in CADN: 1SL/5/203 – *Pensions*. Further reminders from Damascus would continue to reach French Mandate officials as evidenced by the correspondence in the same file at CADN.

[15] The governor requested correspondence from the French High Commissioner's Delegate in Damascus to obtain what he described in Arabic as '*al-ju'zdān wa's-sanadāt ar-rasmiyya al-'āi'de li-rātib taqā'ud 'usrat al-qā'id Aḥmed Effendi 'Aqif*', and provided further details. See the note dated 27 September 1923, from the Governor of the State of Damascus to the French High Commissioner's Delegate in Damascus, in CADN: 1SL/5/203 – *Pensions*.

correspondence over the case continued for years, mainly due to difficulties in determining the identity of the individual and locating the correct archival records pertaining to that particular pension. As late as December 1928, more than five years after the initial request, complexities of the case compelled the French High Commission in Beirut to explain to the French Embassy in Turkey what the Syrian government needed to know exactly.[16] The requested information did eventually reach Damascus, as desired by Ahmed Akif's family, in September 1930.[17] Although the archival research for this study did not yield direct evidence of administrative instructions in this regard, in all likelihood the family began receiving higher amounts of pension payment after this point.

The official correspondence for this case, inside and across the new borders, took place within a diplomatic and legal framework established by the Treaty of Lausanne. Article 139 of this treaty put in place a regulatory framework for reference to 'archives, registers, plans, title-deeds and other documents of every kind relating to the civil, judicial or financial administration, or the administration of Wakfs'.[18] Initiatives to access Ottoman records were

---

[16] See the correspondence dated 11 December 1928, in CADN: 1SL/5/203 – *Pensions*.

[17] See the information conveyed by the French Ambassador in Turkey to the French High Commissioner in Syria and Lebanon on 29 August 1930, which was subsequently forwarded to the High Commissioners' Delegate in Damascus on 30 September 1930, in CADN: 1SL/5/203 – *Pensions*.

[18] Article 139 of the Treaty of Lausanne (Section III, General Provisions) reads as follows:
'Archives, registers, plans, title-deeds and other documents of every kind relating to the civil, judicial or financial administration, or the administration of Wakfs, which are at present in Turkey and are only of interest to the Government of a territory detached from the Ottoman Empire, and reciprocally those in a territory detached from the Ottoman Empire which are only of interest to the Turkish Government, shall reciprocally be restored.

Archives, registers, plans, title-deeds and other documents mentioned above which are considered by the Government in whose possession they are as being also of interest to itself, may be retained by that Government, subject to its furnishing on request photographs or certified copies to the Government concerned.

Archives, registers, plans, title-deeds and other documents which have been taken away either from Turkey or from detached territories shall reciprocally be restored in original, in so far as they concern exclusively the territories from which they have been taken.

The expense entailed by these operations shall be paid by the Government applying therefor.

taken across the envisioned borders even before the Treaty of Lausanne, but only gradually in the course of the 1920s was this framework established.[19] Considering the absence of a ratified peace treaty and established institutional bases for official correspondence, these early initiatives do not neatly fit into the category of diplomatic interaction. Negotiations with the Ankara government for large-scale delivery of Ottoman records began on specific terms only after the ratification of the Treaty of Lausanne in August 1924. The information conveyed to the French and British authorities in the course of these negotiations revealed the vast amount of relevant records. The requested records reached millions when French and British requests combined, and included numerous kinds.[20] Disagreements took place over which Ottoman records were of 'exclusive' interest/concern to which state in former Ottoman domains. Due to these disagreements, and the large costs of producing copies, the French mandate authorities in Syria and Lebanon made numerous requests from the Ankara government over the years, for particular records in relation to particular cases. The request by Ahmed Akif's family was one such case. It was exceptional in how cumbersome the correspondence became, but ordinary in terms of the administrative need that generated the interaction across new borders.

British mandate authorities in Iraq followed a different path in their interactions with the Ankara government for reference to Ottoman records. They took steps in the second half of the 1920s to obtain copies of Ottoman records *in toto*. For instance, in order to deal with cases similar to the case of Ahmed Akif's family, in which Ottoman records were needed to evaluate

---

The above stipulations apply in the same manner to the registers relating to real estates or Wakfs in the districts of the former Ottoman Empire transferred to Greece after 1912'. See Parliament of Great Britain, *Treaty of Peace with Turkey, and Other Instruments signed at Lausanne on July 24, 1923, together with Agreements between Greece and Turkey signed on January 30, 1923, and Subsidiary Documents forming part of the Turkish Peace Settlement* (Treaty Series No. 16, 1923) (London: His Majesty's Stationery Office, 1923), pp. 104–5.

[19] For some of these initiatives predating the Treaty of Lausanne, see, for instance, State Archives of the Presidency of the Republic of Turkey (*T.C. Cumhurbaşkanlığı Devlet Arşivleri*), former Prime Ministerial Archives of the Republic of Turkey (*Başbakanlık Cumhuriyet Arşivi*)) (BCA): 30-10-0-0-262-764-9-(1-8).

[20] See in these regards especially BOA: HR.İM.: 115–37; BOA: HR.İM.: 195–97; and BOA: HR.İM.: 199–5.

pension-related claims, British authorities requested information about dozens of cases at once, on more than one occasion.[21] These initiatives alone had direct consequences for the families of more than a hundred ex-Ottoman functionaries living in places near, and far from, the new borders. Of great consequence for even a higher number of people were initiatives the British authorities took with respect to Ottoman records pertaining to land and property. At the end of protracted negotiations and formalities, officials from Iraq visited Istanbul in 1926–27 and took back to Iraq copies of numerous records of various types, including 250,000 entries in the registers of title deeds.[22] Reference to Ottoman records was important in efforts to prevent forgery and establish proof of entitlement, whether in claims to modest sums of money in the form of retirement pensions, or to rights of ownership over large swaths of land.

These initiatives by states, and often the prior initiatives taken by their subjects who requested these initiatives, were essentially efforts to cope with state succession. In former Ottoman domains, the former state had generated multiple links with society through its complex bureaucracy. To varying degrees in different cases, states and their subjects relied on interaction across the new borders to find solutions to pressing problems of governance. While almost everything about the Ottoman Empire was portrayed as backward and corrupt in former Ottoman domains in the 1920s, numerous initiatives were nonetheless taken to utilise the empirical knowledge produced by this defunct empire. For states, initiatives to access Ottoman records were important not least for their 'production of bureaucratic authority'.[23] Being

---

[21] See in this regard especially the British requests from Turkish authorities in October and November 1926, in BOA: HR.İM.: 254–101 and BOA: HR.İM.: 255–47 respectively.

[22] In regard to this visit, see especially United Kingdom National Archives (The National Archives) TNA: FO 371/12277 - E_2217; BCA: 30-10-0-0-258-737-14-3; BOA: HR.İM.: 207–42; BOA: HR.İM.: 256–20; and the remarks pertaining to 'Records Obtained from Constantinople Under the Treaty of Lausanne', in 'Report by His Britannic Majesty's Government . . .' in Robert L. Jarman, (sources in the collection established by Jarman), *Iraq Administration Reports 1914–1932*, Vol. 8: 1925–27 (Slough: Archive Editions, 1992), pp. 469–70.

[23] See the use of this term by the historical anthropologist Ilana Feldman in her *Governing Gaza: Bureaucracy, Authority, and the Work of Rule, 1917–1967* (Durham, NC: Duke University Press, 2008), pp. 3, 31–3.

able to utilise the records of even 'the previous era' would contribute to states' administrative capacity, and thus authority and legitimacy. For their subjects, access to Ottoman records could potentially yield at least a say on how broader political transformations affected them.[24]

As people such as the family of Ahmed Akif would know all too well, correspondence across the new borders bespoke the very existence of those borders, not the possibility of easily reaching beyond them. Having to go through extra stages of correspondence and wait long periods of time to obtain results were reminders of the new reality of a recently bordered polity. They remained exposed to new paths of official correspondence – and to the power dynamics these paths represented – even as they hoped for a favourable outcome from lands now beyond a border. This exposure, even in the form of expectation, impressed upon former Ottoman subjects the terms of their new contexts of interaction with state authorities.

A couple of further remarks on the 'particularity' of these contexts will be useful before proceeding onto the next part. The challenge of dismantling an empire was certainly not unique to former Ottoman domains after the First World War. Neither was the need to access imperial records in successor states. This need was encountered and addressed in former Austria-Hungarian lands as well, for example.[25] 'Particularity' rather than 'uniqueness' of historical context is therefore the preferred term in this discussion's contextualisation of borders in terms of their role in the dismantling of an empire. This historical particularity can be further qualified through comparisons with other contexts of imperial collapse, and through enquiries into how specific aspects of

---

[24] It should be noted that efforts to consult Ottoman records did not work the same for everyone. Depending on how state officials evaluated an individual's allegiance and sincerity, reference to Ottoman records could be much more difficult for some former Ottomans than it was for others. Moreover, reference to Ottoman records did not guarantee solutions to problems, but it could facilitate executive and legal action if state authorities wanted to address a problem.

[25] See article 93 in Great Britain Parliament, *Treaty of Peace between the Allied and Associated Powers and Austria, together with Protocol and Declarations annexed thereto, signed at Saint-Germain-En-Laye, September 10, 1919* (Treaty Series No.11, 1919) (London: His Majesty's Stationery Office, 1919), p. 25.

the interactions examined above shaped specific visions of governance, such as those pertaining to nationality.[26] Notwithstanding the exciting prospects of future discussions along these lines, the next part advances a more basic point about borders, new legal regimes and nationality. It underlines the role borders played in making nationality a forceful legal category among the former subjects of an empire that was still in the process of being dismantled.

## Upholding New Legal Regimes: Reinforcing the Significance of Nationality

The interactions state succession necessitated across the new borders were not only about records concerning administrative aspects of governance. States and their subjects engaged in cross-border interaction also as part of concerted efforts to cope with changes in legal regimes. Service of legal documents across the new borders exposed former Ottomans to new circuits of communication and power as did initiatives for reference to Ottoman administrative records. In a context where former imperial subjects' existing social relations (to each other and to the land) transcended the new borders, the significance of nationality as a forceful social and legal category was often put to test. The new borders played key roles in reinforcing difference among former imperial subjects as categorised and legalised through nationality. The specific cases discussed below will help demonstrate this point. Treated first is a cross-border dispute over maintenance support between two former Ottomans who became subjects of different states after the Ottoman demise and were residing in Istanbul and Baghdad respectively when the dispute began in 1923. Attention is then drawn to the case of a landowner notable who resorted to nationality status and sought French legal support in 1928 to defend his lands against 'his' peasants near the present-day border between Turkey and Syria. As these cases highlight,

---

[26] I am thankful to the anonymous reviewer for her/his expression of interest in the latter path of enquiry. Essential to an endeavour as such would be to demonstrate causal relations between specific aspects of Ottoman state practice in the final years of the Empire – e.g. in records-keeping, institutional frameworks, bureaucratic mechanisms – and the specific conditions these practices brought about when determining new nationalities for former Ottoman subjects. In my above-cited dissertation I have taken what I believe are preliminary steps in this direction.

in the 1920s the borders between Turkey and the Mandates were means of not only bordering but also of 'ordering' and 'othering' on the basis of difference in terms of nationality.[27]

The dispute between Saadet Hanum and Muhiddin Bey over maintenance support is one of the pivotal cases that led to diplomatic agreements on execution of foreign judgements in former Ottoman domains. It is a case in which two ex-Ottomans who got divorced in Damascus subsequently became Turkish and Iraqi nationals respectively. As such, the case is a poignant reminder of the ties which continued to connect the lives of some ex-Ottomans even after the Ottoman demise. Following the partition of imperial domains, these ties had to be managed across the new borders. As in similar cases in the 1920s, the dispute began with efforts to figure out whether or not the (former) husband was still alive after the war. The starting point was an initiative by Saadet Hanum's mother, who reached out to the Turkish Red Crescent in Istanbul in 1923.[28] Based on the unverified information Saadet Hanum's mother provided, the Turkish Red Crescent corresponded with the Directorate of the Police and the Municipality in Baghdad.[29] Officials in Baghdad confirmed Muhiddin Bey's health, which set the stage for further correspondence.[30] These initial stages in the dispute are highly noteworthy. Conventional diplomatic channels were clearly not

[27] As Daniel Meier describes, 'bordering' refers to the definition of, and sovereignty over, a particular space. 'Ordering' refers to identity building and power over that social construction. 'Othering' is a dimension of collective identity construction in relation to a specific territory, referring to the making of the foreigner, the neighbour, the other. See Meier, 'Introduction to the Special Issue', pp. 500–2. See in this regard also the following seminal work; Henk van Houtum and Ton van Naerssen, 'Bordering, Ordering, and Othering', *Tijdschrift voor Economische en Sociale Geografie*, Vol. 93, No. 2 (2002), pp. 125–36; and the recent forum reflecting on the significance of this work, introduced in Rianne Van Melik, 'Introduction to the Forum: Bordering, Ordering and Othering', *Tijdschrift voor Economische en Sociale Geografie*, Vol. 112, No. 1 (2021), pp. 1–3.

[28] Regarding the initiative taken by Saadet Hanum's mother (Fehime) in this case, see *Türk Kızılayı Arşivi* (Archives of the Turkish Red Crescent) (TKA): 281–208.

[29] See the letters these institutions sent to the Turkish Red Crescent, in TKA: 281–210 and 281–210.1.

[30] See especially the letter dated 23 November 1923 (in Arabic) from the Directorate of the Police in Baghdad to the Turkish Red Crescent, in TKA: 281–210.1.

the only means for interaction with authorities on different sides of the envisioned borders.[31]

The complex set of interactions and correspondence that characterised this dispute may test the reader's patience. However, at least an outline of its multiple stages is worthy of close attention. This is essential for gaining a sober sense of what state succession could imply for former Ottomans whose ties with each other transcended the new borders. By the time Saadet Hanum learned that Muhiddin Bey was alive and well in Baghdad, Muhiddin Bey had become a lieutenant colonel in the Iraqi army. He confirmed that he had a wife residing in Istanbul named Saadet, whom he divorced in the Sharia Court of Damascus in 1918.[32] Neither of the former spouses contested that they were properly divorced in Damascus in May 1918. By May 1924, after ascertaining the whereabouts of her ex-husband, Saadet Hanum began her efforts in Istanbul to send Muhiddin Bey an invitation to court for an increase in the maintenance support for their daughter.[33] Muhiddin Bey was informed about this invitation by September 1924, via legal authorities in Turkey, the Delegation of the Ankara government to Istanbul, and the British officials in Turkey and Iraq.[34] The next month Saadet Hanum took further steps. She had the Turkish authorities in Istanbul record that Muhiddin Bey was ordered by Ottoman courts as of February 1918, before their divorce in May the same year, to pay maintenance support for his wife as well as for his child; following which Muhiddin Bey's salary from the Ottoman state was impounded. Calculations in October 1924 suggested that there was an amount of money Muhiddin Bey still owed to Saadet Hanum, and she demanded him to pay.[35] In December

---

[31] Indeed, interaction involving officials of multiple states does not necessarily mean 'diplomatic' interaction. The 1920s in former Ottoman domains was a period when institutional bases of interaction across the new borders were not stable, but rather in the process of consolidation.

[32] See the letter (in Arabic) dated 28 January 1924, from the Municipality of Baghdad to the Turkish Red Crescent, in TKA: 281–210.

[33] See the note dated 29 May 1924, sent to the Ankara government's Delegation to Istanbul by court officials in the city, in order for a legal notification to be made in Iraq, in BOA: HR.İM.: 106-28.

[34] See the correspondence in this regard in BOA: HR.İM.: 106-28 and BOA: HR.İM.: 117–78.

[35] See especially the information recorded on the back of Saadet Hanum's petition to legal authorities in Istanbul dated 25 October 1924, in BOA: HR.İM.: 124-58-1.

1924 Turkish officials in Istanbul contacted the British diplomatic mission in the city with a request for their intervention to secure the payment of this amount to Saadet Hanum.[36] Months passed without a response. A reminder was sent in March 1925.[37] In contrast to the earlier instance when Muhiddin Bey was only informed about an invitation to court, this time the Ankara government was requesting help for the execution in Iraq of a judgement emanating from a court in Turkey. This took the issue to another level, especially since Muhiddin Bey's response to Saadet Hanum was to argue that the couple had an agreement when they got divorced. He would request the handing over of their daughter to the father if Saadet Hanum had changed her mind.[38] This must have sounded to Saadet Hanum more as a threat than an expression of willingness to share responsibility.

In a dispute like this Muhiddin Bey had reasons to feel armoured by the state institutions he had been, and was still, a member of – first as an Ottoman then as an Iraqi army officer. He had years of past service behind him, he knew people, he was a part of the state apparatus. In the absence of formal procedures to execute the court decisions Saadet Hanum obtained in Turkey, Muhiddin Bey's response from beyond the border could defer her claims indefinitely. This is why the matter was evaluated by British and Iraqi officials in Iraq in the context of execution of foreign judgements, along with a similar case involving a woman in Damascus named Suad and another officer in the Iraqi army named Mahdi.[39] The latter case was as consequential

[36] See the note drafted at the Delegation to Istanbul and sent to the British Diplomatic Mission in the city on 2 December 1924, in BOA: HR.İM.: 124-58-2.

[37] See the note of reminder sent from the Delegation to Istanbul to the British Diplomatic Mission in the city on 7 March 1925, in BOA: HR.İM.: 134–78.

[38] See Muhiddin Bey's statement as attached to the note from the British Embassy in Turkey on 16 April 1925 to the Ankara government's Delegation to Istanbul, in BOA: HR.İM.: 134–78. See it enclosed also in the correspondence dated 23 March 1925 between the Ministry of Defense and the High Commission in Baghdad, in The National Archives of India (NAI), Baghdad Residency Records (1918-33) (BRR), Judicial Matters, Execution of foreign judgments in Iraq, 8/145, 1924–32.

[39] See the dispatch dated 21 January 1925 from the Iraqi Ministry of Justice to the Secretary to the British High Commissioner for Iraq, and the memo dated 3 February 1925, from the Secretariat of the High Commissioner to the Iraqi Ministry of Justice, in NAI, BRR, Judicial Matters, Execution of foreign judgements in Iraq, 8/145, 1924–32.

as the case of Saadet Hanum and Muhiddin Bey in bringing about conventions for execution of foreign judgements. A notion in all likelihood shared by Muhiddin Bey was actually made an explicit reference point by the Iraqi officer in that case. In addition to stating that the claim against him was fabricated, the officer stated that as an Iraqi national he was 'not subject to the jurisdiction of the Damascus government'.[40]

The gist of disputes such as these had to do with the difficulty of executing judgements by what had become foreign courts. Borders played an essential role in making these courts 'foreign' to each other, even if they were Sharia courts. They helped frame Ottoman territories as separate political entities under separate legal regimes. Cross-border legal disputes placed former Ottoman subjects in situations where one's nationality mattered not less than one's religion. For some, borders were barriers that needed to be overcome for material support; for some they were reasons to feel armoured. Both ways, the new borders upheld new legal regimes and entrenched the legal significance of difference in terms of nationality. These were among the key ways in which borders shaped the 'lived experience of territoriality' for former Ottoman subjects.[41]

Borders' role in upholding new legal regimes and reinforcing the significance of nationality status can be observed in a wide range of social relations, involving a wide range of social actors. It will be useful to consider in this regard the case of a landowner sheikh named Mahmud, who belonged to the prominent Ansari family and possessed large tracts of land on the Turkish as well as the Syrian side of the border. In July 1928 Sheikh Mahmud wrote a letter to the French High Commissioner in Beirut from the village of Amuda in Syria (about seventy kilometres north of al-Hasaka, fifty kilometres southeast of

---

[40] See the protest signed by Mahdi al-Rahhal as attached to the correspondence dated 23 January 1926 between the Iraqi Minister of Justice and the Secretary to the British High Commissioner in Baghdad, in NAI, BRR, Judicial Matters, Execution of foreign judgements in Iraq, 8/145, 1924-32.

[41] 'The lived experience of territoriality' is a term Matthew Ellis uses, building on the work of scholars including Charles Maier and Will Hanley, as 'the conceptual lens that best enables scholars to capture the dynamic interaction between state and local actors in the forging of modern bordered political identities'. See Matthew H. Ellis, *Desert Borderland: The Making of Modern Egypt and Libya* (Stanford: Stanford University Press, 2018), p. 8.

Mardin). He requested the High Commissioner's help in pursuing legal action against 'one of [his] peasants [*aḥd fallāḥīnī*] who usurped part of his land'.[42] As the lands in question were on the Syrian side of the border, he had appealed to court in the State of Syria. According to Sheikh Mahmud, although it was established that the land was indeed usurped, the judge ordered adjournment of the trial 'on the basis of the decision prohibiting Syrian courts from examining cases pertaining to lands belonging to subjects of the Republic of Turkey'. Sheikh Mahmud thought that the court had made an obvious mistake: 'I am of Arab origin [*'Arab ul-'aṣl*], the place of my residence [*maḥall iqāmatī*] is Syria where my property is, I did not opt for Turkish nationality [within the period allowed for] option [*fī muddat at-tajnīs*], and I registered as Syrian at the time of the census in our village'.[43] Sheikh Mahmud expressed deep resentment that the court in Syria considered him a Turkish subject. He had in fact begun his letter by noting the following: 'it is true that I was formerly settled in the Sandjak of Mardin; but since the armistice I resided at Amuda, where I dispose of my property without contestation or opposition from anyone, like all the other Syrian villagers, and pay the tithes and taxes due to the government'. Being treated as if he was not a Syrian subject, he protested, was a treatment [by the court] that caused him harm impossible to repair in the future, as it emboldened [*tajāsara*] the villagers to usurp his property and land [*ḍabṭ emlākī wa arḍī*].[44]

After receiving the sheikh's letter, the French High Commissioner asked his delegate to the State of Syria in Damascus to enquire into the civil status of

---

[42] See Sheikh Mahmud's request dated 13 July 1928 in CADN: 1SL/1V/2540 – *Turquie; Requêtes*, (subfile *Requête de Cheikh Mahmoud Ansari*).

[43] By the term '*muddat at-tajnīs*' here Sheikh Mahmud was referring to the period of two years allowed for option of nationality after the ratification of the Treaty of Lausanne, as regulated in the Treaty's articles related to nationality (articles 30–36). For the texts of these articles in English, see Parliament of Great Britain, *Treaty of Peace with Turkey*, 26–29. For a contextualisation of the 'right of option' [*droit d'option/ḥakk-ı iḥtiyār*] in broader terms, with references to similar stipulations in other peace treaties at the end of the First World War, see Yaël Ronen, 'Option of nationality', *The Max Planck Encyclopedia of Public International Law* (Oxford: Oxford University Press, 2013), Vol. VII, pp. 995–99.

[44] Sheikh Mahmud's above-referenced request dated 13 July 1928 in CADN: 1SL/1V/2540 – *Turquie; Requêtes*, (subfile *Requête de Cheikh Mahmoud Ansari*).

the sheikh in Syria.[45] It took about two months for the results to be presented, but in the end it was a significant explanation of Sheikh Mahmud's position. The High Commissioner's delegate to Dayr al-Zor, Colonel Callais, prepared a detailed report in which he challenged the central tenets of the Sheikh's claims. Callais began by noting that 'the current situation of this character [Sheikh Mahmud] is similar to that of many notables from [*originaires des*] eastern provinces of Turkey who crossed the border since 1926'.[46] According to the report, Sheikh Mahmud belonged to 'a notable family of Arab race from Mardin [*une notable famille de race arabe originaire de Mardine*]'. He had numerous properties in the region of Mardin, and his wife and children were still residing in the city of Mardin when he submitted his letter to the French High Commissioner. It was in early 1926, following the Sheikh Said Revolt and in apprehension of being deported to western provinces of Turkey that the sheikh crossed the border and came to Amuda.[47] At Amuda, Colonel Callais wrote, the sheikh 'took a second wife, a young Armenian refugee [*une jeune arméniénne réfugiée*] who was raised in a tribe following the exodus and massacres [*l'exode et des massacres*] of 1917'. In contradiction with the sheikh's claim that he resided in Amuda since the armistice, the report stated that he was 'fixed' [*fixé*] in Amuda not before the beginning of 1926, and that he did so primarily due to the political circumstances in the Turkish side of the border.[48]

---

[45] See the dispatch dated 26 July 1928 from the French High Commissioner to his Delegate in Damascus, in CADN: 1SL/1V/2540 - *Turquie; Requêtes*, (subfile *Requête de Cheikh Mahmoud Ansari*).

[46] See the dispatch dated 3 October 1928, sent to the High Commissioner in Beirut from his Delegate to the State of Syria, who passed on the note of information on Sheikh Mahmud prepared by Colonel Callais (the High Commissioner's Delegate at Dayr al-Zor) dated 22 September 1928, in CADN: 1SL/1V/2540 – *Turquie; Requêtes*, (subfile *Requête de Cheikh Mahmoud Ansari*).

[47] The Sheikh Said Revolt began in February 1925 and posed a serious challenge to the Republic's central authority in the environs of Diyarbakır before it was crushed by June 1925. Kurdish (and Zaza) tribes took a leading part in the revolt, in which dissent was voiced through a combination of calls for Kurdish ethnic solidarity with criticism towards the secularising policies of an increasingly more demanding central government in Ankara. For an analysis in English, see Hakan Özoğlu, *From Caliphate to Secular State: Power Struggle in the Early Turkish Republic* (Santa Barbara: Praeger, 2011), pp. 79–121.

[48] See the above-cited report by Colonel Callais, dated 22 September 1928, in CADN: 1SL/1V/2540 – *Turquie; Requêtes*, (subfile *Requête de Cheikh Mahmoud Ansari*).

'It seems,' the colonel wrote, 'that Sheikh Mahmud el Ansari is above all anxious to preserve his properties both in Turkey and Syria.' He believed the sheikh wanted his family remaining in Mardin to take care of his properties in Turkey while he would take care of his properties in Syria. In terms of law (*en droit*), the French colonel did not think the sheikh could be considered a Syrian subject. 'He is registered in Mardin, can return to this city whenever he wants, and will be considered as Turkish,' he wrote. 'The case of Sheikh Mahmud is not unique. This is the case with all the Chelebis of Mardin and Nusaybin who have one foot on each side of the border.'[49] A complaint about peasants being 'emboldened' to usurp land and property was a complaint the French mandate officials could not ignore, and they did look into the matter. However, they were careful about which landowner with which allegiance they would be backing exactly. The archival records consulted in relation to the case did not include any evidence of the French support Sheikh Mahmud expected. Apparently the border mattered more than what the sheikh was willing to acknowledge in his deeds. He claimed the benefits of a particular nationality status, under a particular legal regime. However, the border and the sheikh's attitude towards it played the key role in shaping the fate of that claim. It was costly to ignore the significance of borders in the ongoing reconfiguration of state-subject relations.

## Conclusion

The functions highlighted for borders in this study echoed the following description by Baud and Van Schendel: 'Borders create political, social, and cultural distinctions, but simultaneously imply the existence of (new) networks and systems of interaction across them'.[50] The discussion in this chapter underscored borders' role in the dismantling of an empire *and* in the construction of new state-subject relations in its former domains. Themselves in need of precise definition even after the Treaty of Lausanne, the borders

---

[49] The French colonel used the following phrase here: '*tout les Tchélébis de Mardine et Nissibin*'. It is difficult to come up with a precise translation of the word '*çelebi*' in this context. It seems to have been used in the sense of men of higher social status, such as landowner notables. See Callais's above-cited report, ibid.

[50] Baud and Van Schendel, 'Toward a Comparative History of Borderlands', p. 216.

between Turkey and the Mandates were reminders of far-reaching changes that still continued. They represented a political status quo, but one that was in-the-making throughout the 1920s and beyond.

This is why these borders were contextualised in this chapter with an emphasis on their role in ongoing processes: state succession and changes in administrative and legal regimes. Their consequences were illustrated and discussed through specific cases where the contexts of claims and disputes transcended the new borders. The first part highlighted the case of Ahmed Akif's family as an example of numerous cases where former Ottomans had to request cross-border correspondence for reference to Ottoman records. Similar interactions took place with the purpose of managing a wide range of hardships related essentially to state succession. While some of the negotiations for large-scale delivery of Ottoman records in the 1920s yielded positive results, some failed and led to numerous requests over the years in relation to specific cases. The second part offered further insights into how borders compartmentalised former Ottoman lands into countries under different administrative and legal authorities. As illustrated with reference to cross-border disputes over maintenance support, courts in former Ottoman domains became 'foreign' to each other with the passing of new borders between them. If separated by these new borders, former Ottoman subjects would now have to interact in contexts where difference in terms of nationality status was of paramount significance in shaping the fate of their legal claims. The case of Sheikh Mahmud was highlighted as part of that same emphasis on borders' role in materialising post-imperial settings of subjecthood to state authority. The sheikh may have wished to have one foot on each side of the border. But this made it difficult for him to receive the precious legal support he expected from a particular state on the basis of a particular nationality status. The cross-border mobility he wished to exercise defied the essential changes borders were there to implement.

In a nutshell, then, borders between Turkey and the Mandates necessitated new paths of official communication and new regimes of mobility in former Ottoman domains. Experiences of these necessities were pressing reminders of changes in patterns of administrative and legal interaction. These reminders reinforced the significance of difference in terms of nationality among people who were previously not different from each other in that sense. At a time when new divisions came to separate 'external' and 'internal' spheres of administration, law and politics more broadly, borders in former Ottoman domains shaped lives in accordance with those new divisions.

# 3

# THE LAST OTTOMAN MERCHANTS: REGIONAL TRADE AND POLITICS OF TARIFFS IN ALEPPO'S HINTERLAND, 1921–29

## Ramazan Hakkı Öztan[1]

On 21 March 1925, the Zaloom Brothers, a company that specialised in the import of pistachios from Aleppo, contacted the American consulate in the city to inquire 'if Aintab and Marach [*sic*] are commonly known to be a part of Syria'. Joseph A. Zaloom, who emigrated to New York City only few years prior, was curious, in part because of the growingly competitive local pistachio trade in the US, where the imported crop was incorrectly marketed to American consumers as Cilician nuts. Zaloom hailed from Aleppo and knew that the pistachios feeding the city's exports mostly originated from Aintab and Marash, but it was the American consulate that had to inform him that 'neither Aintab nor Marash are in Syria'.[2] In late May of the same year, the American consul received a similar letter, this time from the International Transportation Association which had forwarded the

[1] I would like to thank Remzi Çağatay Çakırlar, Jordi Tejel, Samuel Dolbee, Orçun Can Okan and Alexander Balistreri for their help and suggestions.

[2] The National Archives and Records Administration (hereafter NARA) College Park, Record Group 84, Consular Aleppo, Syria, Vol. 116: 'Zaloom Brothers Company to American Consulate, Aleppo', 21 March 1925; 'American Consulate, Aleppo, to Joseph A. Zaloom', 16 April 1925.

information it compiled on travel conditions and touristic sites in Syria to be double-checked for any errors before the publication of their handbook. In its response, the consulate noted that 'the city of Aintab which you have listed as being located in Syria is in Turkey', suggesting that it should instead 'be included in the section on Turkey'.[3]

Back in October 1921, namely four years before the exchange of these letters, the Ankara government and France had agreed that the Turkish–Syrian border would pass just north of Aleppo, following the tracks of the Berlin–Baghdad railway from the Çobanbey station until Nusaybin in the Jazira. The railway, which was foreseen in the early 1900s as a project that could help reinvigorate the Ottoman Empire by linking its incongruent units to one another, ironically became the very site of the empire's definitive dismemberment after the First World War.[4] The railway-cum-border practically divided the Ottoman province of Aleppo into two, separating the commercial hub that the city of Aleppo was from its southern Anatolian hinterland, where the cities of Aintab and Marash were located. The letters that the American consulate received in later years makes sense only in this context of post-Ottoman territorial divisions that ruptured what was once a connected regional economy – one the Zaloom Brothers knew by heart. For them, infrastructural investments, such as roads and railways, had made considerable strides since the late nineteenth century in making the disparate units of the empire increasingly interdependent, facilitating a range of everyday mobilities that ultimately defined the practical meaning of imperial rule. This chapter primarily asks what happened to these mobilities in the absence of the empire.

To be sure, we have come a long way as a field in our approaches to the end of imperial rule and emergence of nation states, increasingly wary of neat depictions of the transition between the two. In particular, scholars continue to explore Ottoman legacies and continuities in the making of the Middle

---

[3] NARA, College Park, Record Group 84, Consular Aleppo, Syria, Vol. 120: 'International Transportation Association to American Consulate, Aleppo', 25 May 1925; 'American Consulate, Aleppo, to International Transportation Association', 27 June 1925.

[4] Sam Dolbee, 'The Locust and the Starling: People, Insects, and Disease in the Late Ottoman Jazira and After, 1860–1940', (PhD thesis, New York University, 2017), pp. 13–14.

East, a growing literature rooted in, but also going well beyond, the earlier critiques of official nationalist narratives.[5] Most recently, Michael Provence examined the post-imperial odysseys of what he called the last Ottoman generation, reconstructing the stories of how the Ottoman military and civilian elites, educated and socialised in imperial academies, eventually came to terms with the collapse of the empire by trying to carve out a career for themselves in the emerging cadres of leadership across the Middle East.[6] Yet, what about a more 'ordinary' generation of Ottomans, such as merchants, peasants and townspeople, who were less under the influence of an imperial education? What did the end of imperial arrangements mean to them? Keith Watenpaugh had already shown what it was like for the inhabitants of Aleppo to get disconnected 'from the ideological and cultural networks binding them to the Ottoman centre'.[7] This chapter seeks to contribute to this strand of literature by tracing how the end of imperial rule unfolded in the realm of economy, examining particularly the ways in which it ruptured the world of commercial mobilities that the Aleppines, such as Zaloom Brothers, had navigated for generations.

In pursuit of this line of enquiry, the choice of focusing on Aleppo is a strategic one, for it had historically been an imperial hub of mobility that not only connected the caravan routes from Iraq to Syria but also stood at the centre of a voluminous import and export trade that fed into various regional and transnational nodes of commerce. Aleppo therefore holds an empirical promise that could help chart the complex politics of post-Ottoman mobilities. Yet, Aleppo is also historiographically relevant, particularly as to the way we could re-think the end of Ottoman rule in the Middle East. Even if the notion of an Ottoman decline has been discredited

[5] Erik Jan Zürcher, *The Unionist Factor: The Role of the Committee of Union and Progress in the Turkish National Movement, 1905–1926* (Leiden: Brill, 1984); L. Carl Brown (ed.), *Imperial Legacy: The Ottoman Imprint on the Balkans and the Middle East* (New York: Columbia University Press, 1996).

[6] Michael Provence, *The Last Ottoman Generation and the Making of the Modern Middle East* (Cambridge, Cambridge University Press, 2017).

[7] Keith David Watenpaugh, *Being Modern in the Middle East: Revolution, Nationalism, Colonialism and the Arab Middle Class* (Princeton: Princeton University Press, 2006), p. 125.

for the past few decades now,[8] historians continue to make sense of the collapse of the empire by synchronising it with political and socio-economic processes that presumably underlay the empire's disintegration.[9] As the interwar economic history of Aleppo will illustrate, however, the collapse of the imperial rule was far from being a uniform experience across the Ottoman domains. It was in fact particularly contentious in places which had once been at the core, but were ultimately reduced to peripheral status as a result of post-Ottoman territorial divisions. I argue this was particularly the case in Aleppo, where the post-war settlements ruptured the very connections that had long defined the city's central position within the Ottoman East.

The first section below first seeks to substantiate the claim that the Ottoman domestic economy indeed got increasingly intra-connected and interdependent. After sketching the broad outlines of this nineteenth-century development, and Aleppo's significance within it, we will see that this intertwinement continued uninterrupted during the First World War. The second part of the chapter will then examine the economic policies that informed the post-war settlements, particularly paying attention as to how the mandatory powers sought to secure the continuity of interregional economic ties across the Ottoman Middle East. While these efforts bore fruit in some regions, the case of Aleppo will show the contentious ways in which this episode had eventually unfolded. More often than not, the economic future of the city had become a bargaining chip during protracted negotiations that sought to revise the post-war settlements in the Middle East in general and along the Turkish–Syrian border in particular. We will examine this process by tracing the negotiations on tariff policies by Turkey and French Syria, the two new states that came to control the northern and southern portions of the Ottoman province of Aleppo. As the chapter will ultimately seek to illustrate,

[8] David A. Howard, 'Ottoman Historiography and the Literature of "Decline" in the Sixteenth and Seventeenth Centuries', *Journal of Asian History*, Vol. 22, No. 1 (1988), pp. 52–76; Donald Quataert, 'Ottoman History Writing and Changing Attitudes towards the Notion of "Decline"', *History Compass*, Vol. 1 (2003), pp. 1–9.

[9] For a critique, see Ramazan Hakkı Öztan, 'Point of No Return? Prospects of Empire after the Ottoman Defeat in the Balkan Wars', *International Journal of Middle East Studies*, Vol. 50, No. 1 (2018), pp. 65–84.

the Ottoman Empire did not 'collapse' like a house of cards, but rather get disentangled, particularly in places like Aleppo where imperial rule was less of an imagined affair than a connected one.

## Towards an Ottoman Single Market

The emergence of the Ottoman Middle East as a single market and Aleppo's place within it was not a historical given, but rather a long drawn-out outcome borne out of a particular conjecture. Back in the late eighteenth century long-distance trade across the Ottoman Empire did certainly exist in the form of trans-desert caravans, but the volume and frequency of this trade were far from creating interdependent markets. Even though the caravans linked the land ports of Aleppo and Damascus to Mesopotamia and Hijaz, they often brought in luxury goods that were not consumed locally but instead transited to Constantinople as well as other major European markets. At a time when transport costs were prohibitive, Middle Eastern cities largely met their subsistence needs by cultivating limited dependencies with their 'green belts' – immediate rural hinterlands whose *raison d'être* was their proximity to urban markets.[10] Any agricultural and manufacturing surplus from these suburban zones of cultivation was in turn earmarked for the army, the palace and the metropole, as well as other provincial capitals – a system that was in line with the traditional Ottoman economic policy of provisionism.[11] In this system, which was configured on maintaining self-sufficient administrative units, domestic trade was given secondary importance, as it was kept subject to internal duties – collected both on overland routes and along the coast – which made interregional commercial exchange costly and therefore limited to luxury goods that were light in bulk but high in value.[12]

---

[10] James A. Reilly, 'Regions and Markets of Ottoman Syria: Comparisons and Transformations', *Chronos*, Vol. 10 (2004), pp. 111–44.

[11] Mehmet Genç, 'Economy and Economic Policy', in Gabor Agoston and Bruce Alan Masters (eds), *Encyclopedia of the Ottoman Empire*, (New York: Facts on File, 2009), p. 192. In the far-flung Arab provinces of the empire, the rural and urban surplus formed the backbone of struggles among a number of powerful households that sought to maximise their share of the surplus. See Roger Owen, *The Middle East in the World Economy, 1800–1914* (London: I. B. Tauris, 2002), pp. 18–22.

[12] Mehmet Genç, 'Osmanlı Devleti'nde İç Gümrük Rejimi', *Tanzimat'tan Cumhuriyet'e Türkiye Ansiklopedisi*, Vol. 3 (İstanbul: İletişim Yayınları, 1985), pp. 786–90.

The Industrial Revolution in Europe, with its growing need for raw material, had significant consequences for the provisionist Ottoman economy, as the prices increased at home due to rising external demand. The Ottoman state accordingly began to embrace a set of interventionist policies into changing market dynamics, seeking to limit the access of foreign merchants into the Ottoman interior. This situation changed radically in the decades after the Treaty of Baltalimanı (1838), however. While maintaining the pre-existing lower tariffs for imports, the treaty opened up the Ottoman markets to foreign traders by removing the limits placed on the export of raw material, bringing the Ottomans into the fold of export-orientated European mercantilism.[13] In the absence of provisionist policies, merchants across the Middle East first began to channel themselves towards port cities where agrarian surplus became the return cargo of ships that had brought in machine-made manufactured goods from the West. Interstate conflicts, such as the Crimean War (1853–56) and the American Civil War (1861–65) deepened this dependency, facilitating the export of Ottoman cereals to meet the wartime necessities.[14] Increasingly connected to the world markets, but also meeting the needs of the region's growing local populations, cereals became the engine of agricultural growth in the Eastern Mediterranean, registering a nearly threefold increase of output from 500,000 tonnes in the 1830s to 1,300,000 tonnes by 1914.[15]

Growing output of cereals as well as other agricultural produce throughout the second half of the nineteenth century was interlinked to a host of crucial processes that in one way or another related to developments borne out of war-making. For one, the Ottoman state, increasingly eager to revitalise its economy, became deeply invested in its attempt to institute greater

[13] Seyfettin Gürsel, '1838 Osmanlı-İngiliz Ticaret Antlaşması', *Tanzimat'tan Cumhuriyet'e*, pp. 688–90.

[14] Françoise Métral, 'Changements dans les routes et les flux commerciaux du désert syrien, 1870–1920: Le sort incertain des oasis du nord de la Palmyrène', in Thomas Philipp and Birgit Schaebler (eds), *The Syrian Land: Processes of Integration and Fragmentation: Bilād al-Shām from the 18th to the 20th Century* (Stuttgart: Franz Steiner Verlag, 1998), pp. 41–42.

[15] Linda Schilcher, 'The Grain Economy of Late Ottoman Syria and the Issue of Large-Scale Commercialisation', in Çağlar Keyder and Faruk Tabak (eds), *Landholding and Commercial Agriculture in the Middle East* (Albany: State University of New York Press, 1991), p. 174.

public security across its provinces in pursuit of greater sources of manpower and taxation.[16] This was particularly visible in the outlying arid sectors of the Aleppo province from the 1860s onwards, a time when 'the state needed the frontier . . . while the frontier might not have needed the state'.[17] In this effort, the authorities were aided by the adoption of new rifle technologies that made it easier to extend military control over tribal zones, which began to be dotted with military outposts that sought to secure trade routes.[18] A similar, but much more concentrated effort at state penetration took place in the Northern Caucasus by Tsarist Russia, which had led to the displacement of nearly one million Muslims until 1914. Their resettlement by the authorities across Ottoman Syria became an important way in which the Sublime Porte implemented its goal of expanding cultivable land, while also increasing rural population numbers.[19]

This process went hand in hand with attempts to encourage sedentarisation of tribes as well. After all, the Ottoman Empire was as much a pastoral empire as an it was an agrarian one.[20] While these efforts by the Porte to colonise 'empty' lands through sedentarisation certainly resulted in conflicts over lands and resources, they also expanded networks of capital, creating more interdependent regional markets.[21] In Aleppo, these interlinked

[16] Bruce Masters, 'Aleppo: The Ottoman Empire's Caravan City', in Edhem Eldem, Daniel Goffman and Bruce Masters (eds), *The Ottoman City between East and West: Aleppo, Izmir and Istanbul* (Cambridge: Cambridge University Press, 1999), pp. 66–67.

[17] Eugene L. Rogan, *Frontiers of the State in the Late Ottoman Empire: Transjordan, 1850–1921* (Cambridge: Cambridge University Press, 1999), p. 9.

[18] Norman Lewis, *Nomads and Settlers in Syria and Jordan, 1800–1980* (Cambridge: Cambridge University Press, 1987), pp. 46–48.

[19] Vladimir Hamed-Troyansky, 'Imperial Refuge: Resettlement of Muslims from Russia in the Ottoman Empire' (PhD thesis, Stanford University, 2018); Patrick J. Adamiak, 'To the Edge of the Desert: Caucasian Refugees, Civilization, and Settlement on the Ottoman Frontier, 1866–1918' (PhD thesis, University of California, San Diego, 2018).

[20] Reşat Kasaba, *A Moveable Empire: Ottoman Nomads, Migrants & Refugees* (Seattle: University of Washington Press, 2009).

[21] Yücel Terzibaşoğlu, 'Landlords, Nomads, and Refugees: Struggles over Land and Population Movements in North-Western Anatolia, 1877–1914', (PhD thesis, University of London, 2003); Nora Elizabeth Barakat, 'An Empty Land? Nomads and Property Administration in Hamidian Syria', (PhD thesis, University of California, Berkeley, 2015).

developments manifested themselves in the realm of imperial estates, as the Ottoman sultans began to acquire large plots of lands starting from the mid-nineteenth century. This policy reached a peak during the reign of Abdülhamid II, whose properties constituted the majority of lands to the east and south of Aleppo. These estates not only came with the added benefit of increased security in the shape of gendarmerie posts, but also provided cheaper rates to those who were willing rent and toil smaller plots, including, but not limited to, the incoming flows of Circassian refugees. The Land Law of 1858 consolidated the trend, whereby important Aleppine families also began to expand their own landholdings around the city.[22]

These developments not only expanded the cultivation of lands beyond the traditional bounds of green belts that had surrounded Middle Eastern cities for generations, but also created conditions conducive for interregional trade. To be sure, the centres of textile manufacturing such as Aleppo had been losing their market outlets in Europe since the late eighteenth century, but the Aleppine merchants sought to compensate their losses by seeking new markets both for transit goods and locally manufactured commodities. The coming of the Long Depression (1873–96) in particular became the most opportune moment, as the radical drops in the purchasing power of Ottoman consumers naturally curtailed the volume of imported goods, since the latter remained well beyond their reach.[23] Ottoman manufacturers stepped in to fill the gap by beginning to exercise a variety of cost-cutting techniques, ultimately producing cheaper clothes that catered towards a local, but impoverished clientele across southern Anatolia, Iraq, Syria and Egypt.[24] Many smaller cities, such as Aintab, Urfa and Marash, which were previously Aleppo's markets for textiles, slowly developed their own manufacturing capacities too, forming new divisions of labour among neighbouring cities in textile production.[25] This level of market integration was further aided in

[22] Lewis, *Nomads and Settlers*, pp. 49–54.

[23] Donald Quataert, *Ottoman Manufacturing in the Age of the Industrial Revolution* (Cambridge: Cambridge University Press, 1993), p. 68.

[24] George Hakim, 'Industry', in Said B. Himadeh (ed.), *Economic Organization of Syria* (Beirut: American Press, 1936), p. 121.

[25] Quataert, *Ottoman Manufacturing*, p. 103.

1874 by the abolition of internal customs duties that ceased to be collected in internal ports of trade such as Aleppo.[26]

Yet, Aleppine merchants did not solely sell manufactured textiles to an expanding hinterland. Like other artisanal centres across the Ottoman Empire throughout the second half of the nineteenth century, Aleppo, too, began to develop a growing dependency with the coastal regions where cultivation had already shifted to cash crops of cotton and silk. The corresponding increase in demand for foodstuffs in these littoral zones were in turn met by the increasing engagement of animal husbandry in areas that once stood on the margins of agriculturally productive zones.[27] Accordingly, Aleppo also emerged as an important commercial centre where livestock merchants bought sheep from the plains of Eastern Anatolia and northern Iraq – most notably Mosul – for the growing consumption needs in the littoral. While the wool processed in Aleppo found export markets across the globe and the sheep guts were earmarked for export to the West to be used as sausage casings, the rest of the animals supplied the growing demand for meat down south in Syria and as far as Egypt. This interdependence between Aleppine merchants and pastoral herders even led to the formation of long-term partnerships, whereby merchants began to own their own flocks of sheep tended by nomads – an arrangement through which the urban commercial elites and the Bedouins shared the risks posed by climatic conditions and rustling.[28]

On the eve of the First World War – the conflict that would eventually bring an end to the Ottoman rule – Aleppo's economy was not one of decay and ruin that foreshadowed an empire on the verge of collapse. The city was instead more connected to its hinterland than a century before, enjoying interdependent commercial networks that deeply embedded the surrounding rural economy to its urban centre. The population statistics confirmed the trend. In 1908 Aleppo reached the population levels it had known back in the seventeenth century, since the city began to tap into flows of rural

---

[26] Genç, 'Osmanlı Devleti'nde İç Gümrük', p. 787.

[27] Faruk Tabak, 'Local Merchants in Peripheral Areas of the Empire: The Fertile Crescent during the Long Nineteenth Century', *Review (Fernand Braudel Center)*, Vol. 11, No. 2 (Spring 1988), pp. 179–214.

[28] Sarah D. Shields, *Mosul before Iraq: Like Bees Making Five-Sided Cells* (Albany: State University of New York Press, 2000), pp. 170–79.

to urban migration.[29] Various railway building schemes underway also bore fruit from the early 1900s onwards, as Aleppo became connected to Damascus as well as Tripoli on the coast. By the end of the Ottoman rule, the Arab provinces of the empire were not only more integrated into the global circuits of trade, transport and communication than a century before, but they were also much more connected internally with a greater level of market cohesion. As James Reilly noted:

> By 1914, the local economies of Syria had ceased to be self-subsistent. They had been linked in regular and significant ways with neighboring regions and with the world market. Syria itself was developing into an interconnected market, tied to global economic forces as well as linked regionally to Anatolia, Mesopotamia, and Egypt.[30]

Unlike one might expect, the outbreak of the First World War had a similar function in facilitating regional integration across the Middle East. From autumn 1914 onwards the Ottoman war effort quickly led to the improvement and extension of infrastructure across the region.[31] Cemal Pasha's description of the journey from Istanbul to Damascus – the headquarters of the Fourth Army he was appointed to command – was dotted with myriad difficulties he encountered while travelling through the patchwork of an incomplete transport network. As Cemal crossed the Dörtyol-Alexandretta branch line in a handcar at night, observing the enemy boats anchored only some miles ahead, he became determined to turn his tenure in Damascus into a programme focusing on improved transport.[32] This he did across a region that became more interconnected as the empire came to a close.[33] As Edward F. Nickoley noted, 'never before had roads been in such good

---

[29] Masters, 'Aleppo', p. 72.

[30] Reilly, 'Regions and Markets', p. 139.

[31] Cyrus Schayegh, *The Middle East and the Making of the Modern World* (Cambridge, MA: Harvard University Press, 2017), pp. 96–123.

[32] Cemal Paşa, *Hatıralar: İttihat ve Terakki, 1. Dünya Savaşı Anıları*, Alpay Kabacalı (ed.) (İstanbul: Türkiye İş Bankası Kültür Yayınları, 2001), p. 169.

[33] Hasan Kayalı, 'Wartime Regional and Imperial Integration of Greater Syria during World War I', in *The Syrian Land*, pp. 293–306; M. Talha Çiçek, *War and State Formation in Syria: Cemal Pasha's Governorate during World War I, 1914–1917* (New York: Routledge: 2014).

condition as they were in 1918'.[34] The efforts of Germany, the Ottoman ally in the war, certainly contributed to this trend. The engineers and labourers working on the German designed, financed and constructed Berlin-Baghdad railway continued their work throughout the war, working on the tunnels that cut through the Taurus and Amanus mountains, but they only managed to finish the project in August 1918.[35] In other words, only by the end of the war did Aleppo become better connected to Cilicia in its northwest and Nusaybin in its northeast. While this was no doubt ironic, it also foreshadowed the protracted trade wars that were to come, as the railway that was supposed to interconnect Aleppo's markets further became the very site separating the city from its southern Anatolian hinterland.

## Parameters of Post-war Economic Reconstruction

The world economic order that the outbreak of the First World War disrupted was one that was based on the principles of free trade and open markets propagated by Britain, the hegemonic power of the nineteenth century. The Paris Peace of Conference of 1919 essentially sought to restore this economic order, taking the reconstruction of 'the pre-war multilateral trading system as a priority on both economic and political grounds'.[36] The outlines of what this restoration would look like in the Middle East became clear to all parties in late 1917, when the Bolsheviks published the full texts of the Sykes–Picot Agreement (1916). In addition to establishing zones of direct and indirect control by Britain and France, this secret agreement stipulated that the existing Ottoman tariffs would remain in force for a period of twenty years across the Middle East, unless Britain and France would bilaterally agree to change them.[37] The later Treaty of Sèvres, too, signed with the Ottomans in 1920, included similar clauses that required the continued application of Ottoman

---

[34] Nickoley, 'Transportation and Communication', in *Economic Organization*, p. 178.

[35] Sean McMeekin, *The Berlin-Baghdad Express: The Ottoman Empire and Germany's Bid for World Power* (Cambridge, MA: The Belknap Press of Harvard University Press, 2010), p. 341.

[36] Barry Eichengreen, 'Versailles: The Economic Legacy', *International Affairs*, Vol. 95, No. 1 (2019), pp. 7–24, 11.

[37] Sykes–Picot Agreement, 1916 <https://avalon.law.yale.edu/20th_century/sykes.asp>

tariffs of 1907.[38] The developments in the course of the war and the post-war resistance to the scramble of the Middle East ensured that both the Treaty of Sèvres and Sykes–Picot Agreement remained a dead letter. Yet, the mindset that had shaped these diplomatic arrangements deeply informed how the economy of the Ottoman Middle East was ultimately restructured in ways to serve the larger imperial interests.

For one, the mandate charters that established colonial oversight over former Ottoman territories promised 'an open-door policy' that aimed to provide all members of the League of Nations as well as the US equal access to the mandated territories, where they would enjoy lower duties on their imports.[39] This open-door policy was initially championed by the US, largely influenced by the Secretary of State John Hay's 'Open Door Notes', which had underlined the guidelines for US trade relations with the Far East.[40] Much like in China, where the Great Powers exercised different spheres of influence within a single market zone, the introduction of open-door policy to the Middle East intended to divorce politics from commercial competition by promising equal tariff rates to all parties that were part of the post-war reconstruction. In countries such as Egypt and Turkey, however, whose independence were recognised in 1922 and 1923 respectively, open-door policies would have to take a different form. While politically independent, both countries were forced to accept the continued application of the latest Ottoman tariff of 1916 for a five-year period. For Egypt, the lower tariffs were accordingly fixed at 8 per cent *ad valorem*, which would expire on 16 February 1930,[41] while the arrangements for Turkey would terminate some months earlier on 6 August 1929.[42] Bluntly

---

[38] Centre des Archives Diplomatiques de Nantes (hereafter CADN), *Ankara Ambassade*, 36/ PO/1, 146, 'Note sur les Arrangements Douaniers à Faire avec la Turquie', p. 3.

[39] Roza I. M. El-Eini, 'Trade Agreements and the Continuation of Tariff Protection Policy in Mandate Palestine in the 1930s', *Middle Eastern Studies*, Vol. 34, No. 1 (1998), pp. 164–91, 179.

[40] Bruce A. Elleman, *International Competition in China, 1899–1991: The Rise, Fall and Restoration of the Open Door Policy* (London: Routledge, 2015), pp. 13–17.

[41] Middle East Centre Archive, St Antony's College, Oxford (hereafter MECA), Eden Tatton-Brown Collection GB 165-0433, 5 Memoirs, p. 43.

[42] The Turkish Republican Archives of the Prime Ministry (hereafter BCA), 30.10.0.0, 179-238-10, 8 August 1933, p. 11.

put, while Britain and France chose to do away with the Ottoman Empire in the aftermath of the First World War they wanted to keep intact its economic networks and their time-hardened privileges within them.

For mandatory authorities, 'the central problem', as Cyrus Schayegh noted, 'was how to square Bilad al-Sham's considerable degree of economic integration with its political division'.[43] These considerations quickly drove the British and French as early as 25 August 1921 to establish a customs union between Syria and Palestine, since the latter was seen as an indispensable market of the former.[44] To be sure, imperial powers were first and foremost motivated by their own economic interests in pursuing these policies. In commenting on Transjordan, for instance, the Acting High Commissioner argued against its existence as 'a separate political entity'. He reasoned that 'economically Trans-Jordania should continue to be bound up closely with Palestine', in part because the precious mineral deposits on either side of the Dead Sea should be subject to a single regulation.[45] The French embraced a similar attitude towards its mandates, too, as it sought to restore the former position of Syria as an intermediary of trade between Europe and Asia, from which France could then claim a fair share.[46]

These self-serving positions – coupled with an awareness of the broader risks involved with the economic impact of the partitioning Ottoman territories – drove the mandatory authorities to develop policies geared towards absorbing associated economic shocks of the transition from an empire to a world of nation states.[47] As a result, the continuity of imperial commercial links had become the hallmark of mandatory policies in restructuring the economy

---

[43] Schayegh, *The Middle East*, p. 157.

[44] This customs agreement included many arrangements that enabled duty-free exchange of locally manufactured goods, in addition to establishing rules for the conduct of transit trade between the two countries. The National Archives (hereafter TNA), CO 733/22, 32026, 'Report on Administration for Period 1st July 1920 – 31st Dec 1921', ff. 500–501.

[45] TNA, CO 733/22, 27135, 26 May 1922, f. 257.

[46] CADN, *Ankara Ambassade*, 36/PO/1, 136, 'Bulletin Périodique no.69, Période du 26 juillet au 1er septembre', Aley, 4 septembre 1923, p. 11.

[47] The mandatory agreements, for instance, also included an optional clause that allowed the conclusion of special customs treaties with states that neighboured the mandates, such as Turkey and Egypt. Norman Burns, *The Tariff of Syria, 1919–1932* (Beirut: American Press, 1933), p. 41.

of the post-Ottoman Middle East. These were the plans for Aleppo as well, despite its division into two by a national border. Yet, their execution would prove more contentious than the French had anticipated, for commerce was inextricably linked to politics in the eyes of Turkey. After all, Ankara was home to a burgeoning nationalist elite that saw the granting of economic concessions to the West as a prelude to later political domination, a lesson they learned all too well as participants of the late Ottoman political economy.

## Aleppo in the Post-war (Dis)order

On 7 September 1920, one-and-a-half months after the French military took control of the city, proclamations were posted on the streets of Aleppo, where General Gouraud framed the French presence as 'the fulfillment of the wishes of the local people', promising the Aleppines economic prosperity concomitant with the natural and financial resources of the province.[48] Yet, these were not the only placards decorating the streets of Aleppo. Local resistance committees announced their anti-French slogans through similar means, while situating themselves as part of a wider Ottoman struggle against the institution of colonial rule.[49] Led by the former Ottoman officers under the leadership of Mustafa Kemal, Ottoman resistance managed to push the French out of Marash, Urfa, Aintab and Kilis – cities that formed the northern rim of Aleppo's hinterland.[50] The invasion of western Anatolia by Greek forces and the start of their offensive, however, turned the focus of the organised resistance away from Aleppo, where the struggle instead began to take the form of low-intensity guerrilla warfare conducted by roaming bands originating from the Turkish sector. The ensuing insecurity delivered a severe blow to Aleppo's interregional commercial links, as trade became stagnant and largely restricted to 'a radius of some twenty miles from the town'.[51]

---

[48] TNA, FO 861/68, 'Aux Habitants du Vilayet d'Alep et du Sandjak d'Alexandrette', 7 September 1920.

[49] For the complex dynamics of mass politics in the period preceding the French occupation, see James L. Gelvin, *Divided Loyalties: Nationalism and Mass Politics in Syria at the Close of Empire* (Berkeley: University of California Press, 1998).

[50] Watenpaugh, *Being Modern*, p. 172.

[51] TNA, FO 371/6454/E5774, 23 April 1921, f. 156.

Amidst rampant insecurity on the roads, the goods that would normally get exported abroad piled up in the Syrian interior, with only few camel convoys transporting them to Aleppo.[52] The situation did not fare any better for the import of goods from Europe, as the risks associated with political unrest drove the costs of camel transport between Alexandretta and Aleppo to considerable levels, leaving only the links to Tripoli and Beirut viable for trade.[53] But even then, the shipment of goods to Beirut remained prohibitive for merchants due to exorbitant freight rates. The state of things was certainly made worse by the ongoing military requisitioning of the railway infrastructure.[54]

The burgeoning discontent of the Aleppine merchant community was the outcome of this growingly contentious relations between the Kemalists and the French. When General Gouraud visited Aleppo in late June 1921 its inhabitants quickly aired discontent and complained how often the roads to the city were cut off, a situation that brought commercial activity to a standstill. The merchants noted their desire for peace and political settlement instead. A month of 'unusual calm' earlier in May had already translated into an increase in the numbers of Turkish traders who purchased local goods, and eventually raised hopes of Aleppo's residents 'that the commercial barriers between Aleppo and the Turkish zone were [finally] broken down'.[55] The resumption of banditry, as it often did with the coming of summer months, however, quickly overrode these short-term improvements.[56]

Ankara's tacit support for the ongoing activities of armed bands in northern Syria was no doubt a way of pressuring the French to a diplomatic resolution of the conflict. The attempts to do so already bore its first fruit on 9 March 1921 after the negotiations in London between the Turkish foreign minister

---

[52] NARA, College Park, Record Group 84, Consular Aleppo, Syria, Vol. 74: From Consul Jackson, 21 April 1921.

[53] NARA, College Park, Record Group 84, Consular Aleppo, Syria, Vol. 78: From Consul Jackson, 30 November 1921, p. 3.

[54] Ibid., Vol. 74: From Consul Jackson, 21 April 1921.

[55] TNA, FO 371/6455/E9105, 23 July 1921, ff. 150–52.

[56] On the cyclical nature of banditry in northern Syria, see Jean-David Mizrahi, 'Un "Nationalisme de la Frontière": Bandes Armées et Sociabilités Politiques sur la Frontière Turco-Syrienne au Début des Années 1920', *Vingtième Siècle Revue d'Histoire*, Vol. 2, No. 78 (2003), pp. 19–34.

Bekir Sami Bey and the French premier Aristide Briand. This was when France accepted to forgo its claims on the zones already occupied by Turkish forces and promised to evacuate Cilicia in exchange for a range of economic concessions.[57] In turn, this agreement projected for the very first time the institution of a Turkish–Syrian border along the tracks of the Baghdad railway.[58]

The news of such a settlement which would divide the Ottoman province of Aleppo into two, quickly created a backlash in the local Aleppo press. '[Fifty per cent] of the goods, exported by Aleppo to Europe and America,' Le Franco-Syrien noted, 'are brought from the territories which the recent Franco-Turkish agreement puts under Turkish dominion, and will be separated from Syria by a line of custom houses.'[59] Statistics were harnessed to make the case: based on the 1913 figures of the Aleppo Chamber of Commerce, Southern Anatolia was indeed the only provider of nearly all tragacanth gum, raisins, yellow berries and gall nuts that came to Aleppo for export, while the region also supplied to local and foreign markets through Aleppo more than 50 per cent of pistachio nuts, wool, almonds, animal skins and liquorice root, among many other products.[60]

Even if the fears of the Aleppine mercantile community were indeed well justified, the agreement in March ultimately failed to get ratified by the National Assembly in Ankara due to the extent of economic concessions it had granted to the French.[61] Yet, the agreement foreshadowed two things. First, the institution of a border between the two countries would eventually

---

[57] The possibility of a French withdrawal from Cilicia in exchange of economic concessions has a longer history going back to early December 1919 when it was first suggested by F. Georges-Picot during his visit to Mustafa Kemal in Sivas. See Sina Akşin, 'Franco-Turkish Relations at the end of 1919', in Hamit Batu and Jean-Louis Bacqué-Grammont, L'Empire Ottoman, la République de Turquie et la France (Istanbul: ISIS Press, 1986), p. 442.

[58] BCA, 930.2.0.0, 1-7-1, 9 March 1921.

[59] NARA, College Park, Record Group 84, Consular Aleppo, Syria, Vol. 74; Paul Burain, 'Alep Menacée de Ruine', Le Franco-Syrien, 27 Mars 1921.

[60] Ibid., 'Provenance de certains produits exportés par Alep'.

[61] For instance, its clauses also stipulated the conclusion of a special customs arrangement between Turkish and Syrian districts, while also giving concessions to French companies in Cilicia and southern Anatolia. BCA, 930.2.0.0, 1-7-1, 9 March 1921. After the rejection of the agreement by the parliament in Ankara, Bekir Sami Bey also resigned from his post. See Türkiye Büyük Millet Meclisi Gizli Celse Zabıtları (hereafter TBMMGCZ), 12 May 1921, p. 73.

separate Aleppo from its south Anatolian hinterland. Second, the Kemalists would resist any French attempts to carve out a zone of economic influence in southern Anatolia that would not only lessen the impact of a border on Aleppine merchants, but also help advance French interests.

Despite the standing differences in principles, geopolitics dictated the necessity of rapprochement between the two parties. Two months after the rejection of the London Agreement, Ankara handed in a counter-proposal to the French and by June, Henry Franklin-Bouillon arrived in Ankara to start bilateral negotiations once again, this time directly with Mustafa Kemal.[62] While the parties agreed on basic terms of the agreement, Franklin-Bouillon left Ankara for further consultations with Paris.[63] Only in September 1921 did the developments bring these diplomatic talks towards more conclusive directions. This was when the Turkish armies managed to repulse the Greek advances away from the doorsteps of Ankara – a victory which made it clear that military coercion alone would not suffice to dislodge the Kemalists. On 20 October, a week after signing the Treaty of Kars with the Bolsheviks, Ankara also concluded the long drawn-out talks with the French and signed the Treaty of Ankara, which formally instituted the Turco-Syrian border. While the treaty did not include any customs arrangements between Syria and Turkey, and left the matter to be decided later on in mixed commissions, Mustafa Kemal's address to the deputies in Ankara made the Turkish position clear:

> I openly shared with Franklin-Bouillon our position on the customs question – that we do not accept the institution of a special sphere of influence [in Aleppo's Anatolian hinterland]. We told him we are afraid that by making us agree to such a principle – however limited it may initially be – they could then use it as a basis to argue for a larger sphere of economic influence that will stretch to our entire country.[64]

[62] For the timeline and details of these negotiations, see Bige Yavuz, '1921 Tarihli Türk-Fransız Anlaşması'nın Hazırlık Aşamaları', *Atatürk Araştırma Merkezi Dergisi*, Vol. 8, No. 23 (1992), pp. 273–308.

[63] For the depiction of his journey and the negotiations in Ankara in early June 1921, see Yusuf Kemal Tengirşenk, *Vatan Hizmetinde* (İstanbul: Bahar Matbaası, 1967), pp. 246–53.

[64] *TBMMGCZ*, 18 October 1921, p. 362.

The French continued to hope otherwise. In addressing the notables of Aleppo, French General de Lamothe tried to convince them of the positive benefits of the settlement, highlighting the continued French commitment to prevent the creation of a customs barrier between Turkey and Syria as a result of it.[65] This was not a passing promise made in the heat of the moment, but a genuine French desire dictated by the nature of Aleppo's interregional economy. In fact, two days after the pact with Turkey, General Gouraud issued an arrêté (no. 1079), announcing that 'the refund system', which was already tested between Syria and Palestine, would also be implemented in commercial transactions with Asia Minor.[66] Accordingly, the city's merchants would be able to import goods from abroad as usual and pay Syrian customs upon arrival; if they sell (i.e. re-export) these goods to their usual customers in southern Anatolian hinterland and therefore pay customs duties for a second time on the Turkish side of the border, the merchants will get refunded the original duties paid to the Syrian authorities, as long as they can present original Turkish receipts.[67] The refund system was therefore designed as a temporary relief in case Ankara were to apply tariffs before the conclusion of a customs agreement with the French.

This was exactly what soon happened, as the Turkish authorities in Aintab began to apply 20 per cent *ad valorem* on the goods the merchants brought from Aleppo, effective from 3 December 1921 onwards.[68] The impact of these tariffs was felt well beyond Aleppo. It was reported, for instance, that the port of Beirut produced one million francs less in revenues in January when compared to December, and half a million francs less in the first days of February when compared to early January.[69] The situation was far worse

---

[65] TNA, FO 371/6457, 24 November 1921, f. 176.

[66] CADN, *Ankara Ambassade*, 36/PO/1, 146, 'Note sur les arrangements douaniers à faire avec la Turquie', p. 2.

[67] It should be noted that the refund system only applied to imported goods or raw material that received some level of processing work in Syria. TNA, FO 371/7846/E4798, 24 April 1922, f. 183.

[68] Archives Nationales d'Outre-Mer (Aix-en-Provence) (hereafter ANOM), Papiers de Mougin, 11 APOM 34: Télégramme par le Délégué à Alep, 1 janvier 1922.

[69] ANOM, Papiers de Mougin, 11 APOM 34: Télégramme par Robert de Caix au Délégué à Alep, 16 février 1922.

in Aleppo itself. As Selim Djambart, the chair of the Aleppo Chamber of Commerce, described the situation in mid-February:

> Aleppo market is paralysed, stocks are piling up, bankruptcies have already been declared, and news of fear, panic, and dismay are taking over the once flourishing trade. If protective measures are not taken quickly, people who are disappointed are thinking of an exodus to regions where the business will get redirected. Bitter murmurs rise in this large city that Aleppo is threatened to become an economically poor town, with a desert to its southeast and a closed border to its north.[70]

As planned, the refund system indeed kicked in to rush help to the merchants in this moment of need. Some local companies reported in March and April that they were able to receive reimbursements from the Syrian authorities for the duties originally paid on Syrian ports of arrival. Yet these refunds were far from restoring to Aleppo the historic role it had once played as the entrepôt of the Eastern Mediterranean. For one, the costs of imports were higher for Aleppine merchants than before, since the system did not refund the difference between the low Syrian and high Turkish tariffs. Also, in the absence of a customs agreement, Ankara prohibited the import of a certain class of luxury goods, such as silk textiles among others, which corresponded to a portion of Aleppine re-exports.[71]

A more permanent settlement on the customs question was therefore necessary, not least because Turkish goods continued to come into Syria tax free while Syrian goods were kept subject to high tariffs.[72] In its assessment of the situation, the Aleppo Chamber of Commerce suggested the institution of a free trade zone that would unify the customs of the ports of Alexandretta and Mersin, in addition to establishing free warehouses in Aleppo for re-export trade. Such an arrangement would allow Turkey in turn to claim a fair share in the customs revenues of Syria, which would be proportionate to the value

---

[70] ANOM, Papiers de Mougin, 11 APOM 34: Djambart à Poincaré, 18 février 1922.

[71] TNA, FO 371/7846/E2717, 11 March 1922, f. 40; TNA, FO 371/7846/E4798, 24 April 1922, f. 180–81.

[72] Comte R. de Gontaut-Biron and L. Le Révérend, *D'Angora à Lausanne: Les étapes d'une déchéance* (Paris: Librairie Plon, 1924), p. 48.

of re-exports shipped from the free zone to Anatolia.[73] In fact, the positions of the merchants of Aleppo entirely overlapped with those of the French as both asked for a free trade zone between Aleppo and its Anatolian hinterland.[74] Yet, the exact shape of how this arrangement would look like was yet to be worked out with Turkey.

## Negotiating Aleppo, 1922–26

Throughout the spring of 1922 the French continued their overtures to Turkish authorities, seizing opportunities as they presented themselves to convince Ankara to start trade talks with a view to solving trade limitations that, in the words of Raymond Poincaré, 'created a precarious situation in the region of Aleppo', both politically and economically.[75] These efforts finally bore fruit in late May when a Turkish delegation arrived in Beirut, composed of a handful of experts who had had considerable local experience in Mersin and Adana.[76] In the evaluation of the British, however, the Turkish mission seemed less interested in commercial affairs than in military matters.[77] Seeing the Franco-Turkish rapprochement as a deviation from the post-war order they sought to establish in the region, the British agents speculated that Beirut was 'a pleasant summer resort' to spend an entire summer under the pretext of commercial negotiations, arguing that Ankara not only used their presence in Beirut as a base to spread pro-Turkish propaganda across the Middle East but also repeatedly pressed the French during the negotiations with more concrete demands, specifically eyeing the

---

[73] TNA, FO 371/7846/E4798, 24 April 1922, f. 181–82.

[74] ANOM, Papiers de Mougin, 11 APOM 34: Télégramme par Robert de Caix au Délégué à Alep, 16 décembre 1921.

[75] ANOM, Papiers de Mougin, 11 APOM 34: Poincaré à Mission Française à Adana, 11 mai 1922; For earlier efforts, see CADN, *Ankara Ambassade*, 36/PO/1, 146, 'Mission Française en Cilicie à Monsieur Poincaré', Adana, 25 avril 1922. BCA, 30.18.1.1, 5-18-3, 'Gümrük Komisyonu Reisi Zekai'den Mevrud Şifre', Adana, 27 Nisan 1338, p. 10.

[76] BCA, 30.18.1.1, 5-14-5, Kararname, 7 Mayıs 1338.

[77] Understandably, London was rather anxious of the Turkish-French rapprochement, and its implications for its position in Mosul. TNA, FO 371/7847/E6391, 'Report of Franco-Kemalist Relations and Situation in Syria during the Latter Half of May', 6 June 1922, f. 121.

shipment of war material to Anatolia.[78] To be sure, the Kemalists were busy in preparing a final offensive to force the Greek units out of their holdouts in Western Anatolia and probably needed all the supplies they could get on top of what they had already secured from the Bolsheviks. Yet the evidence the British conclusions were based seemed flimsy at best.[79]

Unlike whatever the British might have thought, the negotiations in Beirut in fact lasted the whole summer due to the complex issues the French and Turkish delegates had on the table.[80] For Turkey, the ultimate goal during the negotiations was not to yield any economic privileges that could compromise its strict rejection of Ottoman capitulations, which only allowed its delegates to concede limited privileges that were valid only for a short period of time; Ankara also asked them to prioritise the protection of native industries at home.[81] Only after the fulfilment of this principle could the Turkish delegation offer some special arrangements for Aleppo and its port Alexandretta – cities that continued to maintain significant trade links to Anatolia.[82] The Turkish position left very little room to negotiate. Ideally, the French delegation sought to secure an arrangement similar to the customs-free zone established between Syria and Palestine back in 1921, which applied to both agricultural products and manufactured commodities.[83] While the Turkish delegation agreed on the duty-free circulation of local agricultural produce in its border zone with Syria, the real contention lay in customs duties on manufactured commodities – namely, over the question if Ankara was ultimately willing to allow Aleppo to play its historic role as a centre of distribution to its Anatolian hinterland

[78] TNA, FO 371/7848/E10961, 3 October 1922, f. 85.

[79] TNA, FO 684/1, 22/7: 'Situation in Syria', Aley, 13 July 1922, f. 4.

[80] On top of commercial issues, the Turkish delegation also saw the customs meeting in Beirut as an opportunity to rectify the Turkish–Syrian border. See CADN, *Ankara Ambassade*, 36/ PO/1, 148, 'Le Haut-Commissaire au Ministre des Affaires Etrangères, 13 juin 1923.

[81] The basic principles of the Turkish delegation revolved around the protection of home industries, particularly that of cotton textiles, the institution of maximum tariffs on silk goods, and the validity of any arrangements only for a period of five years – hence the retention of the right to change commercial policies under changing circumstances. *TBM-MGCZ*, 15 June 1922, pp. 416–17.

[82] BCA, 30.18.1.1, 5-18-3, 'Hariciye Vekaleti'nin Tezkere Sureti' and 'Suriye Mukavelenames-ine Esas Olacak Talimat', pp. 13–18.

[83] ANOM, Papiers de Mougin, 11 APOM 34: Beyrouth, Télégramme du 3 juin 1922.

of manufactured products, whether of local or European origins. The divergence of opinions on this issue prolonged the negotiations considerably, as
the Turkish delegation had to await negative responses from Ankara to each
French counter-proposal.[84] One such proposal that Ankara dismissed involved
a scheme for the transformation of the port of Alexandretta into a free trade
zone which would also feature the presence of Turkish customs officials for the
collection of Ankara's share of customs receipts.[85]

Even though a deal was finally reached on 30 September 1922, curi-
ously the outlines of the agreement were not made public in the upcoming
months.[86] Local newspapers such as *La Syrie* published editorials describing that the deal secured favourable treatment from Ankara towards locally
manufactured silk and cotton goods, among others.[87] The American consulate similarly reported that the deal included clauses for 'the increased use of
the railroad between Aleppo and her natural seaport of Alexandretta, since
this road passes through Turkish territory for a part of the distance'; because
the deal also foresaw the establishment of Aleppo as a port of entry, it was
reported that French authorities soon began to establish bonded warehouses
that could be used in the storage of goods in transit from Aleppo to Turkey.[88]
Despite all these preparations, however, the Turkish National Assembly did
not ratify the customs agreement that had consumed so much energy to
finalise in Beirut.

After all, by the time the deal was agreed upon in autumn 1922, the interstate context had changed radically, as negotiations for a new peace treaty
between Turkey and the Allied Powers began in Lausanne. In this new context, the settlement of commercial disputes with mandatory authorities and
deriving short-term benefits from it was not a priority any longer. Much to
the contrary, the use of armed bands in northern Syria once again emerged as

---

[84] CADN, *Ankara Ambassade*, 36/PO/1, 146, 'Mission Française en Cilicie aux Conseil des
Ministres des Affaires Etrangères', 15 juillet 1922 et 8 août 1922.

[85] CADN, *Ankara Ambassade*, 36/PO/1, 136, 'Mission Française en Cilicie aux Haut-
Commissariat', Adana, 27 octobre 1922, p. 3.

[86] TNA, FO 371/7853/E867, 'Situation in Syria and the Lebanon', 10 January 1923, f. 108–9.

[87] TNA, FO 371/7848/E11883, 18 October 1922, f. 129.

[88] NARA, College Park, Record Group 84, Consular Aleppo, Syria, Vol. 115: 'Annual Report
upon Commerce and Industries in the Aleppo Consular District, 1924', pp. 2–3.

a way of pressuring the French to come to terms with a settlement favourable to Ankara. The British were joyful reporting that the rapprochement between the French and Turks – one that had worked against the British interests for the past two years – was finally coming to an end.[89] In expectation of the imminent *cheta* (armed group) warfare, the French began to install barbed wire and machine gun posts and dig trenches around Alexandretta – the port city whose trade with Aleppo they were seeking to restore to Turkey only a few months earlier.[90]

Indeed, by early 1923 everything seemed to be back to square one. During the negotiations in Lausanne the Turkish delegation requested the revision of the southern border in their favour, but the French did not budge. Ankara was not alone in its desire to revise the border, however. The influential Aleppine politician Ihsan al-Jabiri, who also attended the talks in Lausanne as part of the Syro-Palestinian Delegation, for example, gave an interview, where he claimed that Turkey might be forced to accept a frontier that crossed further in the north.[91] Al-Jabiri's position largely banked upon the souring of relations between Turkey and France throughout the negotiations in Lausanne. Yet, 'except for those who had won their rights by force of arms', as Provence put it, the likes of al-Jabiri would return disappointed from Lausanne.[92]

When they did, the situation was similarly tenuous back home. Some merchants in the Aleppo market had put up portraits of Mustafa Kemal on their windows, much to the chagrin of local French authorities.[93] The discontent of the city's Muslim and Christian merchants, the British concluded, were less rooted in ideology than economic difficulties, as the situation pushed them 'to toy agreeably with the idea of a refound economic unity under the Turkish aegis'.[94] When the French High Commissioner General Weygand visited Aleppo on 20 July, only few days before the signature of the Lausanne

[89] TNA, FO 371/7853/E646, 20 December 1922, f. 5.

[90] TNA, FO 371/9055/E2345, 12 February 1923, f. 81.

[91] TNA, FO 371/9053/E600, 10 January 1923, f. 47. Similar views were expressed in the Aleppo Representative Council by El Sayed Rabih el-Menkari and Subhi Barakat. TNA, FO 371/9053/E12168, 12 December 1923, ff. 215–16.

[92] Provence, *The Last Ottoman Generation*, p. 148.

[93] TNA, FO 371/9055/E2345, 12 February 1923, f. 81.

[94] TNA, FO 371/9053/E6332, 31 May 1923, f. 131.

Treaty, he encountered a barrage of complaints coming from the merchants on issues ranging from customs difficulties with Ankara to rural insecurity in northern Syria and prohibitive railway freight rates to the south. In a bid to appease them, the general noted that with the imminent peace in Lausanne, 'most of the troubles now besetting Aleppo would be swept away'.[95] Weygand practised what he preached in public. In line with his broader optimism on solving problems that beset Syria, he noted that opening up 'the very important field of transactions between Aleppo and the area seceded to Turkey' is indeed a task that attracted all their attention. In his assessment, the six long years of war had devastated much of Anatolia and the opportunity was ripe for the French to control Turkish markets via Syrian merchants, whom the French called 'perfectly aware of the habits of the Turkish customers'.[96]

The short-term developments soon after the successful conclusions of talks for the Treaty of Lausanne seemed to have proved Weygand right. By December 1923 the Kemalists had suppressed the low-profile warfare raging around Aleppo by expelling the *chetas* from the border zones to the interior.[97] With the re-establishment of the rail link from Alexandretta to the Euphrates, too, as Weygand happily noted, 'a considerable movement of cereals was taking place from Birecik to Alexandretta for reshipment by sea to Smyrna and Constantinople'; the customers from southern Anatolia were also slowly trickling in the markets of Aleppo, just 'as in the old days to make purchases and that Aleppo merchants are even granting them credit'.[98] Therefore, by the end of 1923, the Ottoman interregional markets seemed to have become reconnected despite the absence of the empire – or at least it seemed so for the time being. After all, it was clear that the commercial future of Aleppo would remain at the mercy of turbulent Franco-Turkish relations for the months to come.[99] If it took nine months to negotiate the terms of the peace treaty in Lausanne, more than a year had to pass before the ratification of the treaty, since the most contentious issues were actually left unsolved.

[95] TNA, FO 371/9053/E8075, 23 July 1923, f. 144.

[96] CADN, *Ankara Ambassade*, 36/PO/1, 136, 'Bulletin périodique no.69, Période du 26 juillet au 1er septembre', Aley, 4 septembre 1923, pp. 10–11.

[97] Mizrahi, 'Un 'Nationalisme de la Frontière', p. 24.

[98] TNA, FO 684/1, 23/3: French Railway Policy in Syria, Beirut, 13 December 1923, f. 27.

[99] Gontaut-Biron and Le Révérend, *D'Angora à Lausanne*, p. 49.

The French, for one, returned from Lausanne particularly upset over the unclear status of Catholic schools in Turkey as well as the uncertainties as to how Ankara was to pay its share from the standing Ottoman debt, where the French creditors were in the majority.[100] In delaying to ratify the treaty, the French sought to pressure Ankara to attend to these problems, which left very little leverage for Paris to change the situation for the better in northern Syria. On 1 May 1924, for instance, the French increased the general Syrian tariffs and in doing so distinguished member states of the League of Nations (15 per cent) from the non-members (30 per cent) – a measure to check German influence. Despite being a non-member state, Turkey was still given preferential treatment and enjoyed the League rate, while it continued to apply maximum tariffs to Syrian goods.[101] This ultimately illustrated that the French had little muscle to reverse the situation on the ground and Aleppo (and therefore Paris) had more to suffer from a tariff war that could bring Turkey back to the table to negotiate the terms of an open-door policy between southern Turkey and northern Syria.

The situation took a positive turn in late spring 1924, however, when Édouard Herriot came to power in Paris – a welcome development for Ankara. His *Parti radical* not only promoted an ideological outlook that inspired the Kemalist cadres, but also also featured important members, such as Henry Franklin-Bouillon, who enjoyed personal connections to Mustafa Kemal dating back to 1921. In line with the party's broader willingness to compromise on the harsh terms of the Versailles settlement, Herriot announced in early June that France would soon ratify the Treaty of Lausanne.[102] If Herriot's stint as the prime minister provided a window of opportunity to mend relations, Ankara's worsening tensions with Britain over the Mosul question since late 1924 required compromising with the French. The outbreak of the Sheikh

---

[100] TNA, FO 424-538, 'Turkey: Annual Report, 1923', p. 11.

[101] Burns, *The Tariff of Syria*, p. 56.

[102] Remzi Çağatay Çakırlar, 'Radikal Faktör: Tek Parti ve Kemalizm'in Oluşum Sürecinde Radikal Parti Etkileşimleri', in Sevgi Adak and Alexandros Lamprou (eds), *Tek Parti Dönemini Yeniden Düşünmek: Otoriter Devlet ve Toplum* (Istanbul: Tarih Vakfı Yayınları, 2021) pp. 209–36. The Treaty of Lausanne went into effect on 6 August 1924 after Italy, Japan and Great Britain ratified it, which was soon followed by the French ratification.

Said Rebellion in February 1925, for which Ankara blamed British intrigues, helped facilitate the Turkish-French rapprochement, as the French abided by their treaty obligations – much to the irritation of the British – and let 'excessive numbers of Turkish reinforcements' pass via Aleppo on their way to contain the uprising, using the railway-cum-border.[103]

The French High Commissioner of the time was Maurice Sarrail, who had recently been appointed to the post by Herriot and his broader coalition known as the Cartel des Gauches. Sarrail hoped to harness the friendly relations between France and Turkey and convince Ankara to allow Aleppo to be the region's re-export centre by reaching an agreement on customs formalities. In doing so, he also hoped to also solve the series of more practical problems that beset the operation of the border railway line by *Chemin de fer Cilicie-Nord Syrie*.[104] After all, multiple reports continued to suggest that the Turkish customs authorities were prohibitively vigilant with the operation of the railway. Urfa customs, for instance, repeatedly refused to process the certificates of origins for goods re-exported from Syria, on the grounds that the practice had markedly begun to shift international trade away from the Turkish ports to those in Syria.[105] In the face of these problems, Sarrail wrote:

> The overriding need to maintain and, if necessary, increase the flow of trade between the northern Syrian regions and Anatolia – an essential outlet for their traffic – has forced us to separate the customs and economic question from other contentious cases and enter into isolated negotiations.[106]

These talks came to fruition on 26 July 1925 when a customs convention was concluded between Turkey and Syria. Yet, more than a year still had to pass before France agreed to rectify the border to Turkey's favour, which had become Ankara's pre-condition to ratify the agreement. In the absence

---

[103] TNA, FO 424-538, 'Turkey: Annual Report, 1925', p. 11.

[104] CADN, Fonds Beyrouth, 575, Cabinet politique: 1926–1941, de Sarrail à Mougin, 2 mars 1925.

[105] CADN, *Ankara Ambassade*, 36/PO/1, 137, de Jesse-Curely à Sarrail, Beyrouth, 11 avril 1925.

[106] CADN, *Ankara Ambassade*, 36/PO/1, 340, 'Un projet de convention douanière conclu avec la Turquie', Beyrouth, 14 septembre 1925.

of a ratification, Ankara continued to leverage procedural difficulties on the operation of the railway to its benefit, not only stifling the Aleppine trade with Turkey but also creating problems within Syria. For example, when Aleppo merchants shipped goods using the railway to northern parts of Syria, because parts of the railway crossed into Turkey before arriving back into the Syrian territory, Turkish customs authorities demanded a guarantee in cash that equalled the overall value of the goods in transit. Even if the cash guarantee was to be reimbursed after the goods were unloaded on the Syrian side of the border, it amounted to a sum that required considerable capital investments, which was often beyond the reach of many local merchants.[107]

While these commercial difficulties reflected systemic problems in the north, it was in fact the outbreak of the Great Revolt in southern Syria that ultimately motivated the French to settle its differences with Turkey on the northern frontier.[108] The deal reached in February 1926 included, among other things, the rectification of the border around Kilis – a demand long entertained by Turkey, which the French agreed to accept on the condition of the ratification of the customs agreement.[109] After a few more months of delays and considerable French pressure, Ankara finally ratified the customs convention which took effect on 1 September 1926, valid for a period of three years. Similar to the agreement concluded in Beirut back in 1922 – the one that never got ratified by Ankara, the 1926 convention included the circulation of agricultural and animal products on very low tariff rates between Turkey and Syria – an arrangement favourable to Ankara. Similarly lower rates applied to the trade of Syrian textiles into Turkey, but these lower tariffs were only applicable to the textiles that were fully manufactured in Syria.[110] This latter clause, however, kept the majority of domestic Syrian textiles subject to high Turkish tariffs, since

---

[107] CADN, *Ankara Ambassade*, 36/PO/1, 137, de Jesse-Curely à Sarrail, Beyrouth, 25 December 1925.

[108] TNA, FO 424-538, 'Turkey: Annual Report, 1926', pp. 6–7.

[109] Soheila Mameli-Ghaderi, 'Le tracé de la frontière entre la Syrie et la Turquie (1921–1929)', *Guerres Mondiales et Conflits Contemporains*, Vol. 207 (2002–2003), pp. 125–38.

[110] For a full text of the agreement, see 'Türkiye-Suriye Gümrük İtilafnamesi', *Gümrük Mecmuası*, 1 (1 Teşrin-i evvel 1926), p. 5.

the domestic producers in Aleppo and Damascus often imported either yarn or dye, if not both.[111]

The long sought after customs agreement was not necessarily a win-win situation for the parties involved. Statistics proved the pattern. Syria's imports from Turkey already reached its pre-war levels by 1924 and did not fluctuate much thereafter, but Syria's exports to Turkey never recovered its pre-war position, even after the 1926 customs convention.[112] Neither France nor the Aleppine merchants could do much to change the situation. From the very outset, Ankara navigated a careful legal path in order to keep Syrian goods beyond the bounds of the favourable treatment to which Turkey had committed itself back in the Lausanne negotiations.[113] In this sense, unlike what General Weygand predicted, the Treaty of Lausanne did not solve Aleppo's problems; it rather empowered Ankara to keep in check possible French sphere of influence over southern Turkey via Aleppine merchants. Ankara's strategy was successful until late 1929 when the customs convention of 1926 expired. By then, the world had become a radically different place and the restrictions that Turkey would put in place in response to the Great Depression would have the unintended effect of creating a different set of opportunities in the hinterland of Aleppo for those who were willing to navigate them.[114]

## Conclusion

'The most important and richest customer of the pistachio produced in Aintab is North America, which consumes seventy per cent of our total annual yield', the Turkish daily *Cumhuriyet* reported in March 1936. 'Yet, because the export is carried out via Syria, the profits disappear due to the intermediaries and it is the Syrian merchants that benefit the most from this trade'.[115] This small piece of local news in fact spoke to the persistence of commercial ties that had not only

---

[111] For patterns of the Syrian textile industries during the interwar years, see Geoffrey D. Schad, 'Colonialists, Industrialists, and Politicians: The Political Economy of Industrialization in Syria, 1920–1954', (PhD thesis, University of Pennsylvania, 2001), pp. 132–53.

[112] Burns, *The Tariff of Syria*, p. 62.

[113] The Ottoman Archives of the Prime Ministry (BOA), HR. İM. 176–48, 20 Şubat 1926.

[114] See Ramazan Hakkı Öztan, 'The Great Depression and the Making of Turkish–Syrian Border, 1921–1939', *International Journal of Middle East Studies*, Vol. 52, No. 2 (2020), pp. 311–26.

[115] 'Gazi Antebin Ticari Vaziyeti', *Cumhuriyet*, 16 Mart 1936, no 4250, p. 9.

plugged Aleppo into nodes of transatlantic trade since the nineteenth century but also the continued linkages of Aleppine merchants to the city's traditional hinterland in southern Anatolia, which had certainly transformed but not fully disappeared fifteen years after the end of the Ottoman Empire. Since the early 1920s, when the establishment of the Turkish–Syrian border cut the Ottoman province of Aleppo into two, the ascendant nationalist regime in Ankara had sought to disaggregate commercial zones inherited from the empire and re-channel this trade into the hands of their own bourgeoisie who were to operate in port cities that remained solely within Turkish sovereignty.[116] By and large, Turkey had made great strides to do so, but Aleppo continued to be relevant for the Turkish economy well into the 1930s.

The suzerainty of the Ottoman sultans came to an end in 1922 but the economic mobilities that defined their rule in the Middle East did not disappear overnight. Nor did the market dynamics adjust themselves to the new political realities automatically. The emerging political systems in the region had to address the grievances of local producers who once sold their agrarian surplus within a duty-free imperial market, and attend to the problems created by the institution of new borders that suddenly set apart industrial producers and exporters away from their domestic consumers. That being said, the scholarship continues to see the interwar period as a beginning of distinct national beginnings – a time when national histories take over in a bid to recount how nations are made but not how empires were undone. Even if concerns over methodological nationalism are readily and commonly acknowledged, we are less willing to fully let go off the analytic parameters defined by nationalism. It is therefore high time to go beyond what were once certainly useful discussions of imperial legacies and liminal loyalties and frame the emergence of state systems in the region in analytically interactive frameworks.[117] In order to do so, we need to treat the Ottoman Empire not just as a historical backdrop, but rather as a bundle of very real networks, relations and infrastructure that had to be disaggregated and negotiated, which, as a contentious process, helped make the modern Middle East. After all, the Ottoman Empire was as much an imagined community as it was a connected enterprise.

---

[116] For a region-wide assessment, see Schayegh, *The Middle East*, pp. 169–81.

[117] For one such study that makes a case for a connected post-Ottoman history, see Orçun Can Okan, 'Coping with Transitions: The Connected Construction of Turkey, Syria, Lebanon and Iraq, 1918–1928' (PhD thesis, Columbia University, 2020).

# 4

## PERSONAL CONNECTIONS AND REGIONAL NETWORKS: CROSS-BORDER FORD AUTOMOBILE DISTRIBUTION IN FRENCH MANDATE SYRIA[1]

### Simon Jackson

**Introduction: Heavy Ground and Dangerous Zones**

On 23 June 1924 Harold Beazley, a British Ford Company 'Roadman', sat down in Haifa, in British Mandate Palestine, to draft a letter.[2] He wrote to his colleague Mr Ware, in the Sales Department of the Ford Motor Company d'Italia, located in the Adriatic frontier port of Trieste, Italy, but also carbon-copied his missive to the Ford concessionaire Charles Corm, in French Mandate Beirut. In the letter, Beazley reported on an 'Agricultural Exhibition' held from 14 to 29 June 1924 in Aleppo, in the northern part of French Mandate Syria, close to the slowly consolidating new border with Turkey that is a key site of discussion throughout much of this volume. Written, therefore, across mandatory, imperial and regional borders to document the expanding activities of Ford's global commercial empire in the northern Syrian borderlands, and especially the activities of its 'Fordson'

[1] My thanks to the anonymous reviewer for Edinburgh University Press, to the volume editors and to Cyrus Schayegh for helpful criticism on previous drafts.

[2] On Haifa as a regional bridgehead in the British imperial imaginary see Jacob Norris, *Land of Progress: Palestine in the Age of Colonial Development, 1905–1948* (Oxford: Oxford University Press, 2013).

tractors, Beazley's report encapsulates the core concerns of this chapter.[3] We accordingly begin with a close reading of Beazley's words, before laying out the principal arguments.

Beazley divided his report into six sections.[4] Overall, he detailed the successes of Ford at the exhibition, dramatised the failures of French tractors and the fury of certain French imperial officials and indexed the uncertainties of automobile commerce in the French Mandate's new borderland with Turkey. To begin, he noted that the exhibition was at root a French imperial state initiative, nurtured by Charles Pavie, an official of the Mandate's Agricultural and Economic Services.[5] Invitations had been circulated in advance, along imperial administrative channels to 'Divisional Departments of Agriculture throughout Syria', along imperial commercial channels to 'all French manufacturers of Tractors and Agricultural implements TWO MONTHS prior to the exhibition', and along 'Local' commercial channels to '(Syrian) Representatives of Tractors and Farm implements'. It was into this molten latter category, awkwardly and revealingly, that the Lebanese Charles Corm and his British friend and manager Harold Beazley, representatives of the Italian subsidiary of the Ford company, USA, inserted themselves.

The French authorities publicised the exhibition widely in advance using posters (a sample of which Beazley enclosed) 'printed in French and Arabic and distributed over the Country'. Again tellingly, that final geographical designation, 'the Country', though capitalised, remained unspecified. It referred perhaps to the region of Aleppo, or perhaps to wider political or commercial spaces and networks within and beyond the French Mandate or

---

[3] For more see Simon Jackson, *Mandatory Development: French Colonial Empire, Global Capitalism and the Politics of the Economy after World War One* (Cornell University Press, forthcoming, n.d.). On Ford as an empire see Elizabeth D. Esch, *The Color Line and the Assembly Line: Managing Race in the Ford Empire* (Berkeley: University of California Press, 2018), pp. 22, 24, 32–33.

[4] All references to this report are from Harold Beazley (Haifa) to Mr Ware (Trieste), 23 June 1924, Folder 1 – Ford Correspondence, (henceforth 1) Corm Archive, Beirut, Lebanon (henceforth CAB). Capitalisations and underlining are Beazley's own.

[5] See Charles Pavie, *Le Coton dans Le Gouvernement de Lattaquie* (Aleppo: Imprimerie Maronite, n.d.) and for discussion of his work James Long Whitaker, 'The Union of Demeter with Zeus: Agriculture and Politics in Modern Syria' (PhD thesis, Durham University, 1996), p. 112.

Greater Syria.[6] But, in spite of these efforts and notwithstanding the fact that the French Army General in command of Aleppo was the guest of honour, not one French-made tractor was shown off at the Aleppo exhibition, in spite of 'the fact that stocks of RENAULT, SEMIA, and TOURANT LATIL are in the Country operated (or have been) by the French Agricultural Authorities.' By contrast, American Case and Avery tractors, Canadian Massey Harris agricultural machinery and, most of all, Fordson tractors were heavily present, along with hay cutters and rakes, maize shellers and other tractor-powered farming equipment.

Beazley noted that Charles Corm and Company had developed their presence through their dedicated Aleppo branch but that the exhibition had been 'personally attended by the Dealer [Corm], Aleppo staff, Beyrouth mechanics, and writer [Beazley]'. The Ford stand at the exhibition grounds outside Aleppo was decorated with large signs showing 'Fordson' and 'McCormick' (a major US brand of mechanical grain harvesting equipment that Corm also distributed through Ford) in French and Arabic lettering. Some 5,000 booklets on Ford's proposed tractor facilities and service campaign were translated into French and Arabic, with 1,000 distributed in Aleppo. A further 5,000 pamphlets in the same languages covered the Ford car service, spare parts in general and 'GENUINE SPARE PARTS' in particular, with 1,000 distributed at Aleppo and the remainder, in a sign of the networked geography of the Ford empire in the Mandate, 'sent over the branches'. To complete this propaganda effort, a full-page advertisement was placed in 'a well-known Arabic newspaper with good circulation' and two specialist mechanics travelled from the Mandate's new capital at Beirut to support the performance of the Ford machines. Within the wrapper of the French imperial and Mandatory states' efforts to catalyse agricultural renewal in the Aleppo region, in other words, a sophisticated effort to build a node of the Ford commercial empire was under way. This effort translated for local purposes every technique the corporation could offer from its transnational playbook of communications strategies.[7]

---

[6] On the imagined spaces of Greater Syria see Cyrus Schayegh, *The Middle East and the Making of the Modern World* (Cambridge MA: Harvard University Press, 2017), pp. 42–48.

[7] On Ford's advertising repertoire and orientalism see Saima Akhtar, 'Corporate Empire: Fordism and the Making of Immigrant Detroit' (PhD thesis, University of California, Berkeley, 2015).

The opening day of the exhibition saw discussion of the machines around the stands of the exhibition in the presence of Aleppine notables and French military and local civilian officials, before a move was made in the early evening to the 'ploughing spot' outside the city, where the machines were tested. Despite 'soil of stiff pebbly nature, actual soil not being very deep, and never before touched by tractor ploughs', the Fordson's performance attracted 'extreme interest' in Beazley's words, and 'keen appreciation was expressed by the General', although the French agricultural inspector, Pavie, 'met the result with choleric manner, uttering open defiance to the Dealer [Corm] to continue such ploughing over the period of a day.' This challenge, from a French imperial official dismayed by the success of an American and 'Syrian' rival, was taken up on Monday 16 June, in spite of a thunderstorm at midday, which rendered the clay soil very heavy. The French General expressed 'COMPLETE SATISFACTION' on observing an hour's continuous ploughing, carried out, at his request, by 'native Drivers', although an attempt to demonstrate the McCormick mechanical reaper failed, as the machine sank into the mud and could not process a crop that Beazley blamed for being 'exceedingly short.'

Notwithstanding this claimed success, Beazley judged commercial prospects in Aleppo 'DUBIOUS'. Just three possible clients had shown interest at the exhibition: a 'Russian colonist, an Armenian (very doubtful, and wishing not to buy for use but for re-selling) and one native of Aleppo'. Beazley thought the Avery and Case distributors on the retreat, seeking to liquidate their stock rather than develop 'actual SALES, organisation and propaganda'. Crucially for the purposes of this chapter, finally, Beazley noted that of these three prospects, Russian, Armenian and 'native', 'NONE are sure, ALL are asking for credit facilities, and all have ground in dangerous zones . . . *near the Kemalist border*'.[8]

In this brief closing phrase, Beazley combined three key concerns of this chapter: the way that people imagined the Middle East's uncertain political-economic future in the 1920s, the role of credit (both in the financial sense but most especially in the sense of trustworthiness and the durable interpersonal relationships that proved consubstantial with business), and finally

---

[8] My italics here, Beazley's capitals.

the importance of borderlands as sites (both local and dispersed) of interaction, contention and influence in the making of super-posed local, national, regional, imperial, commercial and global spaces.[9]

This chapter contributes to the volume's treatment of the history of borders, mobility regimes and state-building in the Middle East by examining the business relationships of the man Harold Beazley referred to, in the deceptively anonymising jargon of Ford, as 'the Dealer': the Beirut-based Charles Corm. Corm (1894–1963) was a Maronite Christian and the Jesuit-educated son of Daoud Corm, who had been a prominent portrait painter in the late-Ottoman world. The bohemian-bourgeois family mobilised considerable cultural capital but (relatively) less financial capital – Charles' career would accordingly combine a literary-political commitment to Greater Lebanese nationalism with the skilled accumulation of a large fortune as an automobile distributor. A devoted Francophile who preferred to write in French than in Arabic, Corm spent time before 1914 working in a diaspora textile business in New York City. Later he operated both as a food relief coordinator in Beirut in 1918 and, in 1918–19, as the editor of an influential magazine 'The Phoenician Review'. The review, under the ideological banner of 'neo-Phoencianism', advocated for an expanded, Christian-dominated and anti-Arab 'Greater Lebanon'. It also helped catalyse Corm's literary career as a prolific writer of poetry and prose that often eulogised Lebanon as a Europe-orientated Mediterranean land.[10] In a way that nicely captures the intersection of post-war European imperial expansion with post-war opportunities for the creation of new regional business empires, the pages of 'The Phoenician Review' hailed the prospects for modern transport networks in the as-yet undetermined space of Greater Lebanon, lauded the timeless Lebanese patriotism of the (Christian) peasantry and demanded

---

[9] For an incisive discussion of three issues at the Turkish–Syrian border see Ramazan Hakkı Öztan, 'The Great Depression and the Making of Turkish–Syrian Border, 1921–1939', *International Journal of Middle East Studies*, Vol. 52, No. 2 (2020), pp. 311–26.

[10] The best work on Corm's intellectual and political contexts remains Asher Kaufman, '"Tell Us Our History": Charles Corm, Mount Lebanon and Lebanese Nationalism', *Middle Eastern Studies*, Vol. 40, No. 3 (2004), p. 3. For the longer story of Neo-Phoenicianism see Carol Hakim, *The Origins of the Lebanese National Idea: 1840–1920* (Berkeley: University of California Press, 2013).

French military intervention in favour of Greater Lebanon.[11] Corm's neo-Phoenicianism therefore combined a folkloric, conservative call for harmonious social hierarchy with an enthusiasm for modernising technologies: a mix that would propel his own socio-economic ascent and position him on the post-war global wave of illiberal modernism.

From roughly 1920 to 1934 Corm distributed tractors, automobiles and spare parts across a regional network that traversed intra-Mandate and inter-Mandate/inter-imperial borders but was also entangled with the expanding global network of the Ford Motor Company. Illustratively for our purposes in this volume, Corm's business empire encompassed the Aleppo branch discussed above, claimed its commercial hinterland in the Turkish–Syrian borderland, and featured branches across the inter-imperial and inter-Mandate border in British Mandate Palestine, notably at Jaffa and at Haifa, from where Beazley wrote his report above. This latticework of Corm/Ford branches, I propose, should be considered a kind of non-state, commercial 'empire' that overlapped with, helped constitute, and also sprawled past other forms of boundary-making and space-constituting work, such as that undertaken by the Mandatory state powers in this period. Equally, the vehicles themselves were imported from New York City, or Windsor, Canada, via London and Trieste, situating Corm's regional border-crossing in the wider context of imperial and global regimes of mobility shaped by the politics of racialisation, by tariff regimes and by logistics technologies.[12]

Through this material, the chapter offers two arguments. First, it engages with the broad literature on the history of Ford in transnational and global context, and with the rich historiography on technology and the social life of things in colonial contexts.[13] Countering diffusionist accounts of Ford's

---

[11] See for example Sébastien Bargain, 'La Question des transports en Syrie: Débouchés pour l'industrie automobile', *La Revue Phénicienne*, Vol. 1 (1919), p. 215.

[12] On racialisation, see Esch, *Color Line*, p. 6. On logistics and empire see On Barak, *Powering Empire: How Coal Made the Middle East and Sparked Global Carbonization* (Berkeley: University of California Press, 2020). For a classic treatment that pays little attention to the Middle East see Mira Wilkins and Frank Ernest Hill, *American Business Abroad: Ford on Six Continents* (Cambridge: Cambridge University Press, 2011).

[13] Esch, *Color Line*; Stefan J. Link, *Forging Global Fordism: Nazi Germany, Soviet Russia, and the Contest over the Industrial Order* (Princeton: Princeton University Press, 2020). See also

expansion, as well as arguments that the techno-social co-construction of automobiles took place only in Europe or the US, I coin the concept of 'flatpack Fordism', one that alters our view of the Middle East's role in global capitalist restructuring after 1918. Flatpack Fordism was a process that meant not just the reassembly of Ford vehicles, but also the assembly of a form of 'commercial sovereignty' for Corm as the pre-eminent dealer and Ford as the pre-eminent brand of automobiles in the region.[14] This form of claimed sovereignty certainly relied in part on Corm's privileged relationship to French state power but was not synonymous with it, as we saw above in Charles Pavie's anger. Most centrally, it was based on the construction and maintenance of trust in the Ford brand and trust in Corm's ability to uphold certain standards of authenticity and reliability, both across his network of branches and their surrounding territory, and over time. In other words, Corm's commercial sovereignty created and then relied on a regime of mobility that conscripted all those who used or, to a lesser degree, simply witnessed the operation of Ford vehicles. This regime's durability was premised on rapid repairs, consistent supplies and the exclusion of imitation, lower quality spare

Greg Grandin, *Fordlandia: The Rise and Fall of Henry Ford's Forgotten City* (New York: Henry Holt, 2009); Lewis H. Siegelbaum, *Cars for Comrades: The Life of the Soviet Automobile* (Ithaca: Cornell University Press, 2008); Joel Wolfe, *Autos and Progress: the Brazilian Search for Modernity* (New York: Oxford University Press, 2010). On technology see, for example, David Arnold and Erich DeWald, 'Cycles of Empowerment? The Bicycle and Everyday Technology in Colonial India and Vietnam', *Comparative Studies in Society and History*, Vol. 53 (2011), pp. 971–96.

[14] For a useful general framework on forms of graduated political sovereignty and colonial empire see Lauren A. Benton, *A Search for Sovereignty: Law and Geography in European Empires, 1400–1900* (Cambridge: Cambridge University Press 2010). For recent work on 'semi-sovereignty' and segmented, layered and divided sovereignty in the Ottoman centre and provinces see Aimee M. Genell, 'Autonomous Provinces and the Problem of "Semi-Sovereignty" in European International Law', *Journal of Balkan and Near Eastern Studies*, Vol. 18, No. 6 (2016), pp. 533–49. For a useful recent discussion of approaches to sovereignty, with a particular emphasis on provincial notables' adaptations of steam technology (shipping and railways), see Adam Mestyan, 'Domestic Sovereignty, A'Yan Developmentalism, and Global Microhistory in Modern Egypt', *Comparative Studies in Society and History*, Vol. 60, No. 2 (2018), pp. 419–20. I'm grateful to Matt Houlbrook for encouraging my thinking on flatpack Fordism.

parts and unreliable rival dealers, across the expansive, border-crossing Ford empire that Corm built.[15]

Corm presented this need for trust as both specific to the tough commercial and cultural conditions of the region, and as threatened by that specificity. A key site in this respect is Beirut, which I argue we should treat not simply as an analytically pre-supposed and over-studied urban centre, which scholars should interpret as against peripheral borderlands such as the Turkish–Syrian borderlands north of Aleppo. Instead, it should be seen as in itself a borderland, a zone where the customs status of imported vehicles and their physical reassembly were negotiated, and where concerns about border-crossing more generally significantly constituted business culture.[16] Indeed, as historian Peter Leary has pointed out in the context of the Irish borderland, a key element of border-making is its simultaneously specifying and dispersing effect in space, causing, for example, both the building of walls at specific frontiers and the proliferation of sites of suspicion and verification far beyond the wall itself.[17] In this sense, the chapter points towards a need to conceptualise border-making and mobility regimes in the Middle East less in terms of a binary centre-periphery relationship (even a flipped one in which the periphery substantially 'makes' the centre), and more in terms of a rhizomic cartography of dynamically networked nodes. In other words, Corm's network of Ford branches, less obviously politically hierarchical than the relationship between

---

[15] For another context in which capitalists worked to secure exclusive access to rents and licences in colonial contexts see Egypt in the 1920s, where 'local capitalists' 'successfully merged their interests in foreign-backed ventures with their interest in local accumulation' in Robert Vitalis, *When Capitalists Collide: Business Conflict and the End of Empire in Egypt* (Berkeley: University of California Press, 1995).

[16] For a discussion of customs see Cyrus Schayegh, 'The Many Worlds of 'Abud Yasin; Or, What Narcotics Trafficking in the Interwar Middle East Can Tell Us about Territorialization', *American Historical Review*, Vol. 116, No. 2 (2011), pp. 305–6.

[17] Peter Leary, 'Borders and Beyond', *Historians' Watch/Radical History after Brexit* (blog), *History Workshop*, 13 July 2020, https://www.historyworkshop.org.uk/borders-and-beyond/ Leary aptly quotes Marx's point in the *Grundrisse*: 'Capital drives beyond national barriers and prejudices . . . as well as all traditional, confined, complacent, encrusted satisfactions of present needs, and reproductions of old ways of life . . . But from the fact that capital posits every such limit as a barrier and hence gets ideally beyond it, it does not by any means follow that it has really overcome it . . . its production moves in contradictions which are constantly overcome but just as constantly posited.'

political-administrative branches of the imperial or national state, helps us re-imagine the larger cartography of the Middle East and its borderlands.

The chapter's second argument is that the nodes of the Ford network should be thought of not just through border-crossing connections in geographical space, but also taken to include the 'places' and landscapes of individual sub-jectivity, emotion and affect: we need to understand the borderlands between 'borderlanders'.[18] From the fury of Charles Pavie in the ploughing grounds outside Aleppo, to the intensifying, catalysing feelings that existed between Harold Beazley, his wife Miriam Beazley and Charles Corm, the role of Fords in the history of borders, mobilities and state-making in this period cannot be understood without understanding the interpersonal relationships that facilitated their movement. Accordingly, in its second half, the chapter pivots to show how cross-border and border-making flows of vehicles, capital, parts and ideas about Ford products relied on the production and transgression of another type of border – that between individuals. Diversifying our conceptual understanding of border-crossing and mobility regimes, and adopting a global micro-history framework, pivoting on the concept of 'moving stories', the sec-ond section of the paper peoples Corm's Ford empire by parsing the 'capital-ist friendship' between Charles Corm, Harold Beazley and Miriam Beazley.[19] It argues that interpersonal boundaries – the borderlands between individual subject positions – and the related management of the line between business and friendship, guaranteed the macro-dynamics of late colonial capitalism in the region without being wholly subsumed into them. As Will Jackson has argued: 'friendship is no less friendship because it involves the circulation of debts and obligations . . . [it] . . . is both instrumental and affective'. Much like other forms of border work, in fact, it is '*How* these combine in any given social and cultural context [that] determines . . . its simultaneously inclusionary and exclusionary nature.'[20] The chapter thus seeks to place into conversation the

---

[18] On 'borderlanders', see the editors' introduction to this volume.

[19] John-Paul A. Ghobrial, 'Moving Stories and What They Tell Us: Early Modern Mobility Between Microhistory and Global History,' *Past & Present* 242, Issue Supplement 14, (2019), 243–280.

[20] Will Jackson, 'The Kindness of Strangers: Single Mothers and the Politics of Friendship in Interwar Cape Town', *Journal of Social History*, Vol. 54, No. 3 (2021), p. 823; see also Peter Robb, 'Mr Upjohn's Debts: Money and Friendship in Early Colonial Calcutta', *Modern Asian Studies*, Vol. 47, No. 4 (2013), pp. 1185–217.

growing critical literature theorising capitalism and emotion in tandem, with the recent historiography on state formation in the Middle East and the macro-dynamics of capitalism in this period.[21]

To achieve its goals, the chapter relies on primary sources drawn from the Corm family's private archive in Beirut, where the records of Corm's Ford distribution business are held alongside (and have been occluded by) the manuscripts of his much better known published literary work.[22] In one sense, Corm and his records exemplify the methodological problems that historian John-Paul Ghobrial, in a discussion of the micro-historical study of mobility, finds posed by an 'individual about whom we know more than usual, owing to the discovery of an exceptional set of sources'.[23] Such an approach, such a subject and such sources may encourage the historian to exaggerate the incidence of certain forms of mobility, overstate the typicality of highly unusual protagonists such as 'renegades, converts, and "people in between"', and more generally foster a disproportionate focus on the dynamic self-fashioning of unusual individuals at the expense of a focus on the power of structural forces and the experiences of ordinary people.[24] Plainly, Corm (highly educated, increasingly wealthy and, by late 1919, an anti-Arab advocate of French imperial intervention) was a deeply atypical figure – certainly he was no Menocchio.[25]

But I suggest that Corm's business papers, and especially the personal networks that lattice them, nevertheless offer distinctive material through

---

[21] See representatively Martijn Konings, *The Emotional Logic of Capitalism: What Progressives have Missed* (Stanford: Stanford University Press, 2015) and Schayegh, *Making of the Modern World*.

[22] See, symptomatically, Corm's entry in Peter France (ed.), *The New Oxford Companion to Literature in French* (Oxford: Clarendon Press, 1995), p. 528.

[23] Ghobrial, 'Moving Stories', p. 245.

[24] Ibid., pp. 246–47. See also Jill Lepore, 'Historians Who Love Too Much: Reflections on Microhistory and Biography', *Journal of American History*, Vol. 88, No. 1 (2001), pp. 129–44. In Mediterranean historiographies, as Jocelyne Dakhlia has noted, these risks are entwined with an existing tendency to focus on minorities and brokerage in port cities – see Nicolas Delalande and Thomas Grillot, 'Pouvoir et passions en terre d'Islam. Entretien avec Jocelyne Dakhlia', *La Vie des idées*, 28 février 2014. ISSN: 2105-3030. http://www.laviedesidees.fr/Pouvoir-et-passions-en-terre-d.html

[25] Carlo Ginzburg, *The Cheese and the Worms: The Cosmos of a Sixteenth Century Miller*, trans. John and Anne Tedeschi (London: Penguin, 1992).

which to conjure the emergence of a new capitalist-imperialist conjuncture in the Middle East in the years after the First World War. Cached below Corm's more valorised literary estate, his business papers are a 'border archive' of a kind. That is, they are a set of sources significantly structured from above by the power of the French imperial state and by the global Ford corporation and also deeply suffused from below by Corm's national and literary ambitions, yet fully constituted by neither. Moreover, these 'business records' stand at an angle to the Ottoman, French and British state archives through which borderland histories of the region are often written – even within the taxonomy of the private Corm archive these papers are marginal, subordinated to the privileged 'centre' of the literary records. Within this border archive, then, Corm's Ford correspondence freely combines personal and business registers, illustrating the contingencies that shaped the operation of capitalist logic and the play of emotion and friendship that facilitated the movement of Ford products across the region. In these documents, Charles Corm can be grasped not simply as the bard-entrepreneur of a neo-Phoenician Lebanon, nor even as a fascinating and overweening individual whose biography affords a 'window' onto a time of pivotal change in the region, but instead interpreted as a networked capitalist self, a self that was the product of border-crossing relationality and not of self-authored national or personal autonomy.[26] In this chapter the threads of relationality I concentrate on are those that linked Corm to Harold and Miriam Beazley.

### Flatpack Fordism and Regional Networks

As the historian of race, empire and Ford, Elizabeth D. Esch has noted, although Henry Ford himself opposed the First World War, the conflict proved 'good for corporate America in general and especially for Ford'.[27] Ford's pre-war commitment to overseas expansion, marked by the creation of a British subsidiary in 1909 and a factory in Manchester, England, in 1911, and by the 1913 launch of Ford Argentina, presaged explosive growth during and after the conflict. Huge volumes of Ford vehicles supplied the Entente armies, generating some US$78 million of net profit from 1916 to 1918

[26] Katie Barclay, 'Falling in love with the dead', *Rethinking History*, Vol. 22, No. 4 (2018), p. 469.
[27] Esch, *Color Line*, p. 28.

alone. Substantially reinvested in the company, this capital would finance the transformation of Ford's productive capacity in Detroit as well as plans for further global expansion: 'As early as 1920 Ford manufactured most of the nearly 200,000 vehicles exported annually from the United States; by 1923 the company was making a yearly profit of US$50 million from international sales.'[28] This global expansion operated through the creation of factories and through a network of dealerships: the latter often anticipated the former. Even as Ford created factories in the 1920s in 'Port Elizabeth, Copenhagen, Cadiz, Stockholm, Antwerp, Asnières, and Berlin', it also established dealerships in 'more than 2,000 locations worldwide'.[29] Charles Corm's dealerships in French Mandate Syria were among the latter and, as Esch notes, these dealerships could take delivery of Ford products 'from across an ocean if necessary'.[30]

Corm's network rapidly proved successful. By June 1922, for example, approximately a year after Corm received his first major shipment via London, he had ordered some 510 cars, 16 tractors and US$31,000 worth of spare parts in spite of conditions he characterised as 'a terrible period of crisis' marked out by 'political assassinations, insecurity on the roads, the reduction of our territory due to the creation of the new Kemalist frontier in Cilicia, continual emigration and the poverty and ignorance of the population, which hamper the development of all efforts towards progress'.[31] As we shall see, however, 'taking delivery', with its connotation of passivity, does not capture the creative reinvention that characterised the cross-border import and distribution practices Corm's network of branches developed.

Moreover, the movement of these Ford products was achieved within a system of global distribution that can be considered a regime of mobility in and of itself, even as it helped to constitute regional regimes of mobility around the world by providing vehicles in which people could travel at new speeds across border zones.[32] This global system of distribution was crucially laced with tax arbitrage and with the exploitation of imperial tariff regimes

[28] Ibid.

[29] Esch, *Color Line*, p. 29.

[30] Ibid.

[31] Corm, Beirut, to Ford, London, 3 June 1922, CAB 1.

[32] See, for example, César Jaquier's and Lauren Banko's contributions to this volume.

and spaces. Within the Detroit region, for example, Henry Ford played on corporation and municipal tax rate differences between cities and counties, moving his factory from site to site partly via tax deal-making with municipal authorities. At the US-Canada border, meanwhile, Ford was quick to incorporate in 1904 in Windsor, Ontario, just across the border from Detroit. This gave Ford access to British imperial tariff preference across the British Empire, granting Ford Canada responsibility for exports across the empire, from Uganda to Fiji and from Sierra Leone to the Seychelles. Simultaneously, the incorporation of Ford Canada served to constitute the Windsor-Detroit zone on the Canada-US border as 'what came to be known as the Border Cities region, an area that included the newly minted town of Ford City'.[33] State practices of border-making, here as elsewhere in this chapter, presented and shaped opportunities for various forms of cross-border arbitrage and network building by corporate actors of various kinds.

Similarly, in the Mediterranean region after the war, Ford managers such as William Knudsen projected the corporation's future expansion both by exploiting existing colonial empires and by speculating on the likely outcome of the war's geopolitical settlement. As historian and anthropologist Aslı Odman has argued, the 1919 'Knudsen Plan' was the moment when 'the geographical logic of the global expansion of Ford was written black on white for the first time after the First World War, in an international context that allowed for a relatively stable basis of calculation'.[34] Although logistics played a part in Knudsen's ideas, the key influence on his partitioning of the Euro-Mediterranean world was the operation of imperial economic spaces and connections. Thus: 'The British Division would embrace the United Kingdom, Egypt, and Malta, with headquarters in Manchester' while the 'Central Division, with headquarters in Paris, would include France, Belgium, Switzerland, and Algeria' and the 'Southern Division would cover Italy, Spain, Portugal, Morocco, Tunis, and Tripoli, with an assembly plant in

[33] Esch, *Color Line*, p. 26.
[34] Aslı Odman, 'Ford Motor Company's Assembly Plant in Tophane – Istanbul, 1923–44: Territoriality and Automobility during Interwar Global Capitalism' (PhD thesis in progress, Boğaziçi University), pp. 115–16. I am most grateful to Aslı Odman for generously sharing her work-in-progress with me.

a convenient Spanish city'.[35] We should note at once that while Knudsen placed Egypt and Algeria, large prospective markets differently incorporated into their respective imperial formations, into divisions pivoting around their political imperial centres, both Tunisia and Morocco, French Protectorates, were designated part of the Southern Division in Italy and Spain. Ford's logistical and production imperatives could at times plainly supersede the state-based logics of imperial political control.

In the former Ottoman lands, meanwhile, Ford's 1919 partitioning of the commercial space proved more speculative, but broadly tracked the incipient border-making processes set in motion by the entente occupation of parts of Anatolia and the Treaty of Sèvres.[36] Thus, 'the Adriatic Division would embrace Central Europe south of Germany, the Balkan lands, and Asia Minor, and would have headquarters and an assembly plant at Fiume', while 'the Black Sea Division would include the Ukraine, Central Russia, Turkey, Armenia, and the Caucasus, a difficult region for which planning was shadowy, but which Knudsen hoped would develop a centre in Odessa'.[37] While it is striking to see how the Ford manager conceived of the former Russian and Ottoman empires in linked terms, anchored by Adriatic and Black Sea maritime spaces, less defined in Knudsen's vision were the extent of 'Asia Minor' and 'Turkey' and how the two entities would co-exist, while the former Arab provinces of the Ottoman Empire, or nascent Greater Syria, were completely absent.[38] In due course, the re-articulation of regional geopolitics by Turkish nationalist military resistance against the imperialist settlement of Sèvres would, by the time of the Lausanne Treaty's final signature in 1923, lead to a completely different dispensation. Nevertheless, some features of Knudsen's 1919 vision continued to shape Ford distribution in the region in the early 1920s, such as the attachment of parts of what Harold Beazley often called

[35] Allan Nevins and Frank Ernest Hill, *Ford: Expansion and Challenge, 1915–1933* (New York, Scribner, 1957), pp. 358–59, cited in Odman, 'Ford Motor Company's Assembly Plant in Tophane', pp. 115–16.

[36] For an overview see Eugene Rogan, *The Fall of the Ottomans: The Great War in the Middle East, 1914–1920* (London: Penguin, 2015).

[37] Nevins and Hill, *Ford: Expansion*, pp. 358–59, cited in Odman, pp. 115–16.

[38] On Turkey see usefully Lale Duruiz, 'Turkish Men's Affair with Cars: The History of the Automobile in Turkey', *Mobility in History*, Vol. 7, No. 1 (2016), pp. 123–32.

the 'Near East' to an Adriatic headquarters, not at Fiume, destabilised by the experiment of the Free State, but at Trieste.[39] Later in the 1920s and into the 1930s, the Ford network in the Eastern Mediterranean would be further consolidated, with Ford Italia, under pressure from Mussolini's regime and its champion Fiat, moving its headquarters to Bologna, while new factories would be set up both in the tax-free zone of Tophane in Istanbul and also eventually in Alexandria, Egypt, in 1927.[40]

The vehicles, spare parts, Ford agents, techniques and ideas that flowed along this imperially mediated network and into the partitioned 'divisions' of Ford's regionalised commercial spaces in the Eastern Mediterranean often continue to be thought of in existing scholarship in a more or less quali-fied diffusionist model.[41] 'Created' on the Euro-American production lines of Detroit, Michigan, or Dagenham in the UK, Ford products were certainly shipped transatlantic and across the Mediterranean to 'dealerships that could take delivery of "knocked-down" car kits for local assembly, or in some cases would simply sell cars that were imported from regional assembly shops'.[42] Historians such as Robert L. Tignor long ago acknowledged the political-economic power that Egyptians exercised over Ford Egypt, for example, but he still rested on the claim that in the 1920s and 1930s 'most of the cars, trucks and tractors that were exported to Egypt arrived in a "built up" condition

---

[39] On Fiume's late-imperial history see Dominique Kirchner Reill, *The Fiume Crisis: Life in the Wake of the Habsburg Empire* (Cambridge, MA: Belknap Press of Harvard University Press, 2020).

[40] On Italy see Giuseppe Volpato, 'Ford in Italy: Commercial breakthroughs without indus-trial bridgeheads', in Hubert Bonin, Yannick Lung and Steven W. Tolliday (eds), *Ford. The European History 1903–2003*, Vol. 2 (Paris: Plage, 2003), p. 452. On Tophane see the pio-neering work of Aslı Odman, '"Modern Times" at the Galata Docks. Ford's Automotive Assembly Plant in Tophane/Istanbul 1925–1944', in *Ex.Change Istanbul-Marseille: Indus-trial Architectural Heritage Developing Awareness and Visibility* (Istanbul: Çekül Founda-tion, 2011), pp. 94–105; on Egypt see Robert L. Tignor, 'In the Grip of Politics: The Ford Motor Company of Egypt, 1945–1960', *Middle East Journal*, Vol. 44, No. 3 (1990), pp. 382–83.

[41] For an example of the diffusionist approach see Daniel R. Headrick, *The Tentacles of Progress: Technology Transfer in the Age of Imperialism, 1850–1940* (New York: Oxford University Press, 1988).

[42] Esch, *Color Line*, p. 27.

and *required little* to make them ready for purchase'.[43] This approach, I argue, neglects the way in which border crossing re-constituted Ford vehicles physically, symbolically, and as part of a longer term project of commercial sovereignty that played on – but whose borders did not coincide with – French imperial sovereignty in the Syrian Mandate.[44]

Meanwhile, the notion of the reassembly of technological artefacts in colonial contexts has received more attention from scholars such as David Arnold and Erich DeWald, whose work on bicycles in colonial India and Vietnam has analysed the varied symbolic, spatial and social practices that coalesced and evolved around bicycles. Conceding a linear narrative epistemology of Western origination, they initially argue that bicycles in one sense diffused from the Euro-American centre, since 'colonised subjects in India and Vietnam played no part in the initial fashioning and technological evolution of the modern safety bicycle.'[45] But they also chart the wide varieties of creative reinvention that bicycles underwent in colonial India and Vietnam, since these artefacts were

> amenable to local adaptation, to cultural and political appropriation on a grand scale . . . Yet . . . remained machine enough and foreign enough to raise questions about indigeneity, about the merits and demerits of progress, and about gender roles, social hierarchies, and the mechanisms of state power.[46]

Under the umbrella concept of 'flatpack Fordism', I suggest we can envisage the adaptations and transformations Charles Corm wrought across his Ford empire in similar terms, but also carry the argument further. Instead of thinking within a framework of 'initial' metropolitan manufacture and then 'local' tweaking, we ought instead to think of a process of perpetual reassembly and maintenance, across a global network of dealerships and users.

---

[43] Tignor, 'Grip of Politics', p. 383. My italics.

[44] This point re-states, in the realm of material culture, the point made by Robert Vitalis and others in the 1980s and 1990s about the financial power of local/national capital: in focusing 'on the power of the multinationals', we have ignored the 'power, the bargaining leverage, alliances' and other strategies 'of local capital'. Vitalis, *When Capitalists Collide*, pp. 1–2.

[45] Arnold and DeWald, 'Cycles of Empowerment', p. 972.

[46] Arnold and DeWald, 'Cycles of Empowerment', p. 973.

Across this networked circuit of socio-technical reassembly and the ceaseless reattribution of symbolic meaning, the 'American-ness' of the Fords' 'origins' certainly counted for a lot: US vehicles possessed a certain prestige and the Ford corporation wanted dealers to publicise this. But, equally, those American origins 'counted' in ways asserted and negotiated locally. Even the fabled trustworthiness of Ford vehicles, which the corporation made a pillar of its propaganda, had to be maintained, discursively and literally, in necessarily and finally local contexts.[47] In this sense, then, the more Fords crossed borders, the more they acquired significance and constitutive power in the larger landscape of Fordist production and consumption, de-centring classic narratives of technological and political diffusion.[48]

A good example of this phenomenon, and a key node in Corm's network of branches in the French and British Mandates, was Beirut, where Corm developed a small assembly workshop in which vehicles delivered to the Beirut docks as knocked-down kits could be assembled, modified and repaired. This process of reassembling the vehicles from a kit often involved the raising of the chassis, the provision of additional petrol storage, spare lightbulbs, inner tubes, mechanical car horns, electric rear lamps, spare convertible roofs and other changes for long-distance travel, often made at the request of the individual customer and often negotiated as part of the initial sale or ongoing repair contracts.[49] It could also mean the addition of new supplementary pieces of technology, making the Ford vehicles sites of explicit 'experiment'.

Strikingly, these experimental re-mixings of Ford products themselves depended on the cross-border circulation of parts and on the cross-border brokering of relationships. In January 1924 and again in 1925, for example, Beazley and Corm corresponded over the prospective value of a newly available gadget for Ford vehicles, the 'Ruckstell Axle', which allowed vehicles to climb hills more easily by offering a supplementary gearing system that could be added to the existing gearbox. Beazley noted that he had been visited in Trieste by a travelling representative of the 'American Accessories Co.', which

---

[47] My thanks to Cyrus Schayegh for discussion on this point.

[48] For an exemplary reversal of standard accounts of imperial information and transportation see Nile Green, 'Fordist Connections: The Automotive Integration of the United States and Iran', *Comparative Studies in Society and History*, Vol. 58, No.2 (2016), pp. 290–321.

[49] Corm, Beirut, to Beazley, Alexandria, 8 June 1923, CAB 1.

was distributing the new device, 'applicable to the Ford car and Ford truck' and that while

> we do not issue a full recommendation, I can say that the 'Axle' is exceedingly good. Many have been sold in England, and in the hilly districts in Europe. It is just possible the same would be good for the Lebanon work, and help to boost business between Beyrouth and Damascus. I understand that he is arranging for samples to be dispatched to Syria and Palestine, so in the event of your meeting him I should be glad if you would arrange for one of your Service Cars to be fitted up for the experiment.[50]

In this example the Beirut-Damascus road, a key commercial artery that also ran across an intra-Mandate frontier between Syria and Greater Lebanon, became a prospective experimental site for the re-working of Fords circulating in the Mandate, thanks to an added element, the Ruckstell, itself distributed across French Mandate Syria and British Mandate Palestine alike. Furthermore, in the same letter, driving home the mutual focus of Beazley and Corm on the nodal structure of Ford's Eastern Mediterranean network, the former added (wrongly as it turned out) that 'there is no truth in the statement that a plant is to be erected in Alexandria'. Trieste would remain Corm's 'control branch', and the key source of oversight and dispute for the performance of the network of Corm Ford branches in the Mandates.[51]

Beirut, as the location where the flatpack vehicle kits entered the French Mandate, was also significant as the seat of French imperial Mandatory authority, the dominant economic hub of the French Mandate and the 'economic gravitation point of Bilad al-Sham'.[52] It was also the place where tariffs and customs duties were levied and where vehicles could be physically impounded at customs.[53] These border costs were a significant factor

---

[50] Beazley, Trieste, to Corm, Beirut, 4 January 1925, CAB 1.

[51] Corm, Beirut, to Beazley, Alexandria, 8 June 1923, CAB 1.

[52] Schayegh, *Making of the Modern World*, pp. 59–66.

[53] On tariffs see Roza I. M. El-Eini, 'Trade Agreements and the Continuation of Tariff Protection Policy in Mandate Palestine in the 1930s', *Middle Eastern Studies*, Vol. 34, No. 1 (1998), pp. 164–91. See also Ramazan Hakkı Öztan's contribution to this volume. Customs offices also eventually existed elsewhere, for instance at Damascus, but Beirut was the choke point – see Schayegh, *Making of the Modern World*, p. 167.

in determining the eventual retail price of vehicles across the territory, their relative price to other brands in the wider market, the levels of credit that could be offered to customers and the profits that could be secured by Corm and his sales force. As Corm chafed, in a letter to Beazley in June 1923, price differentials between Fords directly imported from New York City and Fords imported (as Beazley wished) from Trieste, were, in combination with the exchange rate, sufficient to wipe out any profit on individual sales when imported from Trieste.[54]

Tariffs also encapsulated the political standing of automobiles and the relative symbolic throw-weights of specific brands of automobile in the developmental ideology of the French imperial and Lebanese and Syrian national authorities. Thus, Corm benefited from his political connections to the French authorities, acquired in his days as a broker of food relief in 1918, to eventually secure the role of

> the official Sworn Expert to General Administration of Customs in Syria and the Great Lebanon, for Automobiles, Tractors, Motors and all that concerns machinery in general. We trust that you will be glad to hear of that mark of high distinction awarded to Mr Corm and that you will appreciate the importance of such an appointment which will so much facilitate our business in the future.[55]

As sworn expert to the customs authorities Corm accordingly became a key gatekeeper in the political-economy of border-crossing, as well as an interested party who himself moved vehicles and spare parts across the frontier, with knock-on effects for the relative competitivity of Fords across the entire network of branches. Here, then, we should take Beirut seriously, too: not as a pre-supposed centre but as a border zone. In this urban political-economic forcefield, automobiles moved across the city from the docks as they were unloaded, passed customs (or were impounded when the importer could

[54] Corm, Beirut, to Beazley, Alexandria, 8 June 1923, CAB 1.
[55] Corm, Beirut, to Ford, London, 3 November 1921, CAB 1. On food relief see Simon Jackson, 'Compassion and Connections: Feeding Beirut and Assembling Mandate Rule in 1919', in Cyrus Schayegh and Andrew Arsan (eds), *The Routledge Handbook of the History of the Middle East Mandates* (London: Routledge, 2014), pp. 87–101.

not pay or lacked connections) and moved through a matrix of paperwork and charges. They were then transported, often with deliberately high visibility, encountering the gaze and shaping the perceptions of Beirut's citizens, through the streets of the interpellated city, for reassembly at workshops such as Corm's in Ashrafieh.[56] The imperial and Lebanese state authorities were certainly present here, but the customs system had been in part captured by Corm, enabling him to shape the imperial-national state's regulatory regime to his own, and Ford's, advantage. Here, Corm's Francophilia, skilled lobbying of French officials and broad support for French power trumped the commercial threat his Fords posed to rival French automobile interests. The 'official line' incarnate in Charles Pavie's anger outside Aleppo was just one thread of a larger bundle, into which Corm spliced his vision. Or, in Cyrus Schayegh's terms, if 'the Mandates were arenas where the European rulers had the last word, but not the only one', then here we have an example of a member of the Mandate elite playing on the tone and controlling the detail of the conversation.[57]

The significance of appearing 'official' was also visible elsewhere in the politics of automobile import at the Beirut border. Corm's assembly workshop may have been tiny relative to the plants created during the 1920s and 1930s at Trieste, Tophane and Alexandria, let alone the behemoths at Dagenham, Manchester or Dearborn, but it was imposingly substantial relative to the interloping rivals Corm feared and who often tried to disrupt his fragile pre-eminence by placing direct orders with Trieste. Seldom did Corm write to Harold Beazley without criticising and dismissing the competition. Moreover, his rivals' failure to develop adequate assembly systems was a key part of that critique, as when he wrote of the

> Ford smugglers [*contrebandiers de l'importation des Fords*] . . . who even assemble the vehicles in the street by the port, in the dust, the filth and the greatest haste, understanding nothing of the requirements of a rigorous assembly, and all they aim for is that the vehicle should be able to roll along, but of course it doesn't do so for long without problems developing, and then we [Corm's

---

[56] On urban border crossing see Kristin V. Monroe, *The Insecure City: Space, Power and Mobility in Beirut* (New Brunswick, NJ: Rutgers University Press, 2016), pp. 69–73.

[57] Schayegh, *Making of the Modern World*, p. 137 and pp. 165–66 on lobbying.

organisation] have to bear the ensuing trouble and the damage to the reputation of the brand.[58]

Smugglers, then, those constitutive figures of borderlands studies, could be found at the Beirut docks and the surrounding streets, just as they were on the other frontiers of the French Mandate, such as that with Mandate Palestine.[59] As Cyrus Schayegh has shown in the case of narcotics smuggling, such practices reveal the superposed forms of territorialisation that existed in different combinations along the Mandate's frontiers and commercial arteries. But the example of the Ford smugglers of central Beirut shows us that those borders could also be found in the city often considered the metropole or the centre of the Mandate states, and that forms of 'commercial sovereignty' were also at stake and in operation there – intercalated with the more recognised imperial, international and regional forms of territorialisation scholars have analysed.[60]

Corm expressed his concerns about smuggling in the Beirut border zone around the docks, and the related problem of lax reassembly of Ford vehicles, in terms of the damage this ultimately did to the reputation of the Ford brand across the nodes of his own empire of branches, but also, by implication, to Ford regionally and globally – which is why he made the point so forcefully to Beazley, certain that his supervisor and friend would recognise the stakes. This point brings us to the way in which border zone practices in Beirut, such as the creative reassembly of Ford vehicles, connected to the wider space of the Mandates and to Corm's network of Ford branches. Flatpack Fordism, I argue, meant not just the experimental physical reassembly of Ford vehicles, in the ways discussed above, but also the assembly of a form of commercial sovereignty for Corm as the pre-eminent dealer and Ford as the pre-eminent

---

[58] Corm, Beirut, to Beazley, Alexandria, 8 June 1923, CAB 1. For a pre-war iteration of the politics of commercial (dis)trust, in which Austro-Hungarian exporters avoided dealing with small Beirut importers, preferring a few wholesalers as intermediaries, see Schayegh, *Making of the Modern World*, p. 63.

[59] See Lauren Banko's chapter in this volume.

[60] See Schayegh, "Abud Yasin', pp. 305–6. See paradigmatically on smuggling Peter Sahlins, *Boundaries: The Making of France and Spain in the Pyrenees* (Berkeley CA: University of California Press, 1989), pp. 129–40.

brand of automobiles across the wider region. This form of sovereignty was based on an always fragile trust in the Ford brand and in the Corm Company's ability to reproduce the perception of authenticity and reliability across his network of branches and over time. In doing so, its mechanics and salesmen created a regime of mobility premised on the assurance, across the Corm empire's territory, of rapid repairs, consistent supplies and the exclusion of imitation, lower quality spare parts and unreliable rival dealers.

Corm presented this fragile form of sovereignty, based on trust, as both specific to the tough commercial and cultural conditions of the region and as threatened by that specificity. As he put it to Beazley, appealing to the latter's orientalist reflexes and to their mutual understanding (of which more below): 'One cannot sell Fords here as one might in Europe or America. To do so requires a unity of command, an uncontested authority, an unbreakable firmness etc. I am sure you understand me.'[61] Or again:

> in this business there are moral and psychological factors, imponderables caused by the habits and the mentality of the population, which all the other manufacturers working in this country have understood and that Ford [i.e. Trieste and London] alone continues to neglect. This is the more unjust since not a single Ford would sell here without us and if we didn't guarantee a flawless repair and replacement service in every one of our branches, God knows at what cost and sacrifice.[62]

Indeed, the elaboration of his Beirut assembly works and his wider network of repair, maintenance and spare parts were conjoined elements of a rhizomic network of branches. Mechanics circulated across each branch's local territory, visiting clients and their machines and keeping the latter, in the words of Arnold and DeWald, 'machine enough and foreign enough' to raise questions to which only Corm's organisation could provide the answers. In the process, Corm and company secured its own commercial sovereignty as a dominant network and indeed renegotiated and reinvented, through local work, the Ford corporation in Detroit's own claims about the universal qualities of its products. As Corm boasted: 'I have

[61] Corm, Beirut, to Beazley, Alexandria, 8 June 1923, CAB 1.
[62] Ibid.

inaugurated a system of tours of inspection to examine the state of every tractor and to undertake free repairs, costing not a penny to the owners for the necessary labour, for feeding our delegated mechanics or for their travel costs.'[63] Put another way, the regional regime of (auto)mobility was secured in part by the roving mobility of mechanics who fanned out from the network of branches, in which Beirut was only one node. As in the example of the customs regime given above, so again here the imperial and national state authorities and infrastructure were important to this system, notably through their road-building programme: 8,400 km of new main and secondary roads were built between 1919 and 1939. But again, Corm's empire drew on state resources and played on state regulatory systems without wholly aligning with French imperial interests; moreover, Corm's mechanics travelled all the way to the tractors, providing coverage beyond the network of state road provision.[64]

Thus, Corm presented himself as the indispensable broker and guarantor of this fragile sovereignty to his superiors at Ford in Trieste and beyond: he hoped one day 'Henry Ford himself will learn of my crusade and congratulate me on it'.[65] But he also felt a clear obligation to cover as much territory as possible, and sought to develop his branches notably in İskenderun (Alexandretta) and Aleppo, despite what he portrayed in 1923 as the insecure conditions there:

> I would like to add 30 cars to my recent order [90 vehicles, mainly Tourings, ordered from New York City via Trieste] for dispatch to Alexandretta, but I'm afraid of what might happen in the region, and that I might lose not only my existing stock in that town but also any new cars I send, and I risk losing too much capital for too little profit given our general costs there. The same goes for Aleppo, where the cost of sending up cars via Beirut [instead of Alexandretta presumably, due to the lack of security on the Alexandretta-Aleppo road] is too ruinous to continue the system.[66]

---

[63] Ibid.

[64] On roads see Schayegh, *Making of the Modern World*, p. 158.

[65] Corm, Beirut, to Beazley, Alexandria, 8 June 1923, CAB 1.

[66] Ibid. On the Alexandretta-Aleppo road's dangers and the resulting difficulty of investing further in Alexandretta see also Beazley to Corm, Beirut, 4 January 1925, CAB 1.

Corm, in another sign of his proximity to the Mandate state authorities, expressed a hope that the government would restore security to Aleppo, where fighting had taken place inside the city in early June, and claimed that 'all the local press and the civil and religious authorities enjoined the government to the greatest severity'.[67]

Significantly, Corm framed this obligation to at least try to cover as much territory as possible, including in the northern Syria border zone, as entwined with his personal obligations to Beazley. Indeed, among their first exchanges was a series of rapid letters sent and received across town in Beirut in the same day, when Beazley was visiting there in 1922. In it, Corm enquired about the limits of his commercial purview in the borderlands north of Aleppo:

> We would be grateful if you can tell us whether we can sell Ford cars, tractors, trucks and spare parts in Urfaj, Diarbekir, Aintab, Killas, Marash [*sic*], through our Aleppo organisation. We draw your attention to the fact that these towns formed part of our territory last year, at least in part, and that the new frontiers of Syria as traced by the Franco-Turkish treaty have placed them outside our territory, though they remain naturally dependent on Aleppo's sphere of economic influence (*champ d'action économique*).[68]

It is perhaps apt to close this section of the chapter on this quotation. Focused on the Aleppine borderlands, Corm's query was doubly constitutive: of the relationship between Beirut business culture and the French Mandate's northern borderlands, and of the siting and limits of the Corm Ford empire within the larger global and regional Ford networks. In other words, this request shows how Corm's distribution network in the northern Syrian borderland was entangled with the staccato rhythm of business correspondence in Beirut, but also with the shifts in the wider capitalist geopolitics of the region. But the distribution network was also entangled with another form of community – when Corm wrote 'our territory' he referred to French imperial, Syrian national and Ford's/his own concession's commercial forms of sovereignty. But he also increasingly referred to another 'our' – the community

---

[67] Corm, Beirut, to Beazley, Alexandria, 8 June 1923, CAB 1.
[68] Corm to Beazley, 12 January 1922, CAB 1.

of friendship that had germinated between Corm and Harold and Miriam Beazley. It is to this capitalist friendship that we now turn.

## Personal Connections and the Borderlands of the Self

'I am sure you understand me,' Corm had written to Beazley in 1923. Detouring into the lexicon of the personal, he thereby appealed for Beazley's continued patronage of the exclusive Corm concession. He also appealed, more epistemologically, to what Corm believed to be Beazley's orientalist understanding of the region as a space in which commercial and political practices alike purportedly required an authoritarian edge.[69] But how could Corm be quite so sure he was understood, and how did his claim that he was sure in fact contribute to the fashioning of their budding mutuality? This second section of the chapter argues that interpersonal boundaries – what we might think of as the border, and borderlands, between individual subject positions – and the related management of another, intersecting frontier, between business and friendship, were both an important part of the macro-dynamics of late colonial capitalism in the region.[70] Moreover, like the uneven consolidation scholars see as symptomatic of the making of physical borderlands, so the capitalist friendship between Corm and the Beazleys took time to develop.[71]

The historian John-Paul Ghobrial has recently deployed the term 'moving stories' to explore the 'mechanics and meaning of mobility' in early modern crossings of the Atlantic and Mediterranean. Helpfully, Ghobrial tacks between global history approaches, concerned with general processes and networks of mobility, such as those associated with long-distance trade, and micro-historical approaches, concerned with individuals about whom, in the tradition of *microstoria*, we may have exceptionally rich sources that

---

[69] Lebanese neo-Phoenicians shared many aspects of such thinking. See Hakim, *Origins of the Lebanese National Idea*.

[70] For a history of friendship that usefully discusses the historically recent specificity of anti-instrumental, egalitarian models of friendship 'for its own sake', see Allan Silver, 'Friendship and trust as moral ideals: an historical approach', *European Journal of Sociology*, Vol. 30, No. 2 (1989), p. 280.

[71] Gideon Biger, *The Boundaries of Modern Palestine, 1840–1947* (London: Routledge Curzon, 2004), pp. 7–12. I thank Alexander E. Balistreri for drawing this work to my attention.

enable a discussion of their often 'normal' lives as they were shaped by major dynamics.[72] Ghobrial argues that we should neither exaggerate the incidence of mobility nor conceive of it primarily in a geographic sense, but instead look at 'moving stories' to understand how globe-spanning processes of displacement and unbelonging are constructed and maintained in specific systems and passing conjunctures: 'concrete, local process of *identification*'.[73] In this section we see how moving stories were told and processes of identification were undertaken by Corm and Beazley alike, but also by Beazley's wife Miriam. And, while Ghobrial's protagonist found himself 'at the mercy of foreign, and often suspicious, regimes of power', Beazley and Corm were in a sense at one another's mercy – Corm as the agent of Ford in the Eastern Mediterranean, obliged to cultivate Ford's regional managers, and Beazley, as a Ford employee who travelled regularly through the region but who also felt isolated at Ford's Trieste head office by the cold culture of the Ford corporation, where he needed to demonstrate the success of the dealerships he oversaw. Moreover, this mutual displacement was not binary but triangular, mediated by Miriam.

In January 1925, Miriam Beazley wrote to Corm from Trieste. She, too, felt displaced in and disappointed by her new home in Italy and journeys were at the heart of her message:

> We have been very disappointed you have not yet visited Trieste but are now hoping you will arrange your journey after Mr Cooper's [another Ford manager based in Trieste] visit to Beyrouth. How I wish he had sent Harold instead for then I should have seen you and all those of your family of whom I have heard so much, and also your beautiful Syria, which Harold so often wishes to see again. In one way the settlement at Trieste was a disappointment to me for I had eagerly looked forward to seeing the lands of the East. I had let my imagination run riot at the prospect of seeing at last all those places of which I had read, and which appealed to me tremendously. And again, I wanted to see your work which to me is so extraordinary. It sounds like magic

---

[72] Edoardo Grendi, 'Micro-analisi e storia sociale', *Quaderni storici*, Vol. 35 (1977), pp. 506–20, cited in Jan de Vries, 'Playing with Scales: The Global and the Micro, the Macro and the Nano', *Past & Present*, Vol. 242, Issue Supplement 14 (2019), p. 28.

[73] Ghobrial, 'Moving Stories', pp. 246–49.

to hear of anyone successfully planting the most progressive Western commercial organisation in a land where Time itself seems to move more slowly
and with gentle touch compared with the rush and whirl in the West which
leaves even those of us who should be used to it tired, and longing sometimes
to glide into a backwater to rest and think a little. It must take all your time
and strength and be a big strain on what Harold calls your 'indomitable spirit
and pluck' to build as you have done, and we watch for every evidence of
your success.[74]

The hierarchical and orientalist, even settler-colonial, underpinnings of
Miriam's letter are clear here in her literary characterisation of the 'lands of
the East' and of the 'magic' through which Corm had improbably prevailed
in his 'planting' of Ford, the 'most progressive' commercial organisation, in
'Syria'.[75] Her words corroborate the ease with which Corm himself could
play on Harold Beazley's view of the 'East' when Corm sought to justify
specific commercial tactics and the need for his own exclusive rights to be
upheld in the borderlands of his Ford network and the French Mandate
space. These orientalist reflexes were cultivated within an intense domestic
intimacy shared by Harold and Miriam in Trieste: 'I try to make our little
home a haven of peace and contentment for him to return to each night for
he needs it badly'.[76] Indeed the mutual identification and trust-building that
Corm and the Beazleys engaged in, as they rendered the borders between
themselves more porous, also rested on a shared, heteronormative consensus
about deeply felt communication within the framework of domesticity.[77]
As recent historians of Ford have noted, the charismatic, mission-driven

---

[74] Miriam Beazley (and postscript Harold Beazley), Trieste, to Corm, Beirut, 23 January 1925,
CAB 1.

[75] On settler colonial automobility see Georgine Clarsen '"Australia – Drive It Like You Stole
It": Automobility as a medium of communication in Settler Colonial Australia', *Mobilities*,
Vol. 12, No. 4 (2017), pp. 520–33.

[76] Miriam Beazley (and postscript Harold Beazley), Trieste, to Corm, Beirut, 23 January 1925,
CAB 1.

[77] Compare here the importance of family ties and the spaces of heteronormative domesticity in the moral economy of smuggling networks and the distribution of illicit textiles in
Southern Turkey. Öztan, 'The Great Depression', p. 319.

managerialism of the corporation was organised in part around the promotion of 'marriage, family and gender-based behaviour at home'.[78]

The Beazleys were typical in this respect, and the way they jointly presented their domestic life to Corm can be used to re-frame Ghobrial's notion of 'moving stories'. Miriam's 'moving story', as written to Corm, of her sojourn in unfamiliar yet insufficiently exotic Trieste, was certainly about the 'meaning of mobility' as she experienced it. But it was also about the importance of sentiment – about *being* moved emotionally by travel and by marriage alike, and about her confidence that Corm would recognise and identify with the importance of that sentiment and its associated practices – which included physical journeys. Miriam again:

> Sometimes I wonder if you ever have time or opportunity to allow the uncommercial side of you to come uppermost and if you find yourself longing to break away from it all to indulge the real bent of your nature. I expect you do. For myself I have revelled in some solitary walks by the sea, with just my thoughts and the beauty of nature and I wonder how I endured so long the rush and turmoil of business life. Sometimes at the weekend when Harold and I have gone up to the hills to rest, we have silently watched and thrilled to the sunset until it seemed that we were thinking with one mind and feeling with one heart and I have felt my hands taken in the grip which you too have felt and which tells so much more than words, of the sympathy and understanding existing.

Here, Miriam staged for Corm's benefit the form of emotional communion she felt with Harold: the dissolving of the borders between two selves through the creation of a shared and exalted interiority, catalysed by the commonplace tropes of a romanticised landscape – sunset from the hills above Trieste, ironically itself a border zone. Such sentiments were hardly uncommon in the 1920s (or today) when the intensification of middle-class labour regimes led to a widespread quest for refuge in the performance of interiority.[79] What marks out

---

[78] Esch, *Color Line*, p. 7. Stefan J. Link, 'The Charismatic Corporation, Finance, Administration, and Shop Floor Management under Henry Ford', *Business History Review*, Vol. 92, No.1 (2018), pp. 85–115.

[79] Robert Wiebe, *Self-Rule: A Cultural History of American Democracy* (Chicago: Chicago University Press, 1995), p. 187, quoted in Cotten Seiler, *Republic of Drivers: A Cultural History of Automobility in America* (Chicago: University of Chicago Press, 2008), p. 34.

Miriam's words here, though, is her commitment to sharing this experience with Corm not just by narrating it to him, but by claiming that he too has experienced elements of this same communion with Harold: 'the grip which you too have felt.' In this sense, Miriam's performance of heteronormative intimacy and boundary-dissolving between husband and wife over-spilled itself, enveloping Charles Corm and Harold Beazley too and bolstering the men's construction of a homosocial and egalitarian friendship that was independent of an instrumental agenda even as it advanced the cause of Corm's Ford empire. In other terms, the trio were thus federated into a triangular relationship, in which the homosocial bond of the two men depended on 'the structural context of triangular, heterosexual desire' and the 'male traffic in women'.[80] We are some distance here from other forms of cross-border trafficking discussed in this volume, but I argue that this understudied form of boundary work, too, was constitutive of the Middle East's wider mobility regime in the interwar period.

Unsurprisingly, given this triangular relationship and blurred interpersonal frontiers, there is a striking analogy between Corm's claim, with which we began this section, that Harold Beazley understood him, and Miriam's claim immediately above, that Corm understood her. 'I expect you do', as she put it, comfortable in her right to speculate on his feelings. Importantly, she claimed this understanding in the context of their shared desire to get away from work and 'indulge the real bent of [their] nature'. As I have argued elsewhere, the apparent frontier Miriam drew, between the breakneck pace and coldly alienating dynamics of capitalist commerce, and the domain of natural, peaceful, human sympathy and interpersonal understanding, was itself an effect of a Fordist mode of capitalism in which emotion and accumulation in fact combined.[81] Therefore, the sprawling regime of Fordist automobility

---

[80] Eve Kosofsky Sedgwick, *Between Men: English Literature and Male Homosocial Desire* (New York: Columbia University Press, 1985), pp. 2, 16. See also Toby L. Ditz, who argues that 'access to women defines masculine privilege; it is what makes men alike as men and secures, however incompletely, the male bond. Correlatively, disparities in the terms of that access are at the core of competing forms of masculinity and the differential claims to masculine privilege associated with them.' Toby L. Ditz, 'The New Men's History and the Peculiar Absence of Gendered Power: Some Remedies from Early American Gender History', *Gender & History*, Vol. 16, No. 1 (2004), pp. 10–11.

[81] Jackson, *Mandatory Development*.

that Corm, Beazley and others helped build across the territorial borders of the French and British Mandates rested on the crossing and blurring of the interpersonal borders between individuals, *and* on the carefully administered but finally fictitious dividing line separating the world of capitalist business from the world of human friendship and sympathy.[82] As the historian Deborah Cohen has argued of another late imperial context, the worlds of 'love and money' here combined such that they became inseparable, a combination paradoxically managed in part by the protagonists' insistence that the two worlds remained fundamentally demarcated from one another.[83] Or, as Corm consoled Beazley in November 1924:

> I understand you well about the [cold] Branch atmosphere at Trieste. Happily there is Her [Elle]! . . . and that must console you for everything, absolutely everything! So I hope you will give as little of yourself as possible to Society Life [in English in the original], and as much as possible to intimate life, to complete fusion, to total and solitary union with her![84]

To deploy the terms that have organised other arguments across this volume, we can think here of Corm and the Beazleys as 'borderlanders', criss-crossing the frontier between love and money, benefiting from the separate sovereignties and disconnected jurisdictions of these two worlds, even as those worlds constituted a single border zone.

[82] We need not presuppose these interpersonal borders as necessarily more local, or more suited to 'micro' analysis than territorial or regional borders, however. For a stimulating and critical discussion of the limits of 'scale' as an analytical concept in global microhistory, see Christian G. De Vito, 'History Without Scale: The Micro-Spatial Perspective', *Past & Present*, Vol. 242, Issue Supplement 14 (2019), p. 353. My thanks to the editors of this volume for drawing my attention to this work.

[83] Strikingly, Cohen, who focuses on hetero-patriarchal marriage in her work on Argentina, tends to hold these motives in tension where I argue for a fuller mix, even as the border between these worlds was maintained: 'the relative significance of ties of family or a love of the country *as opposed to* money-making and business opportunities?' Deborah Cohen, 'Love and Money in the Informal Empire: the British in Argentina, 1830–1930', *Past & Present*, Vol. 245, No. 1 (2019), p. 84 (my italics). See also Andrew Popp, *Entrepreneurial Families: Business, Marriage and Life in the Early Nineteenth Century* (London: Pickering and Chatto, 2012).

[84] Corm, Beirut, to H. Beazley, Trieste, 14 November 1924, CAB 1.

**Conclusion**

This chapter has examined the system of cross-border distribution of Ford vehicles and spare parts in the Eastern Mediterranean region, with a particular focus on the network of Ford branches Charles Corm built up in the 1920s. This commercial empire operated mainly within the territory of the French Mandate in Lebanon and Syria and it plainly benefited from Corm's privileged connections, as a member of the Mandate elite, with the French imperial authorities. But we have also seen that Corm's engagement for the US Ford against rival French manufacturers meant that his relationship to the Mandatory imperial state was ambivalent – recall the wrath of Charles Pavie at Aleppo. Moreover, Corm also developed branches in British Mandate Palestine and sought to extend his reach into Turkey, while he imported his vehicles via Ford's global and regional network, in which Trieste, Tophane and later Alexandria, but also London, New York City and the Detroit-Windsor Border Cities zone, were key nodes.

I argued in a first section that Corm's organisation practised a form of 'flatpack Fordism', in which it reassembled Ford's vehicles, helping devise Ford as a global phenomenon from below, in spite of the diffusionist impression the corporation itself aimed to conjure and that later scholarship has sometimes echoed. Even the fabled 'American-ness' of the vehicles, I argued, had to be renarrated and maintained locally. Simultaneously, Corm's organisation assembled a distinctive form of 'commercial sovereignty' across a rhizomic network of branches that together constituted a space and a regime of mobility that overlapped with, helped enforce and also sprawled beyond the space and mobility regime of the French Mandate itself. In this network, Beirut operated both as an important node and as a key border zone, where the state-framed political-economy of customs acted as a strategic site that Corm strove to police, in order to maintain his exclusive rights against the infiltration of rivals he relegated as frauds or smugglers. The northern border zone between the Syrian Mandate and Turkey also proved important to the construction of this network, not least as a focus for Corm's boastful, uncertain and probing correspondence with his regional managers at Ford, such as Harold Beazley.

In considering that correspondence the chapter pivoted to a second section, arguing that to understand the role of borders in the construction of regimes of mobility in the Middle East, we must take seriously the 'places' and landscapes of individual subjectivity, emotion and understanding, and consider the constitution, evolution and crossing of borders between individuals. Through an exploration of the triangular capitalist friendship between Charles Corm, Harold Beazley and Miriam Beazley, and of the 'moving stories' they told one another, I have aimed to explore a set of such interpersonal borderlands and to historicise the operation of capitalist rationalities as they combined with the play of emotion and sympathy. Paradoxically, this was achieved in part by examining the protagonists' own insistence on a hard frontier between the purportedly partitioned jurisdictions of capital on one side and of nature and humanity on the other.

By linking these different modes of analysis together and by bringing in non-state protagonists, such as low-ranking Ford managerial personnel, this chapter has contributed to this volume's goal of thinking cross-regionally in order to understand the emergence of the modern Middle East in the inter-war years, complicating conventional teleology and neat cartographies. Such an approach also offers food for thought to historians seeking ways to combine micro-histories with global history in ways that, without drifting into linearity or celebration, can convincingly operate diachronically as well as synchronically. As Jan de Vries has argued, micro-historical explorations of the life-worlds of individuals and transnational, comparative and entangled global histories have often tended to share a synchronic framing, offering a vivid snapshot of 'axial moments' but not an account of diachronic change.[85] Mobility regimes, as an object of study, while complex and evolving, are durable social-technical formations entangled in, but not co-extensive with, political forms such as empires and nations. Accordingly, whether considered through the triangular friendship discussed above, or through Corm's regional empire of Fords, or even in terms of modern capitalism as a global corporation (Ford itself) or as a still larger Fordist system of production, distribution and consumption that dominated much of the twentieth century, I suggest that mobility regimes offer a promising site for future global micro-histories that aim to tackle major, long-term transformations.

---

[85] De Vries, 'Playing with Scales', p. 31. For axial moments I draw on Mestyan, 'Domestic Sovereignty', p. 420.

# 5

# POLYSEMIC BORDERS: MELKITE AND ORTHODOX CLERICS AND LAYMEN IN THE EMIRATE OF TRANSJORDAN, 1920s–1940s

## *Norig Neveu*

In the Middle East the end of the First World War and the creation of the French and British Mandates coincided with the radical rupture of mobility regimes and the establishment of international borders.[1] The latter were constantly renegotiated during the Mandate period, as illustrated by the case of the Emirate of Transjordan, where the borders with the Mandate of Palestine were only defined in 1928 by the Transjordan Agreement (see Chapter Nine for further discussion).[2] In recent years, research has highlighted the importance of the Mandate period in reconfiguring socio-spatial structures in the region.[3] In this context, the study of pilgrim mobility has focused mainly

---

[1] Laura Robson, *States of Separation, Transfer, Partition, and the Making of the Modern Middle East* (Oakland, CA: University of California Press, 2017); T. G. Fraser, *The First World War and Its Aftermath: The Shaping of the Middle East* (London: Gingko Library, 2016).

[2] Abla Amawi, 'The Consolidation of the Merchant Class in Transjordan during the Second World War', in Eugene Rogan and Tariq Tell (eds), *Village, Steppe and State. The Social Origins of Modern Jordan* (London & New York: British Academic Press, 1994), pp. 162–87.

[3] Liat Kozma, Cyrus Schayegh and Avner Wishnitzer (eds), *A Global Middle East: Mobility, Materiality and Culture in the Modern Age, 1880-1940* (London: I. B. Tauris, 2014).

on how mobility influenced health standards[4] and reconfigured pilgrimage routes.[5] These studies have also stressed how these boundaries have influenced Mandate transnational religious policies and communal dynamics.[6] Religion played a central role in the political system imposed by the Mandate authorities[7]. In the case of the Emirate of Transjordan and Palestine, this resulted in the confessionalisation of the political field and the establishment of the 'religious minority' category for Christian communities.[8]

The imposition of new borders contravened other administrative realities, notably those of the Christian Churches in the Emirate of Transjordan. In Palestine and Transjordan, after the First World War, Christian institutions found their prerogatives spread over several countries under British Mandate. The Greek Orthodox Patriarchate of Jerusalem was responsible for the Churches of the Emirate of Transjordan and Palestine. The northern and southern parts of the Emirate of Transjordan depended on two different eparchies of the Melkite Church. Both the Melkite and Greek Orthodox churches were undergoing major changes. The Greek Orthodox Patriarchate was in the midst of a deep financial crisis, and was facing a conflict between the Patriarchate of Jerusalem and Arab lower clergy and laity. For its part, the Latin Church had to reconfigure its new missionary strategy by giving a privileged role to the Melkite Church. For both Churches, the transmission of religious knowledge was deeply rooted in a regional or even international space linking Transjordan with Cairo, Jerusalem, Beirut, Harissa and also Rome.

---

[4] Sylvia Chiffoleau, *Genèse de la santé publique internationale. De la peste d'Orient à l'OMS* (Beyrouth: Ifpo/ Rennes: PUR, 2012).

[5] Luc Chantre, 'Se rendre à La Mecque sous la Troisième République. Contrôle et organisation des déplacements des pèlerins du Maghreb et du Levant entre 1880 et 1939', *Cahiers de la Méditerranée, Migration et religion en France II*, Vol. 78 (2009), pp. 202–27.

[6] Toufoul Abou-Hodeib, 'Sanctity across the border: Pilgrimage routes and state control in Mandate Lebanon and Palestine', in Cyrus Schayegh and Andrew Arsan (eds), *The Routledge Handbook of the History of the Middle East Mandates* (New York: Routledge, 2015), pp. 383–94.

[7] Luizard Pierre-Jean (ed.), *Le choc colonial et l'islam. Les politiques religieuses des puissances coloniales en terres d'islam* (Paris: La Découverte, 2006).

[8] Géraldine Chatelard, *Briser la mosaïque. Lien social et identités collectives chez les chrétiens de Madaba, Jordanie (1870–1997)* (Paris: CNRS edition, 2004). On the notion of minority see Benjamin T. White, *The Emergence of Minorities in the Middle East: The Politics of Community in French Mandate Syria* (Edinburgh: Edinburgh University Press, 2011).

At the end of the nineteenth century, missions revived the dynamism of local religious institutions by establishing local clergy. However, the rights granted to local clergy to access the highest ecclesiastical offices depended on their church. Missions were commonly considered as support and relay for European powers.[9] The abolition of the Capitulations by the Treaty of Lausanne in 1923 limited the capacity of these powers to interfere politically. Nevertheless, missions remained a means of disseminating the language of the European powers and of supporting the establishment of these powers in the newly created states.[10]

Representatives of the British Mandate of Palestine, and then of Transjordan, had to respect the management and practices of the religious groups. The Christian nature of the Mandate power influenced the policies implemented in the administered countries. In Palestine, the involvement of local authorities in managing religious issues was limited.[11] This was partly due to the debates concerning the establishment of a Jewish 'national home'. The status of Christians was defined during Herbert Samuel's term, following the Millet system and the Tanzimat reforms. In contrast to the Emirate of Transjordan, no state religion was proclaimed. Communal institutions developed with relative independence, but the intervention of British representatives was significant. Christians represented between ten and fifteen per cent of the population of the Palestine and Transjordan Mandates, and were privileged political intermediaries of the British Mandate representatives. Paradoxically,

---

[9] Karène Summerer Sanchez, 'Action sanitaire et éducative en Palestine des missionnaires catholiques et anglicans (début du XXᵉ siècle)', in Chantal Verdeil (ed.), *Missions chrétiennes en terre d'islam, Moyen-Orient-Afrique du Nord (XVIIe-XXe siècles), Anthologie de textes missionnaires* (Turnhout: Brepols, 2013), pp. 232–82; Jérôme Bocquet, 'Le rôle des missions catholiques dans la fondation d'un nouveau réseau d'institutions éducatives au Moyen-Orient arabe', in Pierre-Jean Luizard (ed.), *Le choc colonial et l'islam. Les politiques religieuses des puissances coloniales en terres d'islam* (Paris: La Découverte, 2006), pp. 327–42.

[10] Helen Murre Van den Berg, Karène Sanchez & Tijmen C. Baarda, *Arabic and its Alternatives: Religious Minorities and their Languages in the Emerging Nation States of the Middle East (1920–1950)* (Leiden, Boston: Brill, 2020).

[11] Nicholas E. Roberts, *Rethinking the Status Quo: The British and Islam in Palestine, 1917–1929* (PhD thesis, New York University, 2010); Daphne Tsimhoni, 'The Status of the Arab Christians under the British Mandate in Palestine', *Middle Eastern Studies*, Vol. 20, No. 4, pp. 166–92.

they did not manage to obtain a leading political role. In Palestine, they did not acquire the same political weight as Muslims and Jews.[12] In both countries, the Christians retained a form of autonomy in their communal space, particularly within the public and political spheres. [13]

This article puts in perspective the (re)development of the Melkite and Greek Orthodox churches in the Emirate of Transjordan during the Mandate period. It addresses the tension between the territorialisation process within national borders and the structural role of transnational networks within the emergence of a political and communal space. The notion of territorialisation is used to describe the establishment of communal spaces, physical or symbolic, through different modes of territorial appropriation at different levels[14]. The territorialisation process will be approached by discussing the concept of transpatialisation[15], considering how the emergence of a national territory and its new capital, Amman, impacted associative, communal and political dynamics. By using a network analysis approach, this article details the plural redefinition of the modes of belonging resulting from constrained mobility regimes and the emergence of national contexts.

The Emirate of Transjordan is considered as a key case study to cross-examine the influence of borders on the reorganisation of regional solidarity networks[16] and to redefine confessional and/or political modes of belonging within young Middle Eastern states.[17] Until the First World War exchanges between Palestine and Transjordan structured the religious, economic and political life of both territories, which did not depend on the same administrative

---

[12] Noah Haiduc-Dale, *Arab Christians in British Mandate Palestine: Communalism and Nationalism, 1917–1948* (Edinburgh: Edinburgh University Press, 2015).

[13] Sasha R. Goldstein-Sabbah and Heleen L. Murre-Van den Berg, *Modernity, Minority, and the Public Sphere: Jews and Christians in the Middle East* (Leiden: Brill, 2016).

[14] Sossie Andézian, 'Introduction; Procès de fondation', *Archives de sciences sociales des religions*, Vol. 151 (September–October 2010), pp. 9–23.

[15] Cyrus Schayegh, *The Middle East and the Making of the Modern World* (Cambridge and London: Harvard University Press, 2017).

[16] Cyrus Schayegh, 'The Many Worlds of Abud Yasin, or: What Narcotics Trafficking in the Interwar Middle East Can Tell Us about Territorialization', *American Historical Review*, Vol. 116, No. 2 (2011), pp. 273–306.

[17] Lauren Banko, 'Refugees, Displaced migrants, and Territorialization in interwar Palestine', *Mashriq & Mahjar*, Vol. 5, No. 2 (2018).

districts.[18] The introduction of borders and passports disrupted this social organisation. For the British Mandate, the constitution of the Emirate of Transjordan had a highly political vocation within their regional competition with the French power. As a result, the country is often seen as a Mandate created from nothing. In Transjordan, in the early 1920s, the representatives of the local churches and laity found themselves separated from the central places of religious and political power (Rome, Jerusalem, etc.) and dependent on constrained mobility regimes. This article questions the establishment of a Transjordanian territoriality as orientated towards a regional space and at the junction of cross-border traffic.[19] Using a bottom-up approach, it also questions the effectiveness of the normative redefinition of modes of belonging during the Mandate period. To do so, this article focuses on the solidarity networks mobilised by Greek Orthodox and Melkite clergy and laypeople at the regional level to establish their churches in Transjordan and to influence national and transnational religious or political debates. Their strategies reflect their perception and use of effective, symbolic and communal borders.

This article is based on interviews conducted in Jordan and Palestine between 2015 and 2019 with members of Greek Orthodox associations and clerics, and also archival documents (Melkite Church, Congregation for the Oriental Churches and Greek Orthodox associations) to determine the polysemic perceptions of borders – may they be administrative, communal or political. The study is also based on the consultation of archives of the British Mandate and the local press, including *Falestin*. Questioning the perception of borders reveals the power dynamics of social groups that were fundamentally rooted in transnational dynamics.

## New Borders and the Establishment of National Churches

In the aftermath of the First World War Middle Eastern churches had to establish new strategies or administrative divisions broadly modelled on the

---

[18] Gideon Biger, *The Boundaries of Modern Palestine, 1840–1947* (London and New York: Routledge Curzon, 2004).

[19] Lauren Banko, 'Claiming Identities in Palestine: Migration and Nationality under the Mandate', *Journal of Palestine Studies*, Vol. 46, No. 2 (Winter 2017), pp. 26–43; Ellis Matthew, 'Over the Borderline? Rethinking Territoriality and the Margins of Empire and Nation in the Modern Middle East', *History Compass*, Vol. 13, No. 8 (2015), pp. 423–34.

borders of the new states. This period was characterised by the consolidation of centralising dynamics, which started at the end of the nineteenth century, and also by the redefinition of missionary strategies. In the 1920s debates emerged on the territorialisation of local churches within national borders and also within urban spaces, such as in Amman, the newly established capital of the Emirate of Transjordan.[20]

### The Melkite study case: the establishment of a national church

From the end of the nineteenth century the establishment of Catholic and Protestant missions revived the dynamism of local religious institutions. The First World War marked a turning point in these missionary policies, particularly for the Latin Church. After the war, and the forced departure of many missionaries from the Middle East[21], the policies of the newly created Congregation for Oriental Churches[22] called into question the former policies of 'Latinisation'. They favoured the deployment of the Melkite Church – perceived as a 'bridge' church between the Latin and Greek Orthodox Churches – according to the developments in papal perspectives.[23] In 1933, a report reviewed the development of the Melkite missions in Transjordan for the Congregation for the Oriental Churches:

> But soon the Melkites arrived in the Holy Land, taking advantage of the freedom that the Latin Patriarchate had fought hard to achieve. The Latin Patriarchate, far from hindering them in any way, helped them to settle in and to rise to the task.[24]

---

[20] Eugene Rogan, 'The Making of a Capital: Amman 1918–1928'. in J. Hannoyer & S. Shami, *Amman: Ville Et Societé* (Beirut: CERMOC, 1996), pp. 89–107.

[21] Roberto Mazza, 'Churches at War: The Impact of the First World War on the Christian Institution of Jerusalem, 1914–1920', *Middle Eastern Studies*, Vol. 45, No. 2 (2009), pp. 207–27.

[22] Tarek Mitri, 'L'uniatisme et le Patriarcat d'Antioche. Note sur l'histoire et la situation actuelle', in Comité Mixte catholique-orthodoxe en France (ed.), *Catholique et orthodoxes. Les enjeux de l'uniatisme. Dans le sillage de Balamand* (Paris: Cerf, Bayard, Fleurus-Mame, 2004), pp. 135–46.

[23] Étienne Fouilloux, *Les catholiques et l'unité chrétienne du XIXᵉ au XXᵉ siècle, itinéraires européens d'expression française* (Paris: Le Centurion, 1982).

[24] Archives of the Archeparchy of Petra and Philadelphia (AAPP), Amman, folder 'Eparchie jordanienne', Statistiques des missions Grecques-catholiques, extrait des rapports annuels envoyés à la Délégation et à la S.C.O. (rep. to S.C. – 15 June 1933. Nº 925/ Rep. to S.C.O. – 11 May 1934 nº 315, Rep to S.C.O. – 6 May N. 1079 /T).

This missionary strategy aimed to 'return' the Greek Orthodox Church to the Catholic Church and considered that adopting the Eastern rite would ease this movement. The Melkite clergy was largely composed of Arab priests, the majority of whom had been trained at the Seminary of St Anne in Jerusalem. This reflects the increased Arabisation of the clergy taken up in the Arab nationalist rhetoric and a central claim of the Greek Orthodox laity in their opposition to the Greek Orthodox Patriarchate of Jerusalem. Some members of the Latin clergy called for Melkite missions to be opened, for example in al-Salṭ in 1906, to welcome Greek Orthodox families in conflict with the Patriarchate of Jerusalem.[25] The Melkite clergy, and in particular the Archbishop of Galilee, Georges Hajjar, who was deeply involved in the development of the Melkite Church in Palestine and Transjordan during the Mandate period, wrote to Monsignor Isaia Papadoupolos, Archbishop Assessor of the Congregation for the Oriental Churches as follows:

> I am happy to report that the movement towards union is continuing among dissidents in Palestine and especially in Transjordan, where my last visit made a deep impression and where many prejudices have fallen. Many villages are sending us petitions and delegations are asking for admission to the Catholic Church.[26]

From the 1920s onwards, the number of Melkite parishes gradually increased throughout Transjordan, as did the number of schools. Until the 1930s, the northern region of the Emirate depended on the Archdioceses of Galilee and Acre, while the south and east were under the authority of the Melkite Patriarch of Antioch. The missions developed asymmetrically over Transjordan according to the hierarchy they depended on. Missions first developed actively in the north before spreading to the south. Soon, this administrative division was seen as slowing down the expansion of missionary activity. Several observers called for an archeparchy to be created with borders matching those of the state.

---

[25] Ibid.

[26] Archives of the Congregation for the Oriental Churches (ACOC), 17967/1926 Caiffa 1/01/1926, Letter of Georges Hajjar, archbishop of Galilee, A Mons Isaia Papadoupolos. Arch, assessor of the ACOC, pp. 1, 2.

In 1950 Pierre K. Medawar, auxiliary to the Patriarch of Antioch and all the eastern region, Alexandria and Jerusalem, mentioned emerging claims concerning the territorialisation of the Melkite Church: 'The idea of restoring a Melkite Eparchy in Transjordan took shape following the Apostolic Visits made in this country either by Mgr. Couturier or by Mgr. Robinson'.[27] Father Paschal Robinson, an Irish Franciscan, was sent on the request of the Congregation for the Oriental Churches to assess the situation of the Melkite missions in Transjordan. The Congregation for the Oriental Churches was one of the first institutions to demand such administrative redistricting. They reasoned that this territory was being neglected because the hierarchical centres were far from Transjordan, resulting in few visits from the Bishop of St John of Acre and the Patriarch.[28] In 1927, Cardinal Michele Lega attributed the difficult development of the missions to the administrative situation of the Melkite Church. He advocated the need to establish a resident authority in Transjordan based in al-Salṭ or Amman. Therefore, the boundaries of a new diocese or eparchy in Transjordan needed to be defined. This institution would have specific funding to finance missions (e.g. schools, orphanages) and guarantee independence from the Franciscan Custody of the Holy Land.[29]

In the 1920s the question of the Melkite Church having administrative autonomy in Transjordan was raised several times. The Congregation for Oriental Churches first postponed this action to the end of the 1930s because the missions lacked proper funding.[30] Discussions about the territorial inscription of the Melkite Church also questioned the ecclesiastical prerogatives over this territory. The Melkite religious authorities perceived this territorialisation as an attempt of the Congregation of the Oriental Churches

---

[27] AAPP, Letter of Pierre K. Medawar to Eugène Tisserant, Damascus, 18 May 1950 /31.

[28] ACOC, Prop, 441, Palestina, Affari Gen, Religiose in Palestina, Ponenze, 1927, (2) Orientali. No. 2, Prot No. 47, p. 127.

[29] Ibid.

[30] Paolo Maggiolini, 'The Archdiocese of Petra and Philadelphia and the Hashemite Emirate of Transjordan. Modern history and ecclesial identity', *Journal of Eastern Christian Studies*, Vol. 65, Nos. 3–4 (2013), pp. 201–29; Norig Neveu, 'Between uniatism and Arabism: missionary policies and diplomatic interest of the Melkites in Jordan during the Interwar period', *Social Sciences and Mission*, Vol. 32, Nos. 3–4 (2019), pp. 361–92.

to take control over territories that had previously been under their jurisdiction. On 8 June 1926 Patriarch Cyril IX sent the following comments to the Congregation for Oriental Churches:

> It would therefore be in our project to appoint a new patriarchal vicar bishop, with the special task of administering those of Transjordan together with the patriarchal missions of Palestine. Most of the year, he would reside in Transjordan, visiting the various localities, inspecting the missions, and confirming new converts. In this way he would prepare Transjordan to become a diocese with a residential bishop.[31]

Beyond the territorialisation of the church within national borders, the prerogatives and status of the authority on which this church would depend was a major issue: should it be an eparchy or a vicariate with an autonomous administration? The Melkite authorities, fearing that the Holy See would retain too tight a control on the Church of Transjordan opposed the establishment of the vicariate. They argued that the administrative structure was not specific to the Melkite Church.[32] In 1950 Pierre K. Medawar mentioned these debates in a letter to Cardinal Tisserant:

> According to my information, the Patriarchate never opposed the creation of the Eparchy. But he did object to this Eparchy being a simple 'Apostolic Vicariate' directly under the Roman Holy See and having with the Patriarchate only the simple link of the episcopal consideration of the Apostolic Vicar. Which Patriarch, which bishop, which priest, which even simple believer would have accepted this 'slap in the face' that was to be given to our community [. . .]. But as soon as it was understood that the new Eparchy would be equal to all the other Melkite Eparchies and that the Roman Holy See, in

---

[31] ACOC, Prop, 441, Palestina, Affari Generali, Religiose in Palestina, Mouvement vers l'union. Son étendue, Num V, Lettera del Patriarca Cirilo IX sulla Transgiordania, Rome, 8 June 1926.

[32] Paolo Maggiolini, 'The Influence of Latin-Melkite Relations in the Land of Transjordan, From the Rebirth of the Latin Patriarchate to the Foundation of the Archdiocese of Petra and Philadelphia (1866–1932)', in Anthony O'Mahony (ed.), *Christianity in the Middle East: Modern History and Contemporary Situations* (Essex: Living Stones Yearbook, 2012), pp. 165–99.

its charity and understanding of its needs, would provide it with the necessary funds for its existence, the Patriarchate made no opposition to its creation, he discussed in a clever and enthusiastic way with the Holy See on the choice of the candidate to be nominated for the first time, and, [. . .] he restored the hierarchy in the country by uniting the Archeparchy of Petra (now in ruins) with the Bishopric of Philadelphia or Amman.[33]

As a result of these debates the Greek-Catholic Archeparchy of Petra, Philadelphia and the whole of Transjordan was established with administrative borders corresponding to the boundaries of the state in 1932. Father Paul Salman, trained at St Anne of Jerusalem and former priest of al-Salṭ and Huṣn, was appointed archbishop on 5 June 1932. Thus, between the 1920s and 1930s, the Melkite Church asserted itself as a National Church. This territorialisation of the Church began with developing missions with their churches, schools and presbyteries, a movement that grew after 1932.

*The Greek Orthodox laity: claims for the territorialisation of the Church*

For the Greek Orthodox Church, the question of territorial affiliations arose differently. After the First World War the Patriarchate of Jerusalem remained in charge of the Greek Orthodox community of the Mandates of Transjordan and Palestine. At this time, the Patriarchate was facing a major financial crisis.[34] This led the High Commissioner of the British Mandate to appoint the Bertram-Young Commission of Inquiry to evaluate the economic situation of the Patriarchate.[35] As early as 1919, Athens offered donations as the Greek state was trying to emerge as the new privileged interlocutor of the Patriarchate of Jerusalem. The Autocephalous Church of Greece was to replace the Ecumenical Patriarchate of Constantinople, which had faced difficulties spreading its influence from Kemalist Turkey.[36] The Greek state also

---

[33] AAPP, Letter of Pierre K. Medawar to Eugène Tisserant, Damascus, 18 May 1950/31.

[34] Konstantinos Papastathis, 'Church Finances in the Colonial Age: The Orthodox Patriarchate of Jerusalem under British Control, 1921–1925', *Middle Eastern Studies*, Vol. 49, No. 5 (2013), pp. 712–31.

[35] Bertram and Luke, 1921.

[36] Daphne Tsimhoni, 'The Arab Christian and the Palestinian Arab National Movement During the Formative Stage', in Gabriel Ben-Dor (ed.), *The Palestinians and the Middle East Conflict* (Ramat Gan: Turteldove Publishing, 1978), pp. 73–98.

took advantage of the decrease in missionary activities of the Russian imperial society. After the Bolshevik revolution, the Russian imperial society closed most of its schools and missions in Palestine and Transjordan.[37] The British authorities aimed to limit foreign influence and encourage the Patriarchate of Jerusalem to refuse the financial aid proposed by the Greek state and accept the support of American Protestant churches. The latter's influence was considered to be more compatible with British political interests.[38]

The Mandate authorities also based their decision on the conflict that broke out at the end of the nineteenth century between the higher Greek Orthodox clergy, notably the Brotherhood of the Holy Sepulcher and the lower Arab clergy and laity. The latter demanded an Arabisation of the ecclesiastical hierarchy. Their claim also concerned the internal organisation of the Church and in particular the development of communal institutions. In 1875, with the Ottoman Fundamental law, the Patriarchate of Jerusalem took control of the Church's properties. After 1908 and the Ottoman constitution, the Greek Orthodox laity of Palestine and then Transjordan played a central role in the organisation of the Church's life and the community's demands. The laypeople became increasingly important within the movement, especially Palestinian intellectuals such as Ya'qūb Farraj, Khalīl al-Sakākīnī[39], Yūsuf and 'Isā al-'Isā[40]. Since the beginning of the twentieth century they had all been closely involved in the Arab nationalist movement and the struggle against Zionism. For instance, 'Isā al-'Isā defined Orthodox Christianity as indigenous and rooted in the region since the Byzantine period, in opposition to Catholicism.[41]

---

[37] Derek Hopwood, *The Russian Presence in Syria and Palestine 1843–1914. Church and Politics in the Near East* (New York: Oxford University Press, 1969); Elena Astafieva, 'La Russie en Terre Sainte: le cas de la Société Impériale Orthodoxe de Palestine (1882–1917)', *Cristianesimo nella storia*, Vol. 1 (2003), pp. 41–68; Raouf Abujaber, *Arab Christianity and Jerusalem* (London: Gilgamesh, 2012).

[38] Chatelard, 2004.

[39] Emanuel Beška E, 'Khalil al-Sakakini and Zionism before WWI', *Jerusalem Quarterly*, Vols. 63–64 (2015), pp. 40–52; Nadim Bawalsa, 'Sakakini Defrocked', *Jerusalem Quarterly*, Vol. 42 (2010), pp. 5–25.

[40] Noha Tadros Khalaf, *Les Mémoires de 'Issa al-'Issa. Journaliste et intellectuel palestinien (1878–1950)* (Paris: Karthala, 2009).

[41] Salim Tamari, 'Issa al Issa's Unorthodoxy: Banned in Jerusalem, Permitted in Jaffa', *Jerusalem Quarterly*, Vol. 59 (2014), p. 18.

The period of the British Mandate opened up new political perspectives for the laity and lower clergy. An Orthodox fraternity (*jama'iyyat al-ikhā al-urthūduksiyya*) in charge of local matters was established with local committees in Palestine and Transjordan parishes. In July 1923 the first Arab Orthodox congress was organised in Haifa. Discussions addressed the territorial organisation of the church and the community. The congress stipulated the need to form community councils in each parish to support local matters. In addition, an executive committee of the congress was established. It was composed of ten members, including seven Palestinians and three Transjordanians; this committee confirmed the structure of the movement, beyond the newly established borders.[42] The congress resolutions also indicated the need to appoint an Arab metropolitan for Transjordan, echoing the territorialisation process described earlier in the case of the Melkite Church.

From 1926 onwards, the executive committee of the congress systematically opposed the representatives of the Greek Orthodox Patriarchate of Jerusalem. British representatives and Emir Abdullah tried to serve as intermediaries to solve the conflict. Thus, the report of the Bertram-Young Commission proposed that members of the Brotherhood of the Holy Sepulcher could adopt Palestinian nationality. It also indicated that Greek Orthodox lay associations should be in charge of managing educational institutions.[43]

Since these recommendations were not taken into account by the Patriarchate, they were reiterated at the second Orthodox congress held in 1931 in Jaffa. In addition to Palestinian members, eight representatives from Transjordanian committees were sent. The congress was held just after the death of Patriarch Damanios; thus, members could question how the Patriarch was elected and call for the recommendations of the Beltram-Young Commission to be applied.[44]

In the same year, a delegation was sent by the executive committee of the Greek Orthodox congress to present the memorandum adopted during its last session to the Palestinian government and Emir Abdullah in Amman.

---

[42] Sahadeh Khoury and Nicola Khoury, *A Survey of the History of the Orthodox Church of Jerusalem* (Amman: Dar al-Shorouk, 2002), pp. 329–31
[43] Chatelard, 2004.
[44] Robson, 2011.

The delegation reported being warmly welcomed by the Emir, who committed to relaying the demands of the congress to the Patriarchate of Jerusalem.

The issues were addressed in *Falestin* a few years later in 1935:

> His Royal Highness Prince Abdullah stated to the President of the Nahda Orthodox Association in Amman that he was highly preoccupied by bringing the diminished rights of the Arab Orthodox people to Greek priests. And if these priests continue to be intransigent, he is committed to side with the people to the point where he can elect an Arab patriarch who lives temporarily in Amman, pending the return of the right to his people.[45]

The Emir's statement did not specify the nationality of the Patriarch to be appointed. However, a few years after the Melkite Archeparchy was created, he insisted on the need for the territorialisation of the church to address the rights of the laypeople. These demands remained unsuccessful but they reveal the entangled modes of belonging of the Greek Orthodox laity. From the 1920s onwards their space of demands and modes of action were fundamentally transnational. They concerned mainly the Arabisation of the clergy and the nationalisation of the Patriarchs and higher hierarchy. They also advocated the creation of a communal space at the local level, through opening schools, building churches and the cultural role of associations.

Beyond these territorial issues, the question of political dependence regarding the Patriarchate was central for the Greek Orthodox laity. The Greek influence was contested. Their political space relied heavily on the support of British Mandate officials and local governments. Regarding power dynamics during the interwar period, a new space was created around members of the Transjordanian and Palestinian intelligentsia who established powerful transnational networks especially through cultural diplomacy.

Putting the Melkite and Greek Orthodox case studies into perspective reveals that the different actors had a common concern for the territorialisation of the churches. These demands questioned the ecclesiastical institutions

---

[45] 'al-Amir 'Abd Allah wa al-qadiyya al-urthūduksiyya', *Falestin*, 13 July 1935, No. 112–2996, p. 5.

in an asymmetrical way. The effectiveness of the church's implantation or its lack of activity served as an argument to justify these projects rooted in Arab nationalist rhetoric but also within missionary and political competitions. This territorial debate illustrated the existing tensions between different religious authorities and institutions. Finally, it confirmed the competitive topography between churches, which increased within national borders.

**Transnational Communities and Local Modes of Belonging**

In the Emirate of Transjordan and Palestine during the interwar period Christian and Muslim religious representatives gathered within various types of societies and associations. These dynamics were encouraged by religious policies as part of the colonial system in the Mandate era. In addition, the Hashemite state developed a legislative body to regulate religious institutions, including the official status of churches. The 1928 organic law guaranteed each church the right to form a community. The 1938 law on the 'formation of the councils of non-Muslim religious communities' specified that each religious community was free to create its internal organisation. It also stipulated the need for each church to have statutes and to set up an executive committee.[46] In this context, the territorialisation within the national or even urban space, in the case of Amman, was based on solidarity networks between clerics or laypeople at a regional scale.

*The Melkite Church: territorialisation through a transnational network*

The creation of the Archeparchy of Petra and Philadelphia generated a new phase of the Melkite Church becoming established in the Emirate of Transjordan. In 1932 nineteen Greek Melkite Catholic schools were opened in Transjordan. They were homogeneously distributed throughout the national territory, but they constantly lacked religious staff. On 8 June 1938 Paul Salman, the newly appointed Archbishop, stated in a letter to the Secretary of the Congregation for Oriental Churches:

> I need three good priests for the three missions to Kerak, Maïn and Zarka. The priest of Kerak is too old and cannot do the right thing. [. . .] Maïn currently has a good priest, but he is sick. [. . .] But with all our missions, we

[46] Chatelard, 2004.

cannot put two or three priests in the same locality and distribute them on Sundays and for feasts in neighbouring parishes as the villages are very far from each other[47].

Several transnational networks were mobilised to ensure the nationalisation of the Church in Transjordan. Religious authorities in Cairo played a fundamental role in fundraising. In a letter to Salman dated 16 June 1932, Balerio Valeri, Apostolic Delegate in Cairo wrote:

> Enclosed you will find a cheque from the 'Banco di Roma', with the sum of fifty thousand Italian pounds, which extraordinarily, the Sacred Congregation has decided to dedicate this year to the needs of the mission of Transjordan.[48]

Despite the creation of the archeparchy, the Melkite and Latin authorities abroad remained a major logistical and financial support until the 1940s. They relied on the committee of missions for Transjordan, founded by laypeople in the 1920s under the authority of A. Delpuch. Mary Khoury, a member of the Melkite bourgeoisie in Cairo, played a central role in this committee. Her commitment was due to a visit she had made to Palestine. In Nazareth, Christian people invited her to develop the Melkite Church in the region.[49] In the 1920s the committee was created to support the development of missions in the north of the Emirate of Transjordan which depended on the Bishop of Acre. However, this committee remained a support after the archeparchy was created, as revealed by several letters exchanged between Mary Khoury and Paul Salman. Salman contacted her several times to ask for financial support for developing certain parishes, give her news of the parishes and later to mention the economic difficulties encountered by the archeparchy because of the Second World War. These letters reveal close ties between these two actors.[50] Until the 1940s Salman relied on diverse solidarity networks based in Egypt; for example, the Daughters of Charity sent a

---

[47] ACOC, Melchita Transgiordania, 292/38, L'ordine basil Savotoriano in transjiordanie, Registre III. No. 291/T. P. Salman à Seg S. C. p E.O

[48] AAPP, 2702/D, Cairo, Zamalik,

[49] AAPP, Num V. Lettera del Comitato del Cairo 'pro Transgiordania', Cairo, 7 May 1925.

[50] AAPP, Letter of Paul Salman to Mary Khalil, Amman – Transjordan, 11 March 1940.

cheque to pay for three masses in 1940[51] and the chapel of the mission of Shatana was built with the financial support of a rich family from Alexandria.[52] Salman also counted on international networks, such as the churches in al-Karak and al-Smakiyya, which were founded with the support of the Archbishop of Milwaukee in the United States.[53]

To ensure missionary activity, Salman relied on more traditional networks such as the Œuvre d'Orient and the French Consulate in Palestine and Transjordan.[54] Although the Church began to recruit national clergy and Transjordanian teachers from the 1930s onwards, tensions still arose between regular and secular clergy, and Salman constantly sought the support of members of Catholic congregations from Egypt, Palestine and Lebanon to send priests to Transjordan. He first relied on the Seminary of St Anne of Jerusalem, opened by the White Fathers in 1882 to train local Melkite clergy. In Lebanon, he could count on the Paulist and Jesuit Fathers. Father Geoffroy de Bonneville was a particularly important interlocutor. He was at the head of the mission in Hauran and Djebel Druze and in charge of inspecting the Melkite schools in Transjordan, including the inter-ritual schools.[55] Several correspondences recorded in the Melkite archives in Amman show his facilitating role with the Jesuits in Cairo, in particular Father Ayout, founder of the Association of the Schools of Upper Egypt and also with the Syrian Seminary in Jerusalem. On 5 August 1930 Anselm Chibas Lassalle, Apostolic Commissioner, wrote to Father Salman:

> I have received your letter of the 23rd of July, in which you ask for my help in procuring three Melkite priests who are needed in your Eparchy following the unification of the Catholic schools that the Apostolic See has just established in Transjordan. Several days ago, in Lebanon, Father G. de Bonneville had already addressed to me the same request. I did not leave him much hope [. . .].

[51] AAPP, Letter of Paul Salman, 19 April 1940, Register IV, N. 223/T.

[52] AAPP, Letter of Paul Salman to Gabriel Boulad, Amman – Transjordan, 3 March 1940.

[53] AAPP, Letter of Paul Salman to Moses E. Kiley, Amman – Transjordan, 11 March 1940.

[54] Norig Neveu, 'Orthodox clubs and associations: Cultural, educational and religious networks between Palestine and Jordan, 1925–1970', in Karène Sanchez Summerer and Sary Zananiri, *European Cultural Diplomacy and Arab Christians in Palestine (1918–1948): Between Contention and Connection* (London: Palgrave Macmillan, 2021).

[55] Henri Jalabert, *Jésuites au Proche-Orient* (Beirut: Dar el-Machreq, 1987), p. 346.

But your needs are urgent, the cases are exceptional, and it is a matter of ensuring a happy start to the new reorganisation. This is why I have already written to the Superiors General of the Alepos and the Chouerites to decide, if possible, to place at your disposal Father Constantin Kallal for Maïn, and Laurent Karam for Fouhais. I still have to contact the Superior General of the Salvadorians who unfortunately has not yet returned from his trip to Europe.[56]

This quote shows the interweaving networks around which communal life and dynamics were structured. At the intersections of this network stood the representatives of the Melkite Church, through their training itineraries, their anchoring to Transjordanian sociability practices and their incarnation of the missionary and reform policies of the Congregation for the Oriental Churches. The complexity and the persistence of these territorial modes of belonging rooted the National Church within transnational solidarity networks and trans-border symbolic, cultural and intellectual spaces. Thus, the National Church was dependent on the policies of the Congregation for the Oriental Churches. The latter promoted both its territorialisation and the externalisation of its rights.

### Greek Orthodox laity: transnational association and communal space

The interwar period marked the advent of a new model of cross-border networks, particularly through the laity becoming involved with communal matters. Family structures and kinship were fundamental in the organisation of local and regional solidarity networks until the 1940s.[57] However, from the first half of the twentieth century, clerics and laypeople carried out their actions and activities through different bodies, including associations and charities.

At this time, religious policies were fundamental in the colonial system.[58] For Palestine, British interventionism was expressed through the establishment of the Supreme Muslim Council. This institution was intended to

---

[56] AAPP, Letter of P. Anselm Chibas Lassalle, Commis Apos to Paul Salman, Jerusalem, Syrian seminary, 5 August 1938.

[57] Olivier Bouquet, 'Famille, familles, grandes familles: une introduction', *Cahiers de la Méditerranée*, Vol. 82 (2011), pp. 189–2011; Beshara Doumani (ed.), *Family History in the Middle East: Household, Property and Gender* (Albany: State University of New York Press, 2003).

[58] See for instance Luizard, 2006.

provide a framework for Muslim religious expression, by confessionalising political intervention. However, it offered some ulemas the possibility to organise against British policies, notably during the 1936–39 revolt.[59] Notables, intellectuals, important families and tribes were linked through religious practices and statuses, locally enrooted due to regional and international interactions. However, limited research has been conducted to analyse the role of the laity within the religious field and their interactions with the ecclesiastical authorities. These relationships remain central to understanding the modes of belonging of these communities. They can highlight the role of the laity in structuring a local, national and transnational communal space during the twentieth century. They also raise the question of the role of borders in reconfiguring the solidarity networks between these actors.

During the interwar period the important Orthodox families of the Mandate of Palestine and Transjordan were closely linked because of economic, matrimonial, cultural and political ties. They developed local associative networks that aimed to develop the Greek Orthodox communal space and spread their political claims, notably through cultural action. Representatives of the British Mandate encouraged the establishment of these faith-based associations. In 1923 the Association of the Arab Orthodox Nahda was one of the first associations to be created in the Emirate of Transjordan. It was officially recognised by the government in 1929.[60] The first founders of these associations came from the Greek Orthodox families of notables, in particular from al-Salṭ and al-Karak, who had settled in Amman when the city had been proclaimed as the capital of the Emirate. The representatives of the associations wished to develop their activities in the country; therefore, they secured the support of the representatives of the government of Transjordan through cultural activities.

Within a regional intellectual space, the first association in Amman emerged from the dynamics of the Greek Orthodox congresses. A significant

---

[59] Uri. M. Kupferschmidt, *The Supreme Muslim Council: Islam under the British Mandate for Palestine* (Leiden/ New York/København: E.J. Brill, 1987); N. E. Roberts, *Islam under the Palestine Mandate. Colonialism and the Supreme Muslim Council* (London: I. B. Tauris, 2017).

[60] Laura Robson, 'Communalism and Nationalism in the Mandate: The Greek Orthodox Controversy and the National Movement', *Journal of Palestine Studies*, Vol. 41, No. 1 (2011), pp. 6–23.

literary and journalistic production also appeared and cultural societies were created which circulated ideas between Palestine and Transjordan. The name of the Transjordanian association echoes the pamphlet of Khalīl al-Sakākīnī entitled *al-Nahda al-urthūdukisiyya fī Filasṭīn* (Orthodox Renaissance in Palestine), published in 1913. For al-Sakākīnī, community identification and nationalism were not compatible. On the contrary, other Palestinian intellectuals, such as Yaʿqūb Farrāj, ʿIsā al-ʿIsā and Emil al-Ghurī refuted this claim, believing that the junction of community identification and nationalism was a way of enabling the Orthodox movement to intervene in the Palestinian political field.[61] The representatives of the Transjordanian association tended to agree with this second perspective.

One of the association's first objectives was to build a church for the Greek Orthodox community in Amman. Until the 1940s this community in Amman found itself in a paradoxical situation: although it was the largest Christian community in the country it had no church in the capital. Amman was a missionary front from the 1920s, and the Latin and Melkite communities had quickly built their places of worship during that period. The association also wanted to open a Greek Orthodox school in the capital. Attempts to build a church in Amman had begun when the association was created. They started with acquiring a plot of land and appointing a leader for the building works. The association relied on fundraising, in particular from Palestinian committees and parishes.[62] The founders of the association had other functions: to ensure the recommendations of the Bertram-Young report were applied, in connection with the Palestinian executive committee and also, at the political level, in the fight against Zionism. Several conferences were organised in Amman on this issue. In 1929, ʿAwda al-Qusūs, then president of the association, called for a boycott of trade with Zionist merchants, in response to the massacres that took place in Palestine in 1929.[63]

[61] Laura Robson, *Colonialism and Christianity in Palestine* (Austin: University of Texas Press, 2011).

[62] Raouf S. Abujaber, *Al-Nahda al-urthūdukisiyya fī ʿarjaʾ al-Batriarkiyya al-Maqdissiyya, 1865–2015*, Vols. 1–2 (Amman: National Press, 2016), p. 158.

[63] Ibid., pp. 150–51.

Other 'Arab Orthodox' associations developed in the country, following similar goals. In 1931, the newspaper *Falestin* mentioned:

> Arab Orthodox Reform Society in al-Salṭ
> Orthodox notables and representatives met in the presence of their spiritual leaders, and after deliberation they decided to form an association to demand the rights of the community, upgrade its affairs, and preserve its endowments.[64]

A few years previously, members of this association sort to preserve and develop the Greek Orthodox school in al-Salṭ. One of the characteristics of the Greek Orthodox laity was its ability to establish a communal space in cities, due to their financial independence from the Greek Orthodox Patriarchate of Jerusalem. The Greek Orthodox laity had economic networks, especially commercial networks, whose income could be mobilised to help the national community, but also in solidarity with community members within this Transjordanian-Palestinian associative space. This independence was also apparent with Arab priests, members of the lower clergy. In 1932, Arab priests organised a conference in Ramallah to demand a better wage and question the status inequalities within the church. The Orthodox executive committee replied to them in the newspaper *Falestin*:

> However, with the intensity of our sympathy for the demands of those calling for the convening of this conference, and the severity of our pain regarding the general situation of the Orthodox community in Palestine and Transjordan due to the intransigence, mismanagement, and national intolerance of the Brotherhood, we do not see any justification for holding this conference today.
>
> First: Because not a single priest attended the General Orthodox Conference that was held in Jaffa in November of last year to consider the general Orthodox issue and improve the status of priests as a whole.
>
> Second: Because the decision to close some Orthodox schools did not find a word of protest from these priests [. . .]
>
> Before deciding to call a conference, it was the duty of the organisers to consult the Orthodox Executive Committee, because this committee should

---

[64] *Falestin*, 25 September 1931, No. 157, p. 2.

consider every aspect of the community's affairs, and the priests' issue is nothing but one of the aspects of the Orthodox issue that requires reform.[65]

Thus, the executive committee claimed hegemony over the revendications of the Greek Orthodox Arab community. Through the interweaving of economic and political networks, and also through extensive cultural diplomacy, its members aimed to acquire this role and status. During the interwar period, they claimed multiple modes of belonging: Arab nationalism, Greek or Arab Orthodox community membership, partisan to Palestinian and Transjordan national issues, and rooted in professional and associative dynamics as local and cross-border actors. Greek Orthodox laypeople and Melkite clerics could rely on cross-border solidarity networks specific to their professional and training itineraries.

The establishment of a Melkite and Greek Orthodox communal space in Amman or, more broadly, in Jordan, in the interwar period underlines different strategies of spatial appropriation.[66] These spatial practices are the result of the social interactions of actors who put forward their local anchorage and mobilised their networks to redefine power relations at the national and transnational levels. They contributed to giving the Transjordanian territory an unprecedented place within the modern dynamics of these churches.

**Cross-border Clergy and Laity: Paths of Solidarity**

Focusing on individuals by studying their religious and social itineraries allows us to identify the networks to which they belong. These networks constitute dissemination channels at a transnational scale. During the Mandate period what are the mediators of dissemination – magazines, books, personalities – who promoted religious, political and cultural circulation? The analysis of networks conceptualises the social world that links the actors and allows us to identify sociability practices.[67] It gives the notions of 'borders' and 'hierarchies' key positions, as 'networks' do not imply an absence of a domination

[65] 'Mu'tamar al-kahana al-'arab', *Falestin*, 6 September 1932, No. 160–2118, p.6.
[66] Didier Guignard and Iris Seri-Hersch, *Spatial Appropriations in Modern Empires, 1820–1960: Beyond Dispossession* (Newcastle-upon-Tyne: Cambridge Scholars Publishing, 2019).
[67] Karen Barkey, 'Trajectoires impériales: histoires connectées ou études comparées?', *Revue d'histoire moderne et contemporaine* 54-4bis: 5 (2007), pp. 90–103.

or competitive regime between the individuals they are structured around.[68] The paths and itineraries of clerics and laypeople who played a major role in structuring the national and transnational communal space reveal the diversity of social inscriptions and modes of actions of these mediators.

*The Melkite clergy: national transborder clerics*

In 1932 the Greek-Catholic archdiocese of Petra, Philadelphia and all Transjordan had new administrative borders following the limits of the state. Its archbishop, Paul Salman, became a key actor in developing the Melkite missions in the country. He was described by the Mandate officials in 1946 as follows: 'Greek Catholic Archbishop of Philadelphia and Petra, born in Lebanon about 55 years ago. Of great learning and piety with considerable personal influence over members of communities other than his own, including many Moslems'.[69]

Salman's personality was considered by British Mandate officials beforehand, in terms of his ability to build networks. His profile and objectives are in themselves indicative of the transnational modes of belonging of Melkite clerics during the interwar period. In 1932 Philippe Gorra resumed his objectives in a book dedicated to the Seminary of St Anne:

> S.E. Archbishop Paul Salman (Ouadih, son of Joseph), Archbishop of Petra, Philadelphia and Transjordan; of the Patriarchal clergy, born in Damascus in 1886; ordained priest at St Anne's on July 20th 1911 by Bishop Paul Abou-Mourad; teacher and headmaster of the school of Salt (Transjordan); in 1914, founder and parish priest of the mission of Maïn and Karak (Transjordan); 1919, parish priest of Zabadani (Damascus), then professor and procurator of the Patriarchal College of Beirut; procurator of the Patriarchate of Damascus and temporary secretary of Patriarch Dimitrios Cadi, parish priest of the parish of Bab-el-Moussallah (Damascus); since April 1926, first Secretary of S. B. Patriarch Kyrillos IX, appointed Archimandrite in Rome on June 29th 1926, the day H.B. received the Pallium of H.H.; consecrated Archbishop on

---

[68] Claire Lemercier, 'Analyse de réseaux et histoire', *Revue d'histoire moderne et contemporaine*, Vol. 2 (2005), pp. 88–112.

[69] National Archives, F.O series: 371, Piece: 52945, Registry number E8470/8470/80, Sir A. Kirkbride, Amman to Mr Bevin, dated 6 August 1946, received 28 August.

June 5th 1932 in Cairo Cathedral by S/B. Archbishop Kyrillos IX; author of an Arabic work: 'Five Years in Transjordan'.

This short biography confirms the importance of the links maintained by Salman with the White Fathers of St Anne of Jerusalem. The question of religious routes is linked to the training centres where the actors could meet, exchange, or share common dogmatic references. The Seminary of St Anne of Jerusalem had a major role in training the Arab Catholic clergy of the Eastern rite. The young novices came from different regions of the Middle East to be trained in Jerusalem for several years. Salman could count on this network throughout his term of office in Transjordan. It gave him a certain importance within the networks of religious authority; however, it could have also been an obstacle because St Anne was associated with the French networks of influence in the region.[70] For Salman, it remained the main training centre for national regular clergy. In 1940, he wrote to Amédée Outrey, Consul General of France in Palestine and Transjordan:

> I have 5 seminarians from the Diocese of Transjordan at the Seminary of St Anne. At the end of this year, I will have a priest from St Anne. I also have a young seminarian at the Oriental Seminary of the P. Jesuits of Beirut. Each year, we prepare students for the Seminary of St Anne.[71]

One of the priorities of the Melkite Church in Transjordan was to increase the number of local clergy and teaching staff post-1932. The process of Arabisation and nationalisation of this clergy had to rely on regional training centres, first in Jerusalem and then in Lebanon.

The Paulist Fathers of Harissa also played a leading role in the establishment of a local clergy, and Salman's career is an example. His first experiences as a priest are observed in the context of the first Melkite missionary offensive in the north of Transjordan at the beginning of the twentieth century, on the initiative of the Paulist Fathers of Lebanon. Subsequently, Salman settled in

---

[70] Anthony O'Mahony, 'Les chrétiens palestiniens: politique, droit et société, 19171948', in Dominique Trimbur and Ran Aaronsohn (eds), *De Balfour à Ben Gourion. Les puissances européennes et la Palestine, 1917-1948* (Paris: CNRS Edition, 2008), pp. 357–404.

[71] AAPP, Amman, Letter of Paul Salman, Register IV, N. 223/T, 19 April 1940.

Beirut for a few years, where he forged links, particularly intellectual links, with the Jesuits of St Joseph. Salman's relations with Father Bonneville have been mentioned earlier. He also participated in an intellectual sphere embodied by Louis Cheikho, the founder of the Oriental Bookshop. From a folklorist perspective, Salman published his first observations on Transjordanian society in the 1920s. They were first published in *al-Mashriq*, a weekly newspaper in Arabic from the University of St Joseph.[72] This newspaper intended to be a space for exchange and intellectual debate between priests, intellectuals and scholars at the regional level. These observations were later published in a book entitled *Five Years in Transjordan* by the Paulist Press in Harissa.[73] Thus, as Robert Frank points out, 'cultural transfers across borders transform spaces'[74] of religious and political action.

Salman's itinerary is marked by mobility and an anchoring within Middle Eastern, North American and European spaces of circulation. This mobility is an integral part of his capacity to establish a communal, religious and symbolic space at a national scale. During the interwar period, the Melkite Church secured the support of the Transjordanian government, in particular through promoting an Arab clergy. In several letters, Salman evokes Emir Abdullah's benevolence towards him, a guarantee of the national expansion of the missions.[75] His privileged position was due to an argument developed very early on by the authorities of the Melkite Church: the need to Arabise and then nationalise its clergy. In the 1920s the Melkite Church used Arab nationalist rhetoric to justify the priority of its development.[76] In this context, Salman acted as a go-between expert between the Congregation for the Oriental Churches, the Melkite religious authorities and the government. In 1932, Emir Abdullah visited Father Salman during the Christmas period to present his wishes.[77] He took the opportunity to state that he considered Salman the representative of the Christians in the country because he was an

---

[72] See, for instance, 'al-Mazārāt fī Sharq al-Urdun', *al-Mashriq*, 1920, No. 11, pp. 900–15.

[73] Paul Salman, *Khamsa a'wām fī Sharq al-Urdun* (Harissa: Saint-Paul Press, 1929).

[74] Robert Frank, 'Conclusion', *Les Cahiers de l'Irice*, Vol. 1, No. 5 (2010), pp. 87–94.

[75] See, for example: AAPP, Amman, Register III, No. 258/T, 21 February 1940, Letter of Paul Salman to T.R.P. A P. Wijnhovern, Secretary of the Apostolate of Holland.

[76] See, for example: ACOC, Melchita Transgiordania, 528/28, I, Erezione di una Diocesi, 1927, Prot. No. 47, No. 336, 8 February 1928, p. 3.

[77] ACOC, Melchita Transgiordania, 528/28, II, No. 609, 4 December 1934.

Arab priest. This ceremony was an opportunity for the Vatican to develop diplomatic ties with the Emir.

In the 1930s and 1940s Salman played a key role in implementing Melkite missionary strategy in Transjordan due to his knowledge of the country, his training at St Anne and his good relations with Emir Abdullah. He became a go-between expert for Christians in the Emirate and their representative for both the Congregation for the Oriental Churches and Emir Abdallah. He was a prominent figure in the political and local dynamics of the Melkite Church in the Emirate of Transjordan during the Mandate period. These modes of belonging and networks established the asymmetrical boundaries of the social, symbolic, religious and political space within which these actors were embedded.

### 'Awda al-Qusūs and Yūsuf al-'Isā as spokespersons of the Greek Orthodox laity

In the case of the Greek Orthodox laity movement, two of the main actors were 'Awda al-Qusūs and Yūsuf al-'Isā. Both actors reflect the ability to act at the regional and local level, due to their engagement within intellectual, commercial and political networks. They played an important role in structuring the communal space in Palestine and Transjordan through media and associations. They were delegated by the secretary of the conference of Arab Orthodox priests to serve as intermediaries to the Greek Orthodox Patriarchate of Jerusalem and to carry out their claims. In 1935, 'Awda al-Qusūs and Yūsuf al-'Isā visited Jerusalem several times to defend the claims of the priests to the Patriarchate. They also sought the support of the representatives of the British Mandate and the Palestinian and Transjordanian governments. The result of this conciliation attempt was published at the request of the executive committee of the Greek Orthodox Conference in the newspaper *Alif Ba'*, founded by Yūsuf al-'Isā in Damascus in the 1920s. This attempt at mediation failed as reported as follows:

> We have become more than convinced that there are people working in secret so that the dispute between the Patriarchy and the Committee only ends except through the courts and the government, because the community has become like the miserable man in the face of the Patriarchate's intransigence and has made its dependence on the courts.[78]

[78] Al-Qusūs al-Halasā, A. S., al-Qusûs al-Halasā, J. N., and Ghassān, S. *Mudhakarāt wa 'awraqhu* (Memoirs and papers). Not published, n.d., copy of a report written by A. al-Qusūs and Yūsuf al-'Isā.

Despite this attempt failing, the profiles of the two protagonists sent by the Executive Committee of the Orthodox Congress are representative of the territorial paradox of the Greek Orthodox community during the interwar period. Both 'Awda al-Qusūs and Yūsuf al-'Isā were members of important families rooted within the entangled networks of interest between Palestine and Transjordan. They embodied the tension within the Greek Orthodox community between the need to be anchored at the local level through communal institutions, and the need to be structured at the regional level to influence the policies implemented by the Patriarchate. Both played a major role in establishing the Greek Orthodox national and transnational communal space.

'Awda al-Qusūs was an influential notable of the Emirate of Transjordan at the beginning of the Mandate period. He was born in al-Karak on 5 October 1877 and studied at the city's Greek Orthodox School. He was one of the few Ottoman Turkish speakers and readers of the city, which gave him local influence during the last years of the Ottoman rule. After his studies he was appointed as a member of the Court of First Instance in al-Karak. After the First World War he was appointed a member of the Amman Appeals Court in 1921.[79]

During the Mandate period, al-Qusūs was one of the privileged interlocutors of the British authorities. He was one of the first representatives of the Transjordanian tribes to meet Herbert Samuel, representative of the British Mandate in Jerusalem in 1920.[80] John Philby's diaries report regular meetings during which al-Qusūs regularly discussed Emir Abdullah's policies towards Christians.[81] Al-Qusūs was also involved in political life as a member of the national party. He advocated for local notables to have a greater role in the political life of the country, instead of the Syrian representatives who had important roles in the government in the 1920s.[82] He held several positions

---

[79] Al-Qusūs al-Halasā, A. S., al-Qusûs al-Halasā, J. N., and Ghassān, S. *Mudhakarāt wa 'awraq-hu* (Memoirs and papers). Not published, n.d.

[80] Ma'an Abu Nowar, *The History of the Hashemite Kingdom of Jordan. Volume 1: The Creation and Development of Transjordan, 1920–1929* (Oxford: Ithaca Press,1989), p. 24.

[81] Saint Antony's college, GB 165-0229 Philby Collection, 1/5/3/3 Transjordan Diary, Vol. 3 and 5, File 3 of 4 (vol. 5, pp. 149–208), 19 and 20 July 1922.

[82] Ma'an Abu Nowar, 1989, p. 101; Tariq Tell, 'The social origins of Mandatory rule in Transjordan', in Cyrus Schayegh and Andrew Arsan (eds), *The Routledge Handbook of the History of the Middle East Mandates* (New York: Routledge, 2015), pp. 212–24.

in the government including member of the Executive Council of the Abū al-Hudā government and Attorney General in the Sirāj government.[83] His memoirs are one of the richest sources on the social history of Transjordan. He also made an important contribution to folklore studies of the region with his book on tribal justice, which was published in 1966. These publications indicate his inclusion within the intellectual preoccupation of his time.

The trajectory of al-Qusūs is representative of the reconfiguration of the political field in favour of the territorialisation and confessionalisation of political identities. Founder of the Association for the Arab Orthodox Nahda in the 1920s, al-Qusūs remained one of its most eminent representatives until his death in 1943. His professional and political networks enabled him to secure the association's rank at the national scale and to push for the communal space in Amman to be structured. To this end, he worked closely with members of Palestinian associations, whose anti-Zionist political demands he conveyed and with whom he made common claims towards the Patriarchate.

For his part, Yūsuf al-ʿIsā is considered as one of the founders of modern journalism in Palestine.[84] He was born in Jaffa at the beginning of the 1880s. Before entering journalism, he worked for the Jaffa-Jerusalem railway company. He became involved in politics when he participated in the local committee of union and progress and he was one of the advocates of Ottoman patriotism. Al-ʿIsā was one of the leaders of the Arab Orthodox Nahda in Palestine and a member of a mixed committee composed of Orthodox laymen and members of the lower clergy who were in charge of local matters.[85]

Yūsuf al-ʿIsā and his cousin ʿIsa al-ʿIsā founded the newspaper *Falestin* in 1911.[86] During the First World War al-ʿIsā took refuge in Syria where he founded the newspaper *Alif Baʾ*. During the Mandate period, *Falestin* was a transnational space for the circulation of ideas among Arab laity, and it reported the decisions of the Arab Orthodox congresses and its executive

---

[83] Betty Anderson, *Nationalist Voices in Jordan: The Street and the State* (Austin: University of Texas Press, 2005).

[84] Emanuel Beška, 'Yusuf al-ʿIsa: A Founder of Modern Journalism in Palestine', *Jerusalem Quarterly*, Vol. 74 (2018), pp. 7–13.

[85] Beška, 2018.

[86] Tadros, 2011.

committee.[87] Very quickly, it was considered as a media to serve the goals of the Arab Orthodox Nahda and many sections were devoted to the life of the association in Palestine and Transjordan.[88] *Falestin* dynamics resonated with the transnational demands of the orthodox laity, which were to represent the Arab nationalist struggle. After the war *Falestin* increasingly integrated an anti-Zionist editorial line.

Both Yūsuf al-ʿĪsā and ʿAwda al-Qusūs contributed to the territorial implantation of the Orthodox Arab Renaissance movement, which they developed through different professional, cultural and intellectual networks, always linked to political commitment. During the interwar period, they established a cross-border intellectual and solidarity space that gave their initiative considerable political weight and maintained the phenomenon of 'transpatialisation' of confessional dynamics while implementing them with territorial demands. Due to their influence, the field of action of the Orthodox association was anchored within a multipolar political and social space.

The Melkite and Greek Orthodox case studies indicate that although the British authorities made the political choice to establish Amman as the capital, the clerics and laity of the Greek Orthodox and Melkite Churches played a determining role in giving the new communal spaces of the city an importance at the regional scale. The redefinition of these symbolic and community boundaries was based on associative dynamics sometimes inherited from the Ottoman period (see Chapter Two for further discussion) and individual networks offering to diversify the political or confessional relays for the demands of these social groups.

## Conclusion

The interwar period for the Melkite and Greek Orthodox Churches is characterised by a process of nationalisation and territorialisation which relied mainly on regional networks and different forms of externalisation of their prerogatives. In this context, borders were polysemic for both churches and

---

[87] Tamari, 2014.

[88] E. Dierauff, *Negotiating Ethno-Confessional Relations in Late Ottoman Palestine: Debates in the Arab Palestinian Newspaper Filastin (1911–1914)*, (PhD thesis, University of Tübingen, 2018).

characterised by the rooting within the Arab nationalist movement and national political claims. The Melkites defined their communal borders through an affirmation of the local nature of their church, in opposition to the Latin nature. The Greek Orthodox laity was cautious to keep an image of social openness to social debates and collaborated with representatives of Protestant churches and associations such as the YMCA. These two dynamics underline the competitive redefinition of symbolic boundaries, particularly within new spaces of power during the Mandate period, notably Amman.

By addressing the narratives of individuals and clerics, and both the Greek Orthodox and Melkite Churches, this article demonstrates how their claims – sometimes contradictory – to establish a national or urban communal space were part of a complex administrative, symbolic and political game of scales. The latter often places local actors at the crossroads of networks of power and solidarity. Both the Orthodox laity and the Melkite clerics relied on their transnational networks in Egypt, Lebanon and Palestine and within North America and Europe to expand their activities in the Emirate of Transjordan. Through these networks they adapted their strategies within new state borders and brought the demands of their community to the fore.

The polysemic borders of these new communal spaces reflect the will to challenge the ecclesial circumscriptions of each church, and the attempts to constitute national but also regional religious communities. Their use, definition and perception depended on their context of production. The national dynamics of these churches cannot be understood without using a connected approach at the regional scale; thus, they also challenge the notion of 'transpatialisation'. Through the connections of individuals and institutions, one perceives the role of the new Transjordanian national churches and laity progressively asserting themselves towards the role of Palestinian institutions and laity. The redefinition of these interrelations and the balance of power on a regional scale call for a consideration of the genealogy of networks to understand the post-1948 and Nakba migration dynamics.

# 6

# CONTESTED TERRAIN: CROSS-BORDER VIOLENCE, POLITICS AND MEMORY IN SYRIA'S KURD DAGH REGION[1]

## *Katharina Lange*

In 1960 Syrian historian Adham al-Jundi claimed that Syria's 'revolt of the North', led by Ibrahim Hanano, had been sparked by the actions of relatively unknown 'Kurdish hero Mahu ibn Ibo Shasho' (Muhammad Ibrahim).[2] Locally known as Meho Îbshashê, Ibrahim was the first man to fire a shot against the French forces that had occupied Ottoman Cilicia and Aleppo

[1] This chapter has been written in spring 2020 and revised in January 2021, as libraries stayed closed and research travel was impossible amidst the Covid pandemic. This, in addition to the situation in Afrin today which precludes field visits, has shaped the way in which this chapter has evolved, and frankly limited the amount of research that could be done. Much of it has been done online and through social media. Without the help and support of Fakhri Abdo, who generously made his networks and notes available, this would not have been possible – I owe him great thanks. I am greatly obliged to Mustafa Hamo, Mihemed Berkêt, Widad Sheikh Isma'il Zada and Serbest Sheikh Isma'il Zada, for sharing their memories and insights with me. Moreover, I thank Fuat Dündar for alerting me to the Turkish historiography on the issues discussed here and Jordi Tejel and Ramazan Hakkı Öztan for their comments and suggestions on an earlier version of this chapter. The chapter was written with support from Leibniz-Zentrum Moderner Orient and the German Federal Ministry of Education and Research through its project 'Normality and Crisis: Memories of Everyday Life in Syria' (funding code 01UG1840X). The sole responsibility for the content lies with the author.

[2] Adham al-Jundī. *Tārīkh al-thawrāt al-sūriyya fī ʿahd al-intidāb al-firansī* (Damascus: Maṭbaʿat al-ittiḥād, 1960).

after the end of the First World War. Moreover, the armed band Meho commanded constituted the very first gang in this region to rise against France. Locally referred to as 'tchete' (Turkish and Kurdish) or ' 'isaba' (Arabic), this organisational form continued previous local forms of action. In the post-war period, it became the organisational backbone of irregular warfare against the French.[3] Al-Jundi's chronology is borne out by the testimony of Yussuf al-Sa'dun, an insurgent leader in Jabal Quseir during Hanano's revolt. Al-Sa'dun, in his memoirs written (but not published) in the 1950s, confirmed that the first gangs that formed to attack the French were initiated by 'two Kurdish leaders', namely Meho and another man called 'Tek Bek Hadji'.[4]

According to local historiography, Meho was born in the village of Baska, located on the Turkish side of today's border.[5] Hailing from a modest, if not poor, background, the family had to leave the village after a conflict in which one of Meho's uncles was killed. They became landless labourers, first in Syria's Harim region, then in the (today Turkish) 'Amq plain. Meho turned to robbing caravans, ending up imprisoned in an Aleppo jail, from which he was freed by the occupying Arab-British forces in October 1918.[6] When France took control over northern Syria and Cilicia, Meho decided to revolt. His resolve, supposedly formed in discussions with Aleppines opposed to French rule, was fuelled by anger over insults to his 'honour and dignity', involving local gendarmerie's offensive behaviour to his wife.[7] Meho and his men,

---

[3] On the structural characteristics and social significance of the 'isaba for anti-French revolt in Syria see Nadine Méouchy, 'Le mouvement des 'isabat en Syrie du Nord à travers le témoignage du chaykh Youssef Saadoun (1919–1921)' in Nadine Méouchy and Peter Sluglett (eds), *The British and French Mandates in Comparative Perspectives* (Leiden: Brill, 2004), and Nadine Méouchy, 'From the Great War to the Syrian Armed Resistance Movement (1919–1921): The Military and the Mujahidin in Action', in Heike Liebau et al. (eds), *The World in World Wars* (Leiden: Brill, 2010), esp. pp. 503–7.

[4] See Nadine Méouchy, 'Les temps et les territoires de la révolte du Nord (1919–1921)', in Jean-Claude David and Thierry Boissière (eds), *Alep et ses territoires* (Beirut: IFPO, 2014), p. 92.

[5] Mihemed Ebdo Elî, *Çiyayê Kurmênc (Efrîn)* (No place [Berlin]: Sersera, 2018), p. 230; Muḥammad 'Abdū 'Alī, *Jabal al-Kurd ('Afrīn),* (Afrin: no publisher, [2003]), p. 583; Sheikhū 'Alī, *Jabal al-Kurd ibān al-intidāb al-firansī* (No publisher, no place, 2003), p. 32.

[6] M. 'Alī, *Jabal al-Kurd*, p. 584.

[7] Al-Jundī, *Tārīkh al-thawrāt*, p. 12.

numbering more than forty, used to ambush French supply caravans crossing the densely wooded ʿAmq plains by laying fire to the surroundings, using the mountainous region of Kurd Dagh as refuge when pursued. As Meho's reputation grew he was joined by another gang leader from the region, Tek Bîqli Haji. Shortly after, Meho joined the Kemalist forces in Cilicia, where he reputedly was raised to an elevated military rank and received the title 'Pasha'. Later, however, he opposed a Turkish army patrol that was scouring the border villages for military recruits; in the ensuing fight, Meho killed a Turkish soldier and was forced to cross back into Syria. Now a fugitive from Turkish as well as French authorities, he found refuge in Kurd Dagh, where he had relatives. Meho died as violently as he had lived, killed by his own brother-in-law in a cave on Qaziqli mountain.[8]

This chapter uses a historical-anthropological perspective to analyse how networks of violence and politics on and across the Syrian–Turkish border enabled and configured struggles against the French mandate in the region of Kurd Dagh between the 1920s and the 1940s. While al-Jundi commemorates Meho's act in the framework of Syrian nationalism, I suggest that it should be seen in a more regional and, at the same time, transnational context, emerging, as it did, from a border region bridging between emergent Arab and Turkish national movements while being inhabited by a largely Kurdish population. In this border region, men like Meho and Tek Biqlî Haji, oscillating between banditry and revolt, have left their mark on local memory, going back to (at least) late Ottoman times.[9]

Responding to larger debates about the nature of anti-mandate resistance in Syria between religious, local and 'national' scales, the chapter considers the significance of local context and trans-local practices for shaping the actions and networks under investigation. The region of Kurd Dagh, which appears a marginal backwater from the perspective of conventional Syrian historiog-

[8] M. ʿAlī, *Jabal al-Kurd*, pp. 584–86.

[9] Consider famous bandit Etûnê (Abdallah ʿAtûn), from Caʾnika village near Rajo, who cut a Robin Hood-like figure before he was caught and hanged in 1908; Khair ad-Dīn al-Asadī, *Mausūʿat Ḥalab al-muqārina* (Aleppo: Maʿhad al-Turāth al-ʿIlmī al-ʿArabī, 1981–88), see also Elî, *Çiyayê Kurmênc*, p. 230. For a typology of banditry in this context, see Jean-David Mizrahi, *Genèse de l'État mandataire* (Paris: Sorbonne, 2002), pp. 165–66. The figure of the bandit/rebel north of today's border has also been immortalised in Yashar Kemal's literary trilogy around Mehmet Ince.

raphy, was significant for anti-French armed resistance Cilicia and connected to similar movements in northern Syria. The chapter questions how the location on the Turkish–Syrian border impacted and shaped these movements with respect to their practices, relations and networks. Local historical knowledge from the area, rooted in today's Afrin region, offers a range of more or less detailed orally transmitted narratives that communicate information relating to the interwar years. This knowledge can today be accessed through local historiography, interviews with descendants of people who lived during this period, and representations on social media. Read in concert with French archival sources and other contemporary accounts, these narratives indicate that while the Turkish–Syrian border cut off historical economic, social and political relations, it also generated and enabled particular forms of political and military action. They demonstrate that Kurd Dagh saw moments of armed resistance against French rule at the beginning as well as the end of the period during which the Turkish–Syrian border was fixed.[10]

## The Kurdish Mountain

The term Kurd Dagh, 'Mountain of the Kurds', shifted, during the years when the Syrian–Turkish border was established between the end of the First World War in October 1918 and the Ankara agreement of October 1921, from denoting a geographical place (a mountain range in the Syrian–Turkish border region) to referencing an administrative entity on Syrian territory. This shift has shaped and perhaps motivated the actions of the men about whom I write, and it has informed the (local) historiography of the events described in this chapter, complicating my own work in writing about the subject.

Since the establishment of the Syrian state, Kurd Dagh has been a marginal region in a very tangible sense, situated, as it is, on the fringes of both the Syrian state and the governorate of Aleppo of which it formed a part. Yet despite its relative marginality, the region has also been an interstitial space, bridging between Cilicia/Anatolia and Syria. Overland communications between Aleppo and the port of Iskenderun/Alexandretta were maintained by the road that ran through Al-Hammam to the coast; and since 1911/12 a branch of the Baghdad railway crossed the region. Its history in the interwar-period

---

[10] Cf. Soheila Mameli-Ghaderi, 'Le tracé de la frontière entre la Syrie et la Turquie (1921–1929)', *Guerres mondiales et conflits contemporains*, Vol. 207 (2002), pp. 125–38.

(and indeed, in recent times) has been shaped by this dialectical position, oscillating between self-containedness and apartness on the one hand, and the embeddedness in larger political scales on the other.

The eponymous mountain range of Kurd Dagh, paralleling the Amanus at an altitude of 700 to 1260 m, extends across today's Syrian–Turkish border, northwest of Aleppo.[11] During Ottoman times, the villages in this area had been grouped into a number of districts that belonged to the *Qadha* of Kilis, with Kilis serving as the region's administrative, political and also economic centre.[12] Once the border was firmly established, Kilis lost its central relevance for the population on the Syrian side, where a new *Qadha* under the name of Kurd Dagh was founded.[13]

As its name indicated, the Kurd Dagh region was remarkably homogenous in terms of spoken language and ethnicity. French Orientalist Roger Lescot described the region as 'populated entirely by Kurds' in 1940, echoing earlier perceptions by Syrian administrators.[14] In the late 1930s, the population of the new *Qadha* was estimated to number around '50,000 souls'.[15] Ethno-linguistic, religious and tribal affiliations translated into social identities that were shaped by village and family origin, by ties of kin and

---

[11] For cartographic representations see Heinrich Kiepert, *Prof. C. Haussknecht's Routen im Orient 1865–1869 nach dessen Reisen im Orient redigirt. I und II. Nord-Syrien, Mesopotamien und Süd-Armenien* (Berlin: Reimer, 1882); also Vahé Tachjian, *La France en Cilicie et en Haute-Mésopotamie,* (Paris: Karthala, 2004), p. 36.

[12] On the administrative history of the region during the eighteenth century, see Stefan Winter, 'Les Kurdes de Syrie dans les archives ottomanes (XVIIIe siècle)', *Études kurdes,* Vol. 10 (2010), esp. pp. 135–36.

[13] In later years, the *Qadha* was increasingly referred to by its Arabic translation, Jabal al-Akrād, and later by the name of 'Afrīn after its new capital town, named after the eponymous river. In emergent Kurdish historiography, it is referred to as Ciyayê Kurmênc.

[14] Roger Lescot, 'Le Kurd Dagh et le mouvement mouroud', *Studia Kurdica,* Vol. 1, No. 5 (1988), pp. 101–16, 4. On the administrators' perspectives see Arrêté 4276 *Modifiant les limites du Caza de Kurd Dagh* of 26 August 1922, signed by General Governor of the State of Aleppo, Mohamad Kamil al-Qudsi and approved by High Commissioner, Henri Gouraud; published in *Bulletin Hebdomadaire des Actes administratifs du Haut-Commissariat,* No. 41, 8 October 1922, p. 266; BNF (https://gallica.bnf.fr/ark:/12148/bpt6k6486997n, accessed 31 March 2020).

[15] Pierre Rondot, Letter to *Le Temps,* 77: 27556 (16 February 1937, 2) BNF, (https://gallica.bnf.fr/ark:/12148/bpt6k263122d/f2.image, 5 April, 2020).

descent, and structured through socio-political hierarchies. At the beginning of the mandate, Kurdish (Kurmancî) and Ottoman Turkish, rather than Arabic, were the languages spoken and understood by the inhabitants, who thus differed ethno-linguistically from that of neighbouring regions in the south and east. Yet the area has also, geographically as well as historically, been set apart from other Kurdish communities in Syria.[16] As described for other Kurdish areas, political influence was held by (tribal) Aghas and (Sufi) Sheikhs, but in Kurd Dagh, this influence had a distinctly local flavour.[17] Compared to other regions, tribal belonging did not have the same meaning for political mobilisation; and relations between tribe members were increasingly structured by internal socio-economic inequalities and hierarchies. Since the nineteenth century, tribal leaders had turned into a stratum of wealthy landowners who distinguished themselves with regards to wealth, influence and social status, as well as habitual dispositions, taste and comportment.[18] In confessional terms, the majority of the inhabitants were Sunni Muslims, while the region was also home to Yezidis,[19] Alevi/Kizilbash and, especially after the First World War, Armenians.[20]

[16] Cf. Jordi Tejel, *Syria's Kurds* (London: Routledge, 2009).

[17] Martin van Bruinessen, *Agha, Shaikh and State* (London: Zed Books, 1992).

[18] On similar shifts among Syria's Arab tribes, see Dawn Chatty, 'Leaders, Land, and Limousines: Emir Versus Sheikh', *Ethnology*, Vol. 16, No. 4 (1977), pp. 385–97; see also Katharina Lange, 'Heroic Faces, Disruptive Deeds: Remembering the Tribal Sheikh on the Syrian Euphrates', in Dawn Chatty (ed.), *Nomadic Societies in the Middle East and North Africa* (Leiden: Brill, 2006).

[19] On Sunni Muslims in the late 20th/early 21st century, see Paulo Pinto, 'Kurdish Sufi Spaces of Rural-Urban Connection in Northern Syria', *Études rurales*, Vol. 186 (2010), pp. 149–67. On Yezidi communities, see Sebastian Maisel, 'Syria's Yezidis in the Kūrd Dāgh and the Jazīra: Building Identities in a Heterodox Community', *The Muslim World*, Vol. 103, No. 1 (2013), pp. 24–40.

[20] In 1915 tens of thousands of Armenians deported from Anatolia were held under terrible conditions in camps at Rajo and Katma; see Raymond Kévorkian, *The Armenian Genocide* (London: I. B. Tauris, 2011). A few years later, the French retreat from Cilicia caused an influx of Armenian refugees (Tachjian, *La France en Cilicie*, pp. 223, 358), many of whom settled in Afrin. Between the 1940s and 1960s this community dispersed to Soviet Armenia (see Jum'a Abd al-Qadir, *Afrin awakhir al-arba'iniyat . . . awa'il al-khamsiniyat fi'l-qarn al-ishrin* [Aleppo: Dar al-nun 2008], pp. 73–75) and to Aleppo, Lebanon and the USA (Thomas Schmidinger, *Kampf um den Berg der Kurden* [Vienna: Bahoe books, 2018], pp. 28–29).

## Drawing Lines

The Turkish–Syrian border gradually emerged and became reality over a period of three years, between the end of the First World War in October 1918 and the Ankara agreement in October 1921. Local memory in Kurd Dagh recognises the significance of the last days of the war, when Mustafa Kemal (later Atatürk) and the retreating Ottoman troops withdrew north from Aleppo. They were pursued by imperial British troops from the Fifteenth Imperial Service Cavalry Brigade, composed of Mysore and Jodhpur Lancers. On 26 October 1918, the two sides clashed along the road to Kilis north of Haritan in what was to be remembered as 'the last battle of the war' in the Middle East. As Kemal withdrew further north through Deir Jmal, he finally made his headquarters in Katma, 46 km north of Aleppo, where the retreat came to a halt. Four days later, the armistice of Moudros formally marked the end to the war for the Ottoman Empire.

This 'last battle of the war' is, in Anglophone sources, commemorated as the battle of Haritan, while Turkish historiography remembers nearby Katma as the place where Kemal 'drew a line with Turkish bayonets' – a line that was to become the basis for the later Syrian–Turkish border.[21] Katma – locally referred to as Qitmê – was of strategic importance as a station on the Baghdad railway and home to an Ottoman army post.[22] Moreover, it was located beyond the invisible ethnolinguistic boundary separating Arab- and Kurdish-speaking villages in Aleppo's northern countryside; its population could therefore be expected to be less sympathetic to the Anglo-Arab side than the (Arabic-speaking) inhabitants of Deir Jmal and Haritan.

---

[21] Cf. Falih Rıfkı Atay and Mahmut Soydan (eds), *Atatürk'ün Anıları* (Ankara: Olgaç Matbaası, 1983), p. 82; also Mustafa Şahin and Cemile Şahin, 'Suriye'nin son Osmanlı Talisi Tahsin (Uzer) Bey'in Suriye Valiliği ve Mustafa Kemal Paşa ile Buradaki Çalışmaları', *Sosyal Bilimler Dergisi*, Vol. 1, No. 2 (2011), pp. 1–27, 19–20. Sean McMeekin. *The Ottoman Endgame. War, Revolution and the Making of the Modern Middle East, 1908–1923* (London: Penguin Books, 2015), p. 404 takes a sceptical perspective on this claim.

[22] Locally called Qitmê, the town is spelled Katma in Turkish and French sources, and Qatma in Arabic. Names and spellings of places in this border region differ according to the language and political reference system used. Throughout this chapter, I adopt the local place names in their Kurdish spelling, adding other versions as they appear in French, Arabic or Turkish sources.

Local memory marks the demographic boundary in the countryside north of Aleppo, separating between Arab- and Kurdish-settled areas, as significant for the establishment of new borders after the end of the war. This is transmitted through the following anecdote: As a young boy, Mehî Evdî Berkêt witnessed the retreating Ottomans' arrival at his village, Bênê (Arabic: Ibbin), situated northwest of Deir Jmal. Still on horseback, the commanding Ottoman officer reportedly asked the villagers: '*Kurd misin, Arap misin?*' When the inhabitants identified as Kurds, the officer relaxed and signalled the soldiers to settle down. Relieved that they had finally reached a place of safety, his exhausted troops told the villagers that British artillery had continued to shoot at them until nearby (Arab) Deir Jmal, but that the bombardment had ceased when they crossed the (imaginary) line into Kurd Dagh.[23]

More than ninety years later this anecdote was retold by Meho's son, Haj Hisên. Lacking further, corroborating sources, it is impossible to judge its factual accuracy. Having known the late Haj Hisên, I am inclined to believe that while the anecdote may have been narratively honed over the years to provide a better story, the core memory it relates is likely to be true. At least some inhabitants of Aleppo, as well as of surrounding smaller towns and villages, had overtly welcomed and occasionally even joined the Arab troops fighting on the Allied side, thus adding to the pressure on the retreating Ottoman troops.[24] The anecdote related by Haj Hisên reflects, at the very least, the fact that ethnic logics were invoked to justify or contest the later establishment of the Syrian–Turkish border. It also suggests that ethnicity was seen to play a decisive role for political attitudes, as 'Kurds' were supposed to be more loyal to the Ottoman side when compared to their Arab neighbours. And last, but not least, the anecdote certainly shows how this logic – associating ethnicity with political loyalties – was naturalised in the 2000s.

---

[23] From a conversation with Fakhri Abdo (Kokan, 2010) who generously shared his notes and recording with me. More anecdotes about Atatürk's stay in the region have been shared on social media.

[24] Kāmil al-Ghazzī, *Nahr al-dhahab fī tārīkh Ḥalab*, Second Edition (Aleppo: Dār al-qalam al-ʿarabī, 1999 [1929]), p. 502; Muḥammad Fuʾād ʿAintābī/Najwā ʿUthmān. *Ḥalab fī miʾat ʿām, 1850–1950*, 2: 1901–1920. (Aleppo: Maʿhad al-turāth al-ʿilmī al-ʿarabī, 1993), pp. 168–69.

## Fighting (on) the Frontier

Following the end of the war, northern Syria initially stayed under British military control while, in accordance with the armistice terms of 1918, technical service and maintenance of the railway remained in the hands of its former Ottoman personnel. In January 1919 British-French agreements accorded military and administrative control of the railway and the 'Eastern Zone of Occupation' ('*Territoires de l'Est*'), separated from the rest of Cilicia, to Great Britain. This zone was to be controlled by the British Desert Mounted Corps, headquartered in Aleppo.[25] The Kurd Dagh mountain range separated this zone from the rest of Cilicia, placing Meidan Ekbes inside French-controlled Cilicia, while Qitmê/Katma was already in the British-controlled sector.[26] In November 1919 Britain ceded control to France amidst growing unrest and militant resistance against the Allied occupation. French imperial troops (specifically, North African and Senegalese contingents) were stationed at Qitmê and were posted at strategically important points along the railway.

Looking back two decades later, French Orientalist Roger Lescot somewhat ambivalently evaluated the way in which France assumed sovereignty over Kurd Dagh: 'The occupation of the region was accomplished without any great difficulties despite some skirmishes. [. . .] Within a few years, during which gangs equipped and victualled by Turkey maintained a rather great level of insecurity, Kurd Dagh was pacified.'[27]

Considering the situation in 1920, it seems clear that for the contemporaries in the immediate post-war period, said 'gangs' caused considerable problems, rendering the authority of the French military posts, and even their very own security, precarious until well after the French occupation of Aleppo and the battle in Maysalun in July 1920. The years between the end of the war and the formal beginning of the French mandate over Syria were a period of unrest and uncertainty for the region. Foreign presence was precarious and seemed potentially transient; and consequently, the permanence and location of the new borders seemed still in question. When the shift from

[25] Pierre Redan, *La Cilicie et le problème Ottoman.* (Paris: Gauthier-Villars, 1921), p. 77.
[26] See map in Redan, *La Cilicie*, p. 144bis.
[27] Roger Lescot, 'Le Kurd Dagh', p. 103.

British to French control indicated that the presence of foreign troops was to evolve into a more long-term occupation, resistance turned to armed opposition, further facilitated by many local men's military experience and training, and the ready availability of firearms in the wake of the war.[28]

As soon as British troops had withdrawn from the area, armed resistance against foreign occupation grew, reaching a peak in spring 1920. Kurd Dagh held strategic significance for the warring parties because of its geography and its sensitive infrastructural systems. Specifically, the line of the Baghdad railway with its important nodal points, the stations in Meidan Ekbes, Rajo, Qurt-Qulaqê (Kurt Kulak) and Qitmê, and vulnerable railway bridges in remote locations were of vital importance. The insurgents relied on the region's mountainous geography that made deployment of armoured cars or tanks virtually impossible[29], promising refuge to bandits and rebels retreating from pursuing troops or militia.[30] On 28 November 1919, a convoy coming to Islahiye from Marash was attacked by bandits, one of the accompanying soldiers killed and two injured. On 15 December one under-lieutenant, one sergeant and one foot soldier went missing in the vicinity of Qurt-Qulaqê, an area that was described as *'une région parfois peu sure'* (an occasionally insecure region).[31] In late January 1920 the post at Al-Hammam, situated halfway between Aleppo and Iskenderun, was attacked by a force of 600 men on foot and 100 men on horseback, likely supported by Meho, Tek Bîqli Haji and their followers.[32] By February 1920 the region was reported to be in full revolt. When the commanding general of the Fourth Division arrived for an inspection at Qitmê on 12 February he found that bands of 'insurgent villagers' had sabotaged the phone lines,

[28] S. ʿAlī, *Jabal al-Kurd*, p. xx.

[29] Cf. Jamīl Kina al-Baḥrī, *Nubḏa ʿan al-maẓālim al-afransīya biʾl-Jazīra waʾl-Furāt waʾl-madanīya al-afransīya bi-siǧn al-munfarid al-ʿaskarī bi-Qaṭma wa-Khān Istanbul.* (Aleppo: Maṭbaʿat al-Waṭan al-ʿArabī, n. d. [1967]).

[30] 'La vérité sur les derniers incidents militaires', *Correspondance d'Orient* 14 / No. 253, 15 January 1921, pp. 26–27; BNF (https://gallica.bnf.fr/ark:/12148/bpt6k5803675n, accessed 27 January 2021).

[31] Rapport Hebdomadaire, Période du 11 au 18 décembre [1919] SHD/GR 4 H 58/1, 10.

[32] Letter Henri Gouraud to Colonel Cousse at Damascus, Beirut 24 January 1920; CADLC 399 PAAP / 180.

encircled or even beleaguered virtually all French posts, and cut off roads. On the same day, some kilometres to the northwest, an armed group sabotaged the railway between Meidan Ekbes and Qitmê in a valley south of Rajo. The insurgents had removed 150 metres of tracks, causing a transport train to derail. The derailed train was attacked, an Armenian soldier and three employees of the Baghdad railway killed. In addition, one corporal and three men of the Twenty-Second Regiment Tirailleurs Algériens were taken prisoner, robbed of all their possessions, and sent back to their barracks three days later. Subsequently, an auxiliary train that had departed from nearby Qurt-Qulaqê arrived at the site of the attack, only to find that even more tracks had been removed behind the first train, causing this second train to derail as well. Since the Division de Syrie, spread out in fifteen detachments between Alexandretta and Urfa, depended on the railway for its supply, this was a particularly painful coup. Railway traffic resumed on 25 February, but was interrupted again on 2 March, when the tracks were disrupted between Qurt-Qulaqê and Qitmê. By the same token, bridges across the Kara-Su and to the west of Qurt-Qulaqê were burned down. On 6 March the French post guarding the viaduct of Here-Dere (locally referred to as Pirê Hesharkê) was attacked, its thirty-five men driven to flee or taken prisoner, and insurgents moved on to lay siege to the French post at Rajo. Five days later, a relieving force sent from Kilis was finally able to lift the siege whilst railway traffic resumed on 18 March. According to French sources, the insurgents had not only managed to cut the vital supply line of the Baghdad railway for the best part of a month but had also killed two French officers and seven men, wounded eleven, and taken thirty-five prisoners, including an officer. Local bands continued to carry out armed attacks against sensitive communication lines, notably the railway tracks, as well as military posts and patrols. According to a French report, 'the terror they inspired and the violence they used convinced even those inhabitants who had remained unaffected by [anti-French] Kemalist propaganda [to support the insurgency]'.[33] Following a Kemalist attack on the post at Meidan Ekbes on 30 August 1920, nine men of the Second French division, based between Meidan Ekbes and

---

[33] Report on events between 1 February and 15 April, Kilis, 18 April 1920, CADLC 399 PAAP / 184.

the Euphrates, were killed, thirty-six wounded and eight remained missing in action.[34] A French relief force sent by rail from Qitmê was delayed by an attack of several hundred irregulars in the Rajo gorge, preventing them from leaving Rajo station. At the viaduct of Here-Dere, the troops found the post destroyed by cannons, the wooden track-supporting layer of the railway construction burnt, and the Senegalese soldiers manning it killed or missing. Further reinforcements, sent out on 4 September, were attacked near Karababa peak, but managed to relieve Meidan Ekbes two days later, dispersing the attackers to the north and west towards Islahiye. During their return to Qitmê, the relieving force continued to be harried by irregulars.[35] Although French officers hoped to secure the railway through the intercession of influential local Aghas and negotiations with the Turkish side, the region remained unsafe for French communications and officials well into the following year, leading to the installation of an airborne postal service between Aleppo and Alexandretta in spring 1921.[36]

Contemporary French sources clearly considered Kurd Dagh, including the part that was to become Syrian territory, as part of Cilicia, and the insurgent acts of 1920–21 as an extension of the Turkish/Kemalist war against France in that region. Eventually, the Treaty of Ankara, signed on 20 October 1921, formally signalled the end of this war and established a new frontier separating the territories under French and Turkish control. Confirmed on 24 July 1923 in the Treaty of Lausanne, the border now ran squarely across Kurd Dagh. Leaving Meidan Ekbes with its railway station and town just inside the Syrian/French territory and continuing to the southeast, it passed north of the villages Bulbul, Heftaro and Marsa (on the Syrian side). The town of Kilis, but also smaller centres such as Islahiye, became part of the Republic of Turkey.

---

[34] Rapport hebdomadaire, semaine du 1–7 Septembre 1920. Aley, 14 septembre 1920, CADLC 399 PAAP / 186.

[35] Rapport hebdomadaire, semaine du 1–6 septembre 1920. Aley, 7 septembre 1920, CADLC 399 PAAP / 186.

[36] L'Aéronautique No. 23, April 1921, p. 174. BNF (https://gallica.bnf.fr/ark:/12148/bpt6k6555730w, accessed 10 May 2020). Mizrahi, Genèse, pp. 170–71 documents political banditry in the summers of 1922 and 1923 mostly for neighbouring regions but attests to the active role played by 'the guerrilla of Giaour Dagh', specifically its eastern reaches.

## Local Heroes – Translocal Politics

The French archival documents do not tell us much about the identity and personalities of the insurgents, but local memory and historiography do. The rebels were mostly locals who operated on home ground. Often, but not always, they were led by members of the local elite. The attack on the French transport train near Rajo in February 1920, specifically, is locally remembered as the battle of 'Geliyê Tîra' (the Valley of Arrows) and is attributed to a group of several hundred men led by Ehmedê Rûtê (Ahmad Rutu). A notable from Amara village, Rûtê had previously held office as the president of Kilis municipality. Together with him, other insurgents from landowning backgrounds are remembered: Seydê Dîkê, for instance, an influential Agha from the Amka tribe who was able to draw on traditional loyalties to recruit a considerable number of followers,[37] and Haj Henan Sheikh Isma'il Zada from the Biyan tribal group.

To an extent, these men represented a rural version of the 'last Ottoman generation' described by Provence.[38] Yet, similar to the tribal milieus of eastern Syria, they relativise Provence's contention that 'Ottoman officers and veterans led all the movements of armed resistance and national liberation'.[39] They represented a rural elite whose ties of allegiance to the Ottoman polity were less cultivated through individual formation in Ottoman schools or the army: the local *cheta* leaders typically had neither enjoyed much, or even any, formal schooling, nor had they spent formative years in Istanbul or in other metropolitan centres of the empire; at least some of them had even managed to avoid conscription during the war. Rather, it seems likely that the insurgents were driven by a collective sentiment of belonging and a sense of defiance towards foreign invaders that for many carried religious overtones.

Yet not all rebel leaders came from the elite, as the example of Meho Îbshashê, discussed at the beginning of this chapter, shows. Among the men whom Ehmedê Rûtê, Haj Henan and also Meho Îbshashê led were army veterans such as Evdî Khejê, a man from a well-to-do family in Chobana village who had served as a corporal (*onbaşı*) in the Ottoman army, taking

---

[37] Dominique Fradet, *Le montagne kurde* (Clamecy: Impr. Laballery, 2018).

[38] Michael Provence, *The Last Ottoman Generation and the Making of the Modern Middle East* (Cambridge: Cambridge University Press, 2017).

[39] Michael Provence, 'Ottoman Modernity, Colonialism, and Insurgency in the Interwar Arab East', *International Journal of Middle East Studies*, Vol. 43 (2011), pp. 205–25, 207.

part in the battle of Gallipoli (Çanakkale) before deserting and awaiting the end of the war in his native village.[40] There were also young 'foot soldiers' from modest social and economic backgrounds without any previous military training or experience. Among them was twenty-year-old Omar Etûnê, son of bandit Abdallah Etûnê, who had been hanged by the Ottoman authorities in 1908.[41] Another fighter was Rashîd Îbo, born in Bilêlka village near Rajo in 1902. Many years later, Îbo declared in an interview with Syrian newspaper *Tishrin* that he decided to join the insurgents after hearing Ibrahim Hanano speak to an audience of about fifty local men in the Kurd Dagh village of Ma'ratê.[42]

Lacking contemporary testimonies, the motivations and political affiliations of the insurgents in Kurd Dagh are difficult to excavate today; but it seems clear that they were heterogeneous. Kemalist structures and propaganda played a significant role for organising and sustaining insurgent actions, and troops under Kemalist command acted in concert with irregular bands.[43] According to local memory, after the demise of the Ottoman Empire at least some of the men were incorporated into Turkish insurgent structures:

[40] Online interview with his grandson, Mustafa Hamo, on 17 May 2020. Evdî Khejê's older brother, who had been drafted previously, had been killed in Mesopotamia, leaving Evdî's mother without any support or even knowledge of her son's fate. Concern for her, his grandson emphasised, was Evdî's main motive for deserting. Tragically, she died just before Evdî reached home.

[41] Elî, *Çiyayê Kurmênc*, XX; also Pîr Rustum, Al-mudawwana al-'arabiyya (2015), https://pirkurdi.wordpress.com/2015/11/02/%D8%B9%D8%A8%D8%AF-%D8%A7%D9%84%D9%84%D9%87-%D8%B9%D8%AA%D9%88%D9%86%D9%88/?f bclid=IwAR2odaa5taOqRm4UkLdJqG-2ntyvzsmg_909Gp5ZxGma-dmFE2P6aP3X1Zo, (accessed 15 May 2020); and Umar Etûnê's veteran's ID card depicted at https://www.tire-jafrin.com/index.php?page=det_gallary&gallery_id=25&category_id=0&prod_id=19&lan g=ar&fbclid=IwAR1ypSCX00WjfAXxJiq-eMfOe7EP7-8gB5dHmpC4FlpDeulbzbrHeZ-rUyNs (accessed 15 May 2020).

[42] Muṣṭafā Al-Najjār, 'Aḥad qādat al-thaura fī Ḥalab yitaḥaddath 'an al-ma'ārik wa'l-buṭūlāt al-latī saṭṭarahā al-muqātilūn ḍidd al-musta'mir al-ajnabī.' *Tishrīn* 18 April 1986, p. 4.

[43] Rapport hebdomadaire, semaine du 10–24 août 1920. Aley, 24 August 1920, CADLC 399 PAAP / 186. An additional source unfortunately only came to the author's attention after writing the chapter and therefore could not be included in the analysis; it is a 15-page pamphlet on 'The demands of the people of Kurd Dagh', printed for presentation to the Great Turkish National Assembly in Ankara in 1922 and probably penned by Haj Henan or somebody close to him. It demands the revision of the proposed border to include more Kurd Dagh villages in Turkish territory. The document is available through http://isamveri.org/pdfrisaleosm/R165845.pdf.

Seydê Dîkê, Ehmedê Rûtê, Evdî Khejê and Haj Henan Sheikh Ismail Zada are remembered to have joined one of the founding meetings for the Kuva-yı Milliye, led by Kazim Karabekir Pasha, near Marash.[44]

Religious convictions seem to have played an ambiguous role as well. Ehmedê Rûtê is said to have sworn a solemn oath, together with Mustafa Kemal, with whom he was personally acquainted, to remain steadfast allies against the foreign invaders. According to oral historical accounts, Ehmedê sealed his oath by placing his foot, rather than his hand, on the Qur'an, making the gesture both blasphemous and more powerful. Other rebels, such as Haj Henan and Evdî Khejê, are remembered as deeply pious personalities.

The mix of motives evidenced in anecdotal form is consistent with the situation in other parts of northern Syria, which has permitted a variety of scholarly interpretations. Some scholars, following Adham al-Jundî's earlier interpretation, have cast the rebels around Hanano as Arab nationalists.[45] Others have assumed an emergent popular 'Syrian' nationalist affect[46] or emphasised a more regional focus by claiming that the rebels fought 'to forge a new political order in northern Syria'.[47] More recent interventions have underlined the ambiguous and mixed motivations of men who at least initially fought for the sake of a modern(ised) Ottoman polity.[48] This perspective is shared by some interlocutors from the region today, while others – perhaps in response to current developments in the region – suggest that the insurgents of whom this chapter speaks acted out of a desire to safeguard a certain degree of autonomy for their home region.

---

[44] Elî, *Çiyayê Kurmênc*, p. 233.

[45] For a critical take on this, see Keith David Watenpaugh, *Being Modern in the Middle East* (Princeton and Oxford: Princeton University Press, 2006), p. 174.

[46] E.g., James Gelvin: *Divided Loyalties* (Berkeley: University of California Press, 1998), pp. 133–34, Philip S. Khoury, *Syria and the French Mandate, 1920–1945* (Princeton: Princeton University Press, 1987), pp. 105–8.

[47] Fred Lawson, 'The Northern Syrian Revolts of 1919–1921 and the Sharifian Regime: Congruence or Conflict of Interests and Ideologies?', in Thomas Philipp and Christoph Schumann (eds), *From the Syrian Land to the States of Syria and Lebanon* (Beirut: Orient-Institut, 2004), p. 258.

[48] Watenpaugh, *Being Modern*; also Provence, *The Last Ottoman Generation*.

## Living with a New Frontier

Following the Treaty of Ankara of October 1921, France concentrated on consolidating her presence and authority in northern Syria. Employing a tried-and-true strategy, the new mandate power used local political dynamics and allied with influential Aghas to secure the region. Rashid, brother of abovementioned insurgent Haj Henan of the Sheikh Ismail Zada (Şêx Sim'ela) family, became their most important ally. Known as Koreşît (Kor Rashid, 'Rashid the Blind'), he remained one of the most influential Aghas of Kurd Dagh until his death in 1939. In view of their contrasting political positionings, and because Haj Henan was wanted for his rebellion by the mandate authorities, the brothers divided the family's properties, located on both sides of the new frontier. Haj Henan stayed in Qaziqlî village on the Turkish side, while Koreşît resided in Gundî Bêkê, just over the border in Syria. Yet only a few years later, Haj Henan faced persecution in Turkey, possibly due to his alleged sympathies with the Sheikh Said uprising of 1925. Benefiting from an amnesty secured by his brother, he made his peace with France and retreated to Syrian territory, forsaking his properties on the Turkish side. He did not involve himself in local or regional politics until 1946, when he recruited, financed and personally led a voluntary force to join the war in Palestine. According to family members and local knowledge, his motivations then, as well as in the early 1920s, were religious rather than (Arab or Turkish) nationalist: Haj Henan fought to defend Islam, siding with Muslims against non-believers.

Koreşît formulated three conditions for lending his support to French rule, demanding, first, a general amnesty for all men who had fought against the French (a condition that had been stipulated in the Treaty of Ankara as well, and that in this case also benefited his own brother and his men); secondly, the establishment of Turkish as the official language of the area, since the local population did not speak Arabic; and thirdly, the establishment of a separate *Qadha* (Caza, in French sources) that would feature locally recruited officials.[49]

Indeed, a new *Qadha* under the name of Kurd Dagh, comprising almost 370 villages, was established in November 1921; Turkish and Arabic were its

[49] Al-Bahrī, *Nubdha*, pp. 4–5.

official languages and its bureaucrats were required to master both.[50] The new *Qadha* had four districts (Rajo, Katma/Qitmê, Bulbul and Djoum/Cûmê), the exact boundaries of which were yet to be fixed. In 1922 the seat of government, initially at Qitmê and then at Meidanki, was moved to Maabatli/ Mabeta, one of the Sheikh Ismail Zadas' centres of power.[51] The *Qadha*'s territory (corresponding to Syria's later administrative region [*mantiqa*] of Afrin) covered about 3,850 square km. It was defined, in the north, by the Syrian–Turkish border; in the west and south by the border between the state of Aleppo and the sanjak of Alexandretta with its special legal status; the southern and eastern administrative boundaries were drawn across Syrian territory. The official reasoning for the delimitations of the new *Qadha* followed an ethnic logic, claiming that the demographic composition of the region with its Kurdish population made a separate administrative unit necessary: 'Recognising that political and technical considerations make it necessary to unite in one single administrative district the inhabitants of Kurdish race who occupy the northern part of the Sandjak of Aleppo.'[52]

With the sense that French presence in the region was now less precarious, the infrastructure that had been cut and damaged by the rebels was restored

---

[50] Arrêté 1443/647 of 6 November 1921 and Arrêté 4276 *Modifiant les limites du Caza de Kurd Dagh* of 26 August 1922, signed by General Governor of the State of Aleppo, Mohamad Kamil al-Qudsi and approved by High Commissioner, Henri Gouraud. Referred to and published, respectively, in *Bulletin Hebdomadaire des Actes administratifs du Haut-Commissariat* No. 41, 8 October 1922, p. 266; BNF; https://gallica.bnf.fr/ark:/12148/ bpt6k6486997n (accessed 31 March 2020). See also Al-Baḥrī, *Nubdha*, p. 5, Stephen Longrigg, *Syria and Lebanon under the French Mandate*, (London: Oxford University Press, 1958), pp. 370–71 and M. ʿAlī, *Jabal al-Kurd*, pp. 123–25.

[51] Arrêté 4275 *Transférant le Chef du Caza de Kurd Dagh à M'Abadei* [*sic*] of 26 August 1922, signed by General Governor of the State of Aleppo, Mohamad Kamil al-Qudsi and approved by High Commissioner, Henri Gouraud; published in *Bulletin Hebdomadaire des Actes administratifs du Haut-Commissariat* No. 41, 8 October 1922, p. 266; BNF; https:// gallica.bnf.fr/ark:/12148/bpt6k6486997n (accessed 31 March 2020). Also, Ali n.d.: p. 124.

[52] Arrêté 4276 Modifiant les limites du Caza de Kurd Dagh of 26 August,1922, signed by General Governor of the State of Aleppo, Mohamad Kamil al-Qudsi and approved by High Commissioner, Henri Gouraud; published in Bulletin Hebdomadaire des Actes administratifs du Haut-Commissariat No. 41, 8 October 1922, p. 266; BNF; https://gallica.bnf.fr/ ark:/12148/bpt6k6486997n (accessed 31 March 2020).

and improved. Bridges were repaired, barracks and posts renovated and furnished, and lines of communication, notably telegraph and telephone lines, (re)extended.[53] By December 1922 General Gracy was able to report with satisfaction on his inspection visit to the post in Rajo:

> The region of KURD DAGH is absolutely calm; influential Aghas have come to greet me at Radjou [. . .] I believe that, if we continue the wise policy which we have adopted in this region, the Kurd Dagh could soon be considered as definitely acquired for the French mandate.[54]

During the 1920s the town of Afrin gradually grew into the role of the *Qadha*'s administrative and economic centre (a function that had temporarily been assumed by neighbouring Azaz).[55]

The new border with Turkey represented both a resource and an impediment for the inhabitants of Kurd Dagh. Physically, crossing from Syrian into Turkish territory was initially experienced mainly as a change in spheres of control. In the hilly, partly mountainous terrain, a line of border posts, rather than pervasive material fortifications, marked the dividing line. The exact delineation of the border remained a subject of debate between French and Turkish representatives for decades.[56] The porous, 'green' character of the frontier, which was to persist until the late 1950s, allowed for cross-border mobility in both directions. In addition to 'regular' cross-border movements for reasons such as maintaining kinship relations through marriage and economic purposes, 'frontier activities' in the region, according to the French delegate at Aleppo in March 1939, consisted of 'smuggling, clandestine

---

[53] Compte rendu de la visite des ponts de la route de Radjou et du poste de Radjou, 23 September 1923; as well as Rapport du Général Gracy, Cdt. de la 4° Brigade à la suite de son inspection des postes de El-Hammam, Kirik-Khan, Hadjilar et Radjou. Both: SHD-GR 4 H 147.

[54] Rapport du Général Gracy, Cdt. de la 4° Brigade à la suite de son inspection des postes de El-Hammam, Kirik-Khan, Hadjilar et Radjou. SHD-GR 4 H 147.

[55] Cf. Ḥuṣṣāf, Ismāʿīl Muḥammad, *Tārīkh Kurdistān Sūriyā al-muʿāṣir, 1916–1946*, Vol. 1 (Erbil: Salahaddin University, 2017), pp. 284–85.

[56] Thus, a frontier commission, made up of Turkish and French (not Syrian) officers, visited Kurd Dagh in January 1939; *Correspondence d'Orient* 32e année, no 493, p. 34; BNF; https://gallica.bnf.fr/ark:/12148/bpt6k5804814z/f36.image (accessed 31 March 2020).

trafficking of arms and munitions, presence of suspects and Turkish propaganda on the frontier, etc. (*commerce de contrabande, traffic clandestin d'armes et de munitions, présence à la frontière des suspects, propaganda turque, etc)'.*[57] Such 'clandestine' practices took place as part of (para)military confrontations on and across the border in the 1930s during the *Mûrûd* movement discussed below; but smuggling more broadly must be seen before the background of shifting economic policies in the region since the late 1920s, related to the Great Depression, as Öztan argues.[58] The frontier presented an opportunity to escape from criminal persecution and social pressures – criminals who were wanted on the Syrian side of the border frequently sought refuge in Turkey while similar movements took place in the other direction; and Tejel shows that women crossed the border seeking to expand their spaces of agency.[59] As political subjectivities and social identities were reordered through the new states of Syria and the Turkish Republic, persons who owned properties on either side of the new border were able to opt for Syrian or Turkish citizenship; a decision which was, more often than not, linked to strategic considerations and projections into the future.

Yet the negative effects of the new frontier could not be denied. Kilis was deprived of a good part of its fertile agricultural hinterland;[60] families were divided and residents separated from their accustomed pastures, fields and properties, which were now subject to different regimes of taxation and legal systems. All this represented not only an economic transformation but gradually lead to a weakening of social ties and cultural shifts.[61]

---

[57] Le Délégué Adjoint du Haut Commissaire pour le Mohafazat d'Alep [Philippe David] à Monsieur le Général Commandant les troupes des territoires Nord Syrie. Aleppo, 2 March 1939. CADN-BEY/CP/507.

[58] Ramazan Hakkı Öztan, 'The Great Depression and the Making of Turkish–Syrian Border, 1921–1939', *International Journal of Middle East Studies*, Vol. 52, No. 2 (2020), pp. 311–26.

[59] Jordi Tejel, 'Des femmes contre des moutons: franchissements féminins de la frontière turcosyrienne (1929–1944)', 20 & 21. *Revue d'histoire*, Vol. 145 (2020), pp. 35–47.

[60] In 1924 French officials estimated that the villages now in Syria had contributed 75 per cent of the caza's harvests (Mizrahi, *Genèse*, p. 166, fn 9).

[61] Hatice Pinar Şenoğuz, *Community, Change, and Border Towns* (London: Routledge, 2018), p. 41.

## Local Discontent and Translocal Politics: The *Mûrûd*

Until the mid-1930s, discontent with French and Agha rule in Kurd Dagh remained relatively muted. Acts of banditry, a persistent feature during the Ottoman years, continued during the mandate – examples are the acts of cross-border raider and smuggler Ali Karo in 1934[62] or those of famous bandit Mustafa Cholaq, native of Chencheliya village near Rajo and a veteran of the *cheta* movement, of whom a popular song still speaks.[63] Retrospectively, these incidents have been interpreted at least as a sign of popular resistance against state power and control[64] if not acts of rebellion against mandate rule; but again, lacking contemporary testimony, it is not possible to assess the extent to which bandits like Cholaq were indeed (partly) motivated by political positionings. While a general opposition to state authority and its institutional practices might have been tinged with resentment of colonial rule, it is also clear that hegemonic discourses prevalent in Baathist Syria, where anti-colonial resistance was highly valued, may have informed the way in which such acts have been remembered in hindsight.

In the 1930s, however, a formidable new movement mobilised local opposition to the mandate. Referred to as *Mûrûd* (referencing the Arabic *mūrīd*)[65], it quickly attracted followers – according to French intelligence sources, by January 1939, 8,000 of Kurd Dagh's estimated 12,000 men adhered to the movement.[66] Among the *Mûrûd* were men who had already fought in the anti-French insurgency in 1920, the most prominent among them the movement's

---

[62] Benjamin Thomas White, *The Emergence of Minorities in the Middle East* (Edinburgh: Edinburgh University Press, 2011), pp. 104–5.

[63] In 1929 Cholaq and his men attacked large, wealthy Kafr Safra village, killing and plundering gendarmerie and tax collectors, supposedly out of opposition to French tax collection practices. See ʿAlī, *Jabal al-Kurd*, 595f.; On Cholaq see also *L'Armée d'Afrique* 6e année, numéro 56, June 1929, p. 200, BNF; https://gallica.bnf.fr/ark:/12148/bpt6k5474491b/f30.image (accessed 1 April 2020).

[64] White, *The Emergence of Minorities*, pp. 104–5.

[65] This refers to the followers of a religious authority, often a Sufi sheikh.

[66] French sources, but also local memory, indicate that while many followed the *Mûrûd* from conviction, others were afraid of violent reprisals if they refused. *Notice sur la confrérie des Muruds du Kurd Dagh*. Le capitaine Girbau (?), Inspecteur des Services Spéciaux due Vilayet d'Alep, 2 January 1939. CADN - BEY/CP/507.

military leader, Rashid Ibo. Yet others who had fought against France in 1920, such as Haj Henan and Seydê Dîkê, kept their distance from the movement and even opposed it, effectively siding against former allies with their former enemy. The reasons for this apparent changing of political sides lay in the internal fault-lines of Kurd Dagh society and politics, in the complex web of relations between its social elite and Syrian nationalists from Aleppo, as well as – last, but not least – political developments across the border in Turkey.

The *Mûrûd* started out as a religious (Sufi) brotherhood, but soon evolved into a social movement with a paramilitary structure. They were led by Sheikh Ibrahim Khalil Soğukoğlu, who came to the region in 1930. Born in 1901 near Izmit, Ibrahim Khalil had served as a non-commissioned officer in the Ottoman Army during the First World War.[67] He had become a disciple to Naqshbandi sheikhs in Homs and Damascus but was expelled from Syria under accusations of fraud and subsequently settled in the region of Islahiye. When he ran into trouble with the authorities for mobilising a religious followership, he clandestinely crossed the border into Syrian Kurd Dagh, where he initially settled under the protection of Faiq Agha from the powerful Sheikh Ismail Zada family.

The movement advocated for religious and spiritual rigour, exhorting people to 'return' to original Islamic practice, such as a strict observation of Ramadan fasting, the five daily prayers, almsgiving etc., but also urging them to give up tobacco, reject profane music and refrain from other frivolous practices. Nevertheless, some other Sufi sheikhs of the region positioned themselves against the *Mûrûd*, many of whom, Lescot noted, had only 'a very vague notion' of Naqshbandi practices. Outwardly, adherents indicated their allegiance by cultivating long beards;[68] and local memory recalls that *Mûrûd* displayed specific habitual characteristics, such as drinking their tea while

[67] For biographical information, I follow Fehmi Soğukoğlu, 'İbrahim Halil Efendi ve Mürit Hareketi'nin Millî Mücadele'ye Katkısı', *Millî Mücadele'de Güney Bölgesi Sempozyumu* (Ankara: Atatürk Araştırma Merkezi, 2015) pp. 237–65; Sheikh Ibrahim's grandson and Lescot who reflects contemporary French intelligence on the Sheikh. Other sources (e.g., Aşmat ʿUmar, 'Ḥarakat al-Mūrīdīn fī Jabal al-Akrād, 1930–1945' *Dirāsāt Ishtirākiyya*, Vol. 5 (1984) differ.

[68] This memory was recurrent in local narratives of the time; see also Roger Lescot, 'Le Kurd Dagh', p. 108.

keeping sugar in their mouths (rather than stirring it into their cups, as was the usual custom).[69]

The movement articulated not only long-standing socio-economic conflicts but worked through the charismatic figure of Sheikh Ibrahim Khalil who promised otherworldly rewards to adherents, as well as military practices and hierarchies, which were implemented and instilled by a former Turkish non-commissioned officer who had taken over military training for the insurgents.[70] When Sheikh Ibrahim temporarily returned to Turkey in 1933, three local men acted as his representatives: Sheikh Hanifa (in charge of spiritual affairs), Rashid Ibo from Bilêlka village and Ali Ghaleb (aka Ali Qurt Ali) from Serinje.[71]

While most of Sheikh Ibrahim Khalil's followers came from Syria, some, often outlaws or army deserters, held Turkish nationality.[72] The movement appealed primarily to poorer and landless peasants, articulating, as it did, long-standing socio-economic grievances: it denounced the glaring economic inequalities between Aghas and poorer peasants, and promised redress for families of women who had been raped by members of Agha families. Geographically, the movement was strongest in the poorer northernmost villages close to the border.[73]

---

[69] I am obliged to Jordi Tejel for pointing out that this echoes practices in other Kurdish regions with a strong Naqshbandi tradition, e.g. areas around Bitlis, Van and on the Turkish-Iranian border.

[70] *Notice sur la confrérie des Muruds du Kurd Dagh*. Le capitaine Girbau (?), Inspecteur des Services Spéciaux due Vilayet d'Alep, 2 January 1939, CADN, BEY/CP/507, 11. The name of this officer which is variously given as Hasan Sidqi or 'Hasan Chaouich', or as Bakr Fehmi, suggesting that there may have been more than one. French sources also refer to him as 'Bakr Sidqi', perhaps confusing him with the well-known Ottoman-Kurdish soldier who served King Faisal in Syria and Iraq.

[71] *Notice sur la confrérie des Muruds du Kurd Dagh*. Le capitaine Girbau (?), Inspecteur des Services Spéciaux due Vilayet d'Alep, 2 January 1939, CADN, BEY/CP/507, 4.

[72] Among those who joined the movement while holding Turkish nationality were Mohamed and Rashid, two of Abdallah Etûnê's sons, brothers of abovementioned Omar who had fought the French in 1920; *Sujets turcs se trouvant avec les Muruds*, Aleppo, 28 January 1939 (Haut Commissariat de la République Française en Syrie et au Liban; Délégation d'Alep; No 391/S.P.); CADN, BEY/CP/507.

[73] Commander of the Sector Kurd Dagh, Mercuit: 'Extrait d'un rapport de Commandant du secteur du Kurd Dagh sur la situation dans le Kurd Dagh à la date du 24 April 1939', 2. CADN, BEY/CP/507.

The Sheikh Ismail Zada family, and especially their most powerful representative at the time, Koreşît, were the main target of *Mûrûd* wrath. Although other Aghas largely sided against the movement, some also sought to benefit from the conflict to settle older rivalries.[74] Within the national arena of the young Syrian state, the movement was allied to the Syrian nationalists organised within the National Bloc, with whom they were united in their opposition to the French mandate. In September 1936, 200–300 *Mûrûd* staged an enthusiastic welcome to the Syrian nationalists' delegation returning from negotiations in Paris when their train passed through Afrin;[75] in the same year, Husein 'Auni (also from an Agha background) with the support of the *Mûrûd* and the National Bloc ran against Koreşît in the parliamentary elections, eventually – and for many, surprisingly – emerging victorious.

Again, Kurd Dagh's liminal position on the border, and specifically the role of Turkey, was key in nurturing local political developments.[76] This was particularly significant considering the simultaneous developments in the adjacent sanjak of Alexandretta, which underwent several stages of gradual autonomy until formally becoming part of Turkey in July 1939. France feared that Turkey aimed at annexing Kurd Dagh too, and that it prepared for a possible referendum in the *Qadha* by fostering anti-French and pro-Turkish sentiments. Local interlocutors and popular local historiography recall that 'Atatürk' sent a great number of 'Turkish hats' to Kurd Dagh, to be distributed among the population by Seydê Dîkê, who had fought against France in 1920. Interlocutors interpreted this as an effort to make the population appear more 'Turkish' by adopting the outwardly signs of Kemalist modernisation. (After some initial hesitation, however,

---

[74] Roger Lescot, 'Le Kurd Dagh', p. 110.

[75] Cf. 'Umar, 'Ḥarakat al-Mūrīdīn', pp. 158–71.

[76] Several communications from the British Ambassador in Ankara, Viscount Halifax, and the British Consul in Aleppo, Davis, and Damascus, Mackereth, in March 1939 indicate the attention that Britain gave to the situation on the Turkish–Syrian border in the light of suspected Turkish ambitions to revise the post-war order on the eve of the Second World War, all in TNA-FO 371/23276.

Seydê Dîkê reportedly understood that Turkey did not have Kurd Dagh's interests at heart either, and ostentatiously burned the hats.)[77]

French officials on the ground were certain that Turkey sought to destabilise the situation in Syria further by actively supporting the *Mûrûd*. While Turkey had initially viewed Sheikh Ibrahim Khalil's activities with suspicion, he was reported to act under orders from the Turkish secret service at least from 1935–36 onwards.[78] Turkish officials, French sources complained, not only turned a blind eye to insurgents' movements across the border, but actively communicated with the rebels, allowing them to acquire additional weapons, ammunition and even 'volunteers' from Turkey.[79] In March 1939 the French ambassador at Ankara, Massigli, presented the Turkish Foreign Minister, Saraçoğlu, with documents, seized in February 1939 with *Mûrûd* leader Sheikh Hanifa, that proved active contacts between the Kaimakam of Kilis and local Turkish officers, on the one hand, and the insurgents, on the other hand.[80] In this light, the synchronicity of the inauguration of the Turkish province of Hatay and the effective end of the *Mûrûd* revolt in Kurd Dagh in summer 1939 have been interpreted as more than coincidental: the

---

[77] Fradet, *Le montagne*; see also a video composed by a local amateur historian, describing the *cheta* and *Mûrûd* movements, at https://www.facebook.com/tirej.raman/videos/2943383019087946 (accessed 15 October 2020).

[78] Roger Lescot, 'Le Kurd Dagh', pp. 111–13. Cf. also Sever Işık, 'Ne Yakın ne Uzak bir Tarihsel Hadise: İbrahim Halil Soğukoğlu ve Kürtdağı Mürid Hareketi', *e-Şarkiyat İlmi Araştırmalar Dergisi/Journal of Oriental Scientific Research*, Vol. 10, No. 3/21 (2018): pp. 1078–1109. Also 'Syrie: La pacification du Kurd Dagh est terminée', *Les Annales coloniales: organe de la 'France coloniale moderne'*, 18 April 1939, année 39, numéro 16, section Echos d'Outre-Mer et des terres étrangères. BNF, retrieved online at https://gallica.bnf.fr/ark:/12148/bpt6k6272132j/f4.image on 31 March 2020. See also Fradet, *Le montagne*.

[79] French patrols reported Turkish government-issued ammunition found with the insurgents, a fighter dressed in Turkish uniform and other indications that appeared to support that belief. *Extrait d'un rapport de Commandant du secteur du Kurd Dagh sur la situation dans le Kurd Dagh à la date du 24 April 1939*. Commander of the Sector Kurd Dagh, Mercuit. CADN, BEY/CP/507. Also see two telegrams (E 1753-266 and 267) from the British consul in Aleppo, Davis, to the British Foreign Office, 9 March 1939; TNA, FO 371/23276.

[80] The French delegate at Aleppo sent a translation of the documents to the French High Commissioner in Beirut on 9 March 1939; CADN, BEY/CP/507.

Turkish government, this perspective suggests, had achieved its aim and did not need to use unrest in Kurd Dagh as a bargaining chip to put pressure on French-mandated Syria anymore.[81]

When Ibrahim Khalil returned to Syria in late 1938, he toured the border villages with his escort, 'dispensing justice' by announcing the 'annulment' of peasants' debts and declaring it legitimate to seize Agha properties as 'reparations' for earlier dispossessions and acts of injustice committed by Aghas.[82] The movement grew increasingly violent. Koreşît and some of his relatives, but also others who sided with the Aghas, received threatening letters;[83] they became the target of economic blockades as well as armed attacks.[84] Over several years, a number of prominent figures on the Agha side were killed, among them Koreşît's brother, Ja'far, his nephew, Sheikho, and even Koreşît himself, who eventually succumbed to a gunshot wound he had sustained during an assassination attempt in October 1938.[85] Not only members of Agha families, but also some of Kurd Dagh's prominent spiritual figures fell victim to *Mûrûd* attacks. Sheikh Isma'il Sheikh Qember, a well-known Sufi sheikh from Xilalka village who sided with the Aghas, was killed together with Koreşît's brother, Ja'far Agha, during an assault on Ja'far's residence in Gundî Bêkê;[86] and Jamil Agha Shamo, head of Kurd Dagh's Êzidî community, was attacked while accompanying Faiq Agha on a car trip.[87]

---

[81] Sever Işık, 'Ne Yakın ne Uzak'.

[82] Roger Lescot, 'Le Kurd Dagh', p. 109.

[83] Letter from Koreşît to the French delegate at Aleppo, Philippe David; Aleppo, 4 January 1939; CADN, BEY/CP/507.

[84] E.g., Information N° 97 from Lt.-Col. Bertschy, commander of the gendarmerie in North Syria, Aleppo, 20 January 1939; Le Délégué-Adjoint du Haut-Commissaire pour le Mohafazat d'Alep à Monsieur le Haut-Commissaire de la République Française à Beyrouth, A/s de la situation au Djébel Akrad (Kurd-Dagh). N° 277/S.P., 21 January 1939; all CADN, BEY/CP/507.

[85] Letter from Koreşît to the French delegate at Aleppo, Philippe David, 4 January 1939; CADN, BEY/CP/507.

[86] Le Délégué-Adjoint du Haut-Commissaire pour le Mohafazat d'Alep à Monsieur le Haut-Commissaire de la République Française à Beyrouth, *Incident de Bey-Obaci (Kurd-Dagh)*, N° 277/S.P. Aleppo 23 January 1939; also CADN, BEY/CP/507.

[87] *Notice sur la confrérie des Muruds du Kurd Dagh*. Le capitaine Girbau (?), Inspecteur des Services Spéciaux due Vilayet d'Alep, 2 January 1939, p. 9. CADN, BEY/CP/507.

Syrian gendarmerie and French troops were deployed against the *Mûrûd*.[88] While Aleppo newspapers were 'forbidden to publish any accounts of military operations or troop movements in this area' beyond those communicated in 'official communiqués', British contemporary sources noted that 'almost the entire garrison of Aleppo has [. . .] been sent out to the area in question' while 'additional French aircraft [were] brought up from Rayak' for 'observation and bombardment'.[89] At the height of the armed confrontations, in 1938 and 1939, these French troops, as well as Syrian gendarmerie, was opposed by bands of *Mûrûd* numbering between 60 and 250 men; battles took place at Nabi Houri/Cyrrhus, Bulbul, the village of Benîrka and in the Parsi mountains. Although French papers reported that 'the pacification of Kurd Dagh had been completed' in April 1939, violent clashes continued until June.[90] The fighting was so intense that the '*militaires des Troupes du Levant*', as well as the '*personnels civils de nationalité française*' who had participated in these so-called '*opérations de police*' in October 1939 received the '*médaille commémorative de Syrie-Cilicie avec agrafe en bronze*' in recognition.[91] In December of that year, a French presidential decree retrospectively granted double pay to the troops involved, recognising that these so-called 'police operations' had in fact amounted to a veritable war.[92]

[88] Mustafa al-Shehabi, Governor (Mohafez) of Aleppo, to the French delegate at Aleppo, Philippe David, 5 January 1939; No 97/26-D. CADN, BEY/CP/507.

[89] Report of the British consul at Aleppo, Davis, to the Foreign Office, 17 March 1939. TNA, FO 371/23276.

[90] 'Syrie: La pacification du Kurd Dagh est terminée', *Les Annales coloniales: organe de la 'France coloniale moderne'*, Vol. 39, No. 16 (18 April 1939). BNF; https://gallica.bnf.fr/ark:/12148/bpt6k6272132j/f4.image, (accessed 31 March 2020).

[91] *La Charente: organe républicain quotidien*, 68 (26 October 1939). BNF; https://gallica.bnf.fr/ark:/12148/bpt6k4665211x/f2.image, (accessed 31 March, 2020). Also *Le Petit Marocain*, 23 October 1939, p. 2. BNF; https://gallica.bnf.fr/ark:/12148/bpt6k4691773b (accessed 5 April 2020).

[92] 'Rapport au Président de la République Française', 6 December 1939; and 'Décret accordant le bénéfice de la campagne double aux militaires ayant pris part aux combats due Kurd Dagh (Levant)' 6 December 1939, both in *Journal Officiel de la République Française. Lois et décrets*, Vol. 71, No. 105 (9 December 1939), 13816. BNF, https://gallica.bnf.fr/ark:/12148/bpt6k57143393/f8.image (accessed 31 March 2020).

Similar to the French modus operandi in other parts of Syria, military reprisals targeted not just the insurgent bands, but also their home villages. '[A]s many as ninety-six light bombs were dropped on MURUD villages and concentrations' in just one day in March 1939.[93] Aerial bombardment on Rashid Ibo's village, Bilêlka, killed his daughter Zulekha and wounded his sister Khadija.[94] The population of 'entire villages', such as Cheikhorzê and Meydanli as well as Bilêlka, fled across the border into Turkey, taking even their livestock, furnishings, linen etc. with them. Yet not only *Mûrûd* and their kin, but also villagers opposed to them fled into Turkey to avoid the fighting. French officials reacted with alarm, fearing that this could serve to support Turkish claims vis-à-vis Syrian territory:

> This [permits] the Turkish government to show that the insecurity is such in KURD DAGH that without any consideration of political sides, the Kurds come to look for support and protection from Turkey; adding to this fact that of the Turkish interests in KURD DAGH, which are at risk of being sacrificed due to the insecurity (Turkish landowners on the border being unable to cultivate their lands located in Kurd Dagh). Turkey could thus justify a demand for armed intervention on Syrian territory as a prelude, as in the SANDJAK [of Alexandretta] to a more complete stranglehold in the future.[95]

With the violent battles of summer 1939, the *Mûrûd* revolt largely came to an end, although occasional attacks and assassinations continued in the 1940s. Sheikh Ibrahim Khalil returned briefly to Kurd Dagh in July 1940, but otherwise remained in Turkey. While most villagers who had fled across the border returned to Syria after a few months, others, in particular active insurgents and their families, continued to seek refuge in Turkey from French reprisals. Most of them, however, returned to Syria by 1944. After living on

---

[93] Report of the British consul at Aleppo, Davis, to the Foreign Office, 17 March 1939. TNA, FO 371/23276.

[94] Najjār, 'Aḥad qādat'.

[95] 'Extrait d'un rapport de Commandant du secteur du Kurd Dagh sur la situation dans le Kurd Dagh à la date du 24 April 1939.' CADN, BEY/CP/507. See also Nāṣir, Ḥasan Taḥsīn, 'Ḥikāyat mujāhid min waṭanī: fī ḥiwār Ibn al-Mujāhid Rashīd Ibo', *Al-Jamahir* 11655 (1 September 2004).

Turkish territory for a duration of five years, they were treated as Turkish citizens, meaning that by 1944 they could be drafted into army service – an obligation they sought to avoid. Their return movement was facilitated by political shifts inside Syria favourable to the former insurgents: not only had the mandate administration shifted from Vichy France to the Free French and the Allies, but the Syrian nationalist movement was becoming stronger, especially after the parliamentary elections of 1943 from which the Syrian nationalists emerged victorious.[96]

## Conclusion: Commemoration and Nationalism

Pending further research, the motives of Kurd Dagh's insurgents to rise against France remain open to interpretation. While we may confidently claim to have a grasp of what they fought *against*, namely foreign, in particular European and non-Muslim, domination and control over their territory, it is more difficult to ascertain what they were fighting *for*. The *Mûrûd* movement of the 1930s and the anti-French uprising of the years between 1919 and 1921 differed from each other in several ways. Although Islamic symbols and sentiments had been invoked during the earlier period as well, and individual rebels such as Haj Henan were certainly pious men, neither contemporary evidence nor local accounts indicate that the role of religion for the ideology or organisation of the *cheta* was as central as in the case of the *Mûrûd*. Another difference is the significance of social and class divisions. While this issue was pivotal to the *Mûrûd* movement, it apparently did not play a role in the immediate post-war uprisings, where Aghas and representatives of influential local families participated alongside men of non-elite backgrounds.

And yet, there are also similarities, if not lines of continuity. One is the geography of revolt, centring in the mountainous areas close to the border, pointing to the significance of proximity to Turkey and the active involvement of Turkish politics in the region. The persistent significance of this point is glaringly obvious as this chapter is being written. From the vantage point of today, the issue of armed resistance against France in Kurd Dagh during the

---

[96] On the situation in Kurd Dagh between 1941 and 1946, see Katharina Lange, 'Peripheral Experiences: Everyday life in the Kurd Dagh (Northern Syria) during the Allied occupation in the Second World War', in Liebau et al., *World in World Wars*, pp. 401–28.

1920s to the 1940s appears more contentious, and more political, than ever. Since March 2018 the region of the former *Qadha* of Kurd Dagh has been under occupation by militias opposed to the Assad regime who claim to act in the name of Islam, and operate with support by, and under control of, the Turkish government. An increasing number of the region's inhabitants have been forcibly displaced to such a degree that not only the political, but even the demographic future of the region is an open question.

Against this background, contested efforts to recover the region's past are newly significant. Divergent interpretations of the motivations that drove the men of whom this chapter speaks mark, in themselves, contested terrain. Significantly, not only the events of the 1920s and 1930s in Kurd Dagh, but also their commemoration have been shaped by the – then emerging, later fixed – border. As far as these events have been remembered at all, they have been viewed through the lenses of the multiple national and ethnic contexts – Turkish, Syrian, including Arab and Kurdish – with which this region is now associated, and between which it has been contested.

This chapter cannot provide a full discussion of the historiography of the events treated here. Suffice it to say that, in the context of independent Syria, the insurgent acts in Kurd Dagh between 1919 and 1921, and even the *Mûrûd* revolt of the 1930s, were largely forgotten. As far as they have been publicly addressed at all, they have been narrated as part of a larger Syrian struggle against colonial domination – a perspective which is demonstrated by Adham al-Jundi's commemoration of Meho Îbshashê cited at the beginning of this chapter; or by Hafiz al-Assad's formal recognition of Rashid Ibo as a veteran of Syria's anti-colonial struggle ('*manaḥ laqab mujāhid*') that was accompanied with the grant of a function in the 'combatants' association' (*rābiṭat al-mujāhidīn*) and a modest pension until Ibo's death, at the age of 102, in 2004.[97] During the Baathist era, a nationalist Syrian perspective was the dominant (and, in fact, the only officially possible) way of commemorating those movements.[98] The additional aspect of a class struggle against the

---

[97] Ḥasan Taḥsīn Nāṣir, 'Ḥikāyat mujāhid min waṭanī: fī ḥiwār Ibn al-Mujāhid Rashīd Ibo' *Al-Jamahir* 11655 (1.9. 2004), see also Al-Najjār, 'Aḥad qādat', p. 4.

[98] Even Rashid Hemo had to cautiously precede his account *Thaurat Jabal al-Akrād – 'ḥarakat al-mūrīdīn*' (No place, no publisher, 2001), which otherwise reflects a Kurdish nationalist perspective, with a preface echoing the Baathist narrative.

'feudalists' was highlighted in a 1984 article by local lawyer and Communist member of parliament, Asmat Umar.

The complex interplay of Turkish perspectives on the events discussed in this chapter deserve an analysis of their own, which the present text cannot provide.[99] Yet it is important to note that there has, besides other perspectives, been a tendency to frame the events of the 1920s and 1930s in the light of Turkish nationalism. Ehmedê Rûtê's actions, for instance, are commemorated today by the town of Kilis as part of Turkey's War of Independence.[100] Sheikh Ibrahim Khalil's grandson, Fehmi Soğukoğlu, has discussed the *Mûrûd* movement in the framework of the Turkish national struggle, suggesting a continuity between Kemal's presence in Kurd Dagh following the First World War, armed action against France in the early 1920s and the events of the late 1930s.[101] In 1995, historian Mustafa Öztürk reviewed the *Mûrûd* as a movement of 'Turkmen', while managing to avoid any mention of Kurds and the name 'Kurd Dagh', even as an administrative term, throughout.[102] Very recently, following the Turkish-led occupation of Afrin in 2018, Turkish media have published reports celebrating Atatürk's stay in the region a century ago,[103] associated with the 'discovery' of Atatürk's erstwhile 'headquarters' amidst calls for its restoration and musealisation.[104] This discursive line seems linked to political attempts to claim the area's historical closeness, if not centrality, to modern, national(ist) Turkish history

---

[99] See for instance Sever Işık, 'Ne Yakın ne Uzak', p. 1093.

[100] 'Kilis'in Batı Cephesi'ndeki Faaliyetler', http://www.kilis.gov.tr/tarihce, (accessed 1 September, 2019).

[101] Soğukoğlu, 'Ibrahim Khalil', p. 259.

[102] Mustafa Öztürk, *1938 Suriye Olayları ve İbrahim Halil Efendi'nin Faaliyetleri* (Ankara: Türk Tarih Kurumu Yayınları, 1995).

[103] E.g., Sinan Meydan, 9 July 2018, 'AFRİN'DEKİ ATATÜRK! Unutulan Qitmê Zaferi', https://www.sozcu.com.tr/2018/yazarlar/sinan-meydan/afrindeki-ataturk-unutulan-Qitmê-zaferi-2509788/ (accessed 26 September 2019).

[104] E.g., 'Military HQ used by Atatürk in WWI discovered in Afrin'; *Daily Sabah*, 2 July 2018; https://www.dailysabah.com/history/2018/07/02/military-hq-used-by-ataturk-in-wwi-discovered-in-afrin; (accessed 23 September 2019); or 'Military base of modern Turkey's founder found located in Syria's Afrin', *Yeni Şafak*, 2 July 2018, https://www.yenisafak.com/en/world/military-base-of-modern-turkeys-founder-found-located-in-syrias-afrin-3425321, (accessed 23 September 2019).

and perhaps, by implication, to Turkey itself – a claim which most of today's inhabitants (and particularly those who were driven out by the Turkish-led military offensive of spring 2018) would probably find problematic, to say the least.

In hindsight, the insurgents of Kurd Dagh have been claimed as part of Syria's as well as Turkey's emancipatory struggles as nascent nation states. These two metanarratives have elided any attention to the local particularities of this region, linked to its demographic and topographic specificities. Yet, following Öztan, clearly the retrospective application of national logics cannot do justice to the mix of motivations, political affiliations and mobilisations in this border region following the First World War.[105]

Alternative interpretations which highlight the significance of the local context and its specificities have, since the 2000s, emerged in local historiography and more recently on social media, reflecting both a resurgent interest in local history in Syria more generally as well as an increasing visibility of Kurdish perspectives in the Syrian public arena.[106] These tend to approach (Syrian) Kurd Dagh as a more or less distinct geographical, cultural and social entity. From such a perspective, it may appear that men like Ehmedê Rûtê, Haj Henan or Rashid Ibo fought primarily to prevent foreign rule over their home territory. Like the other two perspectives, the view that the insurgents fought for a form of local (if not Kurdish) autonomy too would seem to blend retrospective interpretations with recent political experiences and agendas. Yet in an important sense, it draws our attention to an aspect which merits a fuller consideration: the question of what place there could be for the inhabitants of a Kurdish enclave between two emergent national states, tinged by Turkish and Arab nationalism, respectively, in the post-Ottoman order. In effect, this perspective (which

---

[105] Ramazan Hakkı Öztan, 'Nationalism in Function: "Rebellions" in the Ottoman Empire and Narratives in its Absence', in M. Hakan Yavuz and Feroz Ahmad (eds), *War and Collapse. World War One and the Ottoman State* (Salt Lake City: University of Utah Press, 2016), pp. 161–63.

[106] E.g., Hemo, *Thaurat Jabal al-Akrād*; M. ʿAlī, *Jabal al-Kurd*; S. ʿAlī, *Jabal al-Kurd*; which have in turn been cited in more recent overviews such as Ḥuṣṣāf, *Tārīkh* and others.

clearly is also informed by the more recent political history of the region) regards the actions of the insurgent fighters as attempts to actively intervene in shaping their region's political trajectory. In trying to use the interstitial location of this emerging borderland, and the border itself, as assets enabling particular forms of political and military action, they engaged in their own kind o 'border-making from below'.[107]

[107] Jordi Tejel, 'Making Borders from Below: The Emergence of the Turkish–Iraqi Frontier, 1918–1925', *Middle Eastern Studies*, Vol. 54, No. 5 (2018), pp. 811–26.

# PART II

## CROSS-BORDER MOBILITIES

# 7

# BORDERS, DISEASE AND TERRITORIALITY IN THE POST-OTTOMAN MIDDLE EAST

## Samuel Dolbee

In 1925 the Syrian physician and nationalist leader 'Abd al-Rahman Shahbandar discussed the two realms of his expertise: science and politics.[1] 'It cannot be denied,' he told a crowd in Damascus, 'that science is still incapable of formulating exhaustive rules for self-determination.'[2] In doing so, Shahbandar encapsulated the great hope attached to science, which had enabled previously unthinkable technologies and, thanks to germ theory of disease, newly specific understandings of illness. His words drew a sardonic contrast, however, between these possibilities and the disappointing political realities faced by Syrians and others around the world who fought for self-determination.[3] In sum, science did not deliver the liberation Shahbandar and others like him envisioned. Yet, as elsewhere, so too in Syria and Turkey did science and technology come to have quite a lot to do with the borders and territorial

[1] On how these realms are often presented as separate, see Gabrielle Hecht, *The Radiance of France: Nuclear Power and National Identity after World War II* (Cambridge, MA: MIT Press, 1998); Timothy Mitchell, *Rule of Experts: Egypt, Techno-Politics, Modernity* (Berkeley: University of California Press, 2002).

[2] National Archives and Records Administration, RG 84, Baghdad, Iraq, Vol. 166, Dispatch from American Consulate in Damascus, 14 September 1925.

[3] Erez Manela, *The Wilsonian Moment: Self-Determination and the International Origins of Anticolonial Nationalism* (New York: Oxford University Press, 2007). For an important critique, see Hussein A.H. Omar, 'The Arab Spring of 1919', *LRB Blog*, 4 April 2019. https://www.lrb.co.uk/blog/2019/april/the-arab-spring-of-1919 (accessed 7 August 2019).

forms of emerging states, albeit not in the way Shahbandar had hoped.[4] Put differently, self-determination was no science. But science – in the form of the management of disease – came to play a key role in shaping state visions of territory, which might be thought of as, in historian Charles Maier's words, 'space in effect empowered by borders'.[5]

On a global scale, scholars have recognised that new understandings of disease emerging in the late nineteenth century associated with figures like Pasteur and Koch led to both continuities and ruptures. On the one hand, the idea that invisible agents controlled disease overlapped with religious understandings of the world, and people understood germs in these terms.[6] On the other hand, newly specific understandings of disease allowed public health experts to make new kinds of interventions in the world. As historian Linda Nash puts it, germ theory seemed to prove once and for all 'that disease-causing pathogens were situated in human bodies, not environments'.[7] For example, malaria had long been understood as connected to swampy environments and their air, a concept of disease generally referred to as miasma. The disease etiology presents in the word's etymology itself, as it literally means 'bad air'.[8] But germ theory enabled a more specific understanding of the disease as caused by a parasite spread by mosquitoes. The discoveries of the parasite that caused malaria and the mosquito as its vector in the late nineteenth century prompted a collapse of epidemiology and entomology in some places, as disease control amounted to mosquito control, particularly in settings of US colonialism such as the Philippines and Panama.[9] The shift

[4] Fredrik Meiton, *Electrical Palestine: Capital and Technology from Empire to Nation* (Oakland: University of California Press, 2019).

[5] Charles Maier, *Once within Borders: Territories of Power, Wealth, and Belonging since 1500* (Cambridge, MA: The Belknap Press of Harvard University Press, 2016), p. 1.

[6] Nancy Tomes, *The Gospel of Germs: Men, Women, and the Microbe in American Life* (Cambridge, MA: Harvard University Press, 1998).

[7] Linda Nash, *Inescapable Ecologies: A History of Environment, Disease, and Knowledge* (Berkeley: University of California Press, 2007), p. 6.

[8] Frank Snowden, *The Conquest of Malaria: Italy, 1900–1962* (New Haven: Yale University Press, 2006), p. 11.

[9] Warwick Anderson, *Colonial Pathologies: American Tropical Medicine, Race, and Hygiene in the Philippines* (Durham, NC: Duke University Press, 2006), p. 224; Paul Sutter, 'Nature's Agents or Agents of Empire? Entomological Workers and Environmental Change during the Construction of the Panama Canal', *Isis*, Vol. 98 (2007), pp. 735–37.

was perhaps epitomised by Sir Ronald Ross, who won the Nobel Prize in 1902. He articulated the new focus on insects as the enemy with a 1902 pamphlet entitled *Mosquito Brigades and How to Organise Them*, which advocated eradication of the disease-spreading creatures with bluster ('I am preaching a general crusade') and practicality ('every man should be given a badge').[10] The single-minded focus on mosquitoes would later be deemed 'anophelism', and the collapse of epidemiology and entomology was so pronounced that some called to rename malaria 'mosquito fever'.[11] Thus germ theory did not displace old understandings of disease altogether, but it did enable new kinds of responses to disease. It is this dual aspect that prompted historian Aro Velmet to summarise the historiography as insisting that the bacteriological revolution 'simultaneously did not happen and transformed everything'.[12]

Yet in Syria and on its borders in the interwar period, cattle plague and malaria had a different impact, and one, moreover, significant to the formation of borders and constitution of territoriality. To be sure, some people likely understood microbes as manifestations of the unseen, much like Muhammad ʿAbduh and Sayyid Qutb conceived of germs as *jinn*.[13] But when officials grappled with cattle plague and malaria they fought it not primarily on the level of viruses or parasites, as one might expect given some accounts of the impact of the bacteriological revolution. Rather, they fought based on an understanding of disease informed by place and race. With respect to cattle plague, officials on either side of the border between Syria and Turkey developed quarantines to stop the spread of the disease that anchored disease in place. In doing so, they consolidated the newly formed border by cutting down on cross-border movement of nomadic groups. With respect to malaria, miasmatic understandings of the disease figured prominently in

[10] Ronald Ross, *Mosquito Brigades and How to Organise Them* (London: George Philip & Son, 1902), pp. viii, 19.

[11] Hughes Evans, 'European Malaria Policy in the 1920s and 1930s', *Isis*, Vol. 80, No. 1 (1989), p. 48; Rohan Deb Roy, *Malarial Subjects: Empire, Medicine and Nonhumans in British India, 1820–1909* (New York: Cambridge University Press, 2017), p. 249.

[12] Aro Velmet, *Pasteur's Empire: Bacteriology and Politics in France, its Colonies, and the World* (New York: Oxford University Press, 2020), p. 1.

[13] Marwa Elshakry, *Reading Darwin in Arabic, 1860–1950* (Chicago: University of Chicago Press, 2013), p. 177; On Barak, *On Time: Technology and Temporality in Modern Egypt* (Berkeley: University of California Press, 2013), p. 102.

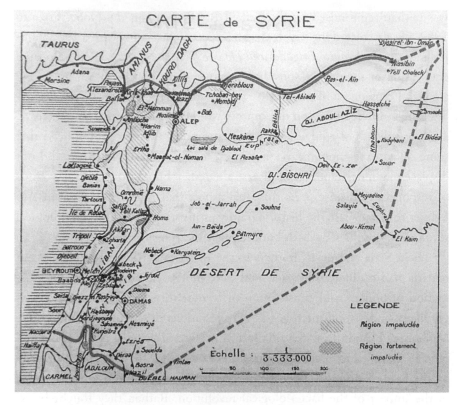

Figure 7.1  Map of malarial regions of Syria, 1926.

Credit: Institut Pasteur Service des Archives, BPT.Doc.62, Delmas and Trabaud, *Contribution à l'Étude Générale du Paludisme en Syrie.*

debates about where Assyrian refugees fleeing Iraq might settle. This aspect on its own was not entirely surprising, given the way germs and miasma overlapped with respect to malaria control whether in Argentina or India.[14] What was remarkable, however, was how often conceptions of race drove these discussions. While in the Philippines and India race had seemed to wane as an explicit interpretive lens even for colonial medicine, race and climate nevertheless accompanied discussion of Assyrian settlements and health in

---

[14] Nandini Bhattacharya, *Contagion and Enclaves: Tropical Medicine in Colonial India* (Liverpool: Liverpool University Press, 2012), p. 149; Eric D. Carter, *Enemy in the Blood: Malaria, Environment, and Development in Argentina* (Tuscaloosa: University of Alabama Press, 2012), p. 48.

many cases, though it was eclipsed increasingly by concern over mosquitoes too.[15] The understandings of disease as rooted in place or environments – as opposed to or alongside viruses or parasites – in many ways echoed Ottoman efforts at disease control, which also involved quarantines and questions about healthy places to resettle refugees. But in the mandate era, these priorities had a different impact. Not only did the League of Nations give a new veneer to disease control as a technical matter seemingly above politics. So too did the understandings of health as place and environmentally based help to shore up the structures of post-Ottoman states, giving shape to both the border between Turkey and Syria as well as the nature of Syrian territory and who could live upon it.

The constitutive role that public health played in borders and territoriality in the interwar period intersects with and extends the interventions of a burgeoning literature on borders in the modern Middle East.[16] Perhaps most

---

[15] Anderson, *Colonial Pathologies*, pP. 208–9; David Arnold, '"An Ancient Race Outworn": Malaria and Race in Colonial India, 1860–1930', in Waltraud Ernst and Bernard Harris (eds), *Race, Science and Medicine, 1700–1960* (New York: Routledge, 1999), p. 138.

[16] Seda Altuğ and Benjamin White, 'Frontière et pouvoir d'état: La frontière turco-syrienne dans les années 1920 et 1930', *Vingtième siècle. Revue d'histoire*, Vol. 103 (2009), pp. 91–104; Reem Bailony, 'From Mandate Borders to the Diaspora: Rashaya's Transnational Suffering and the Making of Lebanon in 1925', *Arab Studies Journal*, Vol. 26, No. 2 (2018), pp. 44–73; Lauren Banko, 'Refugees, Displaced Migrants, and Territorialization in Interwar Palestine', *Mashriq & Mahjar: Journal of Middle East and North African Migration Studies*, Vol. 5, No. 2 (2018); Stacy Fahrenthold, *Between the Ottomans and the Entente: The First World War in the Syrian and Lebanese Diaspora, 1908–1925* (New York: Oxford University Press, 2019); Hilary Falb Kalisman, '"The Next Generation of Cultivators": Teaching Agriculture in Iraq, Palestine and Transjordan (1920–1960)', *Histoire de l'éducation*, Vol. 148 (2019); Robert Fletcher, *British Imperialism and 'the Tribal Question': Desert Administration and Nomadic Societies in the Middle East, 1919–1936* (Oxford: Oxford University Press, 2015); Ramazan Hakkı Öztan, 'The Great Depression and the Making of Turkish–Syrian Border, 1921–1939', *International Journal of Middle East Studies*, Vol. 52, No. 2 (2020), pp. 311–26; Laura Robson, *States of Separation: Transfer, Partition, and the Making of the Modern Middle East* (Oakland: University of California Press, 2017); Vahe Tachjian, *La France en Cilicie et en Haute-Mésopotamie: Aux confins de la Turquie, de la Syrie et de l'Iraq* (Paris: Karthala, 2004); Jordi Tejel, 'Making Borders from Below: The Emergence of the Turkish-Iraqi Frontier, 1918–1925', *Middle Eastern Studies*, Vol. 54, No. 5 (2018), pp. 811–26; Benjamin White, 'Chapter 4: The Border and the Kurds', *Emergence of Minorities in the Middle East: Politics and Community in French Mandate Syria* (Edinburgh: Edinburgh University Press, 2011), pp. 101–20.

notably, Cyrus Schayegh has argued in his pathbreaking work *The Middle East and the Making of the Modern World* that post-Ottoman states divided and integrated the region.[17] By his account, the 'incessant cross-border movement of peoples, animals, goods, and ideas' forced states to 'cooperate . . . on matters as varied as law enforcement and disease prevention'.[18] With respect to epidemics, Schayegh discussed how mandate administration of epizootics in the 1930s led to donkeys being identified as Syrian or Palestinian by way of metal rings placed through their right ears.[19] He suggests that the somewhat 'comical' situation 'accentuated a pattern set in the 1920s', whereby epidemics gave way to 'the bureaucratization of ordinary life . . . to the point of territorializing, indeed nationalizing, animals'.[20]

A sustained look at disease, however, reveals something beyond the profound and absurd reach of post-Ottoman bureaucracy. It shows how disease and public health contributed to the formation of borders and territoriality of post-Ottoman states, building on Ottoman precedents. Cattle plague served as a justification for preventing nomads from crossing borders across which they had grazing rights. As for malaria, notions of disease as connected to climate and race figured prominently in deciding who could go where with respect to refugee resettlement. In short, to rephrase Dr 'Abd al-Rahman Shahbandar's words with which this chapter began, science in relation to disease *did* play quite a role in shaping the territorial forms that ensured that self-determination would not proceed as many had hoped. Cattle plague and malaria helped to determine the formation of borders and resettlement of refugees that were constitutive of the simultaneous disintegration and interconnection of the post-Ottoman Middle East.

### Rinderpest and the Closure of the Border

Bovine plague – also known by its German name of rinderpest – was a virus afflicting cattle and other hoofed animals. Its symptoms proceed from fever and debilitating diarrhoea to a terminal stage in which the animal

---

[17] Cyrus Schayegh, *The Middle East and the Making of the Modern World* (Cambridge, MA: Harvard University Press, 2017), pp. 9–10.
[18] Ibid.
[19] Ibid., p. 261.
[20] Ibid.

bleeds from the rectum, eyes and nose before dying, all in the span of a few weeks.[21] The control of bovine plague – as with many diseases, both human and animal alike – had long been conceived of in terms of political borders, whether in eighteenth-century Venice or nineteenth-century Namibia.[22] The late Ottoman Empire took a similar approach. While attempting to develop new responses to the disease at the Imperial Bacteriology Lab in Istanbul, they also managed quarantines in the provinces.[23] However, nomadic motion and paltry spending meant that control of space – and the disease – was limited.[24]

Both the mandate regimes and the Turkish Republic made a great effort to differentiate themselves from these Ottoman precedents. This process took place even with respect to the name for rinderpest, which the Turkish politician Tunalı Hilmi suggested in 1925 ought to be called not by its Ottoman term (*veba-yı bakari*) but rather the Turkish neologism for it (*sığır vebası*).[25] They may have called the disease by a new name, but the dilemma of controlling cattle plague and mobile human populations remained closely connected to borders, particularly on the edge of the Turkish Republic and the French Mandate of Syria. After all, Article XIII of the 1921 Franco-Turkish Agreement specified that 'sedentary and semi-nomadic inhabitants having the use of pastures or having properties on one or the other side of the line' of the border 'will continue as in the past to exercise these rights'. Meanwhile,

---

[21] John A. Rowe and Kjell Hødnebø, 'Rinderpest in the Sudan 1888–1890: The Mystery of the Missing Panzootic', *Sudanic Africa*, Vol. 5 (1994), p. 151.

[22] Karl Appuhn, 'Ecologies of Beef: Eighteenth-Century Epizootics and the Environmental History of Early Modern Europe', *Environmental History*, Vol. 15, No. 2 (2010), p. 268;

[23] On the Imperial Bacteriology Institute: Seçil Yılmaz, 'Love in the Time of Syphilis: Medicine and Sex in the Ottoman Empire, 1860–1922', (PhD thesis, City University of New York-Graduate Center, 2016), pp. 84–88. On cordons: Başbakanlık Osmanlı Arşivi (BOA), ŞD 2554/6, 7 Mart 1306 (19 March 1890).

[24] On spending: Ahmet Şerif, *Anadolu'da Tanin*, Vol. 1, Mehmed Çetin Börekçi (ed.) (Ankara: Türk Tarihi Kurum Basımevi, 1999), p. 117. On nomads and the disease: BOA, DH.İD 106/11, Assistant of Forests, Minerals, and Agriculture to Interior Minitsry, 6 Temmuz 1327 (19 July 1911); BOA, DH.İ.UM.EK 80/44, 'Aşayır Olan Mahallerdeki Veba-i Bakari', 1 Teşrinevvel 1332 (14 October 1916).

[25] Türk Büyük Millet Meclisi Zabıt Ceridesi (TBMMZC) İ: 12, C: 1, 21.11.1341 (21 November 1925), p. 178.

Article XII of the 1926 Convention of Friendship and Good Neighbourly Relations Between France and Turkey stipulated that the parties would 'prevent the spread of all epizootic . . . diseases', while also remaining in contact regarding 'the sanitary state of the nomadic tribes'. In other words, the dilemma of controlling moving populations across state borders echoed the past. What was distinct, however, was the way that rinderpest would help state officials clamp down on nomadic motion and consolidate the region's post-Ottoman borders.

Even beyond the border between Turkey and Syria state borders structured control of the disease. Indeed, Süreyya Bey of the Turkish Ministry of Agriculture presented rinderpest as not only a health problem, but also a spatial one, having to do with controlling creatures entering the country from the outside. Calling the disease 'the greatest disease . . . in our country for many years', Süreyya described how the disease had typically 'invaded all the way to Rumeli', but for the first time, in March 1925, the state had managed to remain rinderpest free, quite an accomplishment, he insisted, because no other country had been able to do so.[26] The conditions did not last, however, since in June 1925 the disease appeared in Mardin, Diyarbakır and Erzincan, thanks to what Süreyya termed 'the constant traffic in animals from both the border of Mosul and Syria and especially from Iran and Armenia'.[27] The Turkish Department of Agriculture received reports from Aleppo that bovine plague had broken out near Raqqa and was making 'considerable ravages' and in response closed the border to 'animals coming from Aleppo and to nomadic tribes'.[28] Moreover, out of fear that 'animals coming from Iraq' via Nusaybin were infected, the Turkish government proceeded with a 'complete closure of the border of Iraq and Syria to tribes and to the arrival of animals'.[29] Subsequent correspondence of the Agriculture Minister declared that the problem was in fact that 'the animals of the tribes found on the south of our border with Syria were constantly polluted with cattle plague', with the only solution a 'joint border health police' consisting of veterinarians from Iraq, Syria and Turkey, which possibly might be discussed at

[26] Ibid., p. 177.
[27] Ibid.
[28] BOA, HR.İM 148/51, 24 June 1925.
[29] BOA, HR.İM 147/85, 21 June 1925.

the upcoming conference on locusts in Damascus.[30] Factories producing the rinderpest serum would be placed in provinces that had robust cross-border trades in animals, including Diyarbakır, Pendik and Erzincan.[31] Moreover, seeing as 'this disease is entering our country from the outside', Süreyya called for 'three roving veterinary committees' to be installed 'on the border with Syria, on the border with Iran, and around Beyazit'.[32]

British officials charged in response that the animals in question were not actually from Iraq, as no cases of rinderpest had been reported in Mosul since the previous December.[33] They speculated that the real culprit was 'the livestock of nomadic tribes to the north of the Iraqi frontier, who make their winter pasture to the south of the said border'. In other words, it was not Iraqi animals that brought cattle plague to Turkey, the British charged, but rather Turkish animals that brought the disease to Iraq. The British even insisted that the villages that Turkish officials claimed had been infected with rinderpest in Iraqi territory 'could not be found on the maps'.[34] Regardless of the culprit, by October, Turkish officials worried of a spread of cattle plague from eastern Anatolia to central Anatolia, warning that even western Anatolia was 'under threat'.[35] By March 1926 the British wrote that they 'had now been able to identify these villages' that the Turkish authorities had described as being origins of the rinderpest, but they charged that the villages were for the most part found near Nusaybin and, as a result, required discussions with the French authorities in Syria rather than the British in Iraq.[36] In sum, almost all discussions of the disease gravitated to the role of borders in its propagation and prevention.

Süreyya Bey was not the only one who viewed rinderpest as primarily a disease of the border. While Süreyya blamed Syria for rinderpest, in Syria

---

[30] Başbakanlık Cumhuriyet Arşivi (BCA), 30-18-1-1_14-46-14, 26 Temmuz 1341 (26 July 1925).

[31] TBMMZC, İ: 12, C: 1, 21.11.1341 (21 November 1925), p. 177.

[32] Ibid.

[33] BOA, HR.İM 149/47, Embassy of Great Britain in Istanbul to Turkish Ministry of Foreign Affairs, 17 July 1925.

[34] BOA, HR.İM 149/47, Embassy of Great Britain in Istanbul to Turkish Ministry of Foreign Affairs, 29 September 1925.

[35] BCA, 30-18-1-1_16-66-2, 18 Teşrinievvel 1341 (18 October 1925).

[36] BOA, HR.İM 168/37, Embassy of Great Britain in Constantinople to Turkish Ministry of Foreign Affairs, 6 March 1926.

some blamed Turkey for the disease. A native of Latakia by the name of Aly Said made this argument in his 1931 veterinary doctoral thesis at the Faculty of Medicine of Paris. Said suggested that rinderpest emerged in Syria in 1925 because the French imported animals from Turkey to feed its soldiers.[37] When the animals happened to be diseased, 'the plague invaded Syria and spread to all of the regions in the wake of the troops'.[38] It quickly jumped from Kurddağı in the north all the way to the Hawran in the south, the heart of the revolt that emerged at the very same time against French rule. With attention on the rebellion, control of the epizootic was less of a priority. Said was careful to point out that ongoing conflict was not the only reason for the outbreak of disease, seeing as 'Syria was poorly organized, even in a peaceful period, to fight against contagious diseases of livestock'.[39] But he also called for greater vigilance, particularly on the border, where he suggested no animals ought to be able to enter without 'a health certificate issued by the country of origin'.[40] Both those in Syria and Turkey, then, blamed the border for the spread of disease.

But there were other cases where the political exigencies of the border seem to have quite literally created the disease. According to French authorities, in November 1925 two men of Kurdish origin left their village of Hiamli in Syria with a group of mules carrying charcoal and headed to Maydan Akbas, where they hoped to sell their goods.[41] Along the way, they were stopped by what they described as a Turkish gang accompanied by Turkish regular soldiers. The muleteers immediately fled and managed to find enough support among local villages to fend off the soldiers and force them to flee north of the border. By some accounts, some 200 armed Kurds stood along the border

---

[37] On meat consumption and colonialism, see On Barak, *Powering Empire: How Coal Made the Middle East and Sparked Global Carbonization* (Oakland: University of California Press, 2020), pp. 54–82.

[38] Aly Said, 'La Peste Bovine: l'Epidémie de 1925–1927 en Syrie, Bases de la Protection Sanitaire de ce Pays', (PhD thesis, Faculty of Medicine of Paris, 1931), p. 32.

[39] Ibid., p. 36.

[40] Ibid., p. 49.

[41] Centre des Archives Diplomatiques de Nantes (CADN), 1SL/1/V/1000, Monsieur Pierre Alype, Envoyé Extraordinaire du Haut-Comissaire auprès des États de Syrie et du Djébel-Druze to Monsieur le Haut-Commissaire in Beirut, undated.

to prevent any further reprisals and fighting lasted all day. Turkish officials suggested that the root of the conflict was bovine plague; their troops were merely trying to stop potentially diseased animals from entering the country. French officials objected to this excuse on several grounds. First, the men and their mules were in Syria. Second, even if there were threats of rinderpest, the men had mules with them and not cows. Third, and finally, French officials alleged that rinderpest had been present in the Turkish district of İslahiye, yet Turkish humans and animals had continued to enter Syria. The fact that Turkish officials allowed their own citizens to go into Syria freely with animals that would be threatened by epizootics suggested to the French that they did not possess 'real motives' in their seizure of the mules. Henry de Jouvenel, the French High Commissioner, conveyed the same message to the French ambassador in Istanbul, suggesting that

> if the measures of seizure from the Turkish zone were necessitated by an epizootic, the Turkish authorities would had to have warned us, so that we could let relevant populations know, and also, so that we too could ban Turkish subjects who own land in Syrian territory from entering Syria.[42]

At least by the French accounting, then, rinderpest was a useful pretext for the consolidation of Turkish sovereignty over these borderland regions.

Events over the next few years would seem to underscore this point. In the fall of 1927, Turkish officials would deny the Kikiye tribe access to Turkish pastures 'under the pretext of bovine plague' at the Syrian border town of Darbasiyya, even though French officials insisted that 'the allegation of bovine plague decimating the Syrian herds is baseless'.[43] The following spring Turkish officials responded that bovine plague 'was on the verge of complete extinction' in Turkey and so it was only sensible that they not allow animals possibly tainted by the disease in Syria.[44] Moreover, they complained that the French had rebuffed efforts at a joint veterinary conference the previous October, preventing the countries from collaborating effectively on

---

[42] CADN, 1SL/1/V/1000, Monsieur Henry de Jouvenel to Ambassador of France in Istanbul, 24 December 1925.

[43] CADN, 1SL/1/V/1001, Ripert to the High Commissioner, 22 September 1927.

[44] CADN, 1SL/1/V/1001, Note Verbale to the Embassy of France, Ankara, 12 March 1928.

these matters (the French refused because of a denial of a visa to one of their veterinary officials, since he had previously worked in the same capacity in Adana under the French occupation of Cilicia, and had allegedly left without permission from the Turkish state).[45] Again, French officials insisted that their territory was free of plague, with no cases on the Euphrates since July 1926, Alexandretta since November 1926 and Aleppo since June 1927.[46] The 'fallacious pretext' – according to the French – of bovine plague had a purpose, namely that by invoking the disease, Turkish officials 'practically cancelled . . . article XIII of the Ankara Accord allowing the nomadic tribes on either side of the border to maintain their old rights to pasture'.[47]

The use of disease to limit nomadic mobility across borders reflected the tensions that sometimes existed between nomadic groups and local officials, as the contributions to this volume by Robert Fletcher and Laura Stocker underscore. Such measures likely stemmed from a desire to prevent property disputes, in addition to the connection between nomadic groups and various armed political challenges in this period. Meanwhile, Turkish tribes spent 'the great part of the year' south of the border in Syria. And so as retribution the French banned their entry into Syria. 'This measure can only contribute,' they explained sarcastically, 'to the sanitary protection of Turkish livestock, of whom it would be difficult to admit that they should come and go with impunity in territory that the Turkish government claims is contaminated.'[48] By September, Turkish officials moderated their position somewhat. Rather than prohibiting cattle altogether, they allowed them to enter Turkey via one of four border crossings, provided they underwent a quarantine period of twenty days.[49] The French charged that even these reforms made Article XIII 'illusory'. Whether bovine plague itself was illusory is unclear. It was certainly a real concern, even if the ultimate economic impact of cattle traffic

[45] CADN, 1SL/1/V/1001, Note Verbale to the Embassy of France, Ankara, 12 March 1928; Veterinary Major Arzur to Principal Veterinary Director, 12 November 1927.

[46] CADN, 1SL/1/V/1001, Veterinary Principal Director Martin to High Commissioner, 12 April 1928.

[47] CADN, 1SL/1/V/1001, Ripert to the High Commissioner, 23 May 1928.

[48] CADN, 1SL/1/V/1001, Maugras to Nouman Menemenly, Consul General of Turkey in Beirut, 22 June 1928.

[49] CADN, 1SL/1/V/1001, Note for Director of Intelligence Services, 28 September 1928.

between the countries was minimal. But what is clear is that bovine plague – real or illusion – served the purpose of turning the border from an illusion that might be crossed by nomads or landholders into a reality that restricted this kind of movement. The border, then, did not take literal form in relation to disease as, for example, was the case with cholera and the Ottoman–Qajar border.[50] But rinderpest did significantly shape the function of the border, as a tool for keeping nomads and their animals out.

## Assyrians, Malaria and the Miasma of Self-determination

The Christian populations of southeastern Anatolia and what is now north-eastern Syria and northern Iraq have a long history. But like many residents of the Ottoman Empire, their community definition changed greatly thanks to the intersection of imperial modernisation efforts and missionary activity. By the late nineteenth century Chaldeans were associated with Rome and received protection from the French, while those sometimes called Nestorians received attention from Protestant missionaries.[51] Concurrently, archaeologists were unearthing the remains of ancient Assyrian civilisation within the same geography. Deciding that Muslims could not possibly be connected to this legacy, Western travellers and missionaries alike assumed that the Christians around them were the rightful heirs of ancient Assyria, an 'ahistorical identitarian' idea that was on par with most nineteenth-century nationalism and that many local Christians adopted for themselves too.[52] In the process, categories of identity that were distinct in Arabic (*Athuri* people versus *Ashuri* civilisation) blurred into one another.[53]

These Christian communities would be further caught between imperial violence and colonial rule at the end of the Ottoman Empire and in its wake. In the midst of the First World War the Ottoman Empire engaged

[50] Sabri Ateş, 'Bones of Contention: Corpse Traffic and Ottoman-Iranian Rivalry in Nineteenth-Century Iraq', *Comparative Studies of South Asia, Africa, and the Middle East*, Vol. 30, No. 3 (2010), pp. 512–32; Sabri Ateş, *The Ottoman-Iranian Borderlands: Making a Boundary, 1843–1914* (New York: Cambridge University Press, 2013).

[51] Yasmeen Hanoosh, *The Chaldeans: Politics and Identity in Iraq and the American Diaspora* (London: I. B. Tauris, 2019), p. 25.

[52] Ibid., p. 35.

[53] Ibid.

in genocide against Assyrian populations of southeastern Anatolia in what became known as *Sayfo*, killing hundreds of thousands caught between the Ottoman and Russian armies.[54] In the wake of the violence, many fled to Iraq, where they survived in refugee camps.[55] As one French-Assyrian recalled much later, 'They split up the soil of my nation/they separated the Euphrates from the Tigris/One part became the Turks' and Arabs/And another became the Kurds.'[56] The British were happy enough to welcome Assyrians in Iraq for instrumentalist reasons. W.A. Wigram, an Anglican priest and sometime advocate for the population, went so far as to say that 'many a mountaineer from the Assyrian districts . . . looks . . . exactly as if he had stepped down from one of the slabs of the Assyrian galleries of the British museum'.[57] The British attempted to utilise what they perceived as rugged qualities as a means of control, employing the Assyrians as colonial auxiliaries during the 1920 Revolt and throughout the period of British mandatory rule in Iraq. But the Assyrian position with respect to the colonial regime became untenable following the termination of the mandate in 1932. In August 1933 clashes between demobilised Assyrian levies and the Iraqi military on the border with Syria gave way to full-scale massacres of Assyrian civilians at Simele and throughout northern Iraq.[58]

As many fled across the border into Syria, they catalysed a series of questions for the League of Nations that came to have global significance but also

---

[54] B. Beth Yuhanon, 'The Methods of Killing Used in the Assyrian Genocide', in Talay Shabo and Soner Ö. Barthoma (eds), *Sayfo 1915: An Anthology of Essays on the Genocide of Assyrians/Aramaeans During the First World War* (Piscataway: Gorgias Press, 2018), pp. 177, 181.

[55] Robson, *States of Separation*, pp. 36–66; Benjamin Thomas White, 'Humans and Animals in a Refugee Camp: Baquba, 1918–20', *Journal of Refugee Studies*, Vol. 32, No. 2 (June 2019), pp. 216–36.

[56] Antoine Yalap, 'Kim'im Ben', *Hammurabi* 20 (October–December 1998), p. 62.

[57] W.A. Wigram, *The Assyrians and their Neighbours* (London: G. Bell & Sons, 1929), pp. 178–79.

[58] Sargon George Donabed, *Reforging a Forgotten History: Iraq and the Assyrians in the 20th Century* (Edinburgh: Edinburgh University Press, 2015); Khaldun Sati al-Husri, 'The Assyrian Affair of 1933 (I)', *International Journal of Middle East Studies*, Vol. 5, No. 2 (April 1974), pp. 161–76; Khaldun Sati al-Husri, 'The Assyrian Affair of 1933 (II)', *International Journal of Middle East Studies*, Vol. 5, No. 3 (June 1974), pp. 344–60; Sami Zubaida, 'Contested Nations: Iraq and the Assyrians', *Nations and Nationalism*, Vol. 6, No. 3 (2000), pp. 363–82.

remained ever rooted to questions of disease and, with it, race. This was the era of what historian Laura Robson has called the 'transfer solution', a mix of self-determination and imperial settlement schemes that held as a premise that coherent national groups could and should be moved around the world at the behest of empires.[59] At the same time as these global conversations, Syria itself was becoming a haven for refugees, so much so that historian Benjamin White has argued that 'the modern state of Syria was formed around and against refugees'.[60] For both Robson and White, the discussions represent how older imperial concerns smuggled themselves into the novel form of the mandatory regimes and the League of Nations. Yet remarkable about the discussions on the global scale and with respect to Syria is how often miasmatic fears of malaria crept into analysis, often alongside essentialist notions of Assyrian racial identity. Thus like in the realm of the political, in the realm of the medical, too, discussions of health repackaged older ideas of race and environment linked to miasma.

As officials considered where to resettle the refugees, they constantly invoked agriculture, climate and race as primary considerations. As *The Economist* wrote of a scheme to settle the displaced in Brazil, 'it ought assuredly to be possible to plant the Assyrian refugees in Parana'.[61] This scheme fell apart due to what the British officer R. S. Stafford described as 'objections to the entry of any more Orientals into Brazil' ('they are not black as some Brazilians appear to have thought,' Stafford objected).[62] Britain volunteered British Guiana and France portions of Niger as potential sites of resettlement. Of the former, Britain had in mind an interior region known for cattle and indigenous reservations whose 'climate' was 'reputed to be healthy'.[63] The French

---

[59] Robson, *States of Separation*, p. 103.

[60] Benjamin T. White, 'Refugees and the Definition of Syria', *Past & Present*, Vol. 235 (May 2017), p. 143.

[61] 'The Settlement of the Assyrians in Brazil', *The Economist*, Vol. 118, Issue 4718, 27 January 1934, p. 167.

[62] R.S. Stafford, *The Tragedy of the Assyrians* (London: George Allen & Unwin Ltd., 1935), p. 216.

[63] 'Appendix I: Communication from the United Kingdom to the Chairman of the Committee for Settlement of the Assyrians of Iraq, 22 September 1934', in League of Nations, 'Settlement of the Assyrians of Iraq: Report by the Committee to the Council', Geneva, 26 September 1934, p. 4.

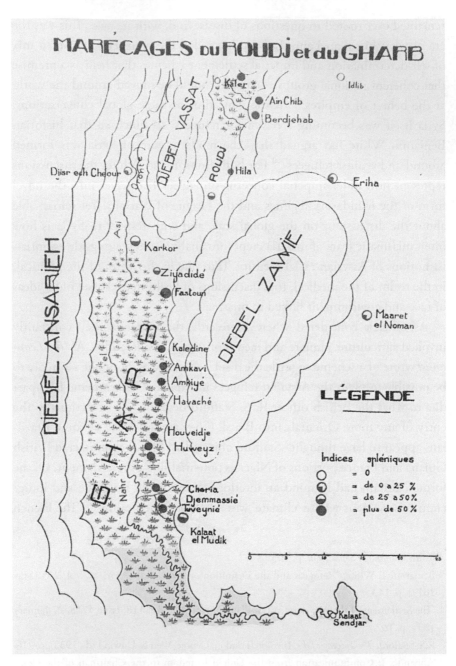

Figure 7.2  Malarial survey of Ghab region (misspelled as Gharb), 1926.

Credit: IPSA, BPT.Doc.62, Delmas and Trabaud, *Contribution à l'Étude Générale du Paludisme en Syrie.*

proposal was more to the point. Placing the Assyrians on a 'bend of the Niger' would require 'careful consideration', René Massigli wrote, given 'the question of their acclimatisation and adaptation to the severe conditions of labour which agriculture in the tropics involves for all colonists of the white race'.[64] Massigli added concerns about the Assyrians dealing with malaria, writing that 'transplantation' only took root when a migrant could find 'a diet substantially the same as that . . . from childhood'. The British officer Stafford believed that 'the Argentine would appear to be ideal, especially in regard to climate', but he believed there was little chance local residents would allow it.[65] None of these plans ultimately proceeded. But they did demonstrate the purchase of the 'transfer solution', while the metaphor of transplantation moreover revealed the significance in the endeavour of disease, underpinned by climate and race.[66]

As the French ultimately considered less far-flung locations, productivity and agriculture continued to shape their thinking. The French had long envisioned how to use Assyrians as part of their rule in Syria. Nearly a decade before they had even considered using a boat to take Armenians from Cilicia part of the way to Armenia, with the boat bringing Assyrians living in Armenia to Syria on its return trip.[67] Thus in 1935, with more than 1,000 Assyrians taking temporary refuge on the Khabur River in northeast Syria, it is perhaps unsurprising that officials planned to transfer the population to a region northwest of Hama known as the Ghab. About 60 kilometres in length and 8–10 kilometres wide, the region was watered by the Orontes River, and was 'half lake, half marsh'.[68] The region was sparsely populated, with some people who raised buffalo, lived in reed huts and caught catfish as well as tillers of land and shepherds who moved towards the edges of the swamp from the surrounding mountains.[69]

---

[64] 'Appendix II: Letter from the French Government, 24 September 1934', in ibid., p. 8.

[65] Stafford, *The Tragedy of the Assyrians*, p. 217.

[66] Robson, *States of Separation*, p. 103.

[67] Tachjian, *La France en Cilicie et en Haute-Mésopotamie*, p. 320.

[68] 'Annex 2: Detailed Study of the Plan for the Settlement of the Assyrians in the Plain of the Ghab', in League of Nations, 'Settlement of the Assyrians of Iraq: Report on the Committee of the Council on the Settlement of the Assyrians of Iraq in the Region of the Ghab (French Mandated Territories of the Levant)', Geneva, 12 September 1935, pp. 11, 14.

[69] Ibid., p. 13.

Moreover, the Ghab possessed ruins that seemed to imply an ancient but fore-gone 'abundant livelihood', always an appealing guide for French officials.[70] The region's malarial present and ancient glory had been known for years, even if initial surveys of the region termed it the Gharb rather than the Ghab (see Figure 7.2).[71] But it was the prospect of Assyrian settlement that prompted one official to remark that 'the science of the modern hydraulic engineer is capable of restoring [the Ghab] to its former prosperity'.[72] The hope was that swamp drainage and irrigation enabled by a dam would not only transform the region but also allow the mandate to resettle refugees on the cheap, seeing as cultiva-tion of cash crops of cotton and rice would allow Assyrians to pay over time for title to the land.

But alongside these discussions there was also anxiety about disease, which manifested itself in ways distinct from the discussions of the transfer of Assyrians to South America or West Africa. Whereas previous accounts focused on the environment and race as determinants for disease, subsequent reports emphasised medical treatment, calling for 'large-scale preventive and curative treatment of the Assyrian colonists against malaria' given that many on the Khabur already suffered from the disease.[73] Further underscoring the shift away from conceiving of malaria as a racial or environmental affliction, one report additionally declared 'there must be no question of creating a new centre of germ-carriers through their settlement in the plain of the Ghab'.[74] In other words, the French hoped to develop the region, but feared that their policies would in fact create 'germ-carriers'.

For all of the ink spilled on the topic of settling Assyrians in the Ghab, it ultimately went the way of similar plans for Guiana and Niger. If the cost of

---

[70] Ibid., p. 18.

[71] Institut Pasteur Service des Archives (IPSA), BPT.Doc.62, Delmas and Trabaud, *Contribu-tion à l'Étude Générale du Paludisme en Syrie* (Beirut: Imprimerie du Bureau Topographique de l'AFL, 1926).

[72] 'Annex 2: Detailed Study of the Plan for the Settlement of the Assyrians in the Plain of the Ghab' in League of Nations, 'Settlement of the Assyrians of Iraq: Report on the Committee of the Council on the Settlement of the Assyrians of Iraq in the Region of the Ghab (French Mandated Territories of the Levant)', Geneva, 12 September 1935, p. 18.

[73] Ibid., p. 25.

[74] Ibid.

the Ghab reclamation project was not enough to dissuade the French, there was also the changing political status of Syria, the independence of which appeared imminent in 1936 (though it would not be ultimately secured until 1946). No small part of this turn of events had to do with rising Arab nationalist opposition to the scheme. Even as some acknowledged Syria's need for labour, they also worried that the formation of 'homogenous blocks' of refugees and minorities might be aimed at curbing Syrian territorial sovereignty.[75] The Damascus newspaper *Al-Qabas* echoed these concerns. Invoking the past glory of the Ghab and the present plight of malaria, one article wondered why the region would only be improved for the purposes of 'an Assyrian colony in the heart of Syria'.[76] Other articles in *Al-Qabas* compared French support of Assyrians to British support for 'the national Zionist homeland' in Palestine, which notably involved extensive drainage and malaria control projects.[77] Meanwhile, the nationalist writer Najib al-Rayyis asked why a group that had been 'colonial soldiers' for the British in Iraq could not have been settled elsewhere in the empire like India, Australia or South Africa.[78]

And so the Assyrians ended up in a place that was intended as a way station rather than a final one, the upper stretches of the Khabur River in northeastern Syria's Jazira region. Their presence in this sparsely populated region allowed the government to assert its authority and thus make these regions 'Syrian' in new ways, as Benjamin White has argued.[79] Alongside this development, discussions of health brought together environmental ideas about disease grounded simultaneously in race and mosquitoes. On the one hand,

---

[75] Mohammed Sarrage, 'La nécessité d'une réforme agraire en Syrie', (PhD thesis, Université de Toulouse, Faculté de Droit, 1935), p. 77; for more on Sarrage's argument, see Elizabeth Williams, 'Contesting the Colonial Narrative's Claims to Progress: A Nationalist's Proposal for Agrarian Reform', *Review of Middle East Studies*, Vol. 44, No. 2 (Winter 2010), pp. 187–95.

[76] 'Sharika taqum bi-tajfif sahal al-Ghab', *Al-Qabas*, 7 (?) May 1936.

[77] 'Hal al-Bilad al-Suriyya watan lil-Ashuriyin?' *Al-Qabas*, 17 May 1936, 1. On malaria and Zionism, see Sandra Sufian, *Healing the Land and the Nation: Malaria and the Zionist Project in Palestine, 1920–1947* (Chicago: University of Chicago Press, 2007).

[78] Najib al-Rayyis, *Al-A'mal al-Mukhtara: Ya Zalam al-Sijn*, Vol. 1 (London: Riad El-Rayyes Books, 1994), p. 314.

[79] White, 'Refugees and the Definition of Syria', p. 163.

League reports revealed continued concern with how the 'mountain origins' of the Assyrians might adversely impact their health.[80] Such concerns echoed the distant and not so distant past. Most of the Assyrian settlements along the Khabur were atop *tall*, the hills that had formed from the ruins of antiquity. The location not only underscored past glory that so often convinced colonial officials of the possibility of present prosperity.[81] It also had health effects, some believed, as it exposed them to better air.[82] Indeed, the Ottomans had long attempted to settle people along the Khabur, starting with Chechen refugees at the source of the river in Ra's al-'Ayn in the 1860s.[83] They suffered epidemics and government officials even refused postings there for fear of 'bad air', a testament to the miasmatic understandings of disease that helped shape the sense that elevation would deliver people from disease.[84] The settlement of Assyrian refugees along the Khabur offers an example of the continued state commitment to exploiting these lands, as well as shifting abilities of states to intervene in these environments. Indeed, while revealing concerns about air and elevation, the League reports also revealed extensive efforts at 'the cleaning of villages and their surroundings' in 1937, including 'leveling, distancing of manure, construction of toilets, relocation of garden patches, closing of canals, various ditches, etc'.[85] They also detailed how 'the

---

[80] 'I. Rapport du Conseil des Trustees sur la Situation, au 31 Juillet 1936, de l'établissement des Assyriens sur le Khabour', *Société des Nations – Journal Officiel*, March–April 1938, p. 251.

[81] 'Annex 1: Report on Visit to the Levant States under French Mandate of the French and United Kingdom Representatives of the Assyrian Committee of the Council of the League of Nations', in League of Nations, 'Settlement of the Assyrians of Iraq. Report of the Committee of the Council for the Settlement of the Assyrians of Iraq', Geneva, 25 September 1937, p. 5.

[82] Ibid., p. 6.

[83] Dawn Chatty, *Displacement and Dispossession in the Modern Middle East* (New York: Cambridge University Press, 2010), pp. 108–9; Chris Gratien, 'The Ottoman Quagmire: Malaria, Swamps, and Settlement in the Late Ottoman Mediterranean', *International Journal of Middle East Studies*, Vol. 49 (2017), p. 590.

[84] BOA, DH.İD 92-1/45, Zor District Governor to Interior Ministry, 4 Kanunusani 1326 (17 January 1911); Council of Zor to Interior Ministry, 24 Kanunusani 1326 (6 February 1911).

[85] 'III. Rapport du Conseil des Trustees sur l'établissement des Assyriens Sur le Khabour Pour la Période Janvier-Mars 1937', *Société des Nations – Journal Officiel*, Vol. XIX, Nos. 3–4, March–April 1938, p. 257.

destruction of larva in stagnant water was undertaken periodically'. In sum, new kinds of environmental control did not altogether displace older ideas of the disease being connected to elevation or race. But they did enable more specific interventions in the environment.

Figures like Bayard Dodge, president of the American University in Beirut, channelled optimism with respect to the Assyrian settlement on the Khabur, calling it, in the midst of the Second World War, 'heart-warming' at a time of 'so much disregard for the rights of minorities and so much brutal exploitation of the weak peoples of the world'.[86] He added, too, that 'malaria is much less of a problem than it is in other irrigated sections of the country'.[87] But Dodge's optimism was premature. At least some of the Assyrian villages on the Khabur met a similar fate as the Ghab. A survey of malaria conducted in the 1940s found that the clay houses built for the Assyrians had left holes along the Khabur, and in the holes mosquitoes bred.[88] Scientists visiting the region noted that those Assyrians still in place 'suffered badly from malaria'. But many had already left, and 'the reason given for the desertion was "malaria"'. In sum, then, officials had talked about both malaria and climate as a guide for where to settle Assyrians, but in the end, neither malaria nor its gloss as climate had resulted in the Assyrians being resettled in a place where they might avoid malaria. Instead, what determined their placement was the colonial desire – itself building on Ottoman precedents – to use refugees to cultivate the Jazira. New understandings of malaria as rooted in mosquitoes rather than air helped enable the transformation, but the memory of these struggles both along the Khabur and in the Ghab would not disappear.[89]

[86] Bayard Dodge, 'The Settlement of the Assyrians on the Khabbur', *Journal of the Royal Central Asian Society*, Vol. 27, No. 3 (July 1940), p. 319.

[87] Ibid., p. 316.

[88] H.S. Leeson, 'Anopheline Surveys in Syria and Lebanon, 1941 to 1943', in *Anopheles and Malaria in the Near East* (London: HK Lewis & Co, 1950), p. 39.

[89] On memory of the Khabur among Assyrian-Americans, see Joash Paul, 'An Open Letter to the Editor', *Assyrian Star*, May 1953. On the Ghab development and its entanglements with the memory of empire and colonialism, see 'Mashru' al-Ghab wa ahamiyyatahu al-iqtisadiyya wa al-ijtima'iyya', *Al-Jundi*, Vol. 10, No. 264, 12 July 1956; Hani al-Shum'a, 'Qisat mintaqat al-Ghab khilal 64 'aman', *Al-Jundi*, 31 December 1964, p. 28.

## Conclusion

In Ömer Zülfü Livaneli's 2017 novel *Huzursuzluk* (*Unease*) the narrator looks out from the southeastern Turkish city of Mardin in the present day and recalls how during his childhood 'red winds would blow from the deserts of Syria, and paint us all in the red dust of the hot desert'.[90] Though the narrator was no longer a child, Mardin – 'lost in time on the Syrian border' – was still 'underneath a layer of red dust'. In so doing, Livaneli deploys a cliché in which Turkey's southeast looms as unchanging. He also uses the symbolism of the wind to convey the danger of blowback. Wind and dust could cross the Syrian–Turkish border, which over the course of roughly a century has progressed from a railway line described by Muhammad Kurd 'Ali as 'not a natural geographical border' to minefields to, most recently, a concrete reinforced wall.[91] Like the wind and the dust, so, too, could the consequences of Turkey's dealings in Syria cross that border.

But the red dust of Syria carried by the wind into Turkey has another resonance. It not only pointed to the shared environment of the region. It also gestured toward the region's shared disease ecology. After all, for centuries before the bacteriological revolution (and even after, given the way researchers – including myself – avoided sitting by the air conditioner at the old Ottoman archives) people have understood air to be one of the crucial factors in health. And at various times air was considered as the driving force behind cattle plague and malaria. The border between Syria and Turkey and the territorial meaning of Syria emerged in dialogue with disease. Cattle plague offered an excuse to close the border to nomadic migrations guaranteed by treaty, while malaria complicated where Assyrian refugees – protested by Syrian nationalists – might settle. In each case, control of disease through climate, place and race remained prevalent. Things would change, of course, with the emergence of new miracle chemicals such as DDT and other organochlorides after the Second World War.[92] The idea of disease as being located

---

[90] Ömer Zülfü Livaneli, *Huzursuzluk* (İstanbul: Doğan Kitap, 2017), p. 18.

[91] Muhammad Kurd 'Ali, *Khitat al-Sham*, Vol. 1, Second Edition (Beirut: Dar al-Qalam, 1969), p. 9. On the border and the wall, see Ramazan Aras, *The Wall: The Making and Unmaking of the Turkish–Syrian Border* (Cham: Palgrave Macmillan, 2020).

[92] For detailed mapping of mosquito ecologies of Syria during the Second World War see The Nations Archives-United Kingdom, WO 177/576.

in the air or the environment fell back, as mosquitoes rose in stature.[93] Public health materials represented DDT as the ace of spades.[94] Miasma offered not the same level of possibility. Thus Livaneli's description of the connection between Syria and Turkey is noteworthy not only because of the way disease had played a role in distinguishing these places. It is also remarkable in the sense that the shared air described by Livaneli did not convey disease. The crucial shifts of the mandate period with respect to disease were the ways that ideas of disease as linked to climate or race and control of disease as connected to place played a constitutive role in consolidating the border between post-Ottoman states while also shaping what the territoriality of these states looked like vis-à-vis refugees. In this way, to recall Shahbandar's words about science not determining self-determination, a certain version of science in fact profoundly affected what the denial of self-determination looked like.

---

[93] Kyle T. Evered and Emine Ö. Evered, 'State, Peasant, Mosquito: The Biopolitics of Public Health Education and Malaria in Early Republican Turkey', *Political Geography*, Vol. 31, No. 5 (2012), pp. 311–23.

[94] Midhat Süyev, *Sıtma Çalışmaları Albümü* (İstanbul: Hüsnütabiat Matbaası, 1953), p. 232.

# 8

# MOTOR CARS AND TRANSDESERT TRAFFIC: CHANNELLING MOBILITIES BETWEEN IRAQ AND SYRIA, 1923–1930

## *César Jaquier*

Ten years ago, cars used to leave Damascus or Baghdad any day of the week to cross the desert, provided they were accompanied by a guide. There were no patrols in the desert, and travellers were vulnerable to gangs or Bedouin vagabonds and looters. Nowadays, the cars only run on two specific days a week and form convoys in which cooperation is guaranteed in the event of a breakdown. Desert police patrols also ensure the safety of passengers and their valuables.[1]

Ameen Rihani – The Heart of Iraq

## Introduction

In February 1932 the Lebanese writer Ameen Rihani drove from Beirut to Baghdad through the desert. He left an account of his journey in *Qalb al-'Iraq* (*The Heart of Iraq*), published in 1935, in which he told the story of his road trip and described how the organisation of motor traffic had changed over the previous decade. Rihani was particularly pleased to note that although the desert crossing had been limited to a few days a week, the route was now patrolled and safe. At the time of his journey, the Baghdad–Damascus route had acquired central importance for the new states of Lebanon, Syria

---

[1] Ameen Rihani, *Qalb al-'Iraq* (Beirut: Ṣader, 1935), pp. 64–65. All translations are mine.

and Iraq, and was intertwined with local, regional and transregional mobility networks. The route cut across the Syrian Desert, thus linking two regions placed under French and British Mandate by the League of Nations after the First World War, as well as crossed the almost entirely delineated Syrian–Iraqi border. As a matter of fact, the development of motorised transport which led to the opening of the Baghdad–Damascus route in 1923 was concurrent with the emergence of new states in the post-Ottoman Middle East. In other words, the introduction of sovereign territoriality, and thus new borders, coincided with an increase in travel opportunities that resulted in new forms of interaction between Lebanon, Syria and Iraq. Against this backdrop, the so-called 'transdesert' route became a matter of concern to local governments and the French and British authorities, who sought to take advantage of the increased movement of people and goods while limiting the negative effects of mobility for their own benefit. This chapter explores the beginnings of the Baghdad–Damascus route in the 1920s by observing how new regimes of mobility took shape. As Tejel and Öztan argue in the introduction to this volume, the formation of states and the creation of borders in the post-war Middle East profoundly reshaped existing regimes of mobility, as the new states – whether independent or under Mandate administration – sought to organise and regulate the flow of people and goods across their borders. In addition to territorial reconfiguration, Tejel and Öztan also point to the extension of colonial rule in the former Ottoman Arab provinces and the persistance of global connections as other elements that contributed to the 're-ordering' of regimes of mobility.

Accordingly, this chapter examines the ways in which the French and British mandatory authorities promoted the development of the Baghdad–Damascus route, organised motor traffic and channelled mobility across their territories. Drawing on the work of Valeska Huber, this chapter understands the 'channelling of mobility' as 'the differentiation, regulation and bureaucratisation of different kinds of movement'.[2] It argues that the interplay between the process of state formation and the growth of mobility resulted in the creation of new mobility regimes governing the movement of travellers through

[2] Valeska Huber, *Channelling Mobilities: Migration and Globalisation in the Suez Canal Region and Beyond, 1869–1914* (New York and Cambridge: Cambridge University Press, 2013), p. 3.

the Syrian Desert, which discriminated between different forms of travel. This does not mean, however, that states always succeeded in shaping mobility as they wished. Rather, this chapter highlights the challenges, negotiations and contestations that played a part in the development of a new mobility network between Iraq and Syria.

The first section shows that the opening up of the Baghdad–Damascus route in the early 1920s offered bright prospects in the eyes of French, British and local officials, who therefore encouraged the development of motor traffic across the region by supporting transport companies and improving travel conditions. As many historians have argued, the coming of new states in the post-Ottoman Middle East did not put an end to regional forms of mobility.[3] This section confirms their statement by examining the development of motorised transport at the regional level. The second section looks at the phenomenon of highway robbery on the transdesert routes and seeks to demonstrate that non-state actors challenged state power in the desert as well as the organisation of traffic. Indeed, tribes, bandits and rebels in the Syrian–Iraqi borderlands started taking advantage of the growing movement of people and goods on the transdesert route by organising hold-ups and robbing passengers. Furthermore, this section explores how the persistence of insecurity led the new states to regulate and organise transdesert traffic in order to ensure the safety of travellers, thus introducing regulations which, in turn, greatly affected the flow of traffic.

---

[3] Seda Altuğ and Benjamin T. White, 'Frontières et pouvoir d'État: La frontière turco-syrienne dans les années 1920 et 1930', *Vingtième Siècle. Revue d'histoire*, Vol. 193, No. [2] (2009), pp. 91–104; Matthew H. Ellis, *Desert Borderland: The Making of Modern Egypt and Libya* (Stanford: Stanford University Press, 2008); Robert S. G. Fletcher, *British Imperialism and the Tribal Question* (Oxford: Oxford University Press, 2015); Mikiya Koyagi, *Iran in Motion: Mobility, Space, and the Trans-Iranian Railway* (Stanford: Stanford University Press, 2021); Ramazan Hakkı Öztan, 'The Great Depression and the Making of Turkish–Syrian Border, 1921–1939', *International Journal of Middle East Studies*, Vol. 52, No. 2 (May 2020), pp. 311–26; Cyrus Schayegh, 'The many worlds of Abud Yasin; or, what narcotics trafficking in the interwar Middle East can tell us about territorialization', *The American Historical Review*, Vol. 116, No. [2] (2011), pp. 273–306; Jordi Tejel, '"Des femmes contre des moutons": Franchissements féminins de la frontière turco-syrienne (1929–1944)', *20&21. Revue d'histoire*, Vol. 145 (2020), pp. 35–47.

The first two sections shed light on how French and British administrators worked together, voluntarily and involuntarily, to secure the routes. By studying cross-border cooperation, the chapter contributes to the study of the League of Nations mandates in the interwar Middle East by moving away from the methodological nationalism that has long characterised research on this subject.[4] As Robert S. G. Fletcher has demonstrated in his influential book, examining mobility across the Syrian Desert offers historians a way to rethink the history of the region by not focusing on 'the political units that later became nation states.'[5] Nevertheless, Fletcher's primary focus on the 'British desert corridor' stretching from Iraq to Egypt through Transjordan and Palestine tends to leave out an important actor involved in the management of movement across the Syrian Desert – that is, the French – and thus overlooks the importance of transimperial mobility and interstate cooperation in the formation of the states of Iraq and Syria. In this respect, the transdesert route enables us to articulate a history of the Middle Eastern mandates that breaches the gap between the history of Iraq and the histories of Palestine, Syria, Lebanon and Transjordan.[6]

Finally, the third section investigates the channelling of transdesert mobility by French and British administrators, who sought to facilitate some forms of movement while restricting others. It will be argued that the French and British authorities regarded Muslim pilgrims as a distinct category of travellers, because they were less important for their political and economic interests and because they posed a particular challenge to the organisation of traffic. By looking into the movement of pilgrims, this chapter underlines the coexistence of different types of mobility on the transdesert routes and highlights the authorities' proclivity to differentiate between them. In other words, while the process of state formation did not necessarily curtail pre-existing and new patterns of movement, it resulted in the coming of new regimes of mobility that introduced 'differential barriers to movement'.[7]

---

[4] Cyrus Schayegh and Andrew Arsan, 'Introduction', in Cyrus Schayegh and Andrew Arsan (eds), *The Routledge Handbook of the History of the Middle East Mandates* (London: Routledge, 2015), p. 13.

[5] Robert S. G. Fletcher, *British Imperialism and 'the Tribal Question'*, p. 69.

[6] Cyrus Schayegh and Andrew Arsan, 'Introduction', p. 15.

[7] Nina G. Schiller and Noel B. Salazar, 'Regimes of Mobility Across the Globe', *Journal of Ethnic and Migration Studies*, Vol. 39, No. 2 (2013), p. 187.

In studying the early developments of the Baghdad–Damascus route, this chapter also contributes to the burgeoning body of research on automobility in the Middle East, which still remains very incomplete.[8] In doing so, it seeks to go beyond the simple 'question of technology' and examine instead the interactions between motor transport technology, travel practices and the organisation and regulation of traffic by states.[9] Admittedly, the technologies of motor transport intensified and accelerated the movement of people and goods between the Mediterranean and Iraq. By reducing travel time, the motor car produced a process of time-space compression that historians of globalisation have widely analysed. Notwithstanding this, the various sections of this chapter question how this process unfolded in the interwar Middle East by showing that time-space compression went hand in hand with cases of re-routing, slowdown and discrimination of mobility.[10]

## Promoting Movement: Imperial Interests and the Beginnings of the Baghdad–Damascus Route

Throughout the Ottoman period, merchants, soldiers and pilgrims crossed the Syrian Desert between present-day Syria and Iraq by following the routes of the trade caravans that circled the centre of the desert to the north.[11]

---

[8] [Special issue], 'The Global Middle East in the Age of Speed', *Comparative Studies of South Asia, Africa and the Middle East*, Vol. 30, No. 1 (2019), pp. 111–69; Frédéric Abécassis, 'La mise en place du réseau routier marocain', *HAL–Archives ouvertes* (2009), https://halshs.archives-ouvertes.fr/halshs-00435869; Nile Green, 'Fordist Connections: The Automotive Integration of the United States and Iran', *Comparative Studies in Society and History*, Vol. 58, No. 2 (2016), pp. 290–321; Kristin Monroe, 'Automobility and Citizenship in Interwar Lebanon', *Comparative Studies of South Asia, Africa and the Middle East*, Vol. 34, No. 3 (2014), pp. 518–31

[9] David Edgerton, 'Creole technologies and global histories: rethinking how things travel in space and time', *Journal of History of Science Technology*, Vol. 1, No. 1 (2007), pp. 75–112.

[10] For a seminal work on the concept of time-space compression see: David Harvey, *The Condition of Postmodernity: an enquiry into the origins of cultural change* (Oxford and Cambridge, MA: B. Blackwell, 1990). For critical studies of the 'time-space compression' narrative see: On Barak, *On Time* (Berkeley: University of California Press, 2013); Liat Kozma, Cyrus Schayegh and Avner Wishnitzer (eds), *A Global Middle East: Mobility, Materiality and Culture in the Modern Age, 1880–1940* (London: I. B. Taurus, 2014); Valeska Huber, *Channelling Mobilities.*

[11] Christina P. Grant, *The Syrian Desert: Caravans, Travel and Exploration* (London: A. & C. Black, 1937).

While scholarship has long asserted that the development of steam navigation and the opening of the Suez Canal in 1869 dealt a blow to the caravan trade in the Ottoman Empire, an increasing number of scholars have
recently refuted the thesis of a decline and shown, on the contrary, that
internal trade remained very important up to the late nineteenth century.[12]
The traditional caravan route between Damascus and Baghdad ran across
the oases of Palmyrena before reaching the Euphrates and following the river
to Hit, Abu Kemal and Baghdad. In the aftermath of the war, relying on
these preexisting networks, motorised transport initially developed between
Aleppo, Mosul and Baghdad.[13] Nevertheless, the car had a decisive advantage over pack animals. By reducing travel time, it soon made it possible
to open a more direct, almost rectilinear route through the heart of the
desert. In October 1923, the Nairn brothers – two New Zealanders who
had previously served in the British Army in the Middle East during the
First World War – managed to open a route linking Damascus to Baghdad
with the help of a Syrian gold smuggler.[14] A few months later, two transport
companies provided a regular passenger and mail service between Beirut
and Baghdad.

At that time, the Arab provinces of the former Ottoman Empire had been
placed under French or British Mandate by the League of Nations. Officially,
the mandates system was framed to guide the trust territories and their inhabitants towards independence, as they were considered 'not yet able to stand by
themselves'.[15] However, the creation of the mandates was also the a posteriori
legitimation by the League of Nations of the conquests made by the Allied

[12] Sarah Shield, *Mosul Before Iraq: Like Bees Making Five-Sided Cells* (Albany: State University
of New York Press, 2000); Philippe Pétriat, 'Caravan Trade in the Late Ottoman Empire:
the 'Aqīl Network and the Institutionalization of Overland Trade', *Journal of the Economic
and Social History of the Orient*, Vol. 63, Nos. 1–2 (2019), pp. 38–72.

[13] Charles Issawi, *The Fertile Crescent 1800–1914: A Documentary Economic History* (New York
and Oxford: Oxford University Press, 1988), p. 219.

[14] Christina P. Grant, *The Syrian Desert*, pp. 274–278; John Munro, *The Nairn Way: Desert Bus
to Baghdad* (New York: Caravan Books, 1980), pp. 35–39.

[15] Article 22 of the Covenant of the League of Nations. Available on the website of the United
Nations Library & Archives Geneva. https://libraryresources.unog.ch/ld.php?content_
id=32971179 (Accessed 6 May 2020).

powers on Ottoman territories during the war.[16] At the end of the war, the regions of present-day Syria and Iraq were entirely occupied by British troops, who withdrew from Syria in 1919 to make way for the French. The deployment of French and British forces between the Mediterranean and the Persian Gulf was mainly aimed at securing imperial trade and communication routes. This has been amply demonstrated by historical studies in the case of the British.[17] As for the French, historians have often asserted that France's increased presence in the Eastern Mediterranean was primarily intended to fulfil a 'civilising mission' and to assert the prestige of the French nation.[18] Nevertheless, France's commercial interests in the region in the early twentieth century should not be overlooked.[19] Crucially, the creation of the mandates was thus the result of a 'compromise' between the great powers, which wanted to annex the territories they had seized from Germany and the Ottoman Empire during the war, and the advocates of international control over the colonies.[20]

The trusteeship entrusted to France and Britain by the League of Nations provided that the mandated territories remained open to international trade and mobility. From an economic point of view, the principle of the 'open-door' required that there should be no discrimination between members of the League with regard to economic access to the trust territories. The mandates system promoted 'freedom of transit' across the mandated territories rather than exclusivist economic policies.[21] Although these commercial rules

---

[16] Pierre-Jean Luizard, 'Le mandat britannique en Irak: une rencontre entre plusieurs projets politiques,' in Nadine Méouchy and Peter Sluglett (eds), *The British and French Mandates in Comparative Perspective* (Leiden: Brill, 2014), p. 366.

[17] Robert S. G. Fletcher, *British Imperialism and 'the Tribal Question'*, p. 35; Pierre-Jean Luizard, 'Le mandat britannique en Irak', p. 366; Jacob Norris, *Land of Progress: Palestine in the Age of Colonial Development, 1905–1948* (Oxford: Oxford University Press, 2013), pp. 10–11.

[18] Michael Provence, *The Last Ottoman Generation and the Making of the Modern Middle East* (Cambridge: Cambridge University Press, 2017), p. 60; Peter Sluglett, 'Les mandats/the mandates', p. 111.

[19] Simon Jackson, 'Mandatory Development: The Political Economy of the French Mandate in Syria and Lebanon, 1915–1939', (PhD thesis, New York University, 2009), pp. 118–97.

[20] Cyrus Schayegh and Andrew Arsan, 'Introduction', p. 2; Susan Pedersen, *The Guardians: The League of Nations and the Crisis of Empire* (Oxford: Oxford University Press, 2015), p. 2.

[21] League of Nations Archives [hereafter LON], Article 11 of the Mandate charter for Syria and Lebanon, August 1922. https://biblio-archive.unog.ch/Dateien/CouncilMSD/C-528-M-313-1922-VI_BI.pdf (Accessed 6 May 2020).

were not always respected by the mandatory powers, the open-door policy contributed to the 'revival of world trade' between the late 1910s and the late 1920s.[22] The emergence of the Baghdad–Damascus route must be understood in this context, where both the mandates system and British and French imperial interests encouraged the development of new regional, if not global communication networks in the region, creating an imperial transit zone transcending to some extent national borders.

During the 1920s, the Baghdad–Damascus route became the main communication axis between Syria and Iraq. From Damascus, travellers could either take the direct route through the desert to Rutbah, Ramadi and Baghdad, or choose to make a detour via Palmyra, where vacationers and tourists could admire its famous ruins before reaching the main track (Fig. 8.1). Although other routes linking Iraq to the Mediterranean emerged during the interwar period – for instance, between Aleppo and Mosul as well as Haifa and Baghdad – they only gained importance in the 1930s. The Baghdad–Damascus route remained the key transdesert route in the 1920s and during most of the interwar years. A few months after the establishment of the Nairn transport service, between 200 and 300 passengers were crossing the Syrian Desert every month.[23] Four years later, in 1927, statistics indicated that an average of about 800 passengers had travelled that year between Damascus and Baghdad. By 1928, the figures had almost doubled.[24] But even more than the volume of traffic, the diversity of travellers is noteworthy, as it ranged from government officials, merchants and tourists to summer vacationers, scouts and pilgrims. Consequently, while the development of motorised transport built on preexisting networks and practices,[25] it also led to a change in the speed, scale and type of movement. In short, the opening of the transdesert route re-shaped mobility across the Syrian Desert.

---

[22] Cyrus Schayegh, *The Middle East and the Making of the Modern World* (London: Harvard University Press, 2017), p. 134.

[23] The National Archives, Kew Garden [hereafter TNA], FO 684/1/24/14, British consul, Damascus to Department of Overseas Trade, 6 November 1924.

[24] TNA, FO 684/7/34/3, report on 'Transdesert Traffic' by Frank H. Todd (British Vice-Consul, Damascus), enclosed in letter from Mackereth (British Consul, Damascus), 26 April 1934.

[25] Robert S. G. Fletcher, 'Running the Corridor: Nomadic Societies and Imperial Rule in the Inter-War Syrian Desert', *Past & Present*, Vol. 220, No. 1 (2013), p. 196.

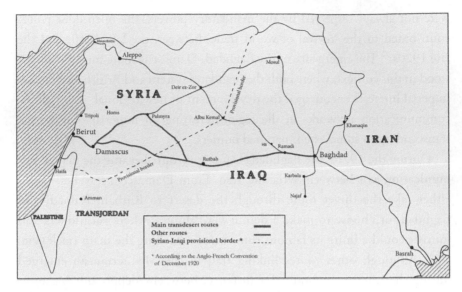

Figure 8.1 Map of transdesert routes (late 1920s).

Credit: Redrawn by the author from Government of Iraq, *Maps of Iraq with Notes for Visitors* (Baghdad: Government of Iraq, 1929).[26]

## *Imperial perceptions*

The sudden success of the first transport companies operating across the desert aroused hopes for the future development of large-scale automobile traffic between the Mediterranean and Iraq, Iran and beyond. Journalists, local government officials and, above all, French and British mandatory administrators shared the conviction that the automobile could overcome the desert, which had been hitherto regarded as an 'impassable barrier' or a 'closed door'.[27] As a newspaper article headlined, the motor car enabled the 'conquest of the Syrian Desert'.[28] In September 1924, the Lebanese newspaper *Lisan al-Hal*

---

[26] Government of Iraq, *Maps of Iraq with Notes for Visitors* (Baghdad: Government of Iraq, 1929).

[27] Cyrus Schayegh, *The Middle East and the Making of the Modern World*, p. 150.

[28] Centre des Archives diplomatiques de La Courneuve [hereafter CADC], 48CPCOM43, 'The Conquest of the Syrian Desert,' reprinted from *The Commercial Motor*, 7 September 1926. For analyses of a similar narrative associated by French officials with the first motor expeditions across the Sahara see: Andrew Denning, 'Mobilizing Empire: The Citroën

expressed hopes that the new route would enable Syria to once again become 'the gateway to the East and its majestic bridge'.[29] Put another way, the trans-desert route was expected to restore Syria's position as a crossroads of regional mobilities, which had been circumscribed by the rise in steam navigation and the opening of the Suez Canal in the nineteenth century.[30] As for French and British Mandate officials, they regarded the Baghdad–Damascus route as a crucial communication route for their respective empires, just as the British had viewed the Suez Canal as a 'highway of the British Empire' in the previous century.[31] In late 1923 the French High Commissioner Weygand stated that the Baghdad–Damascus route was becoming 'the safest, the quickest and the least expensive way' between Iran and Europe.[32] The British, for their part, looked forward to a new 'imperial route to the East' linking the British metropole with India.[33] Furthermore, in the eyes of mandatory administrators, transdesert traffic was likely to mitigate the social and economic damage caused by the establishment of international borders in the Middle East.[34]

Aware that the opening of overland routes in the Middle East served their economic and political interests, local governments and the French and British authorities sought to promote the expansion of traffic across the Syrian Desert. In the mid-1920s their support mainly targeted transport companies

Central Africa Expedition and the Interwar Civilizing Mission', *Technology and Culture*, Vol. 61, No. 1 (January 2020), pp. 42–70; Jacob Krais, 'Mastering the Wheel of Chance: Motor Racing in French Algeria and Italian Libya', *Comparative Studies of South Asia, Africa and the Middle East*, Vol. 30, No. 1 (2019), pp. 143–58.

[29] American University of Beirut, newspaper archives [hereafter AUB], 'Ṭarīq Baghdād', *Lisan al-ḥal*, 29 September 1924, p. 2. Original text in Arabic: bāb al-sharqi wa jisrahu-l-'aẓīm.

[30] CADC, 48CPCOM42, Weygand to French Ministry of Foreign Affairs, 6 August 1924; AUB, 'Ṭarīq ul-qawāfili taslukuhā al-sayyārāt', *Lisan al-ḥal*, 5 June 1924, p. 1.

[31] Valeska Huber, 'Highway of the British Empire? The Suez Canal between Imperial Competition and Local Accommodation', in Jorn Leonhard and Ulrike von Hirschhausen (eds), *Comparing Empires: Encounters and Transfers in the Long Nineteenth Century* (Göttingen: Vandenhoeck & Ruprecht, 2011), pp. 37–59.

[32] CADC, 48CPCOM42, Weygand to French Ministry of Foreign Affairs, 1 December 1923.

[33] Harold L. Hoskins, *British Routes to India* (Philadelphia: Longmans Green, 1928).

[34] TNA, FO 424/632, Satow (British Consul-General, Beirut) to John Chancellor (High Commissioner for Palestine), 16 April 1929; LON, R22/4284/47053, 'Rapport sur la situation de la Syrie et du Liban (année 1924)'.

and took the form of subsidies, contracts for the transport of mail and customs exemptions. The French agreed to provide an annual subsidy to the Eastern Transport Company – a company founded in Beirut by Francis and Alfred Kettaneh – and to entrust the firm with the mail contract for Iraq and Iran in exchange for the addition of French capital to the company.[35] The Nairn Transport Company, for its part, was awarded a contract by the Iraqi government to transport mail between Haifa, Damascus and Baghdad in late 1923.[36] In October 1927, moreover, the French published a first decree granting customs exemptions on cars, tyres, oils and spare parts for the three main transport companies of the time, namely the Nairn Transport Company, the Kawatly Tawil Company and the Makhzumi Company.[37]

Despite the rhetoric of a 'conquest of the desert', travelling through the Syrian Desert in the mid-1920s was an uncomfortable, even dangerous journey. Drivers often had difficulty finding their way through the vast steppe, even more so because of sandstorms that often erased the tracks of cars. Quite often, travellers would get lost in the desert and wander for days without finding a living soul,[38] thus giving full meaning to the nickname attributed by some newspapers to the Syrian Desert: the 'desert of wandering'.[39] In addition, crossing the desert was usually complicated by one or more breakdowns that forced passengers to spend a few extra hours in the Syrian steppe or even abandon their vehicles.

Under these conditions, the development of the transdesert route pursued by the French and British authorities depended on their own capacity to ensure the safety of drivers and travellers across the desert. This common goal prompted French and British officials to collaborate, despite the intense rivalry between the two powers that persisted in the Middle East throughout the interwar period. Taking shape just after the First World War around the

---

[35] TNA, FO 371/10093, memorandum, 'The position and prospects of the Eastern Transport Co', enclosed in letter from Sir Edward Crowe, 11 September 1924.

[36] Christina P. Grant, *The Syrian Desert*, p. 274.

[37] 'Bulletin mensuel des actes administratifs du Haut-Commissariat', decree no. 1607 of 8 October 1927. https://gallica.bnf.fr/ark:/12148/bpt6k64598233 (Accessed 14 April 2020).

[38] AUB, 'Sayyāra ḍā'i'a', *al-Shaab*, 22 August 1927, p. 3.

[39] AUB, 'Ṭarīq al-ṣaḥrā', *Lisan al-hal*, 1 April 1924, p. 1. Original text in Arabic: ṣaḥrā al-ḍalāl.

control of Middle Eastern territories,[40] the Franco-British rivalry developed into a struggle for economic supremacy in the region in the 1930s, crystallising notably around the competition between the ports of Beirut and Haifa,[41] and then reached a peak during the Second World War.[42] Nevertheless, the British Inspector General of the Iraq Police met with French officers in Damascus in November 1923 to discuss the implementation of common regulations and agreed with the French on the need for traffic control and vehicle inspections.[43] In line with their recommendations, the governments of Syria and Iraq issued in 1924 the first legislations on transdesert traffic, which shared numerous provisions. In particular, they compelled any car running across the desert to travel in a convoy, so that passengers would not get lost and would be able to find help in the event of a breakdown.[44] From then on, motor convoys were assembled either in Damascus or Baghdad under the leadership of a convoy leader and embarked on the transdesert route upon notification of their departure to the responsible authorities on the other side of the desert.[45]

## Highway Robberies and the Thorny Problem of Traffic Organisation

The consolidation of the Baghdad–Damascus route did not go without problems, though. Brigands, Bedouins and rebels challenged imperial endeavours while leaving their imprint on the evolution of these desert highways. Already at the end of 1923 there were numerous reports of attacks on cars travelling

[40] Gérard D. Khoury, 'Introduction de partie. Les conditions d'instauration du Mandat français au Proche-Orient après la Première guerre mondiale', in Nadine Méouchy (ed.), *France, Syrie et Liban, 1918–1946: les ambiguïtés et les dynamiques de la relation mandataire* (Damas: Institut français d'études arabes de Damas, 2002), pp. 51–62.

[41] Jacob Norris, *Land of Progress*, pp. 31–33; Cyrus Schayegh, *The Middle East and the Making of the Modern World*, pp. 251–52.

[42] Philip S. Khoury, *Syria and the French Mandate: The Politics of Arab Nationalism, 1920–1945* (Princeton: Princeton University Press, 1987), pp. 583–618.

[43] LON, R58/1/17502/44571, report by His Britannic Majesty's Government on the Administration of 'Iraq for the period April 1923–December 1924, p. 42.

[44] TNA, FO 371/10831, Nairn Transport Company to High Commissioner for Iraq, 28 October 1925.

[45] TNA, FO 684/1/24/14, decree no. 22, 6 February 1924 ('règlementant la circulation automobile sur le territoire de l'État de Damas entre la Syrie et la Mésopotamie').

on the Iraqi road between Fallujah and Deir ez-Zor.[46] With the outbreak of the Great Syrian Revolt in the mid-1920s the Baghdad–Damascus route became the scene of frequent hold-ups. As unrest spread throughout Syria, highway robbers reccurently attacked convoys in the desert, robbing drivers and travellers and sometimes seizing their cars.[47] The largest theft occurred on 26 August 1925 during a violent attack in which several passengers and drivers were injured.[48] On this occasion, the robbers stole a consignment of 15,000 Turkish gold pounds that was being transferred from the Ottoman Bank to the Imperial Bank of Persia.[49] Subsequently, the High Commissioner for Iraq considered that the Baghdad–Damascus route was not safe enough to maintain traffic and decided to temporarily redirect the mail service of the Nairn Transport Company to the Baghdad–Amman route.[50]

Despite the crushing of the revolt, a group of exiled insurgents operating from southern Syria, Transjordan and the Najd gave the French and the British a hard time between 1927 and 1928 by carrying out a few hold-ups on the Baghdad–Damascus route. These rebels had first moved to southern Syria in 1926, before seeking refuge in the camp of Al-Azraq in Transjordan.[51] In the summer of 1927, however, when British forces expelled them from Transjordan, many of these insurgents went further to Wadi Sirhan in the newly created sultanate of Ibn Saud, while others left for Amman, Jerusalem and Cairo.[52] On 10 August 1928 rebels from Wadi Sirhan attacked a mail convoy

---

[46] TNA, FO 684/2/24/109, Bourdillon (Secretary, High Commission for Iraq) to Maigret (French consul, Baghdad), 5 December 1923.

[47] Middle East Centre Archive, St Antony's College, Oxford, Nairn Transport Company Collection [hereafter MECA], 'Desert convoy again attacked: Drivers stripped by raiders', *Times*, 5 September 1925; TNA, Air 5/408, 'Summary of Recent Attacks on Desert Route Convoys', September 1925.

[48] TNA, FO 371/12303, British Consul, Damascus to Foreign Affairs, 26 February 1927.

[49] TNA, FO 371/13072, claim of the Nairn Transport Company for losses in attack on convoy in Syria, 22 December 1927.

[50] TNA, AIR 5/408, telegram from High Commissioner for Iraq to Secretary of State for the Colonies, 2 September 1925.

[51] Michael Provence, *The Great Syrian Revolt and the Rise of Arab Nationalism* (Austin: University of Texas Press, 2005), pp. 142–44.

[52] Laila Parsons, *The Commander: Fawzi Al-Qawuqji and the Fight for Arab Independence, 1914–1948* (London: Saqi, 2017), p. 208.

on the Baghdad–Damascus route, robbed the passengers and took away two cars and the mail bags. Joint investigations conducted by the Syrian, Iraqi and Transjordanian authorities proved that the outlaws were the same that had carried out robberies in March 1928 and that they were operating from Najd territory.[53] This example points out that Bedouins, bandits and rebels who engaged in highway robbery took advantage of the introduction of sovereign territoriality by crossing borders to escape their pursuers. As noted in March 1925 by a British officer concerned about the development of banditry in northern Iraq, bandits used to cross the border into Syria, making desert policing impossible. 'Small bands of brigands will always be able to interfere practically when and where they choose, and the brigands may come from territory beyond the borders of Iraq'.[54] Although collaboration between officers in Syria, Transjordan and Iraq allowed the mandatory authorities to locate the rebel camp in Wadi Sirhan, they could not intervene directly on Najd territory. Instead, the French and British tried to convince Ibn Saud to extradite the rebels or to prevent them from interfering again with the transdesert traffic, to no avail.[55]

Disruption of jurisdiction was not, however, the only challenge that state powers had to deal with in these borderlands; just as travellers used modern technologies to speed up the crossing of the desert, so did bandits and Bedouins.[56] As evidenced by the attacks on convoys by Druze rebels in 1928, local actors managed to use motor cars to carry out activities at odds with the interest of Middle Eastern states and the mandatory authorities. The persistent phenomenon of highway robbery shows that the creation of transdesert routes not only served the political and economic interests of the French and the British in the Middle East but also benefited non-elite groups, who took advantage of the new mobility networks allowed by the spread of motorised transport in their own way. In this regard, the Baghdad–Damascus

---

[53] TNA, AIR 23/390, Major Cones (Iraqi Police) to the Adviser to the Iraqi Ministry of Interior, 30 August 1928.

[54] TNA, AIR 5/408, letter from Webster (British Air Council), 21 March 1925.

[55] TNA, CO 732/33/5, Shuckburgh (Colonial Office) to Mance, 19 December 1928.

[56] Mehdi Sakatni, 'From Camel to Truck? Automobiles and the Pastoralist Nomadism of Syrian Tribes during the French Mandate (1920–46)', *Comparative Studies of South Asia, Africa and the Middle East*, Vol. 39, No. 1 (2019), pp. 159–69.

route carried similar implications to those of various roads built in the late Ottoman period, which, as Fulya Özkan has shown, 'were not only a means of establishing state power, but also an arena that provided the space to contest that power'.[57]

The harm caused by highway robberies prompted the mandatory authorities in Iraq and Syria to take action from 1925 onwards, as more and more travellers were attacked, robbed, injured and sometimes even stripped of their clothes.[58] A particular event became the turning point in the monitoring of these borderlands. In early March 1925 Mrs Maillard, the wife of the French Vice-Consul in Iraq, was killed in a hold-up on Iraqi territory while travelling with the Eastern Transport Company.[59] Against this backdrop, French and British desert police officers reached an agreement in April 1925 on a 'monthly desert liaison', which consisted of detachments of Syrian and Iraqi armoured cars patrolling the desert once a month between October and February and meeting near the temporary border.[60] Despite the patrolling of the desert, however, repeated highway robberies occurred throughout 1925 and again required additional measures. Along the lines of previous arrangements made to secure the Mosul–Aleppo route,[61] the French and British authorities set up in September 1925 a system of escorted convoys of cars on the Baghdad–Damascus route. Every Monday at a fixed time, a convoy left Damascus and another left Baghdad under military escort, the two convoys meeting on arrival near the provisional border.[62] If a convoy did not arrive within forty-eight hours of the scheduled time, motor cars and aircraft could

---

[57] Fulya Özkan, 'Gravediggers of the Modern State: Highway Robbers on the Trabzon-Bayezid Road, 1850s–1910s', *Journal of Persianate Studies*, Vol. 7, No. 2 (2014), p. 225.

[58] MECA, 'Desert convoy again attacked: Drivers stripped by raiders', *Times*, 5 September 1925.

[59] CADC, 48CPCOM3, Bagot (Managing agent in Iraq, Eastern Transport Company) to French Consul in Iraq, 8 March 1925.

[60] TNA, AIR 5/408, 'General Arrangements made for the protection of the desert motor routes from Damascus to Baghdad', Headquarters of the French Army of the Levant, Beirut, 1 April 1925.

[61] TNA, FO 371/7851, written statement by Flaxman (Divisional Adviser, Mosul) and Captain Coux (French Officer), 31 July 1922.

[62] TNA, AIR 5/408, Aubouard (Delegate of the French High Commissioner) to British Consul, Damascus, 14 September 1925.

be sent to search for the missing passengers.[63] These arrangements inaugurated so-called 'protected days' during which cars were allowed to cross the desert and benefited from a military escort. Over time, the mandatory authorities in Syria and Iraq organised the protection of convoys twice and later three times a week to enable traffic to increase.[64]

The need to secure the transdesert route, in addition to giving rise to common practices of traffic organisation between French, British and local administrators, also led the states to renounce the strict assertion of their territorial sovereignty. In 1925, for instance, the French and British chose Bir Mulusa as the meeting point of the Syrian and Iraqi patrols of the desert, even though it was located on Iraqi territory, according to the Anglo-French Convention of December 1920.[65] As the site was the most suitable, however, the British accepted to allow French armoured cars to cross the border in order to meet the Iraqi patrol at Bir Mulusa.[66] Subsequently, the meeting point of the escorts moved to a place called the 'switch road', where the route from Baghdad split between the direct route to Damascus and the longer one via Palmyra, but still remained on Iraqi territory.[67] In August 1928 the French and British authorities renewed their agreement to allow armed escorts to cross the border, if necessary.[68]

## The drawbacks and shortcomings of traffic organisation

Although the French and British were eager to promote (trans)regional movements of people and goods across Syria and Iraq, the measures enforced to ensure safe travel on the transdesert route introduced numerous traffic restrictions and created serious impediments to mobility. In March 1928 only

---

[63] Thomas Cook Archive, Peterborough 'To Baghdad in Nine Days: Further Notes on the Syria-Iraq Motor Route', *The Traveller's Gazette*, Vol. 3 (March 1924), p. 10.

[64] TNA, CO 732/33/5, 'Trans-desert routes', extract from Economic report no. 105, 31 March 1928.

[65] TNA, AIR 5/408, Air staff to Salisbury (British Liaison Officer, Beirut), 30 April 1925.

[66] TNA, AIR 5/408, High Commission for Iraq to High Commission for Syria, 30 April 1925.

[67] TNA, CO 732/33/5, extract from Economic report, 31 March 1928.

[68] TNA, AIR 23/390, 'Notes of conversation with Colonel Le Long, French Chief Staff, Damascus', 11 August 1928.

three escorted convoys per week were organised through the Syrian Desert, leaving Damascus and Baghdad on Tuesdays, Fridays and Sundays.[69] Thus, those wishing to leave Baghdad for Damascus had to wait for the departure of a convoy on one of these days and to comply with the timetables set by the authorities. The restrictions also applied to those travelling in their own car. Maurice Honoré, a Frenchman who travelled from Baghdad to Syria in 1929, was forced to wait several hours in Rutbah for the last car of his convoy to arrive before being allowed to continue his journey. He noted in his travelogue that the system of 'motor caravans' was ill adapted to the situation.[70] To sum up, the organisation of transdesert traffic by the French and British authorities could lead to serious slowdowns in the 1920s.

Moreover, it often produced congestion at the different stages of the journey, in particular at police stations and customs posts, where travellers could observe 'a general gathering of cars of the various convoys'.[71] A frequent spot of congestion was Rutbah, halfway between Baghdad and Damascus in the middle of the desert, where the British built a police post in 1926.[72] The Rutbah Post was later expanded to include a customs post, a health station and, from 1928, a rest house. By the late 1920s, Rutbah was a major location of overcrowding. The Nairn Transport Company – which was in charge of managing the rest house – protested in June 1929 to the British authorities that their clients could not find any accommodation at the Rutbah rest house. 'Native convoys leave one day before us, sleep at Ramadi, and get into Rutba [sic] before the arrival of our convoys, and as accommodation there is limited, Nairn passengers have to go without,' wrote Norman Nairn to one of his associates, forwarding him a letter of complaint from the travel agency Thomas Cook & Son.[73] In the view of the British Adviser to the Iraq Ministry of Work and Communication, overcrowding at the Rutbah rest house was due to the restrictions imposed upon desert crossing. 'If the route was open

[69] TNA, CO 732/33/5, extract from Economic report no. 105, 31 March 1928.

[70] Maurice Honoré, *Vers Bagdad* (Paris: Pierre Roger, 1929), p. 168.

[71] Freya Stark, *Beyond Euphrates: autobiography 1928–1933* (London: John Murray, 1951), p. 81.

[72] CADC, 48CPCOM43, 'The Rutbah Post', *Baghdad Times*, 5 February 1926.

[73] TNA, CO 732/39/11, Norman Nairn to Sir Osborne Mance, 7 June 1929.

every day of the week then there would not be congestion at Rutba [*sic*] and Nairn's staff there would have an easier time'.[74]

In addition, car traffic between Iraq and Syria was likely to increase massively in some months of the year due to the movement of pilgrims heading for Mecca. In May and April 1927, for instance, about two thousand pilgrims left Baghdad for Damascus, thus doubling or even tripling the usual passenger traffic. In the months of July and August, reverse traffic reached a similar level. The British Inspector General of Health in Baghdad, reporting on the motor transport situation in 1927, stated that transport companies plying across the Syrian Desert were able to face such a sudden increase in traffic, as they could 'at very short notice quadruple their transport capacity by hiring cars in Baghdad or in Syria'.[75] Unlike private transporters, however, the authorities met with great difficulty in dealing with the seasonal growth in traffic. As the desert crossing was limited to a few days of the week, any sudden increase in traffic created congestion in various places. In order to minimise the inconvenience, the French authorities in Damascus decided in July 1929, when the returning pilgrimage traffic was at its peak, to allow pilgrims to go to Baghdad on days other than the 'protected' days.[76] On many other occasions, the authorities ended up breaking the rules governing transdesert traffic by allowing cars to drive in the desert outside the prescribed days or hours. The British, for instance, were particularly keen to allow travellers to cross at any time of the day to arrive in Beirut in time to board a ship or to travel during the cooler hours of the day.[77]

As these examples demonstrate, the arrangements made to supervise and protect motor convoys between Syria and Iraq produced unexpected results, ranging from overcrowding to delays, which played against the French and British desire to foster quick and efficient transport across the desert. Although road improvements and new automotive technologies were able to

---

[74] TNA, CO 732/39/11, Wheatley (Advisor, Iraq Ministry of Work and Communication) to Empson (Consular Secretary, High Commission for Iraq), 7 August 1929.

[75] LON, R981-12B-49616-61055, Hallinan (Inspector General of Health, Baghdad) to Major Thomson (President of the Quarantine Board of Egypt), 18 August 1927.

[76] TNA, FO 371/13745, extract from Economic report no. 137, July 1929.

[77] CADC, 50CPCOM358, Paul Lépissier (French Consul, Iraq) to French High Commissioner, 5 November 1929.

reduce the journey time between Damascus and Baghdad, the organisation of transdesert traffic remained a major obstacle to the much-desired 'conquest' of the Syrian Desert. Confronted with multiple obstacles to free-flowing traffic in the late 1920s, the French and British Mandate administrators took more and more unilateral decisions and increasingly violated common regulations on transdesert traffic in order to speed up transdesert mobility.

In this context, a growing number of French and British administrators called for a strengthening of cross-border cooperation. In November 1929 a preliminary meeting was held in Damascus, which paved the way for a broader Desert Traffic Control Conference, convened in the same city on 22 and 23 January 1930. The recommendations of the conference show a mutual willingness to strengthen cooperation and harmonise practices in the field of traffic organisation. For instance, the delegates drew up a draft regulation on the material organisation of traffic that would standardise the rules in force in Syria and Iraq.[78] In addition, these meetings aimed at discussing whether the restrictions on desert traffic should be relaxed to ease traffic flow. At the preliminary session, the British Inspector General of Police, Major Cones, wrote a note in favour of removing the ban on night travel. In his view, allowing it would not only reduce congestion in Rutbah but also significantly reduce travel time between Baghdad and Beirut, which would be greatly appreciated 'in business circles'.[79] Yet the promotion of transdesert traffic went hand in hand with a renewed effort geared towards channelling this mobility.

Indeed, the mandatory authorities and local governments gradually developed ways to regulate and streamline mobility between Syria and Iraq by applying discriminatory treatment to the multiple forms of mobility. Their management of the Muslim pilgrimage to Mecca (the hajj) shows that the promotion of transdesert mobility applied unevenly and selectively to people travelling through Iraq and Syria. The next section thus examines the implementation of bureaucratic measures to regulate the movement of pilgrims on the transdesert routes and aims to show that the channelling of

---

[78] Centre des Archives diplomatiques de Nantes, Nantes [hereafter CADN], SYR-LIB-1v b703, 'Conférence Syro-Irakienne sur le contrôle du Trafic de la route Damas-Bagdad', minutes of the conference.

[79] TNA, FO 371/13745, copy of Major Cones' note on night travel, enclosed in Economic report for the fortnight ending 29 November 1929.

mobility between Iraq and Syria, to quote Valeska Huber, involved 'multiple processes of exclusion and deceleration'.[80]

## Channelling Mobility

In the second half of the 1920s an increasing number of pilgrims from Iraq, Iran and Afghanistan travelled on the Baghdad–Damascus route by car and lorry on their way to Mecca. In 1927 about two thousand Iranians crossed Iraq and Syria towards the Hejaz despite the Iranian government's ban on the pilgrimage to Mecca.[81] These hajj pilgrims benefited greatly from the steady decline, throughout the 1920s, in the fares charged by transport companies for crossing the desert. The increasing opportunities for overland travel in the interwar years also led to a revival of the Indian pilgrimage to the holy cities of Iraq as well as to the Hejaz via Iraq and Syria.[82] As the number of pilgrims circulating on the transdesert route increased, the mandatory authorities in Syria and Iraq began to consider regulating their movements.

These dynamics were by no means new, though. In the nineteenth century, empires ruling over Muslim populations had already become concerned about the regulation of pilgrimage traffic between territories under their control and the Hejaz. The regulation of the hajj intensified in the late nineteenth century, as the mobility of pilgrims was increasingly considered by European powers as a major factor in the spread of epidemic diseases and dissident ideas.[83] In 1865 a cholera outbreak erupted in the Hejaz during

---

[80] Valeska Huber, *Channelling Mobilities*, p. 3.

[81] LON, R2314/6A/6774/655, report to the Council of the League of Nations on the Administration of Iraq for the year 1927, p. 88.

[82] British Library [hereafter BL], IOR/L/E/7/1479, file 6742, letter from Kitching (Administrative Inspector, Diwaniyah) to the Political Secretary to the Government of India, 5 January 1928.

[83] Lâle Can, *Spiritual Subjects: Central Asian Pilgrims and the Ottoman Hajj at the End of Empire* (Stanford, California: Stanford University Press, 2020); Sylvia Chiffoleau, 'Le pèlerinage à La Mecque à l'époque coloniale: matrice d'une opinion publique musulmane ?' in Sylvia Chiffoleau and Anna Madoeuf (eds), *Les pèlerinages au Maghreb et au Moyen-Orient: Espaces publics, espaces du public* (Beirut: Presses de l'Ifpo, 2010), pp. 131–63; Michael C. Low, 'Empire and the Hajj: Pilgrims, Plagues, and Pan-Islam under British Surveillance, 1865–1908', *International Journal of Middle East Studies*, Vol. 40, No. 2 (May 2008), pp. 269–90; Francis E. Peters, *The Hajj: The Muslim Pilgrimage to Mecca and the Holy Places* (Princeton: Princeton University Press, 1996).

the pilgrimage season and spread to Europe, urging the different empires to take sanitary measures along pilgrimage routes.[84] At the time, health control largely focused on the Red Sea, because the maritime routes from India were identified as the main propagation channel.[85] The growth of overland pilgrimage routes in the early twentieth century, spawned by the development of rail and road transport, urged the international community to implement similar measures on the land routes from the 1920s onwards.[86]

At the French initiative, a Conference on the Muslim Pilgrimage was held in Beirut in January 1929, which set the foundations for the channelling of pilgrims' mobility along the new routes that criss-crossed the Middle East. First and foremost, the representatives of Syria and Lebanon as well as Iraq, Transjordan and Palestine defined itineraries for the overland pilgrimage.[87] Moreover, they took a series of bureaucratic measures that specifically applied to pilgrims. Besides requiring their vaccination against smallpox and cholera, the conference recommended the creation of pilgrimage passes that would only be granted upon production of a return ticket and a deposit guarantee.[88] In so doing, Middle Eastern states sought to reduce the number of (mainly Indian) destitute pilgrims, who were expected to increase with the development of cheap means of transport in Iraq.[89]

---

[84] Sylvia Chiffoleau, *Le Voyage à La Mecque: Un pèlerinage mondial en terre d'Islam* (Paris: Bélin, 2017), pp. 163–214.

[85] Eric Tagliacozzo, 'Hajj in the Time of Cholera: Pilgrim Ships and Contagion from Southeast Asia to the Red Sea', in James L. Gelvin and Nile Green (eds), *Global Muslim in the Age of Steam and Print* (Berkeley: University of California Press, 2014), pp. 103–20.

[86] Sylvia Chiffoleau, 'Les quarantaines au Moyen-Orient: vecteurs ambigus de la modernité médicale (XIXe–XXe siècles)', in Anne Marie Moulin and Yeşim Işıl Ülman (eds), *Perilous Modernity: History of Medicine in the Ottoman Empire and the Middle East from the 19th Century Onwards'* (Istanbul: The Isis Press, 2010), pp. 144–45.

[87] Luc Chantre, *Pèlerinages d'empire: Une histoire européenne du pèlerinage à la Mecque* (Paris: Éditions de la Sorbonne, 2018), pp. 255–56.

[88] TNA, CO 732/39/9, 'Conference on the Mohammedan Pilgrimage held at Beyrout on 17–18 January 1929: Regulations passed by the delegates.'

[89] BL, IOR-L-E-7-1558, file 162, 'Memorandum on Pilgrimage to the Holy Cities of Islam in Iraq by British Indians and subjects of the Native States of India', British Consulate, Basra, 21 January 1930.

In order to regulate the movement of pilgrims, the British and the French also resorted to granting concessions to private companies, which were responsible for enforcing the new regulations. From 1928 onwards, the French authorities in Syria began to grant yearly concessions on the transport of pilgrims by ship from Beirut to Jeddah.[90] The same measures were also applied to the transdesert route by the Iraqi authorities, who designated the Mesopotamia Persia Corporation as the official pilgrim transporter in the late 1920s, in order to implement the return ticket system recommended by the Beirut Pilgrimage Conference. Although the company did not provide any transport service between Iraq and Syria, it was entitled to sell return tickets on behalf of other companies.[91] This allowed the Mesopotamia Persia Company to make reservations for the entire journey by land and sea from Baghdad to Beirut, Jeddah and finally back to Bombay.[92]

Testimonies and complaints from Indian pilgrims show how these regulations affected their journey across the Middle East. In late 1928 the government of India opened a position of Protector of Indian Pilgrims in Baghdad in response to the growth of overland pilgrimage through Iraq by their subjects. Tahir Hussain Quraishi, the first Protector, was responsible for providing pilgrims with precise information about road and rail services in Iraq.[93] He also collected their complaints and requests, which he transmitted to the British authorities and the Indian government in an annual report. In 1929 the report mentioned many complaints about the new deposit and return ticket requirements imposed in Iraq on the part of well-to-do pilgrims who 'did not understand why they should be subjected to more stringent regulations than ordinary first-class travellers crossing the desert'.[94] The same year, a well-off

[90] Sylvia Chiffoleau, *Le Voyage à La Mecque*, p. 356.

[91] TNA, FO 371/14456, extract from Economic report no. 4 for the fortnight ended 24 February 1930.

[92] TNA, CO 732/39/9, telegram from High Commissioner for Iraq to Foreign Secretary, India, 6 April 1929.

[93] BL, IOR/L/E/7/1479, file 6742, 'Memorandum regarding the proposed duties of the Protector of British Indian Pilgrims in Iraq' (no date, most likely 1928).

[94] TNA, CO 730/159/2, report for 1929 on the work of the Protector of British Indian Pilgrims, attached to a letter from Empson (Consular Secretary, High Commission for Iraq), 12 August 1930.

Indian pilgrim talked in detail about his journey to Mecca via Iraq to the Hajj Enquiry Committee, which used to collect the grievances of Indian pilgrims. As his testimony goes, Hussain Mohammed Ladhiwalla was asked in Baghdad to make a deposit of 200 rupees and forced to book with the Mesopotamia Persia Company, although he had already arranged for the transdesert journey with another company that charged lower rates. He commented as follows: 'Thus, I think they get a good profit; as, if a Haji can arrange himself, he can easily get the same ticket for about Rs. 200/- and save Rs. 71/-. This is the heavy burden on Hajis travelling by this route.'[95] In Baghdad, Ladhiwalla also refused to make the deposit of 200 rupees per person with the British consulate and was finally exempted after lengthy negotiations with the consul. In all, however, the various formalities took twelve days, during which he had to remain in Baghdad to follow the bureaucratic procedures that now governed the movement of pilgrims. Other evidence points to shortcomings in the regulation of pilgrimage traffic. Some pilgrims with return tickets, for instance, were delayed in Syria on their way back from the Hejaz because transport companies gave priority to passengers paying in cash.[96] It also seems that, despite the return ticket, pilgrims were obliged at each stage of the journey to exchange their tickets with the numerous agents of the Mesopotamia Persia Company, who each took a commission.[97] Unsurprisingly, a British report noted in 1930 that the number of Indian pilgrims performing the hajj via Iraq had decreased and attributed this decline to 'the stories of restrictions and hardships suffered which were circulated by pilgrims on return home'.[98]

The regulation of the pilgrimage was not limited to the introduction of specific bureaucratic formalities and financial guarantees. At the Desert Traffic Control Conference in 1930 the French and British delegates made

---

[95] BL, IOR/L/PJ/7/771-2283, Extract from written statement of Mr Hussain Vali Mohammed Ladhiwalla, attached to letter from the Secretariat of the High Commissioner for Iraq to the Ministry of Interior, Baghdad, 9 December 1929.

[96] BL, IOR/L/E/7/1558, file 162, report for 1932 on the work of the Protector of British Indian Pilgrims.

[97] BL, IOR/L/PJ/7/771-2283, extract from written statement of Mr Hussain Vali Mohammed Ladhiwalla.

[98] BL, IOR/L/E/7/1558, extract from Economic report, 1930 [month unknown], enclosed in letter dated 9 July 1930.

recommendations to improve the flow and speed of traffic across the desert while distinguishing between three categories of transport, namely conventional travellers, pilgrims and goods.[99] As pilgrimage traffic had been identified as a major problem of traffic organisation, the delegates considered its regulation as a precondition for the fluidity of transdesert traffic. In January 1930, Major Cones expressed this Iraqi government's request in these terms:

> The removal of the current restrictions can only be carried out step-by-step and according to transport categories. As an experiment, Iraq would simply be willing, for the time being, to allow the free transport of pilgrims and the movement of goods outside the days of special protection.[100]

French delegate Veber responded that the League of Nations would not appreciate a practice suggesting that the Mandate authorities were less concerned with the safety of pilgrims than with the safety of other kinds of travellers. To the French, moreover, the British Iraqi proposal seemed to serve no purpose other than favouring the leading Iraqi transporter Haim Nathaniel, who was merely catering for pilgrimage and goods traffic.[101] Therefore, they refused the proposal. The French and British delegates did not reach an agreement during the conference but recommended that the Syrian and Iraqi governments should carefully examine whether they wished to allow unrestricted travel for pilgrim convoys. They also agreed, for a transitional period, to allow the organisation of pilgrim convoys outside the prescribed days, if necessary, and on the condition that the Syrian and Iraqi police be notified in advance.[102] In addition, the delegates also recommended that pilgrims travelling to Syria should use the northern route via Mosul and Deir ez-Zor as much as possible, rather than the direct transdesert route, in order to lessen congestion on the Baghdad–Damascus route.[103]

[99] CADN, SYR-LIB-1v b703, 'Note relative à la Conférence Syro-Irakienne des 22 et 23 Janvier 1930 sur le contrôle du Trafic de la route Damas-Bagdad.'

[100] Ibid. Translation is mine.

[101] See the handwritten note added at the bottom of the above-mentioned report ('Note relative à la Conférence Syro-Irakienne'), p. 14.

[102] CADN, SYR-LIB-1v b703, 'Conférence Syro-Irakienne sur le contrôle du Trafic de la route Damas-Bagdad', minutes of the conference.

[103] Ibid.

Crucially, the authorities' attitude towards pilgrims differed greatly from their attitude towards other travellers crossing the Syrian Desert. First, during the interwar period, Middle Eastern states were very keen to encourage European and Arab tourists as well as summer vacationers to visit their countries, aware that they represented a very important economic resource.[104] Local governments and the mandatory authorities considered the creation of national borders and the introduction of documentary and customs regimes as strong impediments to the development of tourism and took measures accordingly to limit administrative and customs complications for tourists. In September 1923 the French High Commissioner argued against the raising of the visa tax for tourists to Lebanon in the French consulates in Egypt and Palestine.[105] The question of the visa fees remained subject to much debate in the territories under French Mandate throughout the interwar years, but the authorities were generally eager to keep them low. In 1935, the French reduced the fees for summer vacationers from Egypt, Iraq, Transjordan and Palestine from 1 May to 1 November so as to encourage summering in Lebanon and Syria.[106] Along the same lines, the French set up facilities for travellers entering the territories under French Mandate with their own cars, most of whom were foreign tourists or well-to-do travellers. In 1926, the authorities decided to exempt motorists affiliated to any tourism company recognised by the Touring Club of Syria and Lebanon from the payment of customs duties on their vehicle upon presentation of a so-called 'tryptique' (travel permit) provided

---

[104] Amit Bein, *Kemalist Turkey and the Middle East: International Relations in the Interwar Period* (Cambridge: Cambridge University Press, 2017), pp. 179–214; Idir Ouahes, *Syria and Lebanon under the French Mandate: Cultural Imperialism and the Workings of Empire* (London and New York: I. B. Tauris, 2018), pp. 65–88; Andrea L. Stanton, 'Locating Palestine's Summer Residence: Mandate Tourism and National Identity', *Journal of Palestine Studies*, Vol. 47, No. 2 (2018), pp. 44–62.

[105] CADC, 50CPCOM310, High Commissioner for Syria to French Ministry for Foreign Affairs, 21 September 1923.

[106] CADC, 50CPCOM544, French Ministry for Foreign Affairs to diplomatic and consular officers in Egypt, Palestine, Transjordan and Iraq, 9 April 1935; NARA, Internal Affairs of Syria 1930–44 (microfilm T1177), roll 4, report by Farrell (American Consul, Beirut), 8 May 1935.

by their association.[107] This measure, which nevertheless took a couple of years to be fully executed, was intended to facilitate customs formalities at the Iraqi border post of Rutbah for motorists travelling between Syria and Iraq.[108] By late 1929 the Iraqi authorities had almost completed similar arrangements with European automobile clubs.[109] Second, at a time when measures governing the passage of pilgrims became increasingly cumbersome – that is, at the end of the 1920s – the French and British authorities initiated discussions to facilitate the movement of government officials, military personnel and high-ranking religious dignitaries between Syria and Iraq.[110] They eventually reached an agreement that granted free visas to various important political, military and religious figures for all travel between the two countries. Lastly, French and British delegates at the Desert Traffic Control Conference were mainly concerned about easing the restrictions on transdesert traffic – especially during the summer months – to promote tourism and business.[111]

## Conclusion

The emergence of territorially bounded states in the interwar Arab Middle East coincided with an increase in travel practices between the nascent states of Lebanon, Syria and Iraq, due in particular to the opening of motor routes across the Syrian Desert. As a result, from the mid-1920s, the Baghdad–Damascus route became a major preoccupation of the French, British and local authorities who endeavoured to channel mobility along

---

[107] 'Bulletin mensuel des actes administratifs du Haut-Commissariat', decree no. 325, 28 May 1926.
https://gallica.bnf.fr/ark:/12148/bpt6k64674508/f3.image.r=triptyque (Accessed 1 May 2020).

[108] TNA, CO 730/129/9, Economic report, 13 October 1928.

[109] Government of Iraq, *Maps of Iraq with Notes for Visitors*, p. 27.

[110] CADC, 50CPCOM544, Sir F. Humphreys (High Commissioner for Iraq) to French High Commissioner, August 1930 as well as French High Commissioner to French Ministry for Foreign Affairs, 2 September 1930.

[111] TNA, FO 371/13745, 'Note on the informal discussions preliminary to the Iraqi–Syrian Overland Route Conference proposed for January next', Damascus, 9 November 1929.

this route in a bid to 'determine the speed, rhythm, routes, and meaning of mobility'.[112]

From the outset, the French and British were very keen to promote the development of motor traffic between Syria and Iraq, since they were aware of the political and economic opportunities that new regional and transregional mobility networks would create. To this end, they sought first and foremost to organise traffic and ensure safe travel conditions across the desert. Analysis of the French and British archives has shown in particular that the need to organise traffic and secure the route led to active cross-border cooperation between mandatory officials and desert administrators in Syria, Iraq and Transjordan, despite the continuing rivalry between France and Britain in the Middle East. Thus, this chapter has helped to show how cross-border mobility led to tensions but also to cooperation between the new Middle Eastern states.[113] As a transregional space, the Baghdad–Damascus route makes it possible to study mobility at the time of state formation while departing from the methodological nationalism that has long prevailed in research on the French and British Middle Eastern mandates.

On the other hand, the increasing involvement of states in the organisation of traffic due to persistent insecurity in the desert seriously hampered mobility, as the authorities introduced numerous restrictions that caused delays and congestion on the route. The frequent highway robberies on the Baghdad–Damascus route in the 1920s also point to the capacity of non-state actors to challenge state power and undermine French and British economic and strategic interests in the region and beyond. These various elements show that the states under French and British Mandate did not always succeed in shaping transdesert mobility according to their interests.

Finally, while this chapter has confirmed the previous findings that state formation and border making in the interwar Middle East did not necessarily curb preexisting and new patterns of mobility, it has highlighted the many-sided and discriminatory nature of the organisation of traffic and the

---

[112] Darshan Vigneswaran and Joel Quirk, *Mobility Makes States: Migration and Power in Africa* (Philadelphia: University of Pennsylvania Press, 2015), p. 20.

[113] Jordi Tejel, '"Des femmes contre des moutons": Franchissements féminins de la frontière turco-syrienne (1929–1944)' *20&21. Revue d'histoire*, Vol. 145 (2020), pp. 35–47.

regulation of mobility by states. The French and British Mandate authorities applied differential treatment to travellers between Iraq and Syria by encouraging and easing the movement of a small number of mostly wealthy travellers – including tourists, government officials and businesspersons – while restricting the mobility of others. This is particularly evident in the case of hajj pilgrims, who had to submit to stricter and heavier bureaucratic formalities than other travellers, not to mention the efforts made to slow down and redirect their movement so as to ease transdesert traffic for others. The contributors to 'Regimes of Mobility Across the Globe', from which the title of this volume derives, call for an approach 'that constantly theorises the relationships of unequal power within which relative stasis and different forms of mobility are constructed and negotiated'.[114] In other words, they encourage scholars to account for the ways in which power dynamics affect the interaction between mobility and immobility or, one might add, with regard to the Baghdad–Damascus route, between acceleration and deceleration of movement. In this respect, it has been argued that the French and British authorities in Lebanon, Syria and Iraq shaped regimes of mobility across the Syrian Desert that excluded certain categories of travellers from a process of acceleration and facilitation of mobility made possible by the development of motorised transport.

[114] Nina G. Schiller and Noel B. Salazar, 'Regimes of Mobility Across the Globe', p. 194.

# 9

# BORDER TRANSGRESSIONS, BORDER CONTROLS: MOBILITY ALONG PALESTINE'S NORTHERN FRONTIER, 1930–46

## Lauren Banko

The opening scene in Khalid Jarrar's 2012 documentary film, *Infiltrators*, is grainy night-time footage of a group of young Palestinian men being smuggled with the help of a couple of other men into East Jerusalem across Israel's concrete separation wall. An interlocutor, his face and body not visible, is asked whether the smuggling jobs pay good money. So-so, he replies, noting, for example, the risks to the smuggled of falling from the high wall. The other risks involve arrest, detention, jail time and hefty fines. As another interviewee explains, it is not only men smuggled into Israel or occupied East Jerusalem but young and older women, too. These Palestinian border-crossers do not have a singular purpose and they certainly do not fit the pictures often painted of them by Israeli media as armed infiltrators. They cross the border wall to visit family, to go to hospital or to pray at al-Aqsa Mosque. The film's chronicle of contemporary transgressions across the separation wall between the West Bank and Israel is not a new story in this geographical space. The same reasons that fuel unauthorised movement in the 2010s existed in the 1930s and 1940s during the British-administered Palestine Mandate. The *raison d'être* behind the regimes of mobility, including regimes crafted by smuggling networks and regimes enforced by police, soldiers, border guards and private contractors, are familiar whether from the interwar period or the post-1967 decades. The human costs of these regimes, so starkly depicted in Jarrar's film, are outweighed in the contemporary era just as they were during the interwar years by the personal, emotional, economic and social potential that lies just across the border.

Palestine's borderland spaces emerged through the mandate era (1920–48) as both geographical and physical, but also social and human. This chapter addresses bordering processes in Mandate Palestine and their subsequent impact from the 1930s to the 1940s on mobility across the territory's northern border with Lebanon, Syria and Transjordan. It focuses on two related aspects of bordering and mobility: the infrastructure of the border and illicit border crossings. This allows for an analysis of the human cost of frontier control in Palestine as reflective of, in the words of anthropologist Madeline Reeves, the everyday workings of power at the edges of states. In addition, frontier control and bordering allow for an interrogation as to when and how certain ideas about the relationship between citizenship, territory and cross-border movement took hold.[1] I also trace examples of the actions and tactics used by individuals 'without papers' to enter or leave Palestine, and the consequences of their crossing the new and often unmarked northern border without passports, *laissez-passer* or visas. The reactions to border transgressions on the part of Palestine's frontier control officers and immigration department are situated in the context of the ever developing border infrastructure such as frontier control stations, bridges, fencing, border passes and the deployment of foot patrols.

The creation of Palestine's borders and the processes that curtailed mobility led to instances in which individuals felt they had no choice but to cross borders illicitly – without passports, visas or border passes. These individuals' experiences tell stories of living 'without papers' in a time of significant transition; however, this transition could sometimes be felt only at the border and only once an individual attempted to cross it without the correct paperwork. As is well known, Palestine's borders, most significantly out of all in the Middle East during the interwar period, facilitated global movements. Histories of

---

[1] Madeleine Reeves, *Border Work: Spatial Lives of the State in Rural Central Asia* (Ithaca: Cornell University Press, 2014), pp. 7, 18.

movement to and from Palestine generally concentrate on the immigration of Jews from Europe and the Americas. The migrants and mobile residents discussed in the chapter, those who crossed Palestine's northern border overland, are not political Zionists, although some were Jewish. Several illicitly left Palestine without proper identity documents and others attempted to enter the territory clandestinely. They included Jews of Middle Eastern origin, Arabs from surrounding territories, members of non-Arab communities from elsewhere in the former Ottoman Empire including Kurds, Armenians and Greeks, as well as Iranians and Muslims and Jews from Central Asia. As such, they rarely appear in the records of the Zionist Organisation and the reasons for their presence in Palestine varied.

The creation of borders made 'difference' official: the state border itself can be a point of reference in response to how identities and national distinctions are constructed and articulated.[2] National borders are important historically as 'political constructs, imagined projections of territorial power', and borders are the ultimate symbol of state power.[3] Undoubtedly, this power is challenged and negotiated when those borders are ignored by the people who cross them. I argue that the movements and circulations across the northern frontier of the Palestine Mandate by non-Zionist Arabs[4], and non-Arab migrants and inhabitants of the borderlands, *did* challenge border infrastructure. Crucially, a borderlands history of Palestine must consider the ambiguities of power that developed almost as soon as the British and French delimited the territory's borders; as a result, migrants and mobile inhabitants directly and indirectly challenged the proposed borders. Additionally, only once governments initiated measures to control movement across frontiers did borders acquire more significant meaning among the communities that

---

[2] Mathijis Pelkmans, *Defending the Border: Identity, Religion, and Modernity in the Republic of Georgia* (Ithaca: Cornell University Press, 2006), p. 14.

[3] Michiel Baud and Willem Van Schendel, 'Toward a Comparative History of Borderlands', *Journal of World History*, Vol. 8, No. 2 (autumn 1997), p. 211.

[4] This is a contentious term. I use it to refer to individuals and communities that had no interest in, and did not come to Palestine for, political Zionism. They did not utilise the immigration system of the Jewish Agency, and when they did enter Palestine they did not do so with intent to join in the building of a Jewish national homeland. This does not negate, however, their possible roles in settler colonialism.

traditionally lived within or exerted control over borderlands in the Arab Middle East.[5] Even so, as Haggai Ram succinctly notes in his work on drugs smuggling, these operations brought to light the 'porous and perforated nature' of the interwar mandates' borders.[6] These porous spaces subverted centrist state power by fostering relationships that went under the radar of the state.[7]

The borderland spaces between Palestine and its neighbours developed a distinct territoriality not entirely due to impositions from the post-Ottoman mandate administrations or other colonial formations such as the British protectorate in Egypt. Instead, these spaces emerged out of, in the words of Matthew Ellis, a 'complex and multilayered process of negotiation'[8] between numerous actors and groups including residents of villages along the new borders, farmers and semi-nomadic Bedouin, merchants, people smugglers and the smuggled, and frequent, undocumented (and usually clandestine) border-crossers. Willem van Schendel's intervention that nothing is passive about borders is applicable to Palestine's northern frontier. In borderlands 'the spatiality of social relations is forever taking on new shapes' and this only continued as British and French infrastructure attempted to pacify movement along each empire's respective mandate boundaries.[9] Similarly

[5] Shamir makes the same argument on the control of borders in Ronen Shamir, 'Without Borders? Notes on Globalization as a Mobility Regime', *Sociological Theory*, Vol. 23, No. 2 (June 2005), p. 204. For a region-specific and new analysis of this, see Ramazan Hakkı Öztan, 'The Great Depression and the Making of Turkish–Syrian Border, 1921–1939', *International Journal of Middle East Studies*, Vol. 52, No. 2 (2020), pp. 1–16.

[6] Haggai Ram, 'Hashish traffickers, hashish consumers, and colonial knowledge in Mandatory Palestine', *Middle Eastern Studies*, Vol. 52, No. 3 (March 2016), p. 550.

[7] Hamalainen and Truett argue much the same in their reassessment of writing North American borderlands history: see Pekka Hamalainen and Samuel Truett, 'On Borderlands', *The Journal of American History*, Vol. 98, No. 2 (September 2011), pp. 338–61.

[8] Matthew Ellis elegantly articulates that the coming-into-being of the border between Egypt and Ottoman Libya in the decades before the First World War was a process of negotiation involving local actors more so than states' governmental actions. Ellis, *Desert Borderland: The Making of Modern Egypt and Libya* (Stanford: Stanford University Press, 2018), p. 8.

[9] Willem van Schendel, 'Spaces of Engagement: How Borderlands, Illegal Flows, and Territorial States Interlock', in Willem van Schendel and Itty Abraham (eds), *Illicit Flows and Criminal Things* (Bloomington: Indiana University Press, 2005), p. 46.

to Ellis, Toufoul Abou-Hodeib shows that for residents and crossers of the northern Palestine-southern Lebanon borderland, lines drawn by the British and French did little to change conceptions of this space and instead played second fiddle to the pre-existing transregional networks of mobility linked to seasonal harvests, pilgrimage and commercial networks.[10] Further to the northeast, on the frontier between Turkey and Iraq, Jordi Tejel convincingly demonstrates that local actors forced (and coerced) concessions from Great Britain, Turkey and the League of Nations regarding the line of the border.[11] Sahana Ghosh emphasises in her work on the Bengal borderlands that studies of border spaces have shown the importance of considering non-state notions of licitness and of legality in conjunction with state regulations defining the illicit and illegal to understand the worldview that underlies the maintenance of cross-border links despite state policies to the contrary.[12] In less than a decade since Asher Kaufman argued that very few studies on the Middle East have dealt with borders or particularly with the relationship between state authority and border populations[13], historians of the region are now asking questions about when state authority began to matter to inhabitants' perceptions of the borderland.

Kaufman's 2014 study of the tri-border zone between Palestine, Syria and Lebanon is instructive in its historicisation of Palestine's northern frontier. The 1920 delineation treaty between Britain and France placed the Jewish settlement of Metullah just inside of Palestine on the northernmost section of the boundary line. This went against the advice of both British and French advisors; in fact, Great Britain successfully pushed Palestine's border further north from its proposed location in the 1916 Sykes-Picot Agreement.

---

[10] Toufoul Abou-Hodeib, 'Involuntary History: writing Levantines into the nation', *Contemporary Levant*, Vol. 5 (2020), pp. 44–53.

[11] Jordi Tejel, 'Making borders from below: the emergence of the Turkish-Iraqi Frontier, 1918–1925', *Middle Eastern Studies*, Vol. 54, No. 5 (2018), pp. 811–26, and Jordi Tejel, 'States of Rumors: Politics of Information Along the Turkish–Syrian Border, 1925–1945', *Journal of Borderlands Studies*, Vol. 35 (2020), pp. 1–20.

[12] Sahana Ghosh, 'Cross-border activities in everyday life: the Bengal borderland', *Contemporary South Asia*, Vol. 19, No. 1 (2011), p. 50.

[13] Asher Kaufman, *Contested Frontiers in the Syria-Lebanon-Israel Region: Cartography, Sovereignty, and Conflict* (Washington, DC: Johns Hopkins University Press, 2014), p. 2.

In practical terms, Metullah remained in French-mandated Lebanon until completion of the Paulet-Newcombe demarcation commission in 1924. Crucially, the population of Metullah and other parts of the northern Huleh Valley received *ipso facto* Lebanese nationality in a 1921 census conducted to define the electorate for Lebanon's legislative assembly.[14] In fact, Britain and Sir Mark Sykes won a significant concession from France to have all of the upper Galilee region and the springs of Jabal al-Shaykh (Mount Hermon) on Palestine's side of the northern frontier.[15] Kaufman notes that the actual border through the tri-border region of the northern frontier remained imprecise through the entire mandate.[16]

Fredrik Meiton's findings elaborate upon the role of Zionist infrastructure in the border-making process: the northern border with Transjordan can be linked not initially to Jewish settlement but rather to Jewish control over water resources needed for an electrification project. Once Britain granted territory for the expansion of the hydroelectric power grid and power stations along the Jordan River, concessionaire Pinhas Rutenberg methodologically planned that Jewish colonisation would follow. Rutenberg joined the Anglo-French negotiations prior to the final demarcation of the northern border with Transjordan in 1923. He also influenced the route of the 1922 eastern border with Transjordan.[17] Metullah then, is a model for what Zionists envisioned as colonisation of the frontier between Palestine and its Arab neighbours – hydroelectricity helped the vision become a reality.

Palestine served as perhaps the most important site in the former Ottoman territories for the immigration and entry and exit of Europeans after 1918. More importantly, while places such as Lebanon and Algeria certainly saw the movement of European citizens and settlers across their borders, the fundamental incorporation of Europeans as naturalised citizens in former Arab provinces happened only on a large scale in Palestine. These citizens were ostensibly

---

[14] Kaufman, *Contested Frontiers*, pp. 15–17.

[15] Matthew Hughes, *Allenby and British Strategy in the Middle East, 1917–1919* (London: Frank Cass, 1999), p. 116.

[16] Kaufman, p. 33.

[17] Fredrik Meiton, *Electrical Palestine: Capital and Technology from Empire to Nation* (Oakland: University of California Press, 2019), pp. 46, 70–73.

on par with Palestine's indigenous inhabitants in terms of their citizenship status and the entailing access to (but not necessarily possession of) passports, travel visas and usage of the British administration's offices for immigration. European settlers in Algeria, for instance, could not claim parity with indigenous Muslim residents in the realm of citizenship as access to border-crossings. However, the focus of this essay is not European Zionist immigrants or indeed European immigrants' mobilities along Palestine's border. Neither do I focus any further on Zionist claims to the border, although Zionist officials clearly influenced the demarcation and eventually the agreements as to the location of Palestine's borders in ways that go beyond simply the movement's wish for a greater amount of territory for a future state.

The first section of the chapter contextualises the boundary delineation between Britain and France in Palestine's northern region from the beginning of the mandate administration, and the on-the-ground changes for mobility as a result of the border demarcation. It then places the experiences of Palestine's residents – whether citizen or not – negotiating the new systems of border controls in order to pass through the northern frontier to and from Transjordan, Syria and Lebanon. The British and French authorities labelled these passages transgressions, or illicit, when they occurred by individuals without the correct paperwork and permissions, or by those who avoided official frontier crossings altogether. These transgressions challenged the northern frontier itself, and the radical re-ordering of space that the creation of border regimes in the interwar Eastern Mediterranean attempted to orchestrate.

## The Ambiguities of Delineating Palestine's Northern Frontier

The border area between the mandates of Palestine, Transjordan, Lebanon and Syria involved substantial revisions and re-routings during the existence of the Palestine Mandate. This area, encompassing what the border in turn shaped into the northern frontier of Palestine, can be better understood as the physical manifestation of the 'borderlands': in the words of Mark Rifkin, a concept which connotes an area at the intersection of claims by multiple sovereign entities or where political sovereignty is indeterminate. Rifkin distinguishes the borderlands from the frontier, referring to the former as a juridical concept that does not name a clear legal or administrative mapping, but is instead a way to envision 'the place . . . [not beholden to] governmental requirements and categories'. The frontier, then, conjures sense of a 'periphery not quite, or perhaps not yet, integrated into the bureaucratic web of the nation's legal geography'.[18] Similarly, Randy William Widdis defines borderland as 'a physical, ideological, and geographical construct, a region of intersection that is sensitive to internal and external forces that both integrate and differentiate communities and eras on both sides of the boundary line'.[19] The British and French administrations never quite agreed on the border's placement and as a result, it remained ambiguously outside of full bureaucratic control. Zionist settlers in the area claimed the northern frontier as well, to the exclusion of its existing Arab inhabitants.

In 1923 Britain and France approved the route of the demarcation commission's boundary for Palestine's northern frontier. The 1923 line diverged from an earlier 1920 delineation agreement in a number of sections, with the greatest distance between the two different lines totaling seven kilometres.[20] Even after 1923, as discussed below, the line remained in flux. In principle, this boundary ran from the Mediterranean Sea incorporating Ras al-Naqura dividing Palestine from Lebanon, to the village and railway station of al-Hamma, south of Tiberias and separating Palestine from Syria and Transjordan.[21] The agreement on the boundary is itself vague: the physical demarcation included cairns, ruins and 'unnamed' wadis as markers.[22] The 1923 agreement shifted an earlier proposed border with Syria northwards between the Yarmuk valley villages of Samakh and al-Hamma, both very

---

[18] Mark Rifkin, 'The frontier as (moveable) space of exception', *Settler Colonial Studies*, Vol. 4, No. 2 (2014), p. 176.

[19] Randy William Widdis, 'Migration, Borderlands, and National Identity: Directions for Research', in John J. Bukowczyk, Nora Faires, David R. Smith and Randy Widdis (eds), *Permeable Border: the Great Lakes Basin as Transnational Region, 1650–1990* (Pittsburgh: University of Pittsburgh Press, 2005), p. 154.

[20] Franco-British Convention, 23 December 1920.

[21] More details can be found in Gideon Biger, *The Boundaries of Modern Palestine, 1840–1947* (London: Routledge, 2004).

[22] League of Nations Report, 1924: Exchange of Notes Constituting an agreement between the British and French Governments respecting a boundary line between Syria and Palestine, March 1923.

much frontiers at the edge of which Syrian territory began. Divergences between the 1920 and 1923 lines occurred, according to the commission, in order to avoid the division of village lands. In at least two cases, the border diverged in order to prevent splitting the land of wealthy and influential Arab owners. In other cases, whole villages that had been considered Syrian or Lebanese for three years became Palestinian, and vice versa. The village of Samakh on the shores of Lake Tiberias moved from the Syrian to the Palestinian mandate frontier, while Syria retained extraterritorial rights up to Samakh's railway station in accordance with the 1920 convention. The northern border with Transjordan took a direct line from Samakh, just south of the Sea of Galilee, along the Jordan River to al-Majame, from there to and including Beisan, and then south to Jericho and along the road to the Jewish kibbutz of Kallia on the north shore of the Dead Sea.

The adjustment significantly impacted border infrastructure: French-administered Syria could police the railway line along the frontier to Samakh. The government of Palestine, then, took responsibility to patrol all of Lake Huleh and Lake Tiberias, while the inhabitants of Palestine, Syria and Lebanon enjoyed fishing and navigation rights on the two lakes.[23] The frontier changes also included moving the Syria-Palestine border in the Galilee inland towards the east in 1923, as it previously cut through Lake Tiberias.[24] Despite the reasoning that the adjustments prevented splits of whole villages, Palestine's northern frontier boundary continued to divide a number of individual villages. Nineteen villages had proportions of land in both Palestine and Lebanon. For instance, while eighty per cent of Metullah's land fell inside Palestine as its northernmost (and Jewish) settlement, twenty per cent fell inside Lebanon. Officials decided to consider it Palestinian. In another case, the French High Commissioner for Syria and Lebanon insisted one village had been split in the mid-1920s between the three mandates which made it difficult to recover taxes. The British responded that such a village did not even exist on their maps.[25]

---

[23] ISA M316/18, Boundary line between Syria and Palestine from the Mediterranean Sea to Hamma.

[24] ISA M107/2, Notes on the variations between the frontier between Palestine and Syria of 1923.

[25] ISA M107/2, High Commissioner for Syria and Lebanon to High Commissioner for Palestine, 30 January 1924.

After a 1926 border adjustment, problems remained: the change still split eighteen villages between Palestine and Syria. The boundary split some villages nearly equally proportioned between the two mandates. Banais, in the Galilee, had forty per cent of its territory in Syria and sixty per cent in Palestine, but officials deemed it as Syrian.[26] Only a dirt path from Metullah to Banais marked this section of the frontier between Palestine and Syria. In 1932, some years after the adjustment, Great Britain received word from the League of Nations that the former never sought official League approval of the Syria-Palestine border. It took two more years for the League to approve the agreement between Great Britain and France and offer official recognition of the border.

Aside from the boundary changes, the region of the northern frontier was one of the most heterogenous of Palestine's borderlands in terms of religious communities, ethnic groups and the presence of nomads, semi-nomadic groups and settled inhabitants.[27] European Zionists, too, added to this demographic diversity. In addition, absentee landowners held hundreds of thousands of dunams there. Most of the absentee owners near Bcisan, for example, were Egyptian.[28] This presented practical problems for those landowners who needed to cross from Egypt through to the north of Palestine and often across into Lebanon or Syria to tend to land and tenancy issues. The annexation of certain lands, such as parts of Huleh to Palestine from Lebanon, added to the border's impact on daily lives in matters of taxation and the evasion of taxation.

The ambiguities of the frontier's placement also impacted frontier officials themselves. In 1937 British Army forces in Palestine began to question the status of the village and train station of al-Hamma.[29] According to the 1923 convention, the Palestinian side of the frontier ended at al-Hamma and maps included it within Palestine. British forces, however, had been informed by Syrian police and railway officials that al-Hamma's railway station and property belonged to Syria. Similarly, the Transjordanian Frontier Force

---

[26] ISA M107/2, Frontier village charts, 1923 and 1926.

[27] Kaufman, pp. 15, 19.

[28] ISA M268/35, Memo, Assistant District Commissioner Tiberias to District Commissioner Galilee, 11 May 1939.

[29] Al-Hamma and Samakh were both stations on the Jezreel Valley Line (*Marj ibn 'Amar* Line) of the Hejaz Railway as it passed through Palestine to Haifa from Dera'a in Syria.

believed al-Hamma to be in Syria. The commander of British forces in the area wrote that this 'appeared to be a small point' – one of its train stations belonging to another state – but from an internal security perspective it needed clarification. In reply, Palestine's chief secretary stated that while al-Hamma and its station lay inside the Palestinian frontier, Syria had extraterritorial rights over the railway and station there.[30] Syrian officials long complained through the British consulate of the frontier 'transgressions' made by Palestinian and Transjordanian frontier guards and police into Syria in pursuit of criminals or to gather intelligence. One complaint by the French consul-general in Jerusalem, followed by Syria opening an investigation, led the British authorities in Palestine to admit that it seemed 'questionable' whether anything entitled its army and mandate officials to cross the frontier without specific approval by Syrian authorities.[31]

Al-Hamma remained a site of tension between Palestine's and Syria's police and frontier officials, specifically the presence of Palestine's immigration officers on the train between al-Hamma and Samakh stations. Whilst the Syrian authorities remained committed to ending smuggling operations along the northern frontier they objected to British methods used to stop such practices. Immigration officers had long carried out passport controls *on* the train from Syria before that train entered al-Hamma, immediately inside the Palestinian border, or Samakh: they boarded inside Syrian territory to check the visas and identity documents of travellers prior to their entry into Palestine. No physical frontier control station existed on the actual railway line, meaning that identity checks could only be carried out before travellers stepped down from the train at al-Hamma. Through the late 1930s, the French objected to the passport checks and surveillance of travellers.[32] Yet Palestine's authorities duly objected to the situation of extra-territoriality.[33] For his part, the French consul general insisted that Palestinian officers could not pass through al-Hamma from Syria to check documents and that this must be instead done only after the train

---

[30] ISA M107/2, Headquarters of the British Forces in Palestine to Chief Secretary, 27 April 1937.

[31] ISA M5842/19, Correspondence, author unknown, 2 December 1937.

[32] ISA M5842/19, Consul-General of France in Palestine to Chief Secretary, 28 November 1939.

[33] The 1920 convention and the 1923 border demarcation articles did give the French the right to police al-Hamma and the railway line on the frontier up to, but not including, Samakh.

departed that station for Samakh. Palestine's Inspector General of Police also objected to the French complaint and insisted it would be impossible for effective passport control to be carried out in the sixteen minutes that it took for the train to travel between al-Hamma and Samakh if frontier control officers boarded only at al-Hamma station. The French eventually yielded, but warned that only specific, unarmed authorities could carry out limited controls on the train, and they could go no further than al-Hamma in their duties.[34]

The above exchange is telling in that it demonstrates frontier officials, the head of the Palestine police and government authorities on both sides of the frontier had unclear and divergent ideas as to the exact location of the borderline between Palestine and Syria and the furthest extent of each mandates' jurisdiction within the frontier despite a series of agreements on these details during the 1920s. The pressure exerted by the Palestine administration on its counterpart in Syria can be traced to the very specific need felt by the former to prevent the entry into Palestine of individuals without the correct paperwork. The Department of Immigration and Travel took this duty very seriously throughout the mandate and attempted to build sufficient border infrastructure to keep out unwanted overland migrants. Yet, at the same time, migrants and borderland residents efficiently and frequently crossed the northern frontier on foot, by car, and even traversed it by boat (both via the Mediterranean and Lake Tiberias) without the permission deemed essential by mandate authorities. The uncertainties of policing the frontier on the part of the French and British mandatory police and immigration guards only increased mobile persons' chances to successfully enter Palestine without the proper permissions. While these uncertainties often worked to migrants' advantages, more often they did not. The rest of the chapter turns to how border infrastructure – both physical and less tangible – impacted notions of licit and illicit crossings along the northern frontier.

## The Infrastructure of Frontier Control

The infrastructure of the borders came into being alongside their demarcation. Bridges over the Jordan, Yarmuk and Zarqa rivers, including crumbling

---

[34] ISA M5842/19, Correspondence on representations made by the Consul General of France on the crossing of the Syrian frontier, March–May 1940.

structures sometimes dating back to Mamluk rule over Syria, became 'official' crossing points. The Department of Public Works constructed small buildings to process exits and entries, some of which eventually encompassed housing for immigration, customs and police officers. Tunnels, such as at Ras al-Naqura, funnelled arrivals and departures between Lebanon and Palestine. In areas of the border, particularly with Lebanon, where the frontier did not follow a river or stream, fencing served as separational infrastructure, as did other outposts built by the British or the French. As Palestine's civil administration grew in the 1930s it constructed new frontier stations and repaired and expanded others when the budget allowed. By the final year of the Palestine Revolt in 1939, thirteen frontier stations existed: five along the northern frontier with Lebanon and Syria, six along the northeastern frontier with Transjordan and parts of Syria, and two along the southern frontier with Egypt. Not all operated on the same terms, as some processed only the entrances of pedestrians; others, pedestrians, livestock and goods traffic. Some closed periodically due to financial problems, damage or insecurity, such as that during the three years of revolt. Throughout the mandate, the most important of these stations in terms of volume of foot traffic was the coastal Ras al-Naqura. In addition, by 1938 the construction of a border fence along the northern frontier by counter-terrorism colonial planner Charles Tegart served the purpose to keep Arab guerrillas out of Palestine. At the same time, it physically separated borderland inhabitants from families and agricultural lands.

To shape and manage border infrastructure, Great Britain implanted a tried and tested colonial vision of frontier political order borrowed from India, Kenya and elsewhere. Extra-judicial regulations, such as the Frontier Crimes Regulation used by the Raj along the northwestern frontier of India, as well as criminal investigation powers, offered illicit migrants a new type of treatment by the Palestine Mandate.[35] Criminal Investigation Department (CID) and immigration officials could deport migrants deemed to be illegally present in Palestine without recourse to Palestine's judiciary or even government offices in Jerusalem and district officials. In cases of deportation the immigration authorities often went above the rulings and acquittals made by

[35] Benjamin D. Hopkins, 'The Frontier Crimes Regulation and Frontier Governmentality', *The Journal of Asian Studies*, Vol. 74, No. 2 (May 2015), pp. 369–89.

Figure 9.1 Ras en Naqura Frontier Post on the border of Palestine and Lebanon.

Credit: American Colony Photography collection, Library of Congress, LC-M31- 3544-[A].

district officials and magistrates regarding the permissibility of migrants to be in Palestine.

Histories of colonialism have demonstrated that through the eighteenth and nineteenth centuries unregulated, indigenous movement made imperial and colonial officials uneasy. Officials believed mobile people and communities, such as those the British in India considered tribes, or the Ottomans considered Bedouin, difficult to control and difficult to incorporate into centralised tax systems.[36] In Palestine, as elsewhere, borders became social institutions in part due to the infrastructures and levels of authority put into place to stop and to surveil undesirable and unmitigated movement. As the Introduction to this volume notes, these practices created new power relations between the state authorities and borderlanders. It also created new social hierarchies between the socio-economic migrants allowed to cross the border licitly and able to afford (and visit the proper offices for) passports and visas, and those people forced to cross into Palestine irregularly.

In a memo to the Palestine police, the Commissioner for Frontier Control (who also served as the Commissioner for Migration and Statistics, the head of Palestine's Department of Immigration), Eric Mills, defined frontier control as 'the complete expression of the interest of the Government in the passage across the frontier of members of the mineral, vegetable and animal kingdom'. In addition, frontier control involved an obligation to keep recorded data of human passages across the frontier. The most significant element of this was to prohibit illicit entry or departure from Palestine.[37]

A memorandum between Britain and France in 1922 initially affirmed the shared importance of this type of security policing along the shared border. Frontier control applied to the boundaries of Palestine in their entirety:

---

[36] Hopkins, p. 374; see also Reşat Kasaba, *A Moveable Empire: Ottoman Nomads, Migrants, and Refugees* (Seattle: University of Washington Press, 2009); Secil Yilmaz, 'Threats to Public Order and Health: Mobile Men as Syphilis Vectors in Late Ottoman Medical Discourse and Practices', *JMEWS*, Vol. 13, No. 2 (July 2017), pp. 222–43; J. Martens, 'Polygamy, Sexual Danger, and the Creation of Vagrancy Legislation in Colonial Natal', *Journal of Imperial and Commonwealth History*, Vol. 31, No. 3 (2003), pp. 24–45; Claude Markovits, Jacques Pouchepadass, and Sanjay Subrahmanyam (eds), *Society and Circulation: Mobile People and Itinerant Cultures in South Asia, 1750–1950* (New Delhi: Permanent Black Publishers, 2003).

[37] ISA M4126/10, Mills to Palestine Police HQ, 19 September 1939.

territorial waters, seaports, land stations and air stations.[38] The immigration department, which governed frontier control actions until the Palestine police took over this service in 1939, mandated that entry into Palestine had to be through specific stations; thus, any entry at other places became an offence. The Department of Customs, Excise and Trade, the Department for Agriculture, the Director of Medical Services and the Inspector General of Police worked within specific frontier stations. These departments carried out the necessary checks regarding the admission of foreigners, goods and animals, and the detention and arrest of persons with warrants against them seeking to leave Palestine and maintenance of public order.[39]

Frontier infrastructure depended on topography and climate. Officials frequently characterised northern frontier posts between Palestine and Transjordan as malarial, which made posts unpleasant sites for both frontier officials and the people who crossed through them. In 1939 Palestine's director of customs derided the state of the frontier control at Ras al-Naqura. After a visit to the post he described his shock at the 'dreadful conditions' – meaning those under which the largely British government officers lived and worked. The conditions were 'a positive disgrace' and the Customs House proved inadequate in size for handling of goods and had inadequate shelter to load and unload transborder lorries. The post had no water supply and so all water came from the Lebanese side of the border or the Palestinian village of al-Bassa.[40]

Other frontier stations on the northern boundary included Metullah, Jisr (Bridge) Banat Yacoub, Rosh Pinna and al-Buwayziyya. The east (and northeast) boundary hosted frontier controls at Allenby Bridge, Jisr al-Majameh, Jisr al-Yarmuk (also known as Jisr al-Saghir), Samakh, Jisr al-Damiya, Jisr Sheikh Hussein and, to the very furthest south on the eastern border, Beersheba. Under the mandate's ever-amended immigration ordinances, the Damiya and Sheikh Hussein bridges were not prescribed places of entry for foot traffic but rather for the movement of animals and livestock. Rosh Pinna, further inside of Palestine, functioned as a secondary check for people and

---

[38] Ibid.
[39] Ibid.
[40] ISA M4126/10, Director Customs, Excise and Trade to Chief Secretary, 19 December 1939.

goods cleared through Metullah or Banat Yacoub. Yet, despite what a map depicted as regular crossing points, the bridges and frontier control stations had arbitrary hours of opening, varying levels of staffing and some were so remote that even nearby villagers experienced difficulties using them to take animals and produce to markets across the borders.

In general, certain persons who wished to enter Palestine across the northern frontier had to possess border passes issued under authority of the 1926 Bon Voisinage Agreement or hold valid travel documents bearing visas issued by British consular officers at Damascus, Aleppo, Beirut or Amman. Residents of the area directly on or along the frontier had more freedom to cross it as they did not require paperwork in the form of passports and visa stamps. The Bon Voisinage Agreement stipulated that inhabitants of the frontier regions of Lebanon, Syria and Palestine could pass freely across the mandates' borders using a system of border passes. The border passes could be annually renewed by Syrians and Lebanese who had land inside of Palestine. On the Palestinian side of the frontier, the task of approving border passes fell to the assistant district commissioners. Even for those border residents who received passes, other infrastructure did not exist to allow swift crossing at official points: while the British and French paved new road networks and encouraged vehicular traffic it often took years for those roads to be completed. Instead of using them, travellers and migrants travelled older routes avoiding border posts.[41]

Further to the east during the 1930s, frontier control stations over the Jordan River grew to encompass formerly private land and bridges, fences, gates, accommodation structures and other outbuildings as Palestine's Public Works financed their construction. Bridge crossings opened during daylight hours only and their methods of operation encouraged clandestine movement into and out of Palestine. Intentionally or not, individuals had no choice but to cross the border without authorisation if they arrived at frontier control stations after sunset. By 1940 the Transjordan boundary with Palestine had four main control points for entry and exit: Samakh train station and al-Yarmuk, al-Majameh and Allenby bridges. Sheikh Hussein bridge closed in 1938 due to lack of available staff for security and remained closed in 1940

---

[41] Abou-Hodeib, 'Involuntary History', p. 49.

Figure 9.2 Allenby Bridge guardhouse during flooding along the Jordan River, 1935.

Credit: Matson (G. Eric and Edith) collection, Library of Congress, LC-M32- 10991.

after it sustained flood damage. Along with al-Damiya Bridge, neither hosted an attached police station. Frontier officials complained about this lack of security. In 1938, just before flooding along the banks of the Jordan, the District Office in Galilee argued that since motor traffic frequently crossed the Sheikh Hussein Bridge, the lack of control staff meant people and arms smuggling could not be prevented. As a result, the bridge closed to all pedestrian and vehicle traffic and officials erected wire barricades at both ends. Those who wished to enter Palestine from points north and east had to pass through crossings further away, such as al-Majameh to the north, instead.[42] The flood damage and abandonment made Sheikh Hussein only more attractive to irregular migrants seeking a way to enter Palestine with minimal risk of surveillance.

Of course, the importance of these crossing points for livelihoods of individuals and communities and the continuation of the local and regional

[42] ISA M230/56, District Commissioner Galilee to Chief Secretary, 24 August 1938.

economy cannot be understated. The closure of frontier control stations created enormous hardship for local traders as well as regular travellers. Sheikh Hussein stood fifteen kilometres south of Jisr al-Majameh and forty-five kilometres north of Jisr al-Damiya. People who normally crossed the northern frontier at Sheikh Hussein could not necessarily travel further south to al-Damiya, itself subject to restricted opening times. On the other hand, the congestion at the closer crossing, al-Majameh, led to exposure and damage for those carrying crops such as grapes and various vegetables.[43] Cultivators and suppliers of produce suffered from delays, opening and closing times that did not align with their journey to markets, repeated closures, and insufficient personnel to process their movements at the bridge crossings. Bridge closures lasted for years in the event of damage or flooding: in 1944, during the continued closure of al-Damiya, the British Resident at Amman received a petition from cultivators located near the bridge to ask for it to be re-opened to traffic. The Transjordan government responded that the re-opening would not sufficiently benefit a large enough swathe of the population to outweigh security concerns due to insufficient staff in the event of its re-opening.[44] Al-Damiya remained closed in 1946 when the Haganah paramilitary forces attacked it and nearly all of the other border bridges along the northern frontier.

For areas of the frontier where bridges or built-up infrastructure did not exist, particularly where the border of Palestine cut through village and grazing lands, other institutions substituted as control mechanisms. By the mid-1920s officials depicted the criss-crossing into and out of Palestine of Bedouin as well as Druze refugees during the Great Syrian Revolt as an acute problem in need of a solution. The 1923 Bon Voisinage Agreement between Palestine and Syria stipulated 'all inhabitants, whether settled or semi-nomadic' could continue to exercise their rights to both sides of the border with their animals.[45] Still, the French Levant army's Contrôle Bedouin established a policing force along the Syrian and Lebanese borders with Palestine and the Syrian border with Transjordan. The imposition of customs barriers and tariffs, enforced at borders, further ended the free trade monopolised by the Bedouin. In 1940, a

---

[43] ISA M230/56, CID to Chief Secretary, 23 January 1940.
[44] ISA M230/56, British Resident, Amman to Chief Secretary, 22 May 1946.
[45] Bon Voisinage Agreement, 3 February 1922.

Figure 9.3 Jisr Sheikh Hussein, on the border of Palestine and Transjordan, 1930s.

Credit: Matson (G. Eric and Edith) collection, Library of Congress, LC-M33- 3250.

reciprocal agreement between Palestine and Transjordan meant that Bedouin tribes could enter each mandate south of the Dead Sea without a passport if they reported to the frontier control or Arab Legion post nearest to their point of entry within a two-week time window.[46]

As Baud and Van Schendel write, new social realities manifested in the borderlands as a result of government intentions in those spaces.[47] Indeed, certain borderlanders and certain migrants could legally pass through the northern frontier's burgeoning infrastructure through the 1930s but many others did not meet the qualifications set by Britain to do so. Bedouin without appropriate documentary identity fell into the latter cohort, as did any

[46] ISA M5844/18, Memo, British Resident at Amman, 11 March 1940.
[47] Michiel Baud and Willem van Schendel, 'Toward a Comparative History of Borderlands', *Journal of World History*, Vol. 8, No. 2 (autumn 1997), p. 212.

mobile person without a visa, passport or border pass. Others could not legally cross the frontier during the set times and through the set points thrust suddenly into their older trajectories of movement. Still others could not produce the correct 'excuse' to receive permission to enter or leave Palestine: the border regime became linked to colonial ideas of which indigenous person should deserve the right to reside in the territory. Absence from spaces claimed as homelands, former Ottoman subjects found it often impossible to prove to the mandate authorities that their brief (or extended) sojourns outside of Palestine did not cause them to lose a sense of loyalty to the territory and thus the right to return to their residences. It is to these stories the chapter now turns.

### Permissibility and the Illicit

The histories of illicit frontier crossings (defined as such by the mandate authorities) offer a framework through which to view the actions of non-state actors as they worked within and outside of pre-mandate regimes of mobility at a time of expanding colonial power over the landscape of the villages, hills, rivers and bodies of water that became borderland. I focus on the line between the permissibility and illicitness of certain crossings: those by residents of Palestine. These residents could be citizens, or simply long-term inhabitants of the mandate whose natal villages or towns were in one of the other post-Ottoman mandates or states, Egypt, Iran, North Africa or Central Asia.

Palestine's immigration and citizenship regulations stipulated a link between habitual residence and the right to claim the nationality offered by the mandatory. This mattered for voting in municipal and legislative councils, but it also mattered at the borders of the mandate. As Jan and Leo Lucassen argue, such links meant the 'alien' held significant importance for nation state governments that had to socially and legally define migrants in order to clearly implement the state's settlement policies.[48] Indeed, defining migrants ensured that immigration and police authorities could better control the frontiers of the state. The need to adhere to a strict immigration policy in Palestine was

---

[48] Jan Lucassen and Leo Lucassen (eds), *Migration, Migration History, History: Old Paradigms and New Perspectives* (Bern: Peter Lang, 1997), p. 26.

paramount: authorities acted against illegal immigration of both Arabs and Jews in order to uphold the terms of the mandate. The lack of a record of Palestinian citizens made it an impossible task for immigration officers to accurately assess the citizenship of individual Arab residents of Palestine when such a resident happened to arrive at the border. Arrivals from neighbouring states and the wider region to frontier control stations faced the possibility of arrest and deportation by the mandate authorities if they could not prove their long residence in Palestine with identity papers or other means. Even those who could prove residence did not necessarily receive permission to re-enter Palestine.[49] Residents without passports or identity documents who returned to Palestine after visiting relatives, conducting business or travelling for religious or social reasons to neighbouring territories could only re-enter through sections of the frontier free from border officers and patrols.

The longest section of Palestine's frontier was its border with Transjordan. While Palestine's immigration department typically recorded more Syrians and Lebanese who illegally entered (and Syrians and Lebanese were generally the most significant groups in lists of monthly deportations), residents of Transjordan faced penalties and deportation orders for crossing the frontier without permission. Despite their common British-run administrations neither Palestinians nor Transjordanians had the right to freely pass through the shared frontier. Still, residents from Transjordan frequently travelled to Palestine for work and long stays, including journeys that ended in settlement in Palestine. Exemplifying this type of journey and its consequences, the following case is instructive. In 1928 a resident of the mandate of Transjordan made a visit to relatives in Jerusalem across the northern frontier. In deciding to remain in Jerusalem with his relatives, he undertook an action that would have been innocuous ten years prior. Only a few years passed since the introduction of passports and visas for travel, and just a few years prior the borders of Palestine remained unofficial. More importantly, Great Britain only carved out Transjordan from Palestine as an entirely separate mandate in 1923. The man from Transjordan, Muhammad Rafat, enlisted with the Palestine police. Upon enlistment, he produced a certification from his village mukhtar (chief)

---

[49] Lauren Banko, '"A stranger from this homeland": deportation and the ruin of lives and livelihoods during the Palestine Mandate', *Contemporary Levant*, Vol. 4 (2019), p. 10.

that inadvertently demonstrated Rafat had not 'conformed' with immigration regulations. He had entered Palestine as a traveller (an immigration category ineligible for residency) and did not return to Transjordan: these contravened regulations and turned Rafat into an illegal migrant. Authorities detained him until a brother-in-law paid bail. After considerable time passed, Rafat found himself unable to leave Palestine, having no documentary paperwork and awaiting legal proceedings taken out against him by the mandate. The police force also could not appoint Rafat into the role for which he applied. This left Rafat in a difficult financial situation, without the means to remain unemployed in Palestine and unable to leave Palestine to find work in Transjordan.[50]

Further to the west, Palestine's northern frontier cut the former Ottoman province of Beirut into two and the border partitioned off several villages into southern Lebanon. The path of the border also shifted through the 1920s, placing some Lebanese villages into Palestine and vice versa. Born in Lebanon to Ottoman parents, the family of Philip 'Abla moved after the First World War to a home in the small borderland village of Abil al-Qameh. 'Abla's mother administered property in the village, located close to Palestine's Metullah. In 1923 after the border demarcation, the village fell within the territory of Palestine, making the family citizens of the latter mandate. A child in 1925, 'Abla moved with his sister and her Palestinian husband to the town of Safed. From there, he went to school in Jerusalem for two years and then moved to Haifa.[51] Over a decade later, 'Abla visited his dying mother, who had since moved across the border to her natal village in Lebanon. Upon his return, the Palestine government issued him a deportation order. 'Abla somehow managed to evade the order for almost three years. In 1941 police in Tel Aviv arrested him on the charge of illegal presence in Palestine. When placed under arrest, 'Abla stated he had lived in Palestine for nearly two decades, since 1925. The CID conferred with its counterpart in Lebanon, the Sûreté Générale, which confirmed 'Abla had been seen in his mother's village in 1938. The CID reported the visit he had made across the northern frontier to Lebanon as grounds for deportation.[52]

---

[50] ISA M860/41, Petition from Mohmmad Rifat to Jerusalem Deputy District Commissioner, 31 August 1928.

[51] ISA M4352/10, Petition, Walid Salah to High Commissioner, 11 April 1941.

[52] ISA M4352/10, CID to Chief Secretary, 18 April 1941.

'The reasons for crossing the northern border without permission ranged. Most were fairly innocent, as in the examples above. For instance, Russian-born monk Michail Nissan left for Palestine in 1929 and made it only as far as Syria where he took up residence, becoming a Syrian subject in 1936. He requested, and was denied, the permission to enter Palestine. Despite this, he found another route across the border. Upon arrival to Jerusalem, he hoped the Greek Patriarchate would house him in the convent and assist in regularising his status. In fact, the Palestine Immigration Department did deliver Nissan a certificate of identity to enable him to *leave* the territory on an emergency visa. Intending to go to Egypt, Nissan soon discovered that because of his irregular position in Palestine, the Egyptian government refused permission to enter. Finding it impossible to travel anywhere but back to Syria, Nissan petitioned the Jerusalem district official to help 'to save me from starvation' before seem-ingly giving up and undertaking the return journey.[53]

It appears that a significant number of northern frontier-crossings were of individuals who sought to obtain employment in Palestine but did not qualify for any visa or permission to enter as workers or labourers. To be sure, many Arab workers entered Palestine clandestinely or without the proper papers, or with forged visas. Others entered across the northern frontier from Syria or Lebanon using smuggling rings or with the help of individuals who styled themselves as smugglers. Drug smuggling has received recent atten-tion in the historiography of the Palestine Mandate.[54] In addition, it is well known that at the height of the Yishuv's (pre-state Jewish community) illegal immigration campaign during the Second World War, Aliyah Bet, Jewish settlements and kibbutzim on the Palestinian side of the northern frontier with Lebanon and Syria served as bases for human smuggling activities. Even prior to Aliyah Bet, Kaufman argues that Zionist smugglers travelled between Beirut and Damascus to bring Lebanese and Syrian Jews to Palestine. These Jews and their Zionist smugglers – working with the help of and knowledge of Syrian and Lebanese Arabs in the borderlands – travelled by car to south

---

[53] ISA M860/41, Petition from Michael Nissan to Jerusalem District Commissioner, 1 July 1938.

[54] Ram, 'Hashish traffickers'; Cyrus Shayegh, 'The Many Worlds of Abu Yasin; or, What Narcotics Trafficking in the Interwar Middle East Can Tell Us about Territorialization', *American Historical Review*, Vol. 116, No. 2 (2011), pp. 273–306.

Lebanon, where locals of the area helped them clandestinely cross the border. Kaufman uses French accounts to paint a clear picture of the activities involved in the 'classic cross-border entrepreneurship' of Shia villages in the Galilee, including Hunin in Palestine, with their counterparts on the Lebanese side.[55] The Transjordanian Frontier Force (TFF), under British control, had orders during the war to stop and arrest smugglers and immigrants for illegal activities along its shared stretch of the frontier.

The regulations for migrants and travellers to Palestine such as the need for specific visas or travel permits with photographs, invitations from employers, new customs controls, time-consuming travel to distant crossing points and the fixed working times of those crossings did little to persuade individuals from soliciting the service of people-smugglers. In 1934, the British government admitted the problem of people-smuggling to the League of Nations and noted most illicit entrances came via its northern and northeastern frontiers. For instance, Palestine authorities traced one dominant father-son smuggling duo in 1932. Criminal investigation officials referred to Abu Fuad, the father, as a professional broker active in the people-smuggling trade for years. Both Syrian nationals, he and his son travelled frequently by train across the northern frontier into Palestine to conduct their operations.[56] In one case, Abu Fuad managed to arrange for the unauthorised passage into Palestine of the elderly and blind mother-in-law of a former dragoman for the United States consulate in Damascus. When a visa request for the elderly woman from Aleppo was denied she illegally entered Palestine with the help of the smugglers.[57] An intelligence report noted that a Baghdadi-born Jewish Iraqi national and a Syrian Muslim resided together and worked in partnership in the Jewish Quarter of Damascus to transport both Jewish and non-Jewish Arabs into Palestine across the same frontier.[58]

British consulates in the neighbouring mandates and the office of the high commissioner for Syria and Lebanon, in correspondence with Palestine's Department of Immigration, attempted to ascertain how the frontier could

---

[55] Kaufman, p. 82.

[56] TNA FO 684/6, Memo, British Consulate to Palestine Government, 20 October 1932.

[57] TNA FO 684/6, Immigrant Smuggling into Palestine memo, CID to British Consulate in Damascus, 15 October 1932.

[58] File from CID to British Consulate, Damascus, 15 October 1932, TNA FO 684/6.

be so easily transgressed. One interlocutor suggested that non-Palestinians conducting smuggling rings made special agreements with frontier agents on both sides of the Palestine-Syria section of the border.[59] Indeed, infra-structure such as frontier guards could and did work against the interests of the colonial state and for their own and local benefits. Ghosh notes that all negotiation and subversion of the law at the margins of the state is a process common to borderlands, including from within the apparatus of the state; for example, border guards are induced by easy profit to work with local smug-gling networks.[60]

The construction of a border fence in the north in 1937 ensured that migrants, as well as anti-colonial rebels, could no longer easily pass unguarded points of the frontier. Palestine's Defence Regulations of 1939, reaffirmed with a government order during the Second World War, made crossing of the frontier illegal, even with a visa, unless it were done at certain cross-ings. These restrictions continued to severely interfere with the agricultural activities of individuals along the frontier and with the everyday movements of inhabitants on both sides.[61] This likely gave more impetus to clandestine crossings of the frontier through the 1940s, albeit through new spots not covered in barbed wire.[62] Constructed during the revolt of 1936–39, the bor-der fence followed a paved road from Ras al-Naqura across Palestine to Nabi Yusha', another village that became part of Lebanon until the 1923 boundary commission shifted Palestine's border northwards, and then south to Lake Tiberias. It excluded the land in the northernmost Upper Galilee along the Lebanese border, and much of the Huleh Valley. During the revolt, British police and security forces restricted the movement into Palestine by Syrian and Lebanese residents of the borderlands. This further cut off access to agri-cultural land across the northern frontier by residents of this area.

---

[59] Ibid.

[60] Ghosh, 'Cross-border activities', p. 57.

[61] See both ISA M716/1, Defence Regulations, 1939; and undated memo ISA M4349/34, 1943.

[62] For more on barbed wire in this same time period in the case of European borders, see Tabea Linhard, 'Moving Barbed Wire: Geographies of Border Crossing During World War II', in Tibea Linhard and Timothy H. Parsons (eds), *Mapping Migration, Identity, and Space* (London: Palgrave Macmillan, 2019), pp. 117–36.

Figure 9.4 Jisr Banat Yacoub damage after bombing by the Haganah, 1946.
Credit: Palestine Chief Secretary's Office, Israel State Archives, M4103/5.

The easternmost frontier could be managed internally between the British administrations in Palestine and Transjordan. This did not, however, make its management easier: both mandates viewed illegal border crossings, smuggling and subversion of the documentary regime as serious problems. This frontier with Transjordan tightened substantially during the 1936–39 Palestine Revolt. Prior to 1939, Palestinians and Transjordanians who lived in the vicinity of the frontier, especially Bedouin who used land on both sides, crossed the border with relative ease. In the aftermath of the Palestine Revolt, the administration expanded the practice of using Bedouin to patrol the frontiers of the mandate. British officials paid stipends to Bedouin sheikhs to police the movement of certain people and goods, particularly across the southern border.[63] Still, throughout the early 1940s, frontier commissions deemed controls along the northern border unsatisfactory, and recommended implementing full police posts at some, barriers across roads at others, and agreements with the French for greater cooperation in patrols.

[63] Mansour Nasasra, 'Ruling the Desert: Ottoman and British Policies towards the Bedouin of the Naqab and Transjordan Region, 1900–1948', *British Journal of Middle Eastern Studies*, Vol. 42, No. 3 (2015), p. 274.

Yet, in summer 1946, Zionist militants blew up nearly every bridge that linked Syria and Transjordan to Palestine. The Allenby, Sheikh Hussein and Banat Yacoub bridges sustained damage to varying extents, and the attacks severed the rail link between Dera'a and Haifa. The northern frontier effectively ceased to function.

## Conclusion

What emerges from a study on the northern frontier during the interwar period is that, in the words of Lara Putnam, there continued to be 'the kinds of migrations that kept borderlands borderlands'.[64] The vast expanse of the northern frontier remained a space that could not come under the regulatory control that the British and French wished for. Border control stations, barriers, barbed wire fencing, increased patrols, or even Jewish settlements did not make the frontier an impenetrable boundary. The northern frontier is important in another way: it offers a glimpse to the past and the present of what Ann Laura Stoler terms 'the carceral archipelago of empire . . . gradated zones of containment that mixed and matched "security" and defense with confinement, abuse, "education," and abandonment'.[65] Frontiers in the Eastern Mediterranean, including in modern day Palestine and Israel, are themselves part of the imperial debris about which Stoler writes. They are part of larger projects of empire repurposed in the post-colonial era as sites to detain, deport, exert high-level security infrastructure over and to readily forget. In being sites of imperial debris, they are also sites of knowledge: these are places where migrants deemed by the British and French colonial empires as illegal and undocumented learned to navigate through, to control, and to present as their own rightful places of passage. Many of the borderland villages, including those next to border crossings, mentioned in this chapter are debris in a more literal sense: in 1948 villages such as Samakh, Abil al-Qameh, al-Majameh, al-Damiya, al-Hamma, Nabi Yusha' and al-Buwayziyya were depopulated by Israeli forces as a result of both overt and subtle Zionist ethnic cleansing operations. Upon the creation of Israel, these sites became

---

[64] Lara Putnam, 'Borderlands and Border Crossers: Migrants and Boundaries in the Greater Caribbean, 1840–1940', *Small Axe*, Vol. 43, No. 1 (March 2014), p. 12.

[65] Ann Laura Stoler, 'Imperial Debris: Reflections on Ruins and Ruination', *Cultural Anthropology*, Vol. 23, No. 2 (2008), p. 213.

strategic due to their locations near the frontiers with the new state's Arab neighbours – and the borders through which the military authorities feared Palestine's refugees would attempt to return.

Unsurprisingly, the Nakba and creation of Israel in 1948 also changed the perception of the border and the people who attempted to cross it. The smuggling of persons and goods across the border continued, this time nearly exclusively on the part of the Palestinian Arabs. Early on, Israel classified this movement as 'infiltration'. The term did not apply only to illegal migration but also to Bedouin movement: tribes that had long grazed their animal herds on both sides of the frontier in the Negev became infiltrators once they passed out of Egyptian-administered territory after 1948. Some of these Bedouin continued the practice of smuggling goods from Egypt and Jordan, and some smuggled weapons and ammunition and acted to sabotage Israeli military installations along the frontier between Gaza and Israel. Even so, 'infiltration' stopped only in the 1950s when United Nations forces began to patrol this border.[66]

On the northern frontier, now the area bordering the 1949 armistice line, a similar situation of cross-border movement continued, classified by the Israelis as infiltration by 'Arab marauders'. In a 1953 memorandum on what the Israelis referred to as 'border incidents' by an Israeli government official to the Hashemite Kingdom, the former claimed infiltration occurred because 'the inhabitants of the border regions have no clear appreciation of the existence and purport of the Demarcation Line'. The official suggested that it 'should be repeatedly explained to the border population that infiltration is illegal, risky and nonprofitable'. The solution, then, was an extensive education programme to change the attitude of the border population towards the demarcation line.[67] Of course, this memorandum assumes, on the part of the Israelis, that border transgressions occurred because the borderland population could not understand the meaning of the border. Yet, for decades the border *had* been understood and a particular relationship assumed between borderland residents and travellers with the frontier and its crossings. It is

[66] Meir and Tsoar, 'International Borders', p. 50.

[67] ISA MFA90/20, Memorandum on proposed measures against infiltration submitted by the Senior Israeli Delegate to the Senior Delegate of the Hashemite-Jordan Kingdom, 25 March 1953.

perhaps only with the end of the Palestine Mandate in 1948 that meanings of citizenship became more firmly linked to territory, as the new post-1948 green line explicitly prevented Arab, or otherwise non-Jewish, cross-border movements. The experiences of early transregional migrants and residents of borderland areas mattered little for the post-colonial decades of territorialised nationhood. Largely because of the creation of Israel but also in line with practices of its neighbouring Arab states after independence, administrative practices at the borders 'territorialised ethnicity'.[68] Whereas this chapter has demonstrated how the creation of and infrastructure along Palestine's northern border did not result in impenetrable space of mandate sovereignty, bordering introduced new forms of mobility regulation and control that existed in cooperation with wider globalised processes.

[68] Reeves, *Border Work*, p. 75.

# 10

## WHEN NOMADS FLEE: 'RAIDER', 'REBEL' AND 'REFUGEE' IN SOUTHERN IRAQ, 1917–30

### Robert S. G. Fletcher

In the Middle East – perhaps more than in any other theatre of the First World War – the dust kicked up by the armies of empires took a long time to settle. Across the 1920s dislocation and displacement remained salient facts of life. Food shortages, political tensions and a recrudescence of violence kept thousands of people on the move. How these movements were managed and understood, however, was refracted through the new state structures, border regimes and prevailing ideologies of statecraft and of empire that now began to take root across the former Ottoman domains.

In recent years, refugee movements in the interwar Middle East have received renewed attention from historians. Innovative attempts to adopt an 'itinerant perspective' have stressed the depth of connection between the history of specific refugee communities and the growth of colonial and international authority in the region.[1] The League of Nations, for example, became

---

[1] Benjamin Thomas White, 'Refugees and the Definition of Syria, 1920–1939', *Past and Present*, Vol. 235 (2017); Keith David Watenpaugh, *Bread from Stones: the Middle East and the Making of Modern Humanitarianism* (Oakland: University of California Press, 2015); Jérôme Elie, 'Histories of Refugee and Force Migration Studies', in Elena Fiddian-Qasmiyeh, Gil Loescher, Katy Long and Nando Sigona (eds), *The Oxford Handbook of Refugee and Forced Migration Studies* (Oxford: Oxford University Press, 2014), pp. 23–35.

a leading centre of calculation for the practice of 'ethnically based mass transfer' of refugees: between Greece and Turkey, in Syria, in Palestine and elsewhere. In the new mandates, the 'refugee regime' for displaced Assyrians, Armenians and Kurds 'quickly became a major *raison d'être* of the League and the British and French mandate authorities alike'.[2] In Syria, the arrival and settlement of successive refugee groups drove processes of territorialisation and the articulation of national identity, so that 'the modern state of Syria was formed around and against refugees'.[3] In Iraq, meanwhile, the rich records of the refugee camp at Ba'quba (1918–20) have granted historians a window onto colonial settlement policies, camp administration, the creation of 'ethnonational enclaves', the discourses affecting refugee groups and the extent of their agency in the most trying of circumstances.[4]

While much of this literature has focused on displaced agricultural communities, and on sites along the borders of Turkey, Syria and northern Iraq, the nomadic societies of the Syrian and north Arabian Deserts also sought refuge from conflict, conscription and dearth. During the First World War the campaigns waged by British and Ottoman forces triggered desperate movements by Bedouin groups between the faltering Anglo-Indian invasion of Mesopotamia in the east and the privations of Djemal Pasha's Greater Syria in the west. Later, the enmity between an expanding Saudi state and the new mandate regimes in Transjordan and Iraq set others in motion between north and south.

The fate of the Bedouin in this new era of emergent states is the subject of a dynamic and growing literature; key themes concern their 'encapsualtion', sedentarisation and implication in the networks and structures of colonial rule. But the scholarship on interwar refugee movements on the one hand, and on nomadic groups on the other, has tended to remain separate. Studies of the interwar Bedouin seldom emerge from refugee or forced migration studies, and are as likely to frame their subjects in terms of state building,

---

[2] Laura Robson, *States of Separation: Transfer, Partition and the Making of the Modern Middle East* (Oakland: University of California Press, 2017), 34.

[3] White, 'Refugees'.

[4] Benjamin Thomas White, 'Humans and Animals in a Refugee Camp: Baquba, Iraq, 1918–20', *Journal of Refugee Studies*, Vol. 32 (2018), pp. 216–36; Robson, *States of Separation*, pp. 35–51.

border tensions, or the place of 'tribe' in regional politics. In this, and in part, the new literature follows the old. Throughout the 1920s and 1930s the League of Nations and the mandate regimes recognised relatively few specific communities as 'refugees'. Bedouin groups do not appear under the main 'refugee' headings of League reports; often, Bedouin were administered (and thus their records were produced) by entirely separate branches of the colonial bureaucracy, reflecting the distinct jurisdictions created for the desert borderlands of many Middle Eastern possessions.[5] Those recognised in Geneva as 'refugees' were usually from non-Muslim communities with historic ties to western Europe and to Anglo-French practices of evangelism and 'protection' in the nineteenth-century Mediterranean.[6] And yet Bedouin groups undoubtedly experienced displacement and forced migration in this period, and nowhere more so than in southern Iraq. On the ground, local mandatory officials and colonial officers spoke often of the 'destitution' driving many Bedouin movements in this period. Tacitly, they recognised how events had created situations in which people could lose everything: their livestock, their grazing grounds, their families and lives. Yet the same officials were inconstant in affording nomads recognition as refugees, specifically; movement, it was thought, was an intrinsic part of their being.

This paper seeks to bring these two contemporary orders of movement – nomadic migration and refugee flight – into the same framework of analysis, by exploring how Bedouin flight was managed and understood. It pays particular attention to the fine line that existed between being treated as 'raider', 'rebel' or 'refugee', and considers how Bedouin options were affected by the new international boundaries taking form across the region. While the literatures on post-Ottoman refugees and nomads have hitherto been largely separate, experts on the former have recognised the potential for making wider comparisons.[7] The camp at Ba'quba, for example, helped establish more

---

[5] Robert S. G. Fletcher, *British Imperialism and 'the Tribal Question': Desert Administration and Nomadic Societies in the Middle East, 1919–1936* (Oxford: Oxford University Press, 2015).

[6] Robson, *States of Separation*. See also: Abigail Green, 'The British Empire and the Jews: an Imperialism of Human Rights?', *Past and Present*, Vol. 199 (2008), pp. 175–205.

[7] There is a contrast here with literature on the pre-war Ottoman Empire, notably: Reşat Kasaba, *A Moveable Empire: Ottoman Nomads, Migrants and Refugees* (Seattle: University of Washington Press, 2009).

general principles in the settlement of displaced populations; its directors spoke of the refugees' distinct 'mode of life', a phrase that also featured prominently in British policymaking toward the Bedouin.[8] More generally, questioning 'the categories adopted at different periods by states and international organisations' has been identified as a key contribution historians can make to the field of refugee studies.[9] The new scholarship on refugees in the mandates has revealed just how restrictive international definitions of a 'refugee' could be; in that respect, the debates conducted by the local mandatory officials within this paper shadow wider international conversations on what constituted a refugee at this time.[10] And yet, as we shall see, application of the term also ran up against Bedouin customs of *dakhala*, or 'entering protection' – a highly sophisticated practice of conflict control and a set of expectations around the relationship of *dakhal* (protector) and *dakheel* (refuge seeker).[11] By examining how local frontier officials improvised, rationalised and disagreed over their own working definitions of a 'refugee', this paper serves to remind us of the interpenetration of imperialism and internationalism in the interwar Middle East.

To explore this, this paper considers three episodes of Bedouin flight that occurred during the long fallout of the First World War. The first concerns the flight from famine conditions of thousands of Bedouin across the Syrian Desert to Mesopotamia in the later stages of the war, and the tacit encouragement, by the British wartime administration, of such movements. The second episode concerns the heated dispute between British authorities and King Fayṣal I of Iraq over the fate of the so-called 'refugee tribes' and their role in the escalating conflict along the Iraq-Nejd frontier. The third episode is that

---

[8] Robson, *States of Separation*, pp. 41, 48; Fletcher, *Tribal Question*, pp. 56–58.

[9] Elie, 'Histories'.

[10] For an exploration of refugee experiences in the wake of the war in Europe, including shifting definitions of 'refugee' itself, see: Peter Gatrell and Liubov Zhvanko (eds), *Europe on the Move: Refugees in the Era of the Great War* (Manchester: Manchester University Press, 2017). For a global perspective, spanning the twentieth century, see: Panikos Panayi and Pippa Virdee (eds), *Refugees and the End of Empire: Imperial Collapse and Forced Migration in the Twentieth Century* (Basingstoke: Palgrave Macmillan, 2011).

[11] Sulayman N. Khalaf, 'Settlement of Violence in Bedouin Society', *Ethnology*, Vol. 29 (1990), pp. 225–42.

of those Ikhwān who sought to flee Ibn Saʿūd's jurisdiction to Kuwait and Iraq in the latter stages of the 'Ikhwān Rebellion'. Here, British ambivalence over how to treat these 'refugees' was particularly exposed, before the ultimate decision to eject them into the waiting arms of Saudi forces. Together, these episodes demonstrate the range of administrative responses to Bedouin migrations in the early decades of the twentieth century. In southern Iraq British imperialism brought local officials into a position whereby they might respond to the evidence of Bedouin flight before them. Colonial categories, priorities and assumptions, however – the lens through which the Bedouin were viewed – made it harder for officials to see nomadic groups as victims of disaster, dearth or oppression, deserving of protection or refuge.

## I. Refuge: The Euphrates, 1917–18

The First World War in the Middle East was fought alongside 'a humanitarian disaster of world-historical proportions'.[12] New histories of the Ottoman Empire at war afford an increasingly detailed picture of its human cost, which intensified as the authorities strained to mobilise resources in Mesopotamia and Palestine.[13] The toll taken by conscription, grain requisitioning and heavy taxation was compounded by drought, the desert locust and the entente's blockade of coastal supplies. In Greater Syria, Djemal Pasha initiated a brutal crackdown on sedition and dissent. As prices skyrocketed and public health declined, populations were left exposed to the ravages of epidemic disease. Estimates vary, but between 1914 and 1923 perhaps a quarter of the total population of the Ottoman Empire – as many as five million

---

[12] Keith David Watenpaugh, 'The League of Nations Rescue of Armenian Genocide Survivors and the Making of Modern Humanitarianism (1920–1927)', *American Historical Review*, Vol. 115 (2010), p. 1316.

[13] Leila Tarazi Fawaz, *A Land of Aching Hearts: the Middle East in the Great War* (Cambridge, MA: Harvard University Press, 2014); Linda Schatkowski Schilcher, 'The Famine of 1915–1918 in Greater Syria', in John P. Spagnolo (ed.), *Problems of the Modern Middle East in Historical Perspective* (Reading: Ithaca Press, 1993), pp. 229–58; Melanie S. Tanielian, *The Charity of War: Famine, Humanitarian Aid, and World War I in the Middle East* (Stanford: Stanford University Press, 2017). For vivid personal testimony of conditions in wartime Greater Syria, see: Salīm Tamārī, *Year of the Locust: A Soldier's Diary and the Erasure of Palestine's Ottoman Past* (Berkeley: University of California Press, 2011).

people – perished. In Greater Syria alone, during just the final three years of the war, approximately 600,000 people may have lost their lives.[14]

Much of this history has focused on the region's towns and agricultural hinterlands. The relief work conducted by the American Colony in Jerusalem, for example, is well known; and new international aid campaigns, such as that coordinated by the American organisation Near East Relief, worked for the benefit of dispossessed Armenians and Assyrians in particular. But the war also caused immense damage to the pastoralist economy, setting thousands of Bedouin in motion across the Syrian Desert. In 1913, for example, Egypt had imported some 33,000 camels from across north Arabia. This important trade all but ceased during the Sinai and Palestine campaigns. The Ottoman Army may have commandeered as many as 85,000 camels from southern Palestine alone in 1915–16, dealing immense damage to the wealth and livelihoods of pastoral nomads.

The plight of nomads was incidental to the work of the international humanitarian organisations that new histories of wartime refugee regimes have uncovered, but other sources are available. Britain's Arab Bureau, for example, may have been established to gather intelligence on 'tribal politics' and to identify potential sheikhs with whom to collaborate; read critically, however, the pages of its *Arab Bulletin* provide useful evidence of how wartime desperation and dearth impacted Bedouin groups. In December 1916, for example, the *Bulletin* relayed word from an informant in Syria on the extent of requisitions and the shortage of supplies. The lack of animals for transport was felt particularly keenly, and 'Southern Syria has been specially hit', so that beyond the supplies held at military depots such as Kerak and Hebron 'there are practically none to be had'.[15] That same month, the *Bulletin* had learned

> from various sources . . . that the Syrian Desert is in an exceptionally anarchic and unsafe state, the traditional conventions, which allow of passage through the tribes under the guarantee of *rafiqs*, being hardly valid anywhere. There has been no such state of things within Bedouin memory.[16]

[14] Watenpaugh, 'League of Nations'; Robson, *States of Separation*, p. 35.
[15] *Arab Bulletin* [*AB*] 33 (4 December 1916).
[16] *AB* 35 (20 December 1916).

As Tariq Tell has shown, insecurity and food scarcity – particularly a lack of grain – played a critical role in bringing the Hejazi tribes within the orbit of the Hashemite cause (and their British backers): 'it was the threat of famine . . . that allowed the sharif to channel local solidarities and rally the bedouin'.[17] Over the course of 1916–17, as Anglo-Indian forces advanced up the Tigris and Euphrates and consolidated their hold over key market towns, a similar dynamic began to develop on the eastern edge of the Syrian Desert. In 1917, for example, Ottoman seizures of grain in the Hauran sent large numbers of Ruwala, one of the most powerful tribes of the Syrian Desert, across to Mesopotamia in a frantic search for supplies. The Sbaʿa and Fadʿān also began to move south and east towards British-controlled Mesopotamia at this time, on account of both the scarcity of provisions and to escape punishment at the hands of Turkish officials angry at the perceived defection of other Bedouin groups. By the time they reached the Euphrates late in the winter of 1917, they 'arrived starving'. The evidence is fragmentary, but points to a great many more Bedouin groups making similar calculations in the latter years of the war. British officials estimated that by the winter of 1917–18 so many had crossed the Syrian Desert west to east that they were feeding up to 100,000 Bedouin.[18]

In offering these groups access to Euphrates markets under the authority of the military administration, and by issuing grants of grain and other food supplies, the British recognised that they were supporting Bedouin movements that did not fit within the 'usual' patterns of pastoral nomadism. Denying such access, on the other hand, was explicitly discussed as a means of applying pressure to more recalcitrant tribes.[19] British officials in Mesopotamia and the Persian Gulf were acutely aware that their commercial blockade had drastically restricted grain supplies to the entire region: an 'irksome' business, wrote one official, but necessary, if it worked to drive desperate populations to abandon

---

[17] Tariq Tell, 'Guns, Gold and Grain: War and Food Supply in the Making of Transjordan', in Steven Heydemann (ed.), *War, Institutions and Social Change in the Middle East* (Berkeley: University of California Press, 2000), pp. 43–44.

[18] India Office Records (British Library [IOR]): L/PS/10/618, anon. [probably Gerard Leachman], 'Anizah on the Iraq Frontier', n.d; Arnold Talbot Wilson, *Mesopotamia, 1917–1920: a Clash of Loyalties* (London: Oxford University Press, 1931), p. 79.

[19] *AB* 5, 'Mesopotamia' (18 June 1916), p. 40.

Ottoman territory for their own.[20] British reports spoke of openly finding the right time 'for bringing in the Arabs of the Syrian Desert'. With famine in Greater Syria and British control of Mesopotamian markets, they reasoned, 'we shall acquire a strong pull on them and their chiefs'.

That control would be exercised through a kind of outsourcing, in which particular sheikhs, selected for their amenability towards the occupying power, were made gatekeepers of relief, through whom the Bedouin received permits to draw supplies from markets under British control. This could drastically boost a sheikh's authority, distorting power relations in the desert for decades. The example of Fahd Ibn Hadhdhāl, sheikh of the 'Amārāt, is illustrative. In 1916 the British thought the 'Amārāt 'rather out of hand and . . . given to brigandage', and doubted Ibn Hadhdhāl would 'come in with us till our frontier on both Euphrates and Tigris is far advanced enough to the northward to control the Amarat markets'.[21] That happened in May 1917, and by the autumn groups of Fad'an and Sba'a were 'drawing away from the Turks in the north and rallying towards Ibn Hadhdhāl'.[22] Before the war, Ibn Hadhdhāl's influence over even parts of his own tribe was open to contestation. By its end he had been granted a near monopoly over the carrying trade between Kuwait and Iraq, seizing contraband, dispatching agents and welcoming Bedouin groups from even further afield.[23] Even the Ruwala, who had long exercised considerable autonomy of the 'Amārāt (and who were 'loath to be beholden [to Ibn Hadhdhāl] in any way') had to set aside their differences with him in order to access Mespotamian markets.[24]

A revealing example of how the British used the grant of supplies to favour and reward particular Bedouin sheikhs came in October 1917. At a time of grain shortages in Najaf, Fahd Ibn Dugheim of the 'Amārāt (Ibn Hadhdhāl's nephew) withdrew a considerable quantity of grain from the town bazaar to support the tribe. The next day, Fahd Ibn Hadhdhāl himself sent in a caravan of 100 camels to withdraw yet more grain, and 'on passes signed by himself'.

[20] Wilson, *Mesopotamia*, p. 79.
[21] *AB* 32, David George Hogarth, 'Syria: the Anazah Tribes and Chiefs' (26 November 1916), p. 491.
[22] *AB* 65 (8 Oct. 1917), 398.
[23] *AB* 70, 'Notes: Koweit Supplies' (21 November 1917), p. 468.
[24] *AB* 65, 'Notes: News of Anazeh Tribes' (8 October 1917), pp. 407–8.

This pushed the townsmen to rise in violent protest against the ʿAmārāt. When their camp was surrounded, shots were fired, and some of their camels were stolen, the British sent a Political Officer to supervise Najaf and the Shāmiyya district 'in view of the great importance of developing the food supplies of the Euphrates and of checking Turkish propaganda'. His first task, however, was to arrange compensation for the ʿAmārāt.[25]

Even after the war, Ibn Hadhdhāl clung to this system of drawing official rations as a way of staying ahead of his rivals in a revived competition for opportunities, resources and patronage.[26] In the process, the British won for themselves a firm friend in the desert; Ibn Hadhdhāl, some were soon claiming, was their 'natural ally', and would feature again in British attempts to manage refugee groups on Iraq's southern frontier.

### II. Relocation: The Shāmiyya, 1925

If this first episode of Bedouin displacement met with a kind of outsourcing, the second led to a debate over the state's use of so-called 'refugee tribes' as a political and even military asset.

In 1920 Abdul Aziz Ibn Saʿūd stuck a major blow against his major rival in northern Arabia, the Al Rashīd, when his forces defeated those of Abdullah ibn Mitʾab, the ruling Amir of the Jabal Shammar. The subsequent siege and fall of Ḥāʾil, and with it the Rashīdi state, had profound consequences for Bedouin throughout north Arabia. As Saudi power was projected into the Syrian Desert for the first time in a century, groups of Shammar fled north across the frontier of the new British mandate for Iraq. Some of these 'Shammar refugees', as they were known, crossed the Euphrates to enter the Jazīra and join the Shammar Jarba living there. Others sought to remain south of the Euphrates, on grazing grounds frequented by the ʿAmārāt and Ibn Hadhdhāl, until they too were ordered across the river and into the Hillah *liwāʾ*. In the years that followed other 'refugee tribes' entered Iraq from Nejd, including groups of Mutayr, ʿAtaibah and Harb. In most cases, these groups were soon found to be raiding back into Nejd across the

[25] *AB* 85 (15 April 1918), pp. 115–19.

[26] Robert S. G. Fletcher, 'The ʿAmārāt, their Shaykh, and the Colonial State: Patronage and Politics in a Partitioned Middle East', *Journal of the Economic and Social History of the Orient*, Vol. 58 (2015), pp. 163–99.

border; and, in most cases, the idea of their relocation became a key part of the British response.

By the mid-1920s the relocation of Bedouin 'refugees' had emerged as a particular technique of British mandatory governance and as something of a practised regime of mobility in itself. It can be viewed alongside the many agricultural resettlement schemes launched in the aftermath of the First World War.[27] But it also acquired a rationale of its own, as conveyed in this report to the League of Nations on the move of the refugee Shammar into the Jazriah:

> We have . . . witnessed during the past year one of those episodes which from time immemorial have populated Iraq – the hungry desert has once more overflowed into the settled lands, to raid, to pilfer, and, finally, through a long and somewhat painful, if ultimately beneficial process of absorption, to settle down to husbandry.[28]

This was an attractive credo, but only a very partial view of the forces at work within these relocations – and of their potential for us as historians. Let us consider one of these in more depth: the move, in the spring and summer of 1925, of around sixty tents (the British estimated some five hundred people) from the southern frontier, across the Euphrates, north towards the Jazīra. In December 1924 and January 1925 three heavy Ikhwān raids struck Iraq's southern frontier. The British viewed these as belonging to a different order of magnitude – more violent, and out of line with the expected conventions of raiding. Judging them a response to provocative raids into Nejd by Iraq's refugee tribes in the autumn of 1923 and the summer of 1924, they now sought to remove these groups to de-escalate the conflict.

First, it is worth noting that these relocations were seldom animated by a spirit of sympathy for the 'refugee tribes' themselves, even when they were on the receiving end of raids from Nejd. While some British officers supervising the 1925 relocation noted the poor condition of the Ikhwān refugees,

---

[27] On these in the interwar Middle East, see: White, 'Refugees', pp. 156–58.

[28] *Report by His Britannic Majesty's Government to the Council of the League of Nations on the Administration of 'Iraq, October 1920 to March 1922* (London: His Majesty's Stationery Office, 1922), p. 122.

they were just as likely to criticise them for having instigated raids in the first place and in defiance of government instructions.[29] One officer could scarce contain his contempt for these 'jackals' and 'traitors', whose actions had brought Nejdi reprisals upon more innocent Iraqi tribes; 'steps must be instantly taken to evict these pests'. There was a prevailing assumption here that 'true' or 'pure' Bedouin like these 'refugee tribes' – and as opposed to 'shepherd tribes' – ought to have been more capable of defending themselves. As 'entirely camel owners . . . capable of covering vast distances across the desert' they were more mobile, better armed and therefore less deserving of government protection or of recognition as victims.[30] This ideal-typical conceptualisation of the Bedouin downplayed their reliance on other groups and relationships, even as it exaggerated their freedom of mobility – but informed British thinking nonetheless.

Indeed, the British coined a new category of 'refugee raiders' specifically to refer to these groups. This was a revealing appellation, for it was the implications for British frontier policy of this otherwise 'motley collection of Akhwan tribesmen' that informed the creation of a collective policy towards them. Relocation contained within it the idea of surveilling, concentrating, and delivering these tribesmen *as refugees*, 'in one large party' if possible, rather than as separate family or tribal groups. This remained British policy despite the frank admission of the officer leading their relocation that, 'through the nature of their existence during the last three years, there is little cohesion amongst them or unity under their leaders', with each tent 'liable to act independently when an opportunity affords'.[31] Indeed, the innumerable attempts by smaller parties to slip away during the course of the relocation operations – and even after its apparent completion – reveal how Bedouin, just like other, better known groups in the region, could oppose interwar British attempts to solidify their status as refugees.[32]

---

[29] The National Archives (UK) [TNA]: AIR 23/82, S.S.O. Ramadi (H. Hindle James), No. HJ/10/5, 'Report for fortnight ending 13/8/25'.

[30] TNA: AIR 23/79, John Glubb, 'Report on the Defensive Operations Against the Akhwan: Winter 1924–25', 16 April 1925. Glubb acknowledged the prevalence of these assumptions, even as he sought to push against them.

[31] AIR 23/82: Guy Moore to Air Staff Intelligence, 'Akhwan Refugees', 10 July 1925.

[32] See: Robson, *States of Separation*, p. 48.

There were numerous other ethnically based population transfer schemes in the interwar Middle East, of course, and under the auspices of the League of Nations, Britain and France often gathered refugees in contested border areas expressly for the purpose of solidifying colonial control there.[33] The relocation of the 'refugee raiders', in contrast, was more about evacuating a space to better assert the supremacy of British authority within it: *ubi solitudinem faciunt, pacem appellant.* Here the British were seeking to remove various groups whose loyalties might all too easily lie elsewhere. Above all, it was these groups' developing relationship with King Fayṣal I of Iraq that alarmed British authorities. While they feared the diplomatic and security repercussions of refugee tribes launching raids into Nejd, the refugees' all too evident hostility to Saudi expansion found a welcome audience at the Palace. In British eyes, the 'refugee tribes' had not merely become 'pawns in the power politics' between the Hashemite and Saudi families; the issue was one of power and patronage as much as it was of dynastic rivalry. British concerns to monopolise political authority along Iraq's sensitive southern frontier grew steadily across the 1920s. As officials' familiarity with desert politics grew, they were less prepared to suffer competing nodes of authority – the Palace and its active patronage networks, above all.

Keen to maintain desert relationships independent of British control, Fayṣal had come to look on the Shammar as his proxy force on the frontier, the best instrument available for checking Saudi power. In 1923 he permitted Shammar groups under ʿAjīl al-Yāwir to raise a desert force to guard the Euphrates. The following year, he invited al-Yāwir to patrol the southern desert and to repel any attacks by Ikhwān from across the border.[34] Before long, he was giving his tacit approval to illicit raids into Saudi territory by refugee Shammar and Ikhwān alike. The British suspected the Palace of supplying some refugee groups with camels, arms and funds for the purpose,

[33] Ibid., pp. 4–5.

[34] TNA: FO 371/1299: 'Short History of 'Iraq-Nejd Relations'; Middle East Centre Archives (Oxford) [MECA]: Glubb papers, Box 206, File 10, John Glubb, 'Notes on Scheme for Tribal Irregulars – Dulaim Division' [nd 1923]; TNA: AIR 23/291, A.T.O. Lees to Air Staff Intelligence, 20 February 1925. For more on Faysal's close relationship with ʿAjīl al-Yāwir, see: John Frederick Williamson, 'A Political History of the Shammar Jarba Tribe of Al-Jazirah: 1800–1958' (PhD thesis, Indiana University, 1975), p. 158*ff.*

too.[35] When the Colonial Secretary later approved the creation of a chain of permanent desert forts along this frontier, it was not merely for the purposes of defending Iraq but also, revealingly, 'to neutralize any possible tendency on the part of King Fayṣal to connive at such raiding by Iraq tribes as an instrument of his personal hostility towards Ibn Saud'.[36]

Indeed, throughout the move, Fayṣal continued to meet with leading 'refugee raiders' and to issue his own instructions about their relocation. The British suspected this would create delay, or confusion; rumours spread among the 'refugee raiders' that the king was cancelling the whole operation.[37] In that sense, the relocation of the 'refugee raiders' can be read as evidence of the weaknesses of Britain's position in Iraq; the anxieties arising from the pluralism of political authority that characterised the mandatory system of government; and the difficulties its officers faced in rendering frontier places and populations 'legible'.

The move began in earnest in the spring of 1925. Special Service Officer (SSO) Guy Moore, the officer responsible for the key early stages, spent weeks corralling the refugee tribes at Abu Ghar, only for the civil authorities at Nāṣiriyya to abruptly change the first rallying point: a 'needless concession', he complained, that would only serve to give some groups an opportunity to slip away. This set the tone for a laborious operation. Between May and October 1925 officers like Moore worked with Iraqi police detachments to reconnoitre the grazing and water resources ahead of the refugees, negotiate their passage through other Bedouin territories, keep the refugee tribes 'in a more compact body' and resist endless refugee requests for deviation or delay ('[this] only affords them a succession of loop-holes for escaping definite orders').[38] Another SSO understood the refugees' reluctance to set out for

---

[35] For example: AIR 23/82, J.M. Kenny-Leveck to Air Staff Intelligence, No. 558/15, 15 July 1925.

[36] TNA: CAB 16/88, Leopold Amery, No. CP 187(28), 'Memorandum by the Secretary of State for the Colonies on the Akhwan Situation', 15 June 1928.

[37] TNA: AIR 23/80, Special Service Officer, Air Headquarters Iraq to Air Staff Intelligence, No. D/1(b), 18 May 1925; Special Service Officer, Shaibah to Air Headquarters, Baghdad, No. A/479, 25 May 1925; Guy Moore to Air Staff Intelligence, No. M/5, 28 May 1925.

[38] AIR 23/80, Guy Moore to Air Staff Intelligence, No. M/4, 'Shamiyah Desert', 10 May 1925; and Guy Moore to Administrative Inspector, Nasiriyah, No. I/651, 7 May 1925.

the Jazīra, for in the north they would be among Shammar sections known to be hostile to them, while the grazing in the south was poor.[39] It took the threat of air action – aircraft flew over the camps at Jalibah – to finally get the groups to set out.[40] Thereafter, progress remained slower than expected, owing to the scarcity of grazing, fears of hostile parties lying in wait, the thinness of civil administration en route, numerous refugee attempts to disperse, contradictory orders from 'Palace agents', and the exhaustion of refugees and their camels alike. At least one whole section succeeded in escaping into Nejdi territory. Others made for Syria and thence to the Hejaz (probably with Fayṣal's assistance), 'to become a thorn in the side of the Akhwan on the other frontier'.[41] It was a diminished group that finally camped near Fallujah in August, where, having secured permission to remain under the supervision of Fahd Ibn Hadhdhāl rather than continue on to the Jazīra, the operation came to an end.

A number of points of wider interest arise from this episode. The first is the striking degree of agency these refugee groups retained even during what was, ostensibly, their forced relocation. Time and again, their leaders succeeded in extracting concessions from Iraqi and British authorities over the route to be followed and the schedule of the march.[42] Within a few months of the end of the operation many of the refugees had successfully re-crossed the Nejd frontier.[43] More broadly, the entire relocation was driven by the actions

---

[39] AIR 23/82, H. Hindle James, 'Report on Akhwan Refugees', No. HJ/10/25.

[40] AIR 23/80, Guy Moore to Aviation Baghdad, No. I/716, 25 May 1925.

[41] AIR 23/82, Guy Moore to Air Staff Intelligence, 10 July 1925; AIR 23/82, SSO Baghdad to Air Staff Intelligence, 21 July 1925.

[42] The change of the initial rally point to Jaliba, for example, owed much to the leaders preference for this site as being 'more accessible to Baghdad for messengers, etc.', where they might continue to plead their case with Fayṣal: AIR 23/80, Guy Moore to Air Staff Intelligence, No. M/4, 'Shamiyah Desert', 10 May 1925.

[43] AIR 23/82, H. Hindle James, No. HJ/10/11, 22 October 1925. This was a theme of a number of such Bedouin relocation operations in the 1920s: plans to 'concentrate' the refugee Shammar in the northern Jazīra, for example, ran against the reality that 'their mobility is so great, and their knowledge of the desert so intimate and extensive that even this remote banishment does not in itself prevent them raiding as far south as Kuwait . . .': *Report by His Britannic Majesty's Government to the Council of the League of Nations on the Administration of 'Iraq, for the Year 1926* (London: His Majesty's Stationery Office, 1926), pp. 32–33.

of the 'refugee raiders' themselves, and by British concerns to frustrate their collusion with Fayṣal and the Iraqi government.

Secondly, the 1925 relocation of the 'refugee raiders' worked to tighten Britain's client relationships with key Bedouin figures – most notably Fahd Ibn Hadhdhāl. Wary of attack by more hostile Bedouin groups, the refugees only consented to advance toward the Jazīra if they could proceed through Ibn Hadhdhāl's territory, and it was his agent at Razaza who arranged to escort the refugees to watering places and pastures at a critical stage of the journey. Ibn Hadhdhāl himself became an important point of contact for British officials keen to learn of the movements of other Bedouin groups, potential rivalries or threats, and current grazing and water conditions along the route.[44] Initially reluctant to take final responsibility for the refugees, Ibn Hadhdhāl's change of heart spared the British the potential embarrassment of resorting to force to drive them on to the Jazīra against their will – and boosted his own authority, in the process.[45] Ultimately, the British reasoned that either Ibn Hadhdhāl could be trusted to prevent the refugees from raiding or would intercede with Ibn Saʿūd to arrange their return to Nejd (their threat to frontier security neutralised, either way).[46]

Finally, managing this refugee relocation made a significant contribution to British knowledge of and confidence in Iraq's southern desert. The challenges of arranging this relocation across multiple administrative districts fed calls for a more unitary approach to the administration of Iraq's southern desert. Pilots gained valuable experience in navigating the southern desert by 'compartments', SSOs produced new maps of its grazing grounds and tribal territories, and the Iraqi police expanded their range of operations (Fig.10.1).[47] British compassion for these Bedouin refugees also grew as the weeks wore on. 'The

---

[44] AIR 23/80, Kinahan Cornwallis, Memorandum No. C/1076/117/55, 4 May 1925; and misc. enclosures in Adviser to the Ministry of the Interior to High Commissioner, Baghdad, 24 May 1925.

[45] TNA: AIR 23/81, Ibn Hadhdhāl to Administrative Inspector, Ramadi, enclosed in Cornwallis to Counsellor to the High Commissioner, 28 May 1925; AIR 23/82, S.S.O. Ramadi (H. Hindle James), No. HJ/10/5, 'Report for fortnight ending 13/8/25'.

[46] AIR 23/82, Adviser to the Ministry of the Interior to Secretary to the High Commissioner, Baghdad, No. 12390, 30 September 1925.

[47] Glubb, 'Defensive Operations against the Akhwan'; AIR 23/80, John Glubb, 'Final Report on Defensive Operations against the Akhwan, Winter 1925–26'.

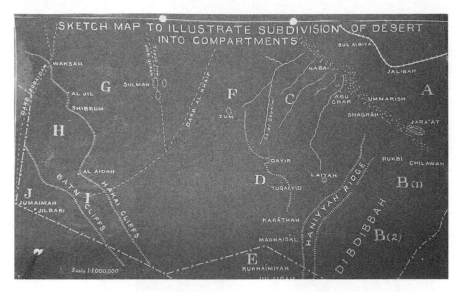

Figure 10.1 Sketch map to illustrate subdivision of the desert into compartments.

Credit: TNA: AIR 23/80, 'Final Report on Defensive Measures against the Akhwan, 1925–26'.

great thing ... is for us to not let them down over their route,' Guy Moore wrote once the move was underway: 'the country has changed a good deal in the last month and I want to be certain of facts regarding water and grazing all along.'[48] At times, the mandate state was virtually acting as a pastoralist itself, taking advice on the quality and extent of grazing resources and learning – through trial and error – when to rest herds and when to move on.[49] While it would not routinely become involved in such fine details of herd management again, a loose surveillance and occasional control of seasonal migrations – as of that of the Shammar out of the Jazīra in 1928 – became part of the repertoires of mobility of the British mandate state.

## III. Rejection: The Iraq–Kuwait Border, 1929–30

If our second episode had occurred as part of the dramatic rise of Saudi power, the third came about amidst the sudden threat of its collapse. In 1927, Ibn

---

[48] AIR 23/81, Guy Moore, unnumbered report of 7 June 1925.

[49] For one example among many: AIR 23/81, Administrative Inspector Diwaniyah to Ministry of the Interior, No. 507, 12 June 1925.

Figure 10.2 Fayṣal al-Dawīsh in 1929, from a sketch by Squadron Leader Harry Stewart (RAF). Stewart's career symbolised both the power and vulnerability of British air control in Iraq: he died when his Wapiti bomber aircraft crashed at Shaiba, where 'on the desert side there is not a single landmark by which an incoming pilot can gauge his progress' (*Baghdad Times*, 6 January 1931).

Credit: From J. B. Glubb, *War in the Desert* (London: Hodder and Stoughton, 1960).

Saʿūd's relationship with the Ikhwān – those tribes who had been so crucial to his earlier expansion – began to unravel. Seeking accommodation with the British and Hashemite territories to the north, Ibn Saʿūd now sought to rein in the Ikhwān by restricting their raiding privileges. The result was a violent revolt, for the next two years, along the frontiers of Saudi authority, led by the Harb, ʿAtaibah and Ajman tribes, but above all by Fayṣal al-Dawīsh of the Mutayr (Fig. 10.2).

At first, the British viewed this latest manifestation of the ʿAkhwan menace' as a frontier security issue and struggled to establish how far these Ikhwān raids were independent of Ibn Saʿūd's control.[50] In late March 1929,

---

[50] For a useful summary of these raids from the perspective of the India Office, see: IOR: L/PS/10/1238, P4224/28, 'Supplementary Memorandum on Koweit, 1908–1928', n.d.

however, Fayṣal al-Dawīsh was wounded and a Mutayr and 'Ataibah force defeated by Saudi forces in the battle of Sibilla. While al-Dawīsh recovered and the Ikhwān rallied to contest Saudi power, the question of what to do about the groups fleeing Ibn Saʿūd's jurisdiction – and what kind of status to afford them – increasingly occupied British officials.[51] A further defeat at Riqai that December proved decisive, and thousands now sought protection in mandatory Iraq and British-aligned Kuwait, fearful of Saudi retribution. J. G. Laithwaite of the India Office summarised the fraught situation:

> Ibn Saud has moved north and has his headquarters about 70 or 80 miles south-east of the Iraq-Koweit frontier, and the same distance inland from the sea. The rebellious forces are to some extent hemmed in, though the area which they occupy is considerable. They have their backs to the Iraq-Koweit frontier, and from time to time cross that frontier, either on raids or in search of water and supplies.[52]

In the winter of 1929–30 British officials found themselves weighing urgent Ikhwān appeals for protection against increasingly strident Saudi demands for the ejection of these 'rebels'. This was precisely the unenviable scenario that the Director of the Arab Bureau had warned his colleagues to guard against, back at the very creation of the mandates.[53] Their disagreements demonstrate just how contested the categories of 'raider', 'rebel' and 'refugee' remained a decade after the drawing-up of new international boundaries.

---

[51] In August 1929 the Kuwait Political Agent recorded his surprise at finding 'the whole rebel force with their camels, women, children and impediments settled comfortable round about Subaihiyeh and the adjacent wells' in Kuwait: IOR: R/15/2/1499, Harold Dickson, Fortnightly Report No. 16 of 1929 (16–31 August 1929).

[52] IOR: L/PS/10/1246, P.87/30, John Gilbert Laithwaite minute, 2 January 1930.

[53] 'No form of boundary settlement will, of course, bring unadulterated peace to Arabia; tribal raids will never go out of fashion, and the need for confining the activities of the Wahabis and Ikhwan will ever be present. We shall, however, need to be most guarded in our promises to assist rulers against acts of aggression on their frontiers; otherwise, every little tribal disturbance will result in a prompt demand for aeroplanes, tanks, and other more or less suitable forms of armed assistance': H. Garland, 'Territorial Disputes in Arabia', in *AB* 4, No. 113 (17 July 1919), p. 106.

Part of the difficulty stemmed from long-standing confusion over the character of the Ikhwān movement.[54] H. R. P. Dickson, the Political Agent in Kuwait, and who would now play a critical role in enforcing the ejection of Ikhwān 'refugees', had earlier argued that 'Ikhwanism does not appear to be the entirely bad movement it is made out to be'.[55] His neighbour in Iraq's Southern Desert, John Glubb, profoundly disagreed, and across the mid-1920s drew his colleagues' attention to 'the particular terrors' of the Ikhwān's brutal raids.[56] If the character of the movement was hard to discern, then judgements about Fayṣal al-Dawīsh were equally contradictory. Officers along the Iraq's southern frontier noted his running grievances against Ibn Saʿūd, even as they continued to doubt the extent of his break with him.[57] Rumours circulated of his removal as 'paramount' sheikh of the Mutayr, only to be swiftly contradicted.[58] Yet most agreed that Fayṣal al-Dawīsh was a leader of 'great intelligence', with 'no mean control over his people', and who maintained sophisticated and long-distance networks of communication and correspondence. An 'astute' and 'magnanimous' figure of consequence – even a 'politician' – his actions could not easily be dismissed as mere raiding.[59]

Throughout 1929 British officers freely admitted their confusion over what was happening in northern Arabia and the difficulties of 'sift[ing] the truth from the falsehood'.[60] At a local level, this created space for individual officers to interpret and narrate Ikhwān movement in a variety of ways. It was

[54] The question was a subject of a paper delivered to the Central Asian Society in 1930: Anon. ('Phoenix'), 'A Brief History of the Wahabi Movement', *Journal of the Royal Central Asian Society*, Vol. 17 (1930), pp. 401–16. Back in 1919 St. John Philby had described them as 'Badawin with bees in their bonnets': *AB* 4, No. 108 (11 January 1919), p. 4.

[55] *AB: Notes on the Middle East* 4 (24 May 1920), pp. 103–12.

[56] Glubb, 'Defensive Operations Against the Akhwan'.

[57] For example: R/15/2/1499, J. C. More, Fortnightly Report No. 23 of 1926 (16–30 August 1929).

[58] R/15/2/1499, J. C. More, Fortnightly Reports No. 22 of 1928 (1–15 November 1928) and No. 23 (16–30 November 1928).

[59] IOR: R/15/5/34, Political Agent, Kuwait to Political Resident in the Persian Gulf, Confidential, 25 November 1929; R/15/2/1499, Harold Dickson, Fortnightly Report No. 12 of 1929 (16–30 June 1929), and No. 18 of 1929 (16–30 September 1929).

[60] For one example among many: R/15/2/1499, J. C. More, Fortnightly Report No. 2 of 1929 (16–31 January 1929).

in February 1929 that local officers began reporting that Ibn Saʿūd may have 'temporarily lost control' over groups of Ajman and Mutayr.[61] Few routinely referred to these groups as 'rebels' before May 1929. While some believed Fayṣal al-Dawīsh's final 'defection' only came in June, others would maintain he had been 'virtually in revolt' for some eighteen months by that point.[62] Thereafter, the British continued to refer to the Ikhwān as variously 'disobedient', 'insurgent', 'recalcitrant' or merely in 'disagreement' with Ibn Saʿūd, and criticism of their actions could be softened by reference to the 'grave and far-reaching discontent against the King'.

Indeed, uncertainty over the likely outcome of this conflict changed officers' views of the Ikhwān movement and helped to temper their criticism. John Glubb considered it as part of the inherent turbulence of Bedouin life – unrest 'in the true Arabian tradition' – but others characterised it as a 'civil war'.[63] With Ibn Saʿūd 'daily losing adherents' in the summer of 1929, Dickson was forced to acknowledge al-Dawīsh's statesmanlike qualities. Faced with such a man, even the High Commissioner in Baghdad thought Ibn Saʿūd's ultimate victory 'uncertain'.[64] Even as the tables turned against them, the manner in which Ikhwān leaders presented themselves continued to shape British understandings of them. In August 1929, for example, it was reported that Ali al-Shuwaribet had taken al-Dawīsh's signet ring to Baghdad to argue, in a document intended for the High Commissioner, that 'just as His Majesty's Government did not take sides in the recent rebellion in Afghanistan', so too Britain ought to observe strict neutrality in northern Arabia. Dickson suspected that this proposed document was in fact intended to present the Ikhwān's case, as refugees, before the League of Nations, but

---

[61] IOR: L/PS/10/1238, Acting High Commissioner of Iraq to Secretary of State for the Colonies, No. 77, 21 February 1929.

[62] R/15/2/1499, Harold Dickson, Fortnightly Report No. 12 of 1929 (16–30 June 1929); L/PS/10/1238, John Glubb to Advisor to the Ministry of the Interior, 'Relations with Kuwait', 12 March 1929.

[63] John Glubb, *War In the Desert* (London: Hodder and Stoughton, 1960), 213; R/15/5/34, C. C. J. Barrett to H. R. P. Dickson, private, 1 November 1929.

[64] R/15/2/1499, Harold Dickson, Fortnightly Report No. 15 of 1929 (1–15 August 1929), and No. 18 of 1929 (16–30 September 1929); R/15/5/34, Hubert Young to Lord Passfield, 21 October 1929.

parallels with the Afghan Civil War (1928–29) were indeed discussed in British circles.[65] Later, when these hopes were dashed, al-Dawīsh proved adept at presenting his cause to maximise its appeal to British audiences. He was 'a man fighting for his liberty', he relayed through Kuwaiti merchant Hillal al-Mutayri, and 'His Majesty's Government were pictured to him as the Government who always came to the help of the oppressed . . .'[66]

For these reasons, there was little consensus on how the Ikhwān were to be treated when their final defeat at the battle of Riqai put them to flight. Pushed north and east to the frontiers of Iraq and Kuwait, Fayṣal al-Dawīsh appealed to Britain's Political Agent at Kuwait for fresh supplies and permission to stay, referring to their arrival as 'the migration of a nation', and stressing that 9,000 women and children were among those urgently seeking shelter and relief. Ibn Saʿūd, on the other hand, demanded Britain deny them both entry and supplies and hand over any groups that succeeded in crossing the border. This was far from the first time Ibn Saʿūd had presented such demands, and British officials had found grounds to resist them before.[67] Most recently, in the spring of 1928, the Jedda Conference had foundered on Ibn Saʿūd's insistence that political offenders be included in any extradition agreement, so that by the time that the Ikhwān rebellion entered its endgame a number of long-standing British and Iraqi reservations had emerged – including that Nejd 'possessed no regularly constituted courts' to meet Iraq's own standards of justice and probity, and that 'to eject from [Iraq's] desert pastures large hordes of nomads' would be 'abhorrent to Arab tradition'.[68] The British framed this impasse in terms of a 'conflict between International and Desert Law', and pointed to the hypocrisy of both parties:

> Ibn Saud's relation to his subjects was in his eyes that of the paramount chief to his tribesmen . . . It was indifferent to him whether they wandered into

[65] R/15/2/1499, Harold Dickson, Fortnightly Report No. 15 of 1929 (1–15 August 1929); L/PS/10/1246, P.87/30, Laithwaite minute, 2 January 1930.

[66] R/15/2/1499, Harold Dickson, Fortnightly Report No. 21 of 1929 (1–15 November 1929).

[67] Saudi extradition requests had contributed to the collapse of the Uqair Conference in 1922 and the Kuwait Conference of 1923–24.

[68] CAB 16/88: Gilbert Clayton, 'Mission to the King of the Hejaz and Nejd (1928)', 18 June 1928; Glubb, *War*, p. 213.

another State . . . But when he asked for the extradition of the Shammar, he was changing his ground and appealing to International Law as against desert usage. The Iraq Government, on the other hand, claimed in the desert a territorial frontier which by the rules of International Law would suffer no infringement . . . But when the delinquencies of the refugee Shammar were broached, the Iraq Government fell back on the code sacred to the desert which refuses to deliver up the fugitive within its tents.[69]

The upshot was that a new refugee crisis was beginning with British officials unclear of the extent of their legal responsibilities. As an India Office hand explained, 'no undertaking has been given to arrest and hand over refugees', and nor could doing so be easily defended 'from the standpoint of international law'. Again drawing on British experience on the northwest frontiers of India, the official explained that ordinarily the British would either intern the Ikhwān or 'take security' from them: a guarantee that they refrain from raiding as long as they remained in British territory. Yet the complexity of Britain's informal empire in the Middle East 'and the specially difficult tribal situation on the frontier' made this situation 'so anomalous as not to be judged by ordinary international standards'.[70] In the absence of certainty, interdepartmental tensions were given full rein (the Foreign and India Offices were more inclined to appease Ibn Saʿūd than officials in Baghdad), and the debate became as much about moral as legal responsibility.

With hindsight, we can see that the British were weighing this decision in the context of having lately intervened in different ways on behalf of other nomadic groups. This was the experience of Britain's interwar 'desert corridor' in microcosm: imperial influence was predicated upon facilitating the movements of some, while militating against the movements of others.[71] The Beni Malik, for example, had recently been afforded refuge in Kuwait after these Iraqi shepherds were raided by the Mutayr before the walls of Kuwait town. The scale of their losses, and British perceptions of them as straightforward 'innocents' – a shepherd tribe rather than a 'pure',

---

[69] *Report by His Britannic Majesty's Government on the Administration under Mandate of 'Iraq for the period April 1923–December 1924* (London: His Majesty's Stationery Office, 1927).

[70] L/PS/10/1246, P.87/30, India Office minute, 3 January 1930.

[71] Fletcher, *British Imperialism*.

martial, camel-breeding one – eased their classification as 'refugees', and arrangements were made both for their relief and for an armed escort on to grazing grounds in northern Kuwait.[72] The Awazim, too, presented a subsidiary problem within the wider displacement attending the final stages of the revolt. They had fought for Ibn Saʿūd at Inqair and, in defeat, surrendered to al-Dawīsh. Despite their active role in the wider conflict, London assented to the Sheikh of Kuwait 'affording shelter' to the 'remnants' of the tribe.[73] There were a variety of factors working to influence this decision: their plausible claim to have 'originally' hailed from Kuwait; their 'low rank in the tribal hierarchy' (the British supposed Ibn Saʿūd would not feel their loss); the unusually heavy casualties they had suffered; the fact that, despite surrendering to the Ikhwān, they could not be regarded as active insurgents either; that refuge would 'neutralise' them from any further part in the conflict; and the revealing observation that they had been shown to fight well at Inqair and so 'might be capable of protecting Koweit' in future (particularly relevant if, when the British mandate for Iraq came to an end, the imperial garrison in that country were significantly reduced).[74]

For his part, Sheikh Ahmad al-Sabah of Kuwait was by no means unsympathetic to the Ikhwān's predicament. The rich grazing resources of Kuwait's hinterland had built long-standing connections with these tribes. Kuwait's merchants had provided them with supplies throughout the course of their rebellion; its ruler saw the advantages of welcoming well-armed tribesmen

---

[72] R/15/2/1499, J. C. More, Fortnightly Report No. 5 of 1929 (1–15 March, 1929); L/PS/10/1238, John Glubb to Advisor to the Ministry of the Interior, 'Relation with Kuwait', 12 March 1929.

[73] R/15/5/34, Secretary of State for the Colonies to Political Resident in the Persian Gulf, No. 340, 1 November 1929.

[74] R/15/5/34, Colonial Office to Under Secretary of State for India, 4 October 1929; Foreign Office to Bond, No. 113, 30 October 1929; IOR: L/PS/10/1244, George William Rendel to Bond, E6096/2322/91, 9 December 1929. Despite British hopes that Ibn Saʿūd would be grateful for ensuring the Awazim could not join the Ikhwān ranks, Saudi criticism came anyway: L/PS/10/1244, Bond to Foreign Office, No. 170 (24 November 1929). In the end, the Awazim were found to have been raiding while under the Sheikh of Kuwait's protection, and so this 'refugee remnant' were re-classified as 'rebels' once more: L/PS/10/1244, Political Resident in the Persian Gulf to Secretary of State for the Colonies, No. T/40, 11 December 1929, and No. 91, 24 December 1929.

as a buffer against his powerful Saudi neighbour.[75] Fayṣal al-Dawīsh worked hard to appeal to these sympathies; indeed, there is evidence to suggest he had learned from the experiences of some of the other groups featured in this paper. Ikhwān refugees, for example, often intermingled with Kuwaiti and Iraqi tribes near the frontier – no doubt mindful of how this had frustrated Saudi attempts at pursuit in the past.[76] In letters to the Sheikh of Kuwait and British authorities in Iraq, al-Dawīsh stressed his keenness to avoid an accidental clash with British forces, the modesty of his requests for supplies and to continue 'a Bedouin life' in the future – and the likely duplicity of Ibn Saʿūd.[77] Throughout his attempts to negotiate entry to Kuwait, Dickson was quietly impressed by the extent of al-Dawīsh's knowledge, authority and control, especially 'when one recollects that to the Bedouin the artificial boundary fixed by us and only visible on maps means nothing'.[78]

There were a number of British officials, too, who could not but express sympathy for the drastic reversal in fortunes of 'the aristocratic Mutair', once 'the crème de la crème of Bedouin'.[79] In January 1930 Harold Dickson reported on the 'very distressing situation' of a group of 'exhausted' and 'weak' women and children at Jahrah, left behind in the wake of al-Dawīsh's hasty retreat. Meanwhile, the countryside around Jahrah remained 'covered with panic-stricken persons out of control, and in terror of attack both from [British] aeroplanes and from Ibn Saud'.[80] In Iraq, John Glubb remembered the effect of the late Ikhwān attacks on shepherd tribes, but nonetheless found the sight of them now 'deeply moving'. 'As a man,' he confessed, 'I found something

---

[75] Robert S. G. Fletcher, '"Between the Devil of the Desert and the Deep Blue Sea": Re-orienting Kuwait, c. 1900–1940', *Journal of Historical Geography*, Vol. 50 (2015), pp. 61–62.

[76] For example: R/15/5/28, Ibn Saʿūd to Political Agent Kuwait, 6 October 1921.

[77] For example: R/15/5/34, Harold Dickson to Political Resident in the Persian Gulf, No. 644, 25 November 1929.

[78] R/15/5/34, Harold Dickson to Political Resident in the Persian Gulf, Confidential, 25 November 1929.

[79] R/15/2/1499, Harold Dickson, Fortnightly Report No. 21 of 1929 (1–15 November 1929).

[80] L/PS/10/1246, Political Resident in the Persian Gulf to Secretary of State for the Colonies, No. 8, 8 January 1930, and No. 11, 8 January 1930. Dickson, together with his wife, arranged for their relocation to become 'refugees at [the British Political] Agency' in Kuwait, and in such a way that the Sheikh be protected from the accusation of 'harbouring rebel women'.

painful and humiliating in seeing other human beings reduced to such a state of abject fear.' The thought of handing them over to Ibn Saʿūd 'to be butchered before our eyes' left him 'distressed'.[81]

Grave doubts also surfaced over the legitimacy of using force to turn back would-be refugees – especially given the 'several thousands of non-combatants all mixed-up with fighting men'.[82] Here, the Air Ministry in London took the lead in requesting the use of aircraft and armoured cars specifically 'for the purpose of excluding refugees', and secured permission in principle in May.[83] Faced with the reality of going through with it, however, British qualms re-emerged. By January 1930 officials acknowledged that the presence of women and children made forcibly ejecting the Ikhwān 'very difficult'; it even prompted admissions of 'the shortcomings of air power as a method of controlling a situation such as the present'.[84] Nonetheless, at London's insistence, the RAF began dropping 'warning bombs' on the Mutayr to drive them back towards the border, targeting 'isolated parties of camels' where possible. An urgent pause was called when the British recognised that their actions now risked the refugees being 'driven into the jaws of Ibn Saud, when H.M. Government will have to face stigma of responsibility for massacre of women and children which may result'.[85] Ultimately, however, bombing resumed as the only way to force the Ikhwān's unconditional surrender, and 'even though it might involve injury to a certain number of women and children'.[86] Difficult as this was, the India Office concurred: it did not anticipate a wider 'Mohammedan reaction' to the bombing of this particular community.[87]

All these reservations were weighed against Ibn Saʿūd's demands that Britain intercept or eject the Ikhwān, in increasingly insistent messages over

[81] Glubb, *War*, pp. 329–30.

[82] R/15/2/1499, Harold Dickson, Fortnightly Report No. 16 of 1929 (16–31 August 1929).

[83] L/PS/10/1238, P.2778/29, J. G. Laithwaite minute, 12 April 1929; Secretary of State for the Colonies to High Commissioner for Iraq, No. 163, 11 May 1929.

[84] L/PS/10/1246, 121/30, J. G. Laithwaite minute, 4 January 1930.

[85] L/PS/10/1246, High Commissioner for Iraq to Secretary of State for the Colonies, No. 20, 7 January 1930.

[86] L/PS/10/1246, J. G. Laithwaite minute, 8 January 1930; Secretary of State for the Colonies to High Commissioner for Iraq, No. 11, 9 January 1930.

[87] L/PS/10/1246, minute on interdepartmental conference, f.347.

the course of 1929. And while there was little new here in terms of argument (much of this had been heard many times since the fall of Ḥā'il and the flight of the Shammar), what was new was the level of British anxiety over the consequences of not meeting them. Few thought the fate of the Ikhwān worth the risk of a more general frontier conflict. 'If someone has, unfortunately, to suffer,' one India Office hand concluded as early as March 1929, 'it is better that it should be the stock or even the tribesmen of the desert . . . than that the whole frontier should be set on fire.'[88] After the battle of Riqai, London looked with alarm on a resurgent Ibn Saʿūd threatening direct intervention in Kuwait and Iraq if the Ikhwān were not promptly rounded up and handed over. From Kuwait, Hafiz Wahba warned darkly that the king would no longer 'watch rebels sheltering and himself stand in front of them with hands tied'.[89] It was this pressure from London, and from the Foreign Office in particular, that proved critical in shaping Britain's ultimate decision to eject al-Dawīsh, and to insist on the hardness of the border in this case. When the Ikhwān leader heard that the British were unable to consider his requests for supplies, for protection, or for asylum for families, the news came as a profound shock. Past experience, it seems clear, had led him to expect a different outcome.[90]

After Riqai, British aircraft and armoured cars arrived in Kuwait from Iraq to deny the refugees key wells and grazing areas. Separate columns concentrated them in northwest Kuwait to prevent them from slipping away into Iraq, in particular. While the Ikhwān were to be contained in areas with adequate water supplies, and where they could be protected from reprisals from other Iraqi and Kuwaiti tribes, even the proponents of this position accepted that it risked exposing Britain to criticism. 'The possibility that tribal custom may prove an obstacle to the surrender of refugees . . . is an additional argument for getting them across the frontier as soon as possible', J. G. Laithwaite advised; the consequences were 'embarrassing whichever way

---

[88] L/PS/10/1238, J. C. Walton, India Office minute, 23 February 1929.

[89] L/PS/10/1246, Political Resident in the Persian Gulf to Secretary of State for the Colonies, No. 5, 3 January 1930.

[90] R/15/5/34, Harold Dickson to Political Resident for the Persian Gulf, No. 635, 19 November 1929.

we turn'.[91] Indeed, Fayṣal al-Dawīsh was specifically warned that the British government could not accept any attempt by him to make *dakhala* on either the Sheikh of Kuwait or British officials there: government policy made that custom 'impossible' in the present circumstances.[92]

It was not merely the fear of being seen to violate Arab custom that troubled these officers. A number of them still expected the Ikhwān to face 'brutal treatment' at Ibn Saʿūd's hands, despite his assurances that their punishment would be 'tempered with kindness and mercy'.[93] In part, this concern had led Iraq's High Commissioner to consider allowing the Ikhwān to surrender on the understanding that they would not be returned against their will – a complication that took much correspondence with London to resolve.[94] Similar fears that the Ikhwān leaders would not receive fair treatment (and thus 'lay H.M.G. open to charge of inhumanity') led the Political Resident in the Persian Gulf to wonder whether they might rather be deported to Cyprus or some other British colony.[95] Instead, he resolved on securing a promise from Ibn Saʿūd to spare the lives of leaders and tribesmen alike, and that whatever punishment he chose to enact be consistent with 'Arab sentiment'.[96] Thus was the final hurdle overcome. By late January 1930 the RAF had shepherded the rebels into a small corner of Kuwait and the main leaders were on their way to Ibn Saʿūd, and jail. The last of the Mutayr and Ajman re-crossed the border on 8 February. Even after the Ikhwān tribes and their leaders had been returned, however, the British attempted to follow the 'many and conflicting' reports of their subsequent treatment.[97] Fayṣal al-Dawīsh died in jail the following year.

[91] L/PS/10/1246, J. G. Laithwaite minute, 8 January 1930.

[92] L/PS/10/1246, Political Resident in the Persian Gulf to Secretary of State for the Colonies, No. 8, 7 January 1930.

[93] R/15/2/1499, Harold Dickson, Fortnightly Report No. 1 of 1930 (1–15 January 1930), and No. 3 (16–28 February 1930).

[94] L/PS/10/1246, P.87/30, J. G. Laithwaite minute, 2 January 1930; High Commissioner for Iraq to Secretary of State for the Colonies, No. 15, 7 January 1930.

[95] L/PS/10/1246, Shuckburgh to Laithwaite, 14 January 1930; High Commissioner for Iraq to Secretary of State for the Colonies, No. 66, 24 January 1930.

[96] L/PS/10/1246, Political Resident in the Persian Gulf to Secretary of State for the Colonies, No. T7, 21 January 1930; and No. 37, 28 January 1930.

[97] R/15/2/1499, Harold Dickson, Fortnightly Report No. 3 of 1930 (16–28 February 1930); L/PS/10/1246, G. E. Crombie minute, 23 February 1934.

## Conclusion

After both the operations to relocate refugee tribes in 1925 and to eject the Ikhwān from Iraq and Kuwait in 1929–30, British officials in Iraq conducted reviews of their performance. New information about the southern desert and its personalities was collected and considered; advice on better movement, by air and by car, was given wide circulation. Some 'lessons' were learned but, in general, the tone was congratulatory: these official reports praised the sterling work done in trying circumstances.[98] This was, of course, but part of the story. The three episodes considered here, and officers' working correspondence as they scrambled to respond to these cases of Bedouin dislocation, reveal a number of less straightforward points for consideration.

The first is that the ontological slipperiness of the 'refugee' – long a feature of our field and of the history of our region – was especially marked when those refugees were also pastoral nomads. British officials on the ground were inconstant in affording displaced Bedouin recognition as refugees and – beyond the subjectivities of individual colonial, mandatory and military officials – it is possible to identify some of the variables involved.

As Laura Robson has argued, the interwar refugee regimes of the League of Nations and the mandates recognised Christians as refugees most freely, a practice informed by a longer history of European exchange with and evangelism among the Christian populations of the Ottoman Empire. Indeed, Christian communities such as Armenians and Assyrians were further identified as 'stateless' refugees – refugees with a claim to being a nation-in-waiting – in ways that displaced Kurdish, Arab and Turkish populations were not, so that the latter group were subjected to sedentarisation and local resettlement schemes, while the former were afforded at least the pretence of resettlement towards a future state of their own.[99]

It was not simply because they were not Christian that the Bedouin of southern Iraq were seldom treated as 'refugees'; it also mattered that they were armed.[100] As the debates over how to respond to the 'refugee tribes'

---

[98] For example: AIR 23/82, R. E. Alden to Secretary to the High Commissioner in Baghdad, 22 July 1925.

[99] Robson, *States of Separation*, p. 43.

[100] White, 'Refugees', p. 147.

of the mid-1920s make clear, the local British officers responsible for making judgements about the Bedouin groups they encountered drew a distinction, informally, between what we might call 'deserving' and undeserving' refugees – rather like their counterparts at home did between the 'deserving' and 'undeserving' poor. The fact that displaced Bedouin groups were armed – like the Kurds of northern Syria – counted against them; it complicated perceptions of them as 'victims' deserving of protection. In 1926, for example, one colonel at Air Headquarters in Iraq objected to an officer's requests that more be done to protect and support groups of Dhafir crossing between Iraq and Nejd. 'An unduly prominent place is given to the Dhafir,' he wrote, 'who as a Bedouin and not a shepherd tribe, should have greater responsibilities for looking after themselves, or of seeking another location if too weak to maintain themselves in their present habitat.'[101] Local officials contested this interpretation, pointing to evidence of vulnerability and destitution before their eyes. But despite such evidence, the prevailing perception of nomads as quintessentially mobile and martial – even predatory – often overrode the concerns that were raised about their safety and their claim upon British protection.

It was here, too, that the colonial fixation with the 'modes of life' also mattered. As I have described elsewhere, this was a powerful ideology of the first half of the twentieth century; the division of colonial subjects into 'nomads' and 'settlers' sat alongside race and gender as lenses through which Britons made sense of their empire, directly informing the policies they prescribed for differently categorised colonial subjects. It was precisely because they were nomads that the Bedouin could not straightforwardly be refugees; mobility was seen as being central to their existence, and wholescale relocation when faced with disaster or oppression 'an ordinary law of self-preservation in the desert'.[102] There was, as it were, no plight in their flight. As some local officers came to appreciate, this way of thinking stemmed from a failure to distinguish between different orders of Bedouin mobility. Seasonal migration was, in fact, predicated on a very specific sense of place, as groups moved between well known, familiar grazing grounds and wells. This bore little relation to the

---

[101] AIR 23/79: Air Staff Intelligence to High Commissioner for Iraq, No. I/3/7, 18 June 1926.
[102] Ibid.

more disrupted and desperate movements forced on many Bedouin groups along the interwar Iraq-Nejd frontier.

It was little wonder, then, that local colonial officials oscillated between describing Bedouin groups as 'refugees' one minute and 'raiders' the next – sometimes in the space of a single report. For our three case studies also illuminate the extent to which the British response to Bedouin dislocation was fractured between a host of political and administrative organisations, institutions and traditions. For the historian, this means working across Colonial Office, Foreign Office, India Office and Air Ministry files and familiarising oneself with the preoccupations and jurisdictions of Special Service Officers, Iraqi Desert Police, Political Residents, Government of Iraq 'Advisers' and many others besides. For the British, this amplified the scope for variation in how Bedouin dislocation was interpreted and handled. Officials in Baghdad and on the frontier alike recognised the 'special difficulties' created by their patchy and incomplete intelligence system.[103] But in lieu of something more comprehensive for Iraq's southern desert – much touted in the later 1920s, but never fully realised – the situation bred much mutual recrimination, including accusations that some local officers, in advocating on behalf of particular Bedouin 'refugees', had lost 'a sense of proportion'.[104]

A second question suggested by our three episodes is what they reveal about the relationship between imperialism and humanitarianism – and its limits. As Abigail Green has shown, the phenomenon of 'the imperialism of human rights' has special relevance for scholars of this region, where Britain's fitful concern to protect select communities in Muslim lands (and to find proxies for its imperial interests) 'dovetailed with anti-slavery, Christian humanitarian activism and the rallying cry of "civil and religious liberty" . . .'.[105] Laura Robson's work demonstrates the myriad ways in which the language of 'refugees', their 'difference' and protection served to legitimate mandatory rule over Arab populations in the era of the League of Nations – just as the practice of pointing to 'minorities' had underpinned the Allies'

---

[103] For example: AIR 23/79, Memorandum to Air Office Commanding, 'Glubb's Final Report on the Akhwan Season', 31 May 1926.

[104] AIR 23/79, untitled Air Ministry minute of 1 June 1926, regarding 'Defensive Operations v Akhwan 1925–1926'.

[105] Green, 'Imperialism of Humanitarianism', 178.

case for a continued role in the Balkans and eastern Europe.[106] Indeed, there is a growing literature on British imperial humanitarianism in the twentieth century, but it tends to focus on actors, organisations and enthusiasms emanating from the British Isles, on the one hand, or as part of international or transnational flows of humanitarian thought and practice. Instead, our episodes offer a view of how the local officials of empire – men who were not necessarily familiar with changing international definitions of the 'refugee' – passed judgement on the ground about the people for whom they were responsible.

They were not without pity. The brutal raiding tactics of the Ikhwān had placed 'the nomad tribes of the southern Shamiyah desert . . . in a constant state of terror and uncertainty'.[107] The activities of the 'refugee raiders' had unquestionably exacerbated tensions between Nejd and Iraq, but officers were still plainly moved by their destitution ('tired, and very poorly equipped; their camels were weak, and they had no food supplies'). And while they complied with the ejection of the Ikhwān 'rebels' from Kuwait and Iraq, some expressed real unease about doing so.[108] These officers saw in Bedouin plight a role for themselves. And yet, on the ground, empathy could still be checked by the momentum of received ideas about empire's subject peoples. Across the nineteenth century Britain had come to view refuge as a national obligation: 'We cannot entertain . . . any demand for the expulsion of refugees,' Lord Malmesbury wrote in 1852; 'You must be aware that no government which complied with such demands could exist a month in England.'[109] The ambivalence with which displaced Bedouin were viewed between the wars helps sketch the interplay of imperialism and humanitarianism, illuminating the circumstances in which Britain's historical commitment to refuge met its match.

Thirdly, our episodes reveal a clear relationship between the state's attempts to manage Bedouin dislocation and its growing capacity to know, act in and exert control over its arid frontiers. Each of our three episodes reveals a new layer being added to the state's involvement in Bedouin politics and in the southern desert itself, even as the setting of each episode itself advances further

---

[106] Robson, *States of Separation*, 30.

[107] AIR 23/79, Glubb, 'Final Report'.

[108] Glubb, *War*.

[109] Cited in Caroline Shaw, *Britannia's Embrace: Modern Humanitarianism and the Imperial Origins of Refugee Relief* (Oxford: Oxford University Press, 2015).

south and west: from the Euphrates markets of 1917, to the new wells and routes mapped during the Shāmiyya relocation of 1925, to the border with Kuwait and Nejd in 1929–30. Across the period, evidence of Bedouin suffering formed part of the case for a permanent administrative presence in Iraq's southern desert.[110]

As Ben White has convincingly argued for interwar Syria, refugee flows can 'attract state authority', engendering new state institutions and making the state more present in people's lives, in a process that often begins at the border.[111] In the Syrian case – and again with reference to Christian refugees further north in Iraq – the League also accumulated knowledge, authority and legitimacy from the management of these refugees. In Iraq's southern desert, however, this concentration of authority was lopsided: British authority was entrenched without a concomitant increase in the supervisory capacity of the League. Managing nomads – even nomadic refugees – was seen as a peculiarly imperial responsibility. In Britain's annual administrative reports to the League, the case of the Shammar refugees and of other displaced Bedouin groups appears in the summaries of foreign policy and defence – that is, matters relating to the Anglo-Iraqi Treaty – and not in sections more amenable to the League's scrutiny. Nor was this an area over which the British were prepared to concede authority to the Government of Iraq. As one report reflecting on the 1925 relocation operations put it: 'The Arab official is somewhat apt to be tainted with bureaucracy, a fatal shortcoming in dealing with savages, where the personal touch is essential. An Englishman might be more successful in this respect'.[112] This attempt by the British to connect the management of displaced Bedouin with their desire to monopolise authority over sensitive frontier zones was made most explicit in the case of the 1925 relocation, and the clearly articulated desire of British authorities in Baghdad to deprive King Fayṣal of a proxy force in, and influence over, the southern desert. But this dynamic was at work in our other examples too, from the currying of favour with Fahd Ibn Hadhdhāl as Britain's particular eyes and ears in the desert, to the attempt to manage the fallout of the Ikhwān Rebellion in line with the demands of British diplomacy.

---

[110] Fletcher, *British Imperialism,* chapter 2.

[111] White, 'Refugees', p. 150.

[112] Glubb, 'Defensive Operations Against the Akhwan'.

There was, however, a downside that followed from Britain's efforts to work the management of displaced Bedouin into its claim to an increased say in desert affairs. Already by the mid-1920s local officials keenly felt that Britain's wider reputation in Iraq, and indeed in the Syrian Desert, hinged on its ability to successfully resolve the very difficult problems presented by Bedouin dislocation. 'I am sorry to have made such an unnecessary fuss of the Refugees,' wrote one officer involved in their relocation. 'The whole desert, however, has been watching them with considerable interest . . . and the success or otherwise of the affair will mean a good deal to the [Bedouin] as regards our control of affairs amongst them.'[113]

The final point raised by these three episodes of Bedouin flight, then, is that of refugees' agency in driving forward the history and shaping the changing forms of political authority within Iraq's southern desert.[114] In reacting to Bedouin use of the border, the state was being drawn, in each of our three episodes, into assuming more authority over desert affairs, and into more complex relationships with Bedouin groups. In this, displaced Bedouin benefited from the divided nature of political authority that existed within the mandates – even without making direct appeals to Geneva, as other refugees in the region did. Throughout the relocation of 1925, for example, the refugees were able to appeal to different authorities in each *liwā'* through which they passed in order to influence the route taken, organise delays and even seek an end to the relocation altogether.[115] Occasionally, our sources permit us a glimpse into the arguments and appeals mobilised by refugees themselves: in December 1929, for example, a deputation of Mutayr fleeing Saudi rule addressed a personal letter to a British officer in southern Iraq in which they asserted a claim to Iraqi nationality, this being the territory to which they were 'always considered to belong'.[116] Displaced Bedouin may have seldom been afforded recognition as 'refugees' – a problem requiring explanation in its own right. But their efforts to seek an accommodation with power, and their place within broader imperial claims to authority, were as significant as that of the other refugees prominent in our emerging, engaging histories of the post-Ottoman Middle East.

---

[113] AIR 23/81: Guy Moore, typescript copy of manuscript report, dated 7 June 1925.
[114] See: Elie, 'Histories', p. 8.
[115] For example: AIR 23/81: Guy Moore to Air Staff Intelligence, 6 June 1925.
[116] Glubb, *War*, p. 314.

# 11

## THE 'CAMEL DISPUTE': CROSS-BORDER MOBILITY AND TRIBAL CONFLICTS IN THE IRAQI–SYRIAN BORDERLAND, 1929–34

### Laura Stocker[1]

The history of Bedouin tribes and tribal-state relations in the Middle East has long been written from a nation-centred perspective, whereby tribes were reduced to 'a negligible factor in state formation'.[2] Recent scholarship on borderland studies, however, has shown that when historians shift their perspective to the margins of states and empires, actors previously considered insignificant suddenly appear to play a much more relevant role than generally acknowledged.[3] As Sam Dolbee has argued for the case of the Shammar tribe in the late Ottoman Empire, 'it is in part the Shammar's place on the margins that gave them power' – a fact that can be easily overlooked if scholars continue to focus on centralised state institutions.[4] Alan Mikhail has similarly suggested that the 'traditional concentration of

---

[1] I thank Jordi Tejel, Johann Büssow, Ramazan Hakkı Öztan and Nadav Solomonovich for their insightful comments on this chapter.

[2] Ronen Zeidel, 'Tribes in Iraq. A negligible factor in state formation', in Uzi Rabi (ed.), *Tribes and States in a Changing Middle East* (Oxford: Oxford University Press, 2016), pp. 171–87.

[3] See e.g. Jordi Tejel, 'Making Borders from Below: The Emergence of the Turkish-Iraqi Frontier, 1918–1925', *Middle Eastern Studies*, Vol. 54, No. 5 (2018), pp. 811–26.

[4] Sam Dolbee, 'The Locust and the Starling: People, Insects and Disease in the Late Ottoman Jazira and After, 1860–1940' (PhD thesis, New York University, 2017), p. 107.

historians on political or administrative territorial division can be bypassed, or at least broadened or balanced' by taking ecological spaces and nomadic groups as analytic units instead.[5] Drawing on this discussion, this chapter looks at Bedouin tribes in the *bādiyat al-Shām*, the desert and steppe region stretching between eastern Syria, western Iraq, northeastern Jordan and northern Saudi Arabia.[6] By looking at the desert borderlands, the chapter seeks to rethink how states extended their sovereignty over people and territory situated at the margins of the newly established states in the Middle East during the interwar period.

This study is mainly concerned with the Bedouin communities that belonged to the ʿAnaza tribes (Arabic: ʿAšāʾir ʿAnaza), which formed one of the largest tribal confederations in the *bādiyat al-Shām* region. After the disintegration of the Ottoman Empire the territories of the migratory circuits of the ʿAnaza were divided by new international borders that defined the mandates of Syria, Iraq and Transjordan as well as the independent kingdom of Saudi Arabia.[7] Yet, the emergence of new state borders did not herald a sudden departure from the existing forms of mobility, as the ʿAnaza tribes continued their regular seasonal migrations across various state territories. Such free movement across international borders was granted to them by the governments of the French and British mandatory powers who primarily aimed to control rather than restrict the cross-border mobility of Bedouin tribes. Since most of the ʿAnaza communities became affiliated either to Iraq

---

[5] Alan Mikhail, 'Introduction – Middle East Environmental History: The Fallow between Two Fields', in Alan Mikhail (ed.), *Water on Sand. Environmental Histories of the Middle East and North Africa* (New York: Oxford University Press, 2013), p. 11.

[6] The Arabic term *bādiya* is generally translated as 'desert'. Hence, there is no fixed geographical definition of what the *bādiya* is. However, it is often used to refer to the larger Northern Arabian desert and steppe region stretching from the Arab Peninsula over the Sinai and Western Iraq until Syria: see Chatty Dawn, *From Camel to Truck. The Bedouin in the Modern World* (Cambridge: White Horse Press, 2013). The *bādiyat al-Shām* accordingly refers to the northern part of this region and is often applied equivalently to the term 'Syrian Desert'. In percentage terms, this region accounted for a relatively large area of the newly established nation states of Syria, Iraq and Jordan.

[7] Saudi Arabia as an independent kingdom was only established 1932 with the unification of the kingdoms of the Najd and the Hejaz.

or Syria, this study focuses mainly on the cross-border dynamics between the territories of these two states.

The emphasis of the chapter is on a short, albeit pivotal, period for state formation processes in the Middle East between the late 1920s and mid-1930s. This period marks a transition from what Cyrus Schayegh has called the 'Ottoman twilight' to an era when the Middle East 'became primarily an umbrella region of nation states'.[8] Across the desert borderlands, too, the consolidation of nation states and the demarcation of state borders went alongside with the tighter control of Bedouin tribes and growing state efforts to implement security. Yet, such processes were not the result of an alleged 'natural course' of state formation, whereby state power expands from the centre to the margins, but rather emerged in conjunction with bottom-up responses from local actors to nationalist and imperial policies.[9] The cross-border position of the Bedouin further complicated this interactive dynamic, as the great mobility of the Bedouin made the objectives of taxing the tribes and restricting tribal raiding largely dependent on transnational cooperation. The cross-border policing of tribes in turn triggered constant disputes of sovereignty and administrative responsibilities over people and territory in the borderlands between the French and British mandates.

This chapter examines such cross-border dynamics by taking a closer look at one episode of livestock raiding that emerged against the backdrop of long-standing conflict between two rival coalitions of the 'Anaza tribes. The affair illustrates how Bedouin cross-border mobility and tribal conflicts increasingly became tools with which imperial and national governments pressured one another and advanced claims for territorial control and state sovereignty along the borderlands. Moreover, it brought to the fore the progressively diverging aims in tribal policing of the French-Syrian and British-Iraqi governments. The conflict took place in the late 1920s during the winter migration of the

---

[8] Cyrus Schayegh, *The Middle East and the Making of the Modern World* (Cambridge, MA: Harvard University Press, 2017). This development, as Ramazan Hakkı Öztan has argued, was closely interlinked with economic policies that developed out of the Great Depression of 1929. See Ramazan Hakkı Öztan, 'The Great Depression and the Making of the Turkish–Syrian Border', *International Journal of Middle East Studies*, Vol. 52 (2020), pp. 311–26.

[9] See also Tejel, 'Making Borders from Below'.

Syrian 'Anaza tribes to Iraqi territory involving tribes from both sides. Two well-informed contemporaries, the British military officer John Bagott Glubb and the German archaeologist Max von Oppenheim both described the episode as the last flare-up of large tribal raiding in the European mandates, which was successfully suppressed by the state government, and further cited the affair as proof that the state had gained the upper hand in the desert borderlands and full control over the Bedouin tribes.[10] Yet, looking at the conflict from a cross-border perspective reveals a more complicated picture and mitigates such narratives of European colonial prowess. Because of its transborder dimensions, the conflict had soon evolved into a major diplomatic issue between the French-Syrian and the British-Iraqi governments. Instead of reverting to international agreements which stipulated the regulation of such disputes through joint transnational conferences, both sides started to interfere directly, seizing large numbers of livestock from the Bedouin of the other state, which led to the naming of the affair as the "Amārāt-Ruwalla camel dispute'.[11] However, the imminent settlement of state borders and the efforts of different governments to secure the loyalty of powerful tribes gave the Bedouin considerable leeway to assert their own interests and get the authorities to act on their behalf. Thus, Bedouin tribes were not simply passive recipients of imperial and central state politics but rather pursued their own political and economic interests. By analysing the episode of the 'camel dispute', the chapter argues that the desert borderlands of the new nation states were a central site and their Bedouin population key actors in negotiating the territorial and political order of the post-Ottoman Middle East.

Tracing Bedouin agency is certainly a difficult task, given the absence of sources written by indigenous actors themselves. One way to capture them, as Pekka Hämäläinen has suggested, is the cross-checking of sources from different imperial powers.[12] This chapter adopts this approach by simultaneously consulting archival material from the French and British mandate administrations, complemented with ethnographies, travelogues and private collections from Arab and European contemporaries as well as tribal encyclopaedias. The first

[10] John Glubb, *Arabian Adventures. Ten Years of Joyful Service* (London: Cassell, 1978), p. 211 and Max Freiherr von Oppenheim, *Die Beduinen. Band 1. Die Beduinenstämme in Mesopotamien und Syrien* (Leipzig: Otto Harrassowitz, 1939), p. 76.

[11] The National Archives (hereafter TNA), FO 371/14556, E5598/251/89.

[12] Pekka Hämäläinen, *The Comanche Empire* (New Haven: Yale University Press, 2008), p. 13.

part of the chapter provides an overview on the course of tribal-state relations since the expansion of modern statehood into the desert and steppe regions of the Middle East. In the second part, the episode of the 'camel dispute' is described in more detail and analysed in its specific context of the consolidation of the Middle Eastern nation states in the late 1920s to mid-1930s. However, before elaborating on these aspects, it is necessary to briefly discuss the terms or the categories 'tribes' and 'tribal confederation' as well as to provide some explanations on how, in this chapter, they are understood and used in relation to the 'Anaza communities.

## The 'Anaza Tribes

European orientalist tradition as well as Arab urban-centred scholarship have long perceived tribes (Arabic: *'ašā'ir or qabā'il*) and tribal confederations as homogenous, primordial groups with a peculiar socio-economic or political structure. Yet, this 'essentialist and ahistorical notion' of tribes has been widely discredited by anthropologists and historians over the past few decades.[13] Instead, scholars began to analyse the concept of 'tribe' in its specific social, economic and political contexts, showing the diversity and fluidity of social formations referred to by this generic term. This chapter builds on this more recent scholarship that conceptualises tribes and tribal confederations as 'social groups that claim descent from a common male ancestor and are connected with a specific territory at a particular time but that are not politically united'.[14]

As a socially constructed unit, the 'Anaza confederation, as Astrid Meier and Johann Büssow have suggested, can thus best be described with Benedict Anderson's concept as 'imagined community'.[15] The 'Anaza tribes were connected to each other by different – real or fictive – genealogical lineages, tracing back to the founding father of the confederation 'Anza Ibn Wail Ibn Qasad.[16] The tribe was further divided into two major divisions,

---

[13] Samira Haj, 'The problems of tribalism. The case of nineteenth-century Iraqi history', *Social History*, Vol. 16, No. 1 (1991), p. 47.

[14] Astrid Meier and Johann Büssow, ''Anaza', in Kate Fleet, Gudrun Krämer, Denis Matringe, John Nawas and Everett Rowson (eds), *Encyclopaedia of Islam, THREE*, <http://dx.doi.org/10.1163/1573-3912_ei3_COM_23785>. First published online 2012 (accessed 31 March 2020).

[15] Ibid.

[16] 'Abbas al-Azzawi, 'Asha'ir al-'Iraq (Baghdad: Matba'at Baghdad, 1937), p. 258.

first, the Ḍanā Bishr, which included the tribes of the Fadʿān, the Sbaʿa and the ʿAmārāt, and second, the Ḍanā Muslim, consisting of the Ruwalla (together with the Muḥallaf they built the Jilās), Ḥasana and the Wuld ʿAlī. Intertribal relations during the interwar years in the *bādiyat al-Shām* were largely shaped by the rivalry and conflicts between these two divisions. However, like tribes themselves, tribal alliances were fluid and based on different, often temporary, economic, political and ecological considerations of tribal groups. Genealogical lineages thereby mostly served as 'reference systems' on which such alliances were founded but did not have to be.[17]

Alongside other tribal confederations such as the Shammar and the Ḍafir, the ʿAnaza tribes belonged to the a*hl al-ʿibl* ('people of the camel'), which denominated 'nomadic, camel-herding tribes'.[18] This was primarily a self-attribution, which distinguished them positively from other allegedly 'less noble' tribes whose socio-economic foundations were mostly based on sheep breeding or temporary sedentariness. From the late nineteenth century onwards, the socio-economic distinction between them increasingly blurred. However, during the interwar period the privileged social and political status of the Bedouin was recognised and reinforced by the European mandate administrations, which relied on the military power and territorial knowledge of these tribes to govern the desert borderlands of the new nation states. In the following section, the course of tribal-state relations from the late Ottoman to the interwar period is examined in more detail.

### Tribal-State Relations in the Middle East from the late Ottoman to the interwar period

*The late Ottoman period*

According to oral traditions recorded by Arab historians and European anthropologists, the ʿAnaza tribes had moved from the southern regions of the Arabian Desert to Syria and Mesopotamia in the early eighteenth century, together with the Shammar, and subjugated the long-time predominant

---

[17] Johann Büssow, 'Negotiating the Future of a Bedouin Polity in Mandatory Syria: Political Dynamics of the Sba'a-'Abada during the 1930s', *Nomadic Peoples*, Vol. 15, No. 1 (2011), p. 70.

[18] ʿAbd al-Jabbar al-Rawi, *Al-Badiya* (Baghdad: Matbaʿat al-ʿAnī, 1949), pp. 109–16.

Mawāli confederation.[19] Henceforward, it was mainly the 'Anaza and the Shammar that controlled the desert and steppe areas of Syria, Mesopotamia, the Najd and Hejaz. With new reform policies from the mid nineteenth century onwards, however, the Ottoman central government began to expand its administrative and infrastructural reach into the eastern Arab provinces. The hitherto largely independent Bedouin communities began to be subject to tighter state control.[20] Ottoman reform policies implied profound transformations of the social, economic and physical landscape of the Arab Middle East. The introduction of a new land code in 1858 and the development of agricultural land underpinned efforts to sedentarise the highly mobile population in order to make it accessible for taxation and conscription. New settlements protected by police posts against Bedouin infringements emerged at the desert's margins and cultivation advanced further into the steppe land.[21]

The Ottoman authorities aimed to restrain the frequently erupting tribal wars between the 'Anaza and the Shammar and to restrict tribal raiding which posed a security threat to the settled communities as well as to the transdesert caravan routes. At the same time, they sought to enforce taxation and conscription among the tribes. Such efforts were mostly of limited success and tribes frequently evaded entirely the access of state authorities. In general, however, tribal-state relations resembled more a partnership than one of unilateral domination.[22] The political, military and economic power position of the 'Anaza in Syria and Mesopotamia, and the fact that important trade,

---

[19] Oppenheim, *Die Beduinen*, p. 68. To be sure, the migration of the 'Anaza and the Shammar Bedouin to Syria and Mesopotamia did not occur all at once but was the result of several waves of migration of these communities. Since there is only incomplete historical evidence, both, the reasons for and the course of these migrations are disputed among scholars. For a detailed study of this context which focuses on the Mawāli tribes, see Stefan Winter, 'Aufstieg und Niedergang des osmanischen Wüstenemirats (1536–1741): Die Mawali-Beduinen zwischen Tribalisierung und Nomadenaristokratie', *Saeculum*, Vol. 63 (2013), pp. 249–63.

[20] Eugene L. Rogan, *Frontiers of the State in the Late Ottoman Empire, 1850–1921* (New York: Cambridge University Press, 1999).

[21] Norman Lewis, *Nomads and Settlers in Syrian and Jordan, 1800–1980* (Cambridge: Cambridge University Press, 1987).

[22] M. Talha Çiçek, *Negotiating Empire in the Middle East. Ottomans and Arab Nomads in the Modern Era, 1840–1914* (Cambridge: Cambridge University Press, 2021).

pilgrim and communication routes passed through their territories, made them essential allies for the central government and other regional power holders.[23] Unable to control the Bedouin with military force, the Ottoman authorities formed alliances with powerful tribes and tribal sheikhs in particular. For the levying of taxes and protection of routes the latter were rewarded by subsidies payment, land concessions and political titles. Such Ottoman policies boosted the authority of a small number of sheikhs and heralded a period retrospectively referred to as 'the age of the sheikhs' (zaman al-shuyūkh).[24] The German archaeologist Max von Oppenheim in 1899 noted that many of the ʿAnaza sheikhs competed for being recognised by the government as the paramount sheikh of their tribe.[25] The important power positions of some ʿAnaza sheikhs, such as Fahd Ibn Hadhdhāl from the ʿAmārāt, Nūrī Ibn Shaʿlān from the Ruwalla and Mujḥim Ibn Muhayd from the Fadʿān in the European mandates of the interwar period thus already dated back to the late Ottoman period.

It was also in this late Ottoman context when significant changes took place in the socio-economic landscape of the desert and steppe land, characterised by a gradual shift from camel to sheep breeding and agricultural cultivation. The greater part of the ʿAnaza, however, continued to depend on camel breeding and the caravan trade. While tensions remained between the settled population and Bedouin due to tribal raiding, the expansion of settlements and cultivated land went alongside increasing socio-economic entanglement between these communities.[26] Many of the growing urban

---

[23] India Office Record/L/PS/20/C131, 'Personalities, Arabia', April 1917, in *Qatar Digital Library*, Qatar National Library (ed.), <https://www.qdl.qa/en/archive/81055/vdc_100000000884.0x000164> (2020), p. 104. (Accessed 20 January 2020).

[24] See e.g. Thorsten Schoel, 'The Hasana's Revenge: Syrian Tribes and Politics in their Shaykhs Story', *Nomadic Peoples*, Vol. 15, No. 1, (2011), p. 102 and Katharina Lange, 'Heroic Faces, Disruptive Deeds: Remembering the Tribal Shaykh on the Syrian Euphrates', in Dawn Chatty (ed.), *Nomadic Societies in the Middle East and North Africa: Entering the 21st century* (Leiden: Brill, 2006), pp. 99–122.

[25] Stiftung Rheinisch-Westfälisches Wirtschaftsarchiv zu Köln, Abt. 601, Nachlass Max von Oppenheim, (hereafter, RWWA 601), 188, 'Aneze-Beduinen' (1899 [1935]), pp. 14–15.

[26] See e.g. Lewis, 'Nomads and Settlers'.

centres and villages developed into new regional trade hubs during the late nineteenth century and became important markets for pastoralist products.[27] In the summer, when the Bedouin tribes moved to the margins of the desert, they sold their livestock products in the cities and villages, rented camels to merchants and pilgrims for the crossing of the transdesert routes and, in turn, purchased manufactured goods. Sheikhs often had their new landholdings cultivated by sedentary farmers or smaller allied tribes with whom they entered into a relationship of tenancy. In sum, the expansion of modern territoriality, as Reşat Kasaba noted, did not always contradict Bedouin interests, but rather they 'came to be embedded in the institutions and practices of modern states in the late and post-Ottoman world'.[28]

## The interwar period

In the political reordering of the Middle East during and right after the First World War the 'Anaza, as Oppenheim noted, 'represented their interests with considerable skill'.[29] Many of these tribes constituted a large military and human force and therefore precious allies for various warring parties. This allowed the sheikhs of powerful tribes, such as Nūrī Ibn Shaʿlān of the Ruwalla, to change sides if necessary and ensure they would eventually be on the winning side of the war.[30] After the disintegration of the Ottoman Empire, however, the Middle East was divided into different spheres of interest by European powers and the newly established states were placed under the mandatory rule of France and Britain – officially commissioned by the League of Nations to administratively and militarily support them until

---

[27] See e.g. Barout Jamal, 'La renaissance de la Jéziré : Deir ez-Zor ottomane, de la désertion à la reconstruction', in Jean-Claude David and Thierry Bossière (eds), *Alep et ses territoires, Fabrique et politique d'une ville (1868–2011)* (Beirut, Damascus : Presses de l'Ifpo, Institut français du Proche-Orient, 2014), pp. 105–19.

[28] Reşat Kasaba, *A Moveable Empire, Ottoman Nomads, Migrants and Refugees* (Seattle: University of Washington Press, 2009), p. 124.

[29] Oppenheim, 'Die Beduinen', p. 75. (All translations by the author, unless otherwise noted.)

[30] Philip S. Khoury, 'The Tribal Shaykh, French Tribal Policy, and the Nationalist Movement in Syria between the Two World Wars', *Middle Eastern Studies*, Vol. 18, No. 2 (April 1982), pp. 180–93.

they would be able to function as independent nation states.[31] In Iraq and Transjordan, the British mandatory power established Arab governments under the Hashemite King Faisal in Iraq and King Abdullah in Transjordan, which were placed under the control of British advisers.[32] The French governed Syria, according to the principle of 'divide and rule', as a loose confederation of multiple states that were united to the Syrian Republic in 1930.[33] In defining the borders of the new states, the location of tribal territories was rarely taken into account. The ʿAnaza migratory circuits spanned across the state territories of British Iraq and Transjordan, French Syria and the Najd. Although the Bedouin continued to migrate across different national borders each tribe was assigned a national affiliation. The reorganisation of the political landscape and of regional power distribution simultaneously caused major shifts in tribal alliances, leading to tribal disintegration. Some ʿAnaza sections moved entirely to the Najd, not only because of Ibn Saud's favourable taxation policies for nomadic tribes but also in the hopes that they could pursue their Bedouin way of life better there than under the European mandates.[34] Most of the ʿAnaza, however, chose to side with the French government in Syria, home to their main market towns and summer grazing lands. Only the ʿAmārāt became British-Iraqi subjects, as they were orientated towards Baghdad and the Middle Euphrates.

In broad terms, European mandatory powers perpetuated the Ottoman tribal policies which not only suited their political, economic and strategic interests, but also proved to be a cost-efficient way to govern and safeguard the vast desert frontiers. Both the French and the British continued to excel on the instrumentalisation of tribal leaders by distributing subsidies and land

[31] For a comprehensive introduction into the mandate system, see Cyrus Schayegh and Andrew Arsan, *The Routledge History of the Middle East Mandates* (New York: Routledge, 2015).

[32] For a study of the British Mandate in Iraq see Peter Sluglett, *Britain in Iraq. Contriving King and Country* (London: I. B. Tauris, 2007).

[33] For a detailed study of the French Mandate in Syria see Philip S. Khoury, *Syria and the French Mandate. The Politics of Arab Nationalism, 1920–1945* (Princeton: Princeton University Press, 1987).

[34] Centre des Archives Diplomatiques de Nantes (hereafter, CADN), Cabinet politique, ISL/1/V 1363, 'Notice Tribu Roualla', 20 août 1934.

concessions for the provision of security of imperial infrastructure in the desert, further consolidating the sheikh's power position. In Syria in particular, the 'Anaza sheikhs acquired important power positions in the administration of the borderlands. In the early mandate period, the administration of the entire desert borderlands in Syria were assigned to Nūrī Ibn Sha'lān, the paramount sheikh of the Ruwalla, and to Mujḥim Ibn Muhayd from the Fad'ān. Although this system only lasted a very short time, both sheikhs remained at the top of the list of French subsidy payments throughout the interwar years. In Iraq, too, the 'Anaza under Fahd Ibn Hadhdhāl had already, during the First World War, become one of the most important British tribal allies in Iraq's southern and western desert. This partnership between the 'Amārāt and the British continued during the interwar years and their relations only cooled off with the expansion of direct state control in the late 1920s.[35]

In addition, the European desert administrators also relied on their own military intelligence officers who were usually assigned as 'advisers' of the sheikhs or local administrators and delivered intelligence on tribal migration, raiding and desert resource distribution.[36] Recent scholarship has argued that rather than working for a single state, the sphere of influence of these officers spanned the entire 'desert corridor'.[37] In Syria, French desert officers operated under the military intelligence service, the 'Service de Renseignement' – which was later transformed into the 'Service Spéciale du Levant' – as well as under the tribal control board of the 'Contrôle Bédouin', established in 1920.[38] The British counterpart in Iraq were the Special Service Officers (SSO) who operated under the command of the Royal Air

[35] Robert S. G. Fletcher, 'The 'Amārāt, their Shaykh and the Colonial State. Patronage and Politics in a Partitioned Middle East', *Journal of the Economic and Social History of the Orient*, Vol. 58, Nos. 1–2 (2015), pp. 163–99.

[36] Martin Thomas, 'Bedouin Tribes and the Imperial Intelligence Services in Syria, Iraq and Transjordan in the 1920s', *Journal of Contemporary History*, Vol. 38, No. 4 (2003), pp. 539–61.

[37] Robert S. G. Fletcher, 'Running the Corridor: Nomadic Societies and Imperial Rule in Interwar Syrian Desert', *Past & Present*, Vol. 220 (August 2013), pp. 185–215.

[38] Christian Velud, 'French Mandate Policy in the Syrian steppe', in Martha Mundy and Basim Musallam (eds), *The Transformation of Nomadic Society in the Arab East* (Cambridge: Cambridge University Press, 2000), p. 70.

Force (RAF). The air force was the central element of British tribal policing in Iraq but was also frequently deployed by the French in Syria. The use of air power was seen as a 'cheap and effective' means to control the vast desert areas and its Bedouin population. The practice of collective punishment of 'unruly' tribes by bombing of tribal camps and villages was almost a daily aspect of life in the desert. Such practices were being justified by the deeply rooted colonial notions that the Bedouin could only be disciplined by the use of force.[39] The idea that they were to be ruled along different governmental rationales than the rest of the population was also reflected in the legal and administrative separation of the Bedouin and the desert borderlands. This kind of 'alternative modes of sovereignty and rule' was in fact a shared feature of many colonial borderlands of the late nineteenth and twentieth centuries and was built on the notion that 'tribal populations' needed to be governed by their 'own laws and customs'.[40] At the same time, this separation was based on a paternalistic, romanticising discourse according to which, as Toby Dodge has noted, the Bedouin tribal organisation reflected a 'democratic system of equality' where 'leaders were naturally selected on the basis of strength of character'.[41] It was this notion of the Bedouin as the 'noble savage' that largely determined the tribal policies of European mandate administrations in the Middle East.

In Syria, the separation of the Bedouin population was implemented in the form of a semi-autonomous state in the desert (*bādiya*) that was divided by a physical boundary from the cultivated areas (*mamūra*). This internal boundary not only separated two different legal spheres but also served as a way of controlling and disarming the Bedouin tribes when they entered the cultivated areas. In many regards this internal boundary was equally, if not more important than international borders for the channelling and control of Bedouin mobility. As for Iraq, the extraordinary legal status of the Bedouin

---

[39] Priya Satiya, *Spies in Arabia. The Great War and the Cultural Foundations of Britain's Covert Empire in the Middle East* (New York: Oxford University Press, 2008), pp. 239–62.

[40] Benjamin D. Hopkins, 'The Frontier Crimes Regulation and Frontier Governmentality', *The Journal of Asian Studies*, Vol. 74, No. 2 (May 2015), p. 370.

[41] Toby Dodge, *Inventing Iraq. The Failure of Nation-building and a History Denied* (New York: Colombia University Press, 2003), p. 77.

was inscribed in the Tribal Civil and Criminal Dispute Regulation (TCCDR) and incorporated into the constitution in 1925. The TCCDR was applied to all members of 'tribal communities', and thus concerned basically the entire Iraqi rural population. As such, it established a general division between the rural and urban population, which reflected one of the most important features of British rule in Iraq.[42] In both states, Bedouin tribes were also granted certain privileges that did not apply to the rest of the steppe population. These included the free movement across state borders and the taxation of livestock in lump sums rather than on a per capita basis.

Until the late 1920s state interference into Bedouin affairs was mostly limited to matters concerning the settled population or the safety of imperial infrastructure. The French and British paid less attention to intertribal raiding, seeing it not as an act of tribal resistance, but rather 'as part of the natural cadences of Bedouin life' which was thus rather 'a force to be managed [. . .] than an object to be eradicated'.[43] The British 'rules for raiders', a legislation that existed for a short period of time in 1925 and established rules for the conduction of intertribal raids, is exemplary for this approach.[44] However, for different reasons, the late 1920s marked a turning point in the administration of the borderlands and in state policing of Bedouin tribes across the region. This was when the state authorities on either side of the Syrian-Iraqi border began to increasingly interfere into 'tribal affairs' and advanced efforts to extend greater security in the desert borderlands, while also trying to extract resources in the form of taxes on livestock. In explaining this shift towards tighter state control in the borderlands, scholars have pointed to a number of episodes. In Syria, for instance, after the Great Revolt that lasted from 1925 to 1927, the French became increasingly afraid of a union of tribal sheikhs with the nationalist urban elite as well as the emergence of powerful tribal alliances. Henceforth tribal misconduct was punished more severely by air bombardment and the politics of 'divide and rule' among the Bedouin was conducted more decisively.[45] Thus, they gradually cut the subsidies of great

---

[42] Ibid., pp. 63–83.
[43] Daniel Neep, *Occupying Syria under the French Mandate. Insurgency, Space and State Formation* (Cambridge: Cambridge University Press, 2012), p. 166.
[44] Fletcher, 'The 'Amārāt', pp. 178–86.
[45] Thomas, 'Bedouin tribes', p. 559.

tribal sheikhs like Nūrī Ibn Sha'lān and Mujḥim Ibn Muhayd and began to distribute them among different leaders of smaller tribes. In British Iraq and Transjordan, it was the Ikhwān revolt from 1927 to 1930, and its devastating effect on the tribes whose grazing lands were placed on the border with Saudi Arabia, that pushed the state expansion into the desert districts.[46]

The reconstruction of the 'Anaza 'camel dispute' below shows yet another reason for this shift in tribal policing of the desert – namely the growing disillusionment with the Bedouin sheikhs who were unable to represent and control the steppe population as hoped. This was not least due to the paradox on which the tribal policy of the European mandate power was based: while it boosted the power of the sheikhs, it also caused them to become increasingly distant from other members of the tribal community. Due to their growing wealth, many sheikhs withdrew into urban life and only occasionally accompanied their communities on their seasonal migrations into the desert. In this context, the differences between the British and French mandate systems, which hitherto had played only a marginal role in tribal policing, came to the fore, with 'the former pursu[ing] an unequal partnership with a dependent élite, [while] the latter required more direct control of the subject population'.[47] Since most studies have examined the evolution of tribal policing within a specific national context, transnational and cross-border perspectives have so far been neglected. Yet, as the 'camel dispute' highlights, interstate and cross-border dynamics were central to tribal-state relations. The episode further illustrates that although these developments restricted Bedouin autonomy, it was specifically in this context of imperial rivalry that tribes could also expand their agency by bringing state authorities to act on their behalf.

---

[46] From 1927 to 1930 the Ikhwān tribes in the Northern Najd and Hejaz revolted against 'Abd al-'Aziz Ibn Saud who had formerly used them to extend the territorial reach of his kingdom. After a peace agreement with the British, Ibn Saud, however, restricted the grazing rights of the Ikhwān, which led to an open rebellion of the latter who started large scale raids into Iraq, Transjordan and Kuwait. For a comprehensive overview on the costs of the Ikhwān attacks on Iraqi tribes see Antony Toth, 'Conflict and Pastoral Economy: The Costs of Akhwan Attacks on Tribes in Iraq, 1922–1929', *Critique: Critical Middle Eastern Studies*, Vol. 11, No. 2 (2002), pp. 201–27.

[47] Martin Thomas, 'French Intelligence-Gathering in the Syrian Mandate, 1920–1940, *Middle Eastern Studies*, Vol. 38, No. 1 (2002), p. 1745.

## The 'Camel Dispute' and Cross-border Policing of Bedouin Tribes

The course of Bedouin migration occurred usually in seasonal circuits. During the hot summer months, when the tribes stayed at the fringes of the desert, the Syrian 'Anaza were distributed along the cultivated areas between the upper Euphrates in the north and the Hauran in the south. The summer residences of the Iraqi 'Anaza, on the other hand, were located in the vicinity of Baghdad, Karbala and Najaf in the Middle Euphrates. In winter, the tribes usually moved towards the Hamad, the desert region located in the borderlands of Iraq, Syria, Transjordan and Saudi Arabia. As such, Bedouin tribes enjoyed free movement over the international state borders of the French and British mandates. Indeed, as Benedetta Rossi has argued, 'in desert-like environments', control over people and movement was more important than control over territory.[48] In the British 'desert corridor', as Robert Fletcher has shown, state officials often saw political boundaries as a factor complicating Bedouin policing, since pastoral patterns of mobility often 'invited and required them to reach out across state borders'.[49] As state borders began to be delimited by the late 1920s, however, the transgression of borders by Bedouin between the French and British mandates was increasingly interpreted as territorial claims, leading to severe interstate disputes. In order to avoid constant diplomatic incidents, cross-border policing of tribes was thus regulated in different agreements and conventions between the French and British mandate administrations. Such interstate regulation determined common procedures for the taxation and for the settlement of tribal conflicts. In 1927 Syria and Iraq signed the 'provisional agreement on the regulation of the frontier tribes' and in 1929 a similar agreement was concluded between Transjordan and Syria.[50] Nevertheless,

---

[48] Benedetta Rossi, 'Kinetocracy: The Government of Mobility at the Desert's Edge', in Darshan Vigneswaran and Joel Quirk (eds), *Mobility Makes States. Migration and Power in Africa* (Philadelphia: University of Pennsylvania Press, 2015), p. 149.

[49] Robert S. G. Fletcher, *British Imperialism and the Tribal Question. Desert Administration and Nomadic Societies in the Middle East, 1919–1936* (Oxford: Oxford University Press, 2015), p. 181.

[50] United Nations Archive, League of Nations, 'Provisional agreement concluded between Iraq and Syria for the negotiation of the affair of frontier tribes', 6 April 1927, Mandates General, 1928–1932, 6A/1294/655, R2314.

unclear responsibilities over people and territory and lacking state capacities in the borderlands often obstructed interstate cooperation. Differing domestic political interests further led to increasingly divergent strategies in tribal policing by the end of the 1920s, which – as the 'camel dispute' illustrates – led to a sharp decline of interstate cooperation with regard to cross-border tribes for several years.

## The beginning of the 'Anaza 'camel dispute'

The main elements of policing Bedouin mobility in the French and British mandates were the detection of general migration patterns as well as intelligence gathering on the state of tribal alliances and the distribution of grazing land that allowed insight into any deviation from these patterns. Yet, European colonial powers often misinterpreted the nature of tribal migrations, understanding them as based primarily on social customs, when in fact, they were mainly defined by the distribution of desert resources and tribal alliances.[51] Martin Thomas has shown that government officials and military officers of the French and British desert administration were often poorly equipped and lacked knowledge of the population and the territory. Additionally, they composed their reports under great time pressure with little space for details, which led to the fact that 'connections within and between tribal groups were frequently missed or misunderstood'.[52] Existing methods of policing Bedouin mobility, as illustrated by the escalation of the dispute between the 'Anaza tribes in 1929, quickly broke down when several unexpected factors or misunderstandings converged.

In January 1929 'practically the whole Ruwalla tribe' came to the Wadiyan area in Iraq where they stayed next to the Iraqi 'Amārāt as well as the Syrian Sba'a and the Fad'ān.[53] The relatively water-rich Gara'a depression in the Wadiyān area, which lay in the western desert of Iraq, was a popular winter residence for many Syrian 'Anaza, in particular for the Sba'a and the Fad'ān, who usually grazed their herds together with Iraqi 'Amārāt to which they were allied through the Ḍanā Bishr descent group. Yet, in the

[51] Haj, 'The problems of tribalism', p. 49 and Thomas, 'Bedouin tribes', p. 551.

[52] Thomas, 'Bedouin tribes', p. 550.

[53] TNA, FO 371/13760/E555/30/93, 'Intelligence Report No. 2 for the fortnight ended the 16th of January, 1929', 18 January 1929, p. 4.

winter of 1928 to 1929, different ecological, political and economic factors gave the impulse for the Syrian 'Anaza including the Ruwalla, to move to Iraq in unusually larger numbers. First, the constant stream of attacks from the Ikhwān tribes on the borders of Saudi Arabia made the grazing lands of the 'Anaza further south unattractive.[54] Secondly, the introduction of a new taxation system in Syria in 1927, which subjected Bedouin to tax payments for their livestock on a per capita basis instead of the traditional lump-sum payments, made it more attractive for the tribes to stay on the Iraqi side of the desert as well.[55] Finally, due to deteriorating weather conditions since the mid-1920s, which had gradually reduced the availability of water and grazing land in the desert areas of the *bādiyat al-Shām*, the tribes mingled on relatively small territory.[56] According to the British intelligence officer appointed to the area, however, there was little reason to be concerned, 'since the Ruwalla and the 'Amārāt which both belong to the 'Anaza were on good terms with each other'.[57] Indeed, the threat of the Wahhabi tribes that affected both the Ruwalla and the 'Amārāt had led to a peace agreement between Fahd Ibn Hadhdhāl and Nūrī Ibn Sha'lān in 1923. The decision of the two sheikhs to shelve off their old enmity had eased the long-standing tensions between the Danā Muslim and Danā Bishr. However, Fahd had died in 1927 and Nūrī mostly resided in Damascus, while his grandson Fawwāz accompanied the tribesmen on their winter migration into the desert. As a result of these developments, the agreement between the 'Amārāt and the Ruwalla lost its significance.[58] The British intelligence officers were dumbfounded when a conflict between the 'Anaza broke out and the long-standing

---

[54] Antony Toth, 'The Transformation of a Pastoral Economy. Bedouin and States in Northern Arabia, 1850–1950', (PhD thesis, University of Oxford, 2000), pp. 214–67.

[55] CADN, Cabinet politique, ISL/1/V, 987, 'Contrôle Bédouin de la Mouvance de Syrie, Année 1927, Rapport annuel', p. 1. TNA, Air 23/91, 'Special Service Office, Ramadi', 16 April 1927.

[56] Middle East Centre Archive, St Antony's College, Oxford (hereafter: MECA), Cecil John Edmonds collection, GB165-0095, Box 3, File 1 'Administration of Iraq 1930–1944. Ministry of Interior', p. 3.

[57] TNA, FO 371/13760/E555/30/93, 18 January 1929, p. 5.

[58] TNA, FO 481/18/E6564/3655/91, 'Annual Report of the Administration of the Southern Desert and the Defence of the Iraq Frontiers from 1st May 1929 to 30th April 1930', p. 3.

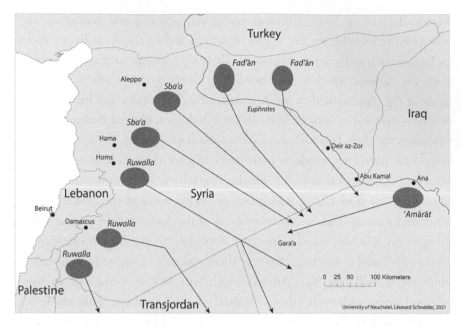

Figure 11.1 Direction of the winter migration of the 'Anaza tribes in the 1930s

Credit: Data compiled from CADN, Cabinet politique, ISL/1/V 552 and Oppenheim, 'Die Beduinen', map in annex titled 'Streifgebiete der Beduinen in Syrien und Mesopotamien'.

dispute between the Danā Bishr and the Danā Muslim coalitions escalated into a larger battle during the winter migration in early 1929.

Raiding incidents from the previous years had already strained the relations between the Syrian 'Anaza with the Ruwalla on the one side, and the Sba'a and Fad'ān on the other. In January 1929 the Ruwalla sought to take revenge from the Sba'a for raids in Transjordan that had occurred some months before.[59] As the Ruwalla attacked the Sba'a, both the Fad'ān and the 'Amārāt quickly got involved into the conflict. The Danā Bishr, together with other Iraqi tribes, built an alliance against the Ruwalla, which in turn began to mobilise other tribes in Transjordan and Syria. The dispute, which had begun with a few raids between the Syrian tribes, therefore escalated into a conflict of two large coalitions in which, according to an article in the Syrian newspaper *al-Nahḍa*, some 40,000 tribesmen

[59] CADN, Cabinet politique, ISL/1/V 1363, 'Notice tribus Roualla' 20 août 1934, p. 5.

were involved.[60] Even though this figure cannot be verified, it reflects, if not the scale of Bedouin tribes' mobilisation capability, at least their success in building a threat potential. As the Iraqi police was considerably overwhelmed with the situation, the Royal Air Force eventually had to intervene, pushing the Ruwalla back over the border.[61] As systems of Bedouin policing broke down, tribal turmoil was often dealt with by the use of the air force and by bombing tribal raiders. European colonial powers justified such acts of state violence less by a lack of state capacity than, as Priya Satia has shown, through the idea that the Bedouin 'could tolerate random acts of violence in a way that others could not'.[62]

Back in Syria, the French gathered the 'Anaza sheikhs and urged them to settle their claims.[63] Like many times before, this agreement did not last long and tensions between the Ruwalla and the Sba'a continued to flare up during the summer grazing season. The British were alarmed by alleged efforts of the Ruwalla to buy large numbers of weapons and demanded from the French to confiscate their machine guns before the tribes' winter migration to Iraq.[64] Yet, due to lack of will and/or capacities of state authorities, such demands often proved in vain or were carried out insufficiently. In late 1929, when the Syrian 'Anaza moved, heavily armed, to the desert, the dispute between the tribes escalated once again and led to the death of two members of the Sha'lān family.[65] This, according to the British reports, prompted the Ruwalla to launch intensive raiding against the Sba'a who resided on the Iraqi territory and also against numerous Iraqi tribes. In early 1930, the British officer Cecil

---

[60] The article is a French translation from Arabic from 'Faik', an informant of Max von Oppenheim. RWWA 601, 158/1, 'Razzu, Rualla, 'Traduction d'un article de journal du journal el Nahda, No 9/5 du 7 avril 1929'.

[61] TNA, FO 481/18/E6564/3655/91, 1 May 1929 to 30 April 1930, p. 3.

[62] Priya Satia, 'A Rebellion of Technology. Development, Policing and the British Arabian Imaginary', in Diana K. Davis and Edmund Burke III (eds), *Environmental Imaginaries of the Middle East and North Africa* (Athens, OH: Ohio University Press, 2011), p. 9.

[63] CADN, Cabinet politique, ISL/1/V 1363, 'Notice tribus Roualla', 20 août 1934, p. 5.

[64] TNA, FO 371/14554/E1226/251/89, 'British consul in Beirut to the French High commissioner', 10 December 1929, p. 130.

[65] CADN, Cabinet politique, ISL/1/V 552, 'Expose de la situation des tribus nomades en 1930', p. 5.

Edmonds reported that 'the Ruwalla were completely out of hand, raiding not only the Sbaʿa but also again the Iraqi ʿAmārāt'.[66]

## The Ruwalla seizure and British-Iraqi tribal policing

The British tended to attribute the main responsibility for the escalation of the conflict to Fawwāz whom they saw as 'spoilt, vain and anxious to make himself a name'.[67] In their view, it was only the power of the two 'great shaykhs', Fahd Ibn Hadhdhāl and Nūrī Ibn Shaʿlān that so far had prevented larger conflicts between the different ʿAnaza branches. The escalation of the dispute also revealed that Maḥrūt Ibn Hadhdhāl, who had replaced Fahd as the sheikh of the ʿAmārāt, did not enjoy the prestige and authority of his father and that his influence over the Iraqi tribes was less considerable.[68] Maḥrūt, who found himself in a quandary between the government's demand not to counter-raid and the interests of his tribesmen in reclaiming the livestock, tried to settle the matter in direct negotiations with Fawwāz. Yet the latter refused to stop the raids as long as Maḥrūt sided with the Sbaʿa and other Iraqi tribes with whom the Ruwalla were at war.[69] It was the British officer John Bagott Glubb who eventually decided to take matters into his own hands.

In 1928 Glubb had been appointed administrator of the newly created district of the 'Southern Desert Province'. In the wake of the deteriorating security situation caused by the Ikhwān attacks, the Iraqi government had agreed to the creation of this new administrative unit in the southwestern borderlands of Iraq and had equipped it with a 200-men strong police unit, the so called 'southern desert force'.[70] In early 1930, when the ʿAnaza conflict escalated in Iraq's western desert, Glubb and the southern desert force had for

---

[66] MECA, Cecil John Edmonds collection GB165-0095, Box 3, File 1, 'Administration of Iraq 1930–1944. Ministry of Interior'.

[67] TNA, FO 481/18/E6564/3655/91, 1 May 1929 to 30 April 1930, p. 3.

[68] Fletcher, 'The ʿAmārāt', pp. 186–93.

[69] TNA, FO 371/14554/E1226/251/89, High Commissioner Baghdad to H.B.M's Consul General, Beyrout', 7 February 1930, p. 161.

[70] 'Report by his Majesty's government in the United Kingdom of Great Britain and Northern Ireland to the council of the League of Nations on the administration of 'Iraq for the year 1928', in ed. Robert L. Jarman (ed.), *Iraq Administration Reports 1914–1932, Vol. 9, 1928–1930,* (Melksham and Oxford: Redwood Press Ltd. & Green Street Bindery, 1992), p. 43.

the first time successfully restricted the Ikhwān raids. Glubb was convinced that in view of the decline of the powerful sheikhs, the establishment of a civil administration and state control was 'the only way of producing a really satisfactory situation in the desert area'.[71] The expansion of state administration into the desert went alongside with the strict prohibition of raiding for Iraqi tribes which was implemented by the 'raiding and plunder law' in 1927.[72] Glubb insisted that the enforcement of the anti-raiding law required that the government takes responsibility for the 'immediate recovery of loots', being 'the only efficacious way of settling intertribal raids'.[73] The raids of the Ruwalla also jeopardised the safety of the overland desert route which 'had become a public highway frequently crossed by convoys of cars and buses'.[74] As multiple attempts of the Iraqi police to intervene into the 'Anaza conflict were of no avail, Glubb, together with heavily armed police cars and the assistance of two airplanes, seized more than 2,000 camels from the Ruwalla, killing 50 tribesmen during the operation. He brought the confiscated animals straight to the British-Iraqi desert post in Ruṭba where he distributed the largest part of them to the Iraqi tribes.[75]

Although the confiscation of livestock was not an uncommon means of punishing tribes or forcing them to cooperate, Glubb's operation – which Antony Toth has aptly described as an 'official raid' – was of a different kind.[76] Instead of making a provisional seizure and resolving the disputes through negotiations in which both sides would file their claims with a joint commission – a process that sometimes took several months – Glubb returned the animals single-handedly and directly to the tribes within a matter of few days. As such, the Ruwalla demands were only considered after the Iraqi tribes had

---

[71] TNA, CO 730/140/8/68058, 'Note on the causes which make it essential to establish and maintain a permanent administration in the desert', 12 June 1929, p. 1.

[72] The 'raiding and plunder law' placed all internal and cross-border raiding under severe punishment, see TNA, FO 371/15360/E3684/8/89, 'Extract from the Iraqi Government Gazette No. 20 dated the 14th of May 1927', p. 14.

[73] TNA, FO 371/14556/E 4555/251/89, 'The Residency, Baghdad to M.D. Tetreau, High Commissioner of the French Republic in Syria', 15 July 1930, p. 3.

[74] Glubb, 'Arabian Adventures', p. 201.

[75] TNA, FO 481/18/E6564/3655/91, 1 May 1929 to 30 April 1930, pp. 13–23.

[76] Toth, 'The Transformation of Pastoral Economy', p. 174.

been fully satisfied in theirs. Meanwhile, the British officer Peake had launched a similar operation on the Ruwalla sections camping in Transjordan whom he accused of raids against the Ḥuwaitāt, a Jordanian tribe.[77] Such operations undoubtedly aimed at gaining tribal loyalties, which had been put at severe risk by the Ikhwān raids and the prohibition of raiding.[78] At the same time, they were clear a demonstration of state power against powerful tribes such as the Ruwalla that still constituted a serious military and political power in the desert borderlands. Most important, they reflected the new course of British tribal policing in which the state was positioning itself as the primary arbitrator in tribal conflicts. From the British point of view, this development was inevitable, given the dwindling influence of the younger generation of Bedouin sheikhs on their tribesmen and their increasing unwillingness to cooperate with the government, as the example of Fawwāz showed. In this sense, they saw in the 'overbearing turbulence of the Ruwalla' an opportunity to 'set an example' and 'to punish some offender'.[79] At the same time, as the subsequent course of the affair shows, the British-Iraqi government sought quick and non-bureaucratic ways to resolve cross-border disputes, resorting to those who were, in their eyes, reliable tribal leaders with sufficient authority. Such strategies increasingly came into conflict with French-Syrian tribal policies. The British narrative portrays the Ruwalla raids in Iraq's western desert as the last raiding incident 'in the vast spaces of the Syrian desert' and the ultimate establishment of state power.[80] A look at this episode from the borderlands, however, challenges such linear narratives of imperial expansion and of alleged 'heroic victories' of British desert officers.

### The 'Amārāt seizure and French-Syrian tribal policing

In the operation against the Ruwalla, a Syrian tribe, the British had deliberately passed over the French-Syrian authorities, which, in the view of the

---

[77] CADN, Cabinet politique, ISL/1/V 552, 'Expose de la situation des tribus nomades en 1930', 1930, pp. 8–10.

[78] Toth, 'The Transformation of Pastoral Economy', p. 175.

[79] TNA, FO 481/18 E6564/3655/91, 1 May 1929 to 30 April 1930, p. 29.

[80] Glubb, 'Arabian Adventures', p. 211. A similar assertion is made by Oppenheim, who pointed out that the dispute was 'the last resurgence of the old conflict between the Bishr and the Ḍanā Muslim', which was 'effortlessly stifled by the French', concluding that the 'power over the desert has eluded the 'Anaza'. (Oppenheim, 'Die Beduinen', p. 76.)

latter, had constituted a breach of the frontier agreement of 1927. The convention stipulated that the settlement of disputes involving tribes from different national allegiances were to be dealt with in conferences from joint arbitrary commissions – a practice that existed since the early mandate period. While such conferences involved a great deal of bureaucracy, including the collection and processing of records and reports dating back several years, they usually had a poor record. Although disputes were in theory often successfully settled, the tribes did not necessarily agree with the results and the government often lacked the will or the means to enforce the decisions. Christian Velud has further pointed out that French tribal policy, driven by growing fears of 'pan-Arab' tribal unions within and across Syria's borders, contributed to the fact that no long-term rapprochement between tribes was achieved.[81] As a result, the same conflicts were resumed over several conferences and their resolution was sometimes postponed for years. The 'Anaza conflict brought to the fore the increasingly divergent opinions between the French and the British on the usefulness of direct interstate cooperation in tribal affairs, especially with regard to such joint conferences for the settlement of cross-border conflicts.

The lengthy bureaucratic efforts involved in these conferences were at odds with the British view that state authority in the desert was to be established 'by acts, not words'.[82] The lack of assertiveness of the French authorities in disarming the Ruwalla after the first conflicts in early 1929 further confirmed the British viewpoint. Instead of turning to the French authorities, Glubb thus approached Nūrī Ibn Shaʿlān in order to settle the outstanding claims of the Ruwalla. Nuri immediately travelled from Damascus to Ruṭba where he negotiated a deal with the British and reconciled with the ʿAmārāt leader, Maḥrūt Ibn Hadhdhāl. The British regarded this gesture as a reprimand against the recalcitrant Fawwāz from Nuri and felt confirmed in their notion that the authority of the 'old' tribal sheikhs was still the safest and fastest way to deal with intertribal raiding.[83] Yet, Nūrī, with his decades of experience in dealing with various state and imperial powers, knew how

[81] Velud, 'French Mandate policy', p. 70.
[82] TNA, FO 481/18/E6564/3655/91 1 May 1929 to 30 April 1930, p. 29.
[83] Ibid.

to play the different sides off against each other in order to assert his own interest and that of his tribe. Back in Damascus he showed no intention of dropping the matter, but instead complained to the French High Commissioner about the British behaviour. The Ruwalla raids, he claimed, had only served to compensate for earlier losses to the Iraqi tribes and made the seizure unjustified.[84] With regard to Peake's operation in Transjordan, too, Nūrī felt unfairly treated, since the raids on the Jordanian Ḥuwaitāt, as he claimed, had not been carried out by his tribesmen but by a dissident section of the Ruwalla who had left him in 1926 to join the Wahhabis in the Najd. The French met Nūrī's complaint with an open ear. The French High commissioner, Henri Ponsot, instantly sent a letter to his British counterpart and the Iraqi minister of interior protesting against Glubb's operation.[85] At the same time, he used the opportunity to urge that the Syrian-Iraqi conference, which should have taken place in February in Abu Kamal, be resumed in order to achieve a final settlement of all existing claims of the tribes on both sides. Since the British and French had been unable to reach an agreement on the preconditions, the conference had been postponed indefinitely.[86]

Other than the British, the French regularly insisted on closer state cooperation in tribal matters not only with regard to tribal raiding but also to tax collection.[87] This was mainly to circumvent the involvement of tribal intermediaries and to maintain control over the British-Iraqi intentions towards the Syrian tribes. Besides the ever-present fear of a union of tribal leaders in Syria, the French also suspected the Iraqi government of seeking to form an anti-Syrian tribal alliance on Iraqi territory. Attempts of the Iraqi government to win tribal loyalties by tax exemptions and gifts to tribal leaders, as well as the British rapprochement with Ibn Saud in 1927, fuelled the paranoiac

[84] TNA, FO 371/14555/E3610/251/89, 'Haute Commissariat de la Republique Française à son Excellence Sir Humphrys Haute-Commissaire de sa Majesté Britannique en Irak, Bagdad', 19 May 1930, p. 2.

[85] Ibid.

[86] CADN, Cabinet politique, ISL/1/V 563, 'Note A.S. de la conférence Syro-Irakienne projetée à Abou-Kemal et de la sasie de gages sur les troupeaux 'Amārāt', 18 avril 1931.

[87] CADN, Cabinet politique, ISL/1/V 561, 'Frontière Syro-Irakienne, Perception de l'oueidi des Chammars', 1930 and TNA, Air 23/158, 'Humphrey, British High Commissionner of Iraq to Ponsot, French High Commissionner of Syria', 17 April 1931.

vision of the French that Syria would soon be surrounded by a pan-Arab tribal union under British tutelage.[88] To satisfy the Syrian tribes in their demands towards the Iraqi tribes was thus also important to ensure tribal loyalties and to prevent further emigration to other state territories. Moreover, there was a danger that the ongoing feuds between the 'Anaza, but also between various other tribes, would get out of control and cause a major split within the Syrian tribes. This, in turn, would have posed a serious threat to the security situation in the desert. The French thus simultaneously made domestic political efforts to defuse the situation and set up a peace conference in Palmyra in May 1930 to which they invited the forty most important tribal sheikhs, forcing them to sign a curfew that would end the state of warfare between them. At the same time, several measures that extended state control over the tribes such as the stricter punishment of raiding and the raising of livestock taxes were implemented and Nūrī's and other tribal leaders' tax share was cut.[89] The restriction of Bedouin autonomy, and of Nūrī's privileges in particular, made it all the more important to represent the interest of the Ruwalla and other Syrian tribes towards the British.

Yet the British-Iraqi authorities rejected Ponsot's suggestion for the reconsideration of the Ruwalla seizure in a joint conference, arguing that the usual procedure would not apply in this case since the raids of the Ruwalla had rather 'the nature of a hostile invasion into Iraq [than of] a conflict between tribes'.[90] Also with regard to the confiscation of the Ruwalla camels by Peake in Transjordan, the British refused to negotiate the matter. In view of the 'obvious ill will' of the British-Iraqi authorities, the French had to look for other ways to satisfy the Syrian tribes and to force the cooperation of the British on the 'Anaza conflict.[91] Such an opportunity was presented to them when the 'Amārāt together with other Iraqi tribes in spring 1930, soon after

---

[88] CADN, Cabinet politique, ISL/1/V 563, 'Compte-rendu de mission', 13 mars 1933.

[89] CADN, Cabinet politique, ISL/1/V, 552, 'Expose de la situation des tribus nomades en 1930', 1930.

[90] TNA, FO 371/14556/E4555/251/89, 'Copy of memorandum NO. C/1955 dated the 18th June 1930, from the Ministry of Interior, Baghdad, to the Ministry of Foreign Affairs, Baghdad', p. 6.

[91] CADN, Cabinet politique, ISL/1/V 552, 'Expose de la situation des tribus nomades en 1930', 1930, p. 13.

Glubb's operation, moved to Sukhna on Syrian territory where grazing conditions were particularly favourable. After having tried in vain to find an agreement with the British-Iraqi authorities on the preconditions for a joint conference, the French commander of the Contrôle Bedouin Colonel Callais proposed to seize camels from the Iraqi tribes in order to restitute them to the Syrian tribes. When the ʿAmārāt raided some smaller Syrian tribes and it became clear that a conference that could have settled the dispute diplomatically was unlikely to happen in the near future, Callais' proposal for the seizure was eventually approved.[92] In August 1930 the French-Syrian authorities thus confiscated more than 800 camels from the ʿAmārāt as well as several hundred from other Iraqi tribes that were camping with the latter and distributed them among the Syrian tribes.

*From a tribal to an interstate conflict in the early 1930s*

At first it seemed that the seizure of the ʿAmārāt camels did not fail in its intended effect as the British-Iraqi authorities eventually agreed to a joint commission meeting that should settle the outstanding claims of the Iraqi and Syrian tribes. However, they refused to enter any negotiations before the camels seized by the French authorities were fully restored to the Iraqi tribes.[93] The fulfilment of this condition encountered several difficulties, such as the refusal of the ʿAmārāt to accept the camels that were returned by the French as they were not the same as those that had been confiscated.[94] Additionally, the Syrian tribes themselves began to make individual arrangements with the ʿAmārāt and the Iraqi authorities for the restitution of the camels, which added to the confusion of the situation.[95] The French suggestion for settling the affair with a lump sum payment helped little to find a way out of the impasse.[96] The longer the affair of the 'camel dispute' dragged on, the more complicated it became to consider the demands of the tribes involved and the less likely it was to find a quick diplomatic solution. As a

[92] CADN, Cabinet politique, ISL/1/V 563, 18 avril 1931.

[93] TNA, FO 371/14556/E5598/251/89, 'From High Commissioner Baghdad to Consul General, Beyrout', 22 September 1930.

[94] CADN, Cabinet politique, ISL/1/V 563, 'Note au sujet des chameaux Amarats', 19 mai 1934.

[95] CADN, Cabinet politique, ISL/1/V 552, 'Sasie effectuée sur Amarat', 22 novembre 1930.

[96] CADN, Cabinet politique, ISL/1/V 563, 'Note au sujet des chameaux Amarats', 19 mai 1934.

result, the planned Syrian-Iraqi conference was postponed repeatedly. Even though, growing presence of police units in areas of potential tribal disturbances impeded larger incidents, raiding between the Syrian and Iraqi tribes, albeit on a smaller scale, went on and added new demands for the restitution of livestock.[97]

What had begun as a dispute between two sections of the ʿAnaza tribes evolved in the early 1930s into an interstate conflict over the question of tribal policies and territorial sovereignty in the Iraqi–Syrian borderland and beyond. In view of the imminent demarcation of state borders, both the French-Syrian and the British-Iraqi government increasingly encouraged Bedouin tribes to relocate to their territory in order to claim tribal lands in the border area. In Iraq, which officially became independent in 1932, King Faisal further saw the predominantly Sunni Bedouin tribes as potential allies to strengthen his position against the national Shiʿi majority and intensified efforts to win the loyalties of the powerful ʿAnaza tribes. Until the mid-1930s, for example, he persuaded a large part of the ʿAbada section of the Sbaʿa to move to Iraq.[98] As for the 'camel dispute', Faisal and the Iraqi government were similarly interested in restoring the good relations with Nūrī Ibn Shaʿlān, which had suffered from the repressive operations against the Ruwalla. In 1932 and 1933 the Iraqi, with Glubb's support, had again confiscated large numbers of camels from the Ruwalla as a compensation for the ʿAmārāt seizure as well as for raids by the Ruwalla on Iraqi tribes that camped in the Najd.[99] However shortly after, Faisal offered Nūrī a compensation payment of 600 lira for the seized camels and restored a third of the animals to the Ruwalla.[100] These deals were usually made on the quiet, without officially informing the French authorities and underlined the claim of the British-Iraqi authorities that tribal affairs on Iraqi territory are their sole responsibility. On another occasion, when the Sbaʿa got raided by the Jordanian Ḥuwaitāt in Ruṭba, the Iraqi authorities applied to Glubb in Transjordan who then forced the Ḥuwaitāt to restitute the livestock to the

---

[97] TNA, Air 23/68, 'Report Western Desert', 13 January 1931.

[98] Büssow, 'Negotiating the future of a Bedouin polity', pp. 81–83.

[99] CADN, Cabinet politique, ISL/1/V 563, Sasie Amarat, 'Note sur les saisies effectuées par le gouvernement irakien sur des tribus syriennes', not dated.

[100] CADN, Cabinet politique, ISL/1/V 563, 'Feuille de Renseignement', 19 mai 1934.

Sba'a. Such actions by the British-Iraqi authorities on behalf of a Syrian tribe without the involvement of the French led to loud protest from the latter.[101]

Other state actors, such as the Saudi government, were simultaneously eager to control tribal affairs on their territory and to safeguard tribal loyalties. When the Ruwalla complained to Ibn Saud that they had been victims of numerous Sba'a raids on Saudi territory, the latter protested to the French-Syrian authorities on behalf of the Ruwalla arguing that 'the existing law in the Najd' would not allow him to 'ignore raids that took place on his territory'.[102] In a similar manner, Ibn Saud negotiated a deal with the British-Iraqi authorities for the restitution of camels to the Dughmān, the Najdi sections of the Ruwalla, whose animals had been confiscated by Glubb. By the early 1930s thus various national and imperial governments had become involved in the 'camel dispute'. Increasing rivalry between different state powers claiming sovereignty over parts of *bādiyat al-Shām* and their efforts to win tribal loyalties offered new spaces of agency for the Bedouin, who got the governments to act on their behalf and represent their interests to the neighbouring states.

In 1932 an international commission deployed by the League of Nations began to demarcate the Iraqi–Syrian border. Yet, it was not until 1934 that the British-Iraqi and the French-Syrian governments resumed direct negotiations with regard to the 'camel dispute'. While the former finally accepted the sum of the French compensation payments for the confiscations of the 'Amārāt camels, the latter consented to refrain from re-negotiating the official seizures of the Iraqi and Transjordan governments on the Ruwalla. In the long term, governments on both sides could not avoid cooperation with regard to cross-border mobility of Bedouin tribes. Among other factors, it was the desert grazing conditions in 1934 forcing many Iraqi tribes to move into Syria that gave the impetus for the British-Iraqi side to acquiesce to a joint conference and led to a rapprochement between the two sides. After a preliminary meeting in Baghdad in May, the actual conference took place in October in Palmyra with the presence of tribal and state authorities from Iraq and Syria as well as Jordanian and Saudi representatives. Eventually, all

---

[101] CADN, Cabinet politique, ISL/1/V 564, 'Rezzou Houeitat sur Sbaa', 9 octobre 1933.

[102] CADN, Cabinet politique, ISL/1/V 564, 'Note sure les renseignements demandés par le Délégue du Nedjd au sujet des biens réclamés aux tribus syriennes par les tribus roualla campant au Djauf', 1934.

claims between the Bedouin tribes were officially settled and the results were stipulated in agreements signed by the paramount sheikhs of the 'Anaza and other tribes.[103] The Palmyra conference did not lift the fundamental mistrust between the governments, nor did it put an end to tribal conflicts and cross-border raiding. Nevertheless, it can be seen as a watershed at the end of a period in which power structures and tribal-state relations in the Middle Eastern borderlands had undergone profound transformations.

By the mid-1930s the desert and steppe region of the *bādiyat al-Shām* was largely pacified. More consistent state intervention reduced the number of raids considerably. Yet, as one of Oppenheim's informants in Iraq claimed, state repression did not completely eliminate the tribal raids but rather led to them occurring more 'in silence'.[104] This was in part due to the fact that the sheikhs who were responsible for their tribe paid high fines for violating the ban on raids.[105] Several external factors contributed to the weakening of the Bedouin tribes, which facilitated the restriction and control of tribal raiding. Thus, many Bedouin tribes had suffered enormous herd losses due to a serious drought that peaked in the early 1930s.[106] At the same time, the world economic crisis of 1929 had begun to take its toll on the pastoralist tribes: the collapse of the wool market in the USA, which was an important place for the export of Middle Eastern wool, meant a severe setback for the pastoralist economy.[107] The stricter enforcement of the raiding ban eventually deprived the Bedouin of what had long been an important means of compensating for losses.[108] The combination of these factors dealt a severe blow to their power and autonomy. As a result, many Bedouin suffered from

---

[103] CADN, Cabinet politique, ISL/1/V 564, Haut Commissaire de la République en Syrie et au Liban à M. le Ministre des affaires étrangères, 8 juin 1934.

[104] RWWA 601, 158, 'Abdul Aziz Reise, Razzu, Schammar', 1937, p. 9.

[105] Ibid.

[106] TNA, Air 23/69, 'Intelligence Report Western Desert from January 1932 February 1932'.

[107] Françoise Métral, 'Transformations de l'élévage nomade et économie bédouine dans la première moitié du vingtième siècle', in Ronald Jaubert (ed.), *Les marges arides du croissant fertile : peuplements, exploitation et contrôle des ressources en Syrie du Nord* (Lyon: Maison de l'Orient et de la Méditerranée, 2006), p. 91.

[108] For the economic function of raiding see: Louise Sweet, 'Camel Raiding of North Arabian Bedouin: A Mechanism of Ecological Adaption', *American Anthropologist, New Series*, Vol. 67, No. 5/1 (October 1965), pp. 1132–1150.

hunger and poverty and migrated to the cities in search of work or became shepherds of the sheikhs and urban notables' herds or tenant farmers on the land of the large landowners. However, from the mid-1930s onwards, favourable weather conditions and a once again flourishing market for livestock products, as well as the relative political stability in the desert and steppe regions, led to a resurgence of nomadic pastoralism.[109] Bedouin tribes continued their seasonal migrations criss-crossing international borders that ran through the *bādiyat al-Shām* throughout the interwar period and beyond. Increasing numbers of police and customs posts, as well as the expansion of the road network, intensified state control and changed mobility regimes in the desert.[110] In many states the Bedouin became important partners of such desert mobility regimes due to their knowledge of the territory and of the tribal landscape.[111] At the same time, they continued to use this knowledge to undermine state structures, for example by evading state authorities and establishing smuggling networks.

During the turbulent period of the Second World War, when Syria and Iraq were (re)occupied by British forces and state control over the desert and steppe lands weakened again, many Bedouin tribes took advantage of the situation to resume their raiding activities.[112] The extended autonomy, however, did not last long. In the post-war period of decolonisation, Arab national governments in Syria began to set up 'new programmes of sedentarisation and detribalisation to bind desert populations to the fate of the nation'.[113] In Syria, all remaining privileges of the Bedouin tribes were officially abolished under the United Arab Republic in 1958, which ultimately led to the migration of many 'Anaza communities to Saudi Arabia. Nevertheless, as research on a more contemporary period has shown, Bedouin identity and nomadic

---

[109] Métral, 'Transformation de l'élévage', p. 93.

[110] See Chapter Eight for further discussion.

[111] The most striking example is the establishment of Glubb's Desert force in Transjordan in 1931, also known as the Arab Legion. The paramilitary force protected Transjordan's desert borderlands and largely consisted of members from Bedouin tribes.

[112] For an overview see TNA, FO 226/271.

[113] Robert S. G. Fletcher, 'Decolonization and the Arid World', in Martin Thomas and Andrew S. Thompson (eds), *The Oxford Handbook of the Ends of Empire* (Oxford: Oxford University Press, 2018), p. 381.

pastoralism continue to exist and exert decisive influence over many states and societies of the Middle East.[114]

## Conclusion

As it has been argued recently, studying the 'Bedouin component' across the desert and steppe regions 'can open new perspectives on important debates in Middle Eastern historiography'.[115] Driven by a similar conviction, this chapter has aimed to explore the roles played by the Bedouin in state formation processes during the interwar years. Focusing on the *bādiyat al-Shām*, and the Iraqi–Syrian borderlands in particular, it has examined two interrelated questions. First, how did states extend their sovereignty over the desert and steppe lands situated at the margins of the post-Ottoman nation states in the Middle East? Second, how did tribal-states relations develop within these processes? In seeking answers to such inquiries, this chapter has zoomed in on an affair known as the 'camel dispute', which took place at a time of regional upheavals during the late 1920s and early 1930s when nation states and state borders were in a process of being consolidated. What started as a dispute between different sections of the 'Anaza Bedouin tribes, as we have seen, soon evolved into an interstate conflict between British Iraq and French Syria.

As this episode has illustrated, the consolidation of state control in the borderlands was not a linear process emanating from the centre to the periphery, but rather one that emerged against the backdrop of negotiations between different state and non-state actors in the borderlands. In particular, as I have argued, it was the cross-border mobility of Bedouin tribes that made them so central to such negotiation processes. Various interstate agreements regulated administrative responsibilities over people and territory in the borderlands. However, as the affair of the 'camel dispute' illustrated, interstate cooperation was often obstructed by differing interpretations and objectives of governments regarding such agreements. The imminent demarcation of state borders moreover intensified the competition for resources and sovereignty in

[114] Dawn Chatty, 'The Bedouin in Contemporary Syria. The persistence of Tribal Authority and Control', *Middle East Journal*, Vol. 64, No. 1 (Winter 2010).

[115] Johann Büssow, Kurt Franz and Stefan Leder, 'The Arab East and the Bedouin Component in Modern History: Emerging Perspectives on the Arid Lands as a Social Space', *Journal of Economic and Social History of the Orient*, Vol. 58, No. 1/2 (2015), p. 1.

the borderlands. Thus, cross-border policing of Bedouin tribes, particularly the regulation of tribal conflicts, became a bone of contention between the British-Iraqi and French-Syrian governments and, at the same time, a means to pressure one another and assert claims of territorial sovereignty.

However, the 'camel-dispute' also highlights that the Bedouin were not merely objects of negotiations between state governments but rather pursued their own objectives. Increasing state rivalries and their free movement across state borders allowed them to advance their political and economic interests within different states. At the same time, they not always relied on state intermediaries but also negotiated directly among themselves when diplomatic channels failed. The comparison of source material from competing imperial powers helps reveal such spaces of agency within which Bedouin tribes operated. Yet, the agencies of ordinary members of tribes appear only fragmentarily, and the sources tend to give more insight into the roles played by Bedouin elite actors such as Nūrī Ibn Shaʿlān. The latter, as we have seen, exploited state rivalries and diverging strategies of tribal policies and in so doing skillfully played off different national and imperial state authorities against each other. Recent studies have shown how the expansion of state control into the desert borderlands of Iraq and Syria have gradually limited the authority and influence of Bedouin sheikhs.[116]

Yet, as the example of Nūrī Ibn Shaʿlān illustrates, the cross-border relationships with various state powers, which sought to secure the loyalty of powerful local actors, also enabled such figures to continue to be influential political actors in the post-Ottoman nation states.

---

[116] See e.g. Büssow 'Negotiating the Future of Bedouin Polity' and Fletcher, 'The ʿAmārāt'.

# AFTERWORD:
# NON/STATE ACTORS, TIMELINES,
# BORDER AND/VERSUS TERRITORY,
# GLOBAL CONTEXTS

## Cyrus Schayegh

Packed with insight and expertly curated by Ramazan Hakkı Öztan and Jordi Tejel, this volume has two fundamental messages relevant to scholars of the post-Ottoman Middle East in particular and to modern historians in general. Borders were shaped by both non-state and state actors, who interplayed; and people experienced life on and across borders in wildly different ways.[1] This was the effect of complex mobility regimes, a concept that, developed in 2005,[2] is analysed in this volume's introduction and brought to life in the chapters.

Having had the privilege to think with those chapters, I have divided my text into four parts. These are exploratory, for an afterword should be short. I start with outlining an ideal-type four-stage approach to interwar *mashriq*

---

[1] As Öztan and Tejel's introduction shows, they build on earlier works such as Inga Brandell (ed.), *State Frontiers: Borders and Boundaries in The Middle East* (London: I. B. Tauris, 2006), on the present times; see also e.g. Sabri Ateş, *Ottoman-Iranian Borderlands: Making a Boundary, 1843–1914* (Cambridge: Cambridge University Press, 2013), p. 3, who 'highlights the role played by borderland communities in the process of [Ottoman-Qajar] boundary making' from the mid-1800s.

[2] Ronen Shamir, 'Without Borders? Notes on Globalization as a Mobility Regime', *Sociological Theory*, Vol. 23 (2005), pp. 197–217.

border-making – an exercise meant to fine-tune the afore-noted issue of the role played by state/non-state actors. Next come two notes on timelines. The interwar *mashriq*'s borders did not develop synchronously, some even having Ottoman roots; and they did not develop linearly. Then, I review the distinction between border and territory, including a discussion of the 'central periphery', a case I explored in a 2017 monograph.[3] I end by zooming out to global contexts.

## 1: State and Non-state Actors in Four Stages of Border Making

Let me begin by noting that it would be fascinating to explore how sea and air border making aligned, and did not, with land borders.[4] As for the latter, there is no doubt that both state and non-state actors made and shaped them, as this volume's co-editors and many contributors expertly demonstrate. Having affirmed this crucial point, volume contributors fine-tuned it, showing that the balance between state and non-state actors as well as the composition of each differed in what we could term different ideal-type stages of border making.

In a first stage, people imagined where a future border may lie.[5] As Alex Balistreri shows, central here, at least in nascent Turkey, were parliamentarians, inter alia those drawing up the 1920 *Misak-ı Millî*, and presumably other politicians and intellectuals writing 'articles' and holding 'speeches' (p. 29). Bureaucrats and officers, too, probably thought of 'nation-state borders as "ideological boundaries"' (p. 31). They and the parliamentarians and politicians, as well as some intellectuals, were state actors who seem to be quite central in this stage. But three qualifications are in order. Turkey was

---

[3] Cyrus Schayegh, *The Middle East and the Making of the Modern World* (Cambridge, MA: Harvard University Press, 2017).

[4] On air, see Priya Satia, *Spies in Arabia: The Great War and the Cultural Foundation of Britain's Covert Empire in the Middle East* (Oxford: Oxford University Press, 2008), p. 7, discussing the relationship between British problems of 'seeing'/understanding the wartime Middle East and its postwar use of air policing, which could not be 'seen', as it were. On the sea, see e.g. Kobi Cohen-Hattab, *Zionism's Maritime Revolution* (Berlin: de Gruyter, 2019).

[5] For an influential related work, see Thongchai Winichakul, *Siam Mapped: A History of the Geo-body of a Nation* (Honolulu: University of Hawaii Press, 1997).

*de jure* recognised internationally only in 1923; hence, at least international legal historians may not see these actors as unproblematically representing a state. (Indeed, historians of different sub-disciplines may always disagree on the stateness of a particular sort of actor.) Moreover, these actors' professional background and their political/bureaucratic role in the nascent state differed: state actors are not identical. And their view of future borders may well have been influenced by the behaviour of, and texts by, non-state actors living on the ground.[6]

A second stage concerned negotiating the border and drawing it on maps. This is when state actors appear most plainly at the forefront. Think for instance of Balistreri's Bekir Sami Bey, Georgiy Chicherin and Henry Franklin-Bouillon. A related point is that, as both Balistreri and Öztan's chapters argue, borders can be a means to a higher political goal. Their course can be sacrificed on the altar of national independence or security, which are ultimately determined by state actors. But also here, there are qualifications. Certainly the actors who led and finalised the negotiations were of the highest rank and they belonged to the government executive: the three afore-mentioned men were two foreign ministers and a plenipotentiary, respectively. In Turkey, the resulting border produced a massive clash with lesser-ranked state actors from another government branch, the legislative. Moreover, a border line on the negotiated map sometimes takes into account and follows on-the-ground stakes, which, however, often need to be large enough for the map-negotiators. That is: they are the stakes not just of any non-state actor but of socio-economically powerful men who hence matter to states. As Lauren Banko reminds us, citing Fredrik Meiton, Yishuvi electricity concessionaire Pinhas Rutenberg 'influenced the route of the 1922 eastern border with Transjordan' (p. 261); Jordi Tejel has shown how 'local community leaders', including Kurds, in and around Mosul helped shape the Turkish-Iraqi frontier.[7]

---

[6] As Ateş, *Borderlands*, pp. 317–18, argues, locals 'at times appropriated and brought the state to the frontier to further their local interests'.

[7] Jordi Tejel Gorgas, 'Making Borders From Below', *Middle Eastern Studies*, Vol. 54 (2018), p. 811. Another, late Ottoman case, in which imperial actors *reacted* to local actors, is Isa Blumi, 'The Frontier as a Measure of Modern Power: Local Limits to Empire in Yemen, 1872–1914', in A. Peacock (ed.), *The Frontiers of the Ottoman World* (Oxford: Oxford University Press, 2009), pp. 303–4.

A third stage may be called implementing the border, that is, actually demarcating the border line and establishing administrative structures. It is here that non-state actors become fully involved. The most fascinatingly intricate case is Katharina Lange's chapter on insurgents in Kurd Dagh, on the Turkish–Syrian border. Their 'motivations [for fighting] . . . were heterogeneous', including local; the border was both 'impediment' and 'resource', including to Turks from further afield who were fugitives; and local leaders like Kor Rashid conditioned supporting France inter alia on 'the establishment of a separate Qadha . . . with locally recruited officials' (pp. 183, 187, 185). Lange also underlines, however, that Turkish officers helped those insurgents. (This pattern held also to the west, across Cilicia, helping to force France to withdraw in 1921.) Certainly imperial French soldiers on the ground would not have categorically distinguished state from non-state soldiers facing them. Moreover, the Kurd Dagh non-state actors may have enjoyed particular leverage because the two bordering states were informally at war and, in this case, did not want to unduly alienate the local population.

The fourth stage, the focus of most chapters here, concerns the long-term administration of, and life in and across borders: 'the lived experience of territoriality'.[8] Characterised by 'contested processes' rather than being 'fixed facts', and by 'interaction[s] between types of territorialities' rather than negotiations of only one, the state's, type of territoriality, this is the most complex stage.[9] State authorities, among other things, enjoyed a 'growing capacity to know, act in and exert control over . . . arid frontiers', erected a complex 'infrastructure of frontier control', and used science, medicine and technology as reasons and pretexts to police borders (Robert Fletcher, p. 316; Banko, p. 267; Sam Dolbee). Meanwhile, people's 'movements and circulations . . . did challenge border infrastructure' and even Bedouin refugee groups kept a 'striking degree of agency', among other examples (Banko, p. 258; Laura Stocker, p. 299). Several aspects deepen this complexity. One was inter-state cooperation across borders, to the point of coordinating trans-

---

[8] Matthew Ellis, 'Over the Borderline? Rethinking Territoriality at the Margins of Empire and Nation in the Modern Middle East (Part I)', *History Compass*, Vol. 13, No. 8 (2015), p. 411.

[9] Ibid., pp. 411, 412, 415 (citing 'Negotiating Territoriality', in Ismael Vaccaro, Charles Dawson, and Laura Zanotti (eds), *Negotiating Territoriality* (New York: Routledge, 2014), p. 1).

desert travel schedules (César Jaquier, pp. 242–43). Another was circularity. State and non-state actors did not simply shape borders in parallel. Rather, their actions were often mutually constitutive, often involving a time lag. Thus, Turkey complicated access by Aleppine merchants – their complaints eventually made France create a refund system – but its ineffectiveness soon forced Aleppines to try staying in business in new ways (Öztan, pp. 97–98). Another example was Bedouin attacks on Syrian-Iraqi desert automobile convoys. This eventually triggered state countermeasures; these in turn eventually made attackers adapt and, as those measures discriminated against (i.e. slowed down) people secondary to imperial interests, such as Indian Muslim pilgrims, these eventually started using additional, alternative routes, in this case to travel from India to Mecca (Jaquier, p. 249).

Yet another aspect concerns how borders affected collective social structure. In Aleppo, some merchants were much more hurt than others.[10] Some Kurd Dagh religious movements 'denounced the glaring economic inequalities between Aghas and poorer peasants' (Lange, p. 191). And in the 1930s, especially in Iraq the 'reorganisation of the political landscape and of regional power distribution simultaneously caused major shifts in tribal alliances, leading to tribal disintegration' (Stocker, p. 328). Last, borders smudged the line between state and non-state actors. Some of the latter turned into – and some continued being – para-state actors. Consider tribal leaders. Some, like Fahd Ibn Hadhdhāl, became state clients, and states 'outsourc[ed]' key policies to 'gatekeepers' and used some leaders as 'proxy force[s]' vis-à-vis other states (Robert Fletcher, pp. 293, 293, 297). Vice versa, a state like Iraq turned (what likely was a specific version of) tribal custom into constitutional law (Stocker, p. 331). And military intelligence officers embedded with tribes (Stocker, p. 329) probably had to adapt to be effective.[11] In sum, the new borders did not simply bring non-state and state actors into more contact. Rather, they

---

[10] Besides Ramazan Hakkı Öztan's chapter, see also Frank Peter, *Les entrepreneurs de Damas: nation, impérialisme et industrialisation* (Paris: L'Harmattan, 2010), esp. pp. 205–7; Geoff Schad, 'Colonialists, Industrialists, and Politicians: the Political Economy of Industrialization in Syria, 1920–1954,' (PhD thesis, University of Pennsylvania, 2001), p. 261.

[11] Or at least thought they adapted: Satia, *Spies*, p. 5: 'long immersion in the desert would, they thought, allow them to replicate the apparently intuitive knowledge-gathering and navigational practices of nomadic Arabs'.

helped bring about various new informal deals in which the very nature of what and who the state and social groups were, and how they interacted, was partially renegotiated.

## 2: Timelines

This development may be framed as a continuation of an earlier new deal, in Ottoman Arab cities from the mid-1800s, between the 'recentralizing' Ottoman central state and well-rooted, powerful urban elites, especially notables, in Arab provinces.

> As Istanbul was penetrating its provinces more forcefully, and with more institutions, it also had to engage – with carrots as much as sticks – the deeply rooted urban notable elites . . . [E]ach city's elite became administratively and socio-culturally more strongly intertwined with Istanbul, which many more than ever got to know first-hand. 'The Ottoman state [and] . . . local elites' were tightly joined as 'unequal parties to self-serving bargains'.[12]

Another new unequal bargain transpired around the same time in the Ottoman-Iranian borderlands. Its manifold people's 'territorial strategies and rationalities' helped shape its halting but real transformation by Istanbul and Tehran, from the 1840s, into a harder, partly demarcated boundary; and a new type of state-society relationship rose in the process.[13] Another new, rather 'equal' bargain linked the Ottomans and the Rashidis of Najd, an area in which Istanbul, fearing British encroachment, took increasing interest from the 1880s.[14]

---

[12] Schayegh, *Middle East*, p. 37; internal quote: Elizabeth Thompson, 'Ottoman Political Reform in the Provinces: the Damascus Advisory Council in 1844–1845', *IJMES*, Vol. 25 (1993), p. 472. See also 'Introduction', in Jens Hanssen, Thomas Philipp and Stefan Weber (eds), *The Empire and the City. Arab Provincial Capitals in the Late Ottoman Empire*, (Würzburg: Ergon, 2002), p. 19; and, already in 1968, Albert Hourani, 'Ottoman Reform and the Politics of Notables', in William Polk and Richard Chambers (eds), *Beginnings of Modernization in the Middle East* (Chicago: University of Chicago Press, 1968), p. 43.

[13] Ateş, *Borderlands*, pp. 5–6.

[14] M. Talha Çiçek, 'The Tribal Partners of Empire in Arabia: the Ottomans and the Rashidis of Najd, 1880–1918', *New Perspectives on Turkey*, Vol. 56 (2017), p. 108.

Yes: postwar borders did signal a departure from late Ottoman times. At the same time, functionally, the continuous renegotiation of state-society relations in and across postwar borders can be seen as part of the aforementioned longer process of re-bargaining, which had started in cities and their rural surroundings and by the later 1800s reached frontier zones.[15] Moreover, many authors in this volume – most explicitly Stocker, on state-tribal relations – see certain late Ottoman realities persisting in the 1920s; real change started around 1930. This periodisation sits well, Stocker notes (p. 321; also Öztan and Tejel, p. 5), with my characterisation, elsewhere, of the 1920s as an 'Ottoman twilight'.[16]

Three additional notes on timelines concern borders more specifically.[17] First, the interwar *mashriq*'s borders did not develop synchronously. In the 1920s–30s some were formally fully delineated much later than others: the Syrian–Turkish border in 1940, for instance. Second, interwar border management developed non-linearly, that is, it was in some ways and times reversible. A good example is the Second World War. In 1941–45 Britain, with considerable success, organised a single wartime Middle East/North Africa-wide economic-administrative area of production, exchange and consumption. Many border arrangements changed. Thus, Turkey, under great war-related economic pressure, joined that area and opened up its southern border. Many Aleppine traders and some manufacturers profited.[18]

The third note echoes this section's first paragraph. Interwar *mashriq* borders did not quite pivot away from late Ottoman reality. Rather, they sharpened processes well underway, though this process, to repeat, remained

---

[15] Eugene Rogan, *Frontiers of the State in the Late Ottoman Empire, 1850–1921* (New York: Cambridge University Press, 1999); Vladimir Hamed-Troyanski, 'Imperial Refuge: Resettlement of Muslims from Russia in the Ottoman Empire, 1860–1914', (PhD thesis, Stanford University, 2018); Nimrod Luz, 'The Remaking of Beersheba', in Itzchak Weismann and Fruma Zachs (eds), *Ottoman Reform and Muslim Regeneration* (London: I. B. Tauris, 2005), pp. 187–209; Janet Klein, *The Margins of Empire: Kurdish Militias in the Ottoman Tribal Zone* (Stanford: Stanford University Press, 2011). See also Reşat Kasaba, *A Moveable Empire: Ottoman Nomads, Migrants, and Refugees* (Seattle: University of Washington Press, 2009).

[16] Schayegh, *Middle East*, chapter 3.

[17] See also Ellis, 'Borderline', p. 413, on periodisation; here, regarding the question of how different disciplines periodise borderlands differently.

[18] Schayegh, *Middle East*, pp. 307–8.

heterogeneous and reversible rather than inexorably leading to ever more state control.[19] Sure, the Ottoman Empire, like other nineteenth-century states, 'failed to realize comprehensive control over bounded political space'.[20] And yet, the late Ottoman *mashriq* had shared international borders with Iran and Egypt. The aforementioned Ottoman-Iranian(-Anglo-Russian[21]) negotiations regarding, and administration of, these borders presaged certain post-war developments; so did an Ottoman-Anglo-Egyptian agreement, under British pressure, in 1906 on the Rafah-Aqaba border and administrative consequences, which was predated by Egyptian khedival attempts since the early 1800s to gain control over the Sinai.[22] In sum, the Ottoman Empire, which had always known a wide 'diversity' of territorial *limes*,[23] was not quite 'borderless' (Öztan and Tejel, p. 3) – certainly not in its last decades. (More broadly, Sabri Ateş argues, territorial sovereignty, including attempts to control frontiers better, started in the Ottoman east, as across Eurasia, in the mid-1600s.[24] This picks up Charles Maier's famous argument about

---

[19] Ellis, 'Borderline'.

[20] Ibid., p. 415, referencing *The Transformation of the World*, Jürgen Osterhammel's magnum opus. A recent study which, however, sees policy changes within the Hamidian period and between it and the Young Turk period is David Gutman, 'Travel Documents, Mobility Control, and the Ottoman State in an Age of Global Migration, 1880–1915', *Journal of the Ottoman and Turkish Studies Association*, Vol. 3, No. 2 (2016), pp. 347–68.

[21] The British and Russian Empires were parties to Ottoman-Iranian border delineation negotiations in the 1840s and to border demarcation commissions in the 1910s: Ateş, *Borderlands,* chapters 2, 5, 6.

[22] Ibid.; Nurit Kliot, 'The Evolution of the Egypt-Israel Boundary', *Boundary and Territory Briefing*, Vol. 1, No. 8 (1995), pp. 1–10; Yitzhak Gil-Har, 'Egypt's North-Eastern Boundary in Sinai', *Middle Eastern Studies*, Vol. 29, No. 1 (1993), pp. 135–48; Yuval Ben-Bassat and Yossi Ben-Artzi, 'The Collision of Empires as Seen from Istanbul: the Border of British-controlled Egypt and Ottoman Palestine as Reflected in Ottoman Maps', *Journal of Historical Geography*, Vol. 50 (2015), pp. 25–36. For 'continuity between imperial and national states' border making, see Liam O'Dowd, 'From a "borderless world" to a "world of borders"', *Environment and Planning D: Society and Space*, Vol. 28 (2010), p. 1042; similarly: Pekka Hämäläinen and Samuel Truett, 'On Borderlands', *Journal of American History*, Vol. 98, No. 2 (2011), p. 340.

[23] A. Peacock (ed.), 'Introduction' in *Frontiers of the Ottoman World* (Oxford: Oxford University Press, 2009), p. 3; also Kemal Karpat and Robert Zens (eds), 'Introduction' in *Ottoman Borderlands* (Madison: University of Wisconsin Press, 2003), p. 1.

[24] Ateş, *Borderlands*, p. 24.

changing modes of territoriality, with different modern stages starting in the mid-1600s, to the late 1700s and 1850s–70s, but not 1920s[25]). An interpretation of the interwar years as sharpening an extant process also explains why the post-Ottoman 'transition . . . to a bordered Middle East' (p. 3) was 'gradual' (Öztan and Tejel, p. 3) and, indeed, incomplete. Even in the 1930s, '*la frontière turco-syrienne n'est . . . pas . . . une ligne fixe et précisément définie [mais] une zone de contention*',[26] and 'although [cross-border tribal] disputes were in theory often successfully settled, the tribes did not necessarily agree with the results, and the government often lacked the will or the means to enforce the decisions' (Stocker, p. 341).

## 3: Borders and/versus Territories

While many contributors to this volume argue and/or show that state initiatives and state-societal interactions formed mobility regimes around borders, many also state or in effect demonstrate that those regimes were not necessarily specific to borders. Rather, those regimes also covered other areas, in however different ways. This view – which is reflected also in classic works on territoriality and on mobility regimes in non-Middle Eastern monographs,[27] and in recent Middle Eastern historical reviews[28] – is here most explicitly embraced by Simon Jackson. He shows that a political centre like Beirut, the French Mandate capital, could also be a 'border zone', as it was an international port city (p. 127). He cites Peter Leary to the effect that 'border making [has] simultaneously specifying and dispersing effect in

---

[25] Charles Maier, 'Transformations of Territoriality, 1600–2000', in Gunilla Budde et al. (eds), *Transnationale Geschichte* (Göttingen: Vandenhoeck & Ruprecht, 2006), pp. 32–55.

[26] Seda Altuğ and Benjamin White, 'Frontières et pouvoirs d'État: La frontière turco-syrienne dans les années 1920 et 1930', *Vingtieme Siecle*, Vol. 103, No. 3 (2009), p. 103.

[27] Maier, 'Transformations.' Shamir, 'Without Borders', pp. 199, 205–8, talks of local, national and regional boundaries and of hyper-ghettos (entire countries) and gated communities. Benjamin Hopkins, *Ruling the Savage Periphery: Frontier Governance and the Making of the Modern State* (Cambridge, MA: Harvard University Press, 2020), argues that nineteenth-century frontiers were less a space and more a set of practices. Each practice was found elsewhere; their combination created a frontier.

[28] Ellis, 'Borderline', p. 411, stresses the 'relationship between borderland identities and modern discourses and practices of territoriality'.

space, causing, for example, both the building of walls at specific frontiers *and* the proliferation of sites of suspicion and verification far beyond the wall' (p. 116). And he invokes a 'rhizomic cartography of dynamically net-worked nodes' (p. 116); a case may be Rutbah (Jaquier, p. 244).

Other contributors to this volume show the blurriness between borders and other areas more implicitly. Bedouin refugee relocations linked border-lands and other areas (Fletcher, pp. 295–301). And Franco-British coordi-nation in managing the Syrian-Iraqi borderlands radiated deep into both countries, affecting spatial organisation of convoys gathered as far back as Baghdad and Damascus (Jaquier, p. 245). On a related note, Stocker men-tions late Ottoman police posts fighting Bedouin tribal raiders (p. 325).[29] Other Middle Eastern historians have noted the blurriness too. Studying the Syrian–Turkish border, Seda Altuğ and Benjamin White have argued that 'the creation [of post-Ottoman borders] forms part of state efforts to impose its authority on the national territory and its populations . . . not only in the border regions but across the entire territory'.[30]

Another example is the area I have called the central periphery, encom-passing southern Lebanon, northern Palestine, southwestern Syria and north-western Transjordan. Here, multiple police tools and tactics were at work. Many were used across Mandate territories. The reason was that the afore-mentioned four areas were not simply peripheral to, and marginal in, their respective country. They also together 'formed a transnationalized transport cross-road at the center of a still firmly integrated *Bilād al-Shām* [Syria, Pales-tine, Lebanon, and Transjordan]. [This] somewhat attenuated their peripheral position within their respective nation-state'. This was the case partly because considerable trade crossed this area, involving not only local but international trajectories, and included illicit goods such as Turkish and Lebanese hashish transported to Egypt. Moreover, activists from one country in *Bilād al-Shām* often crossed the central periphery to be politically active or fight in another

---

[29] For 1920s adaptations of late Ottoman policing, including the re-use of old Ottoman police stations, see Schayegh, *Middle East*, p. 185.

[30] Altuğ and White, 'Frontières,' p. 92. See also Zeynep Kezer, 'Spatializing Difference: The Making of an Internal Border in Early Republican Elazığ, Turkey', *Journal of the Society of Architectural Historians*, Vol. 73, No. 4 (2014), pp. 507–27.

*shāmi* country, triggering considerable police and military interventions also across border lines.[31]

## 4: Global Contexts

What may future research look like? This question evidently has many answers. One concerns global contexts and linkages (see Öztan and Tejel, p. 4).

Contributors mention several developments. Jackson explicitly states the global dimension of the Ford franchise, unpacking how a global economic capitalist map was superimposed on – and to a point interacted with – the geopolitical map after the First World War. More implicit is Jaquier's argument that the 'interplay between the process of state formation and the growth of [automobile] mobility resulted in the creation of new mobility regimes that governed the movement of travellers through the Syrian Desert while discriminating between different forms of travel' (p. 229). An interesting question here would be how automobility and the new state techniques it engendered here compared to, and was in interplay with, other regions, especially imperial ones, in the world. One may pose a similar set of questions to Dolbee's account of the role that veterinary medicine played in legitimising and shaping border management techniques.[32]

Moreover, modern Middle Eastern nationalists' and nationalist politicians' and bureaucrats' thinking about borders and territoriality surely was globally embedded. Did non-Middle Eastern models inform their thinking? Did some confer with, learn from, non-Middle Easterners?

Last, as contributors to this volume and other historians argue, the *mashriq*'s interwar borders were not simply those (characteristic) of nascent

---

[31] Schayegh, *Middle East*, p. 17 (quote), pp. 85–87, 182–83, 242–43, 258–63; Schayegh, 'The Many Worlds of Abud Yasin, or: What Narcotics Trafficking in the Interwar Middle East Can Tell Us about Territorialization', *American Historical Review*, Vol. 116, No. 2 (2011), pp. 273–306. Also Haggai Ram, *Intoxicating Zion: A Social History of Hashish in Mandatory Palestine and Israel* (Stanford: Stanford University Press, 2020); Asher Kaufman, *Contested Frontiers in the Syria-Lebanon-Israel Region: Cartography, Sovereignty, and Conflict* (Baltimore: Johns Hopkins University Press, 2014).

[32] Related, see Aro Velmet, *Pasteur's Empire: Bacteriology and Politics in France, its Colonies, and the World* (New York: Oxford University Press, 2020), showing how Institut Pasteur researchers around the French empire became colonial players.

nation states. Rather, they were shaped by the imperial interests and policies of the European mandate powers too.[33] And crucially, in the interwar decades empires still helped shape, and were shaped by, modes of globalisation and deglobalisation.[34] Let us not 'ben[d too much] toward the telos of the nation', then.[35] This crucial, globally embedded imperial dimension included thinking with, and applying, old and contemporary models – what Jeremy Adelman has called mimesis and which is the subject of a burgeoning literature on interimperial relations.[36] In our case, for instance, some French border specialists were interested in Ancient Rome's use of agricultural-military colonists to secure borders; and the British used British Indian police officials to 'better' police Palestine, including its borders, during the 1936–39 revolt.[37]

To conclude, this wonderfully productive volume has shown that the interwar Middle East is and remains a fascinatingly complex field for studying borders and borderlands. All sorts of societal actors were involved, some turning para-state actors in the process; nascent nation state actors emerged; post-imperial Ottoman issues echoed; European imperial actors and policies mattered; and in various ways new international organisations, especially the League of Naions, played a role, too.

---

[33] Altuğ and White, 'Frontières', pp. 91, 100, invoke a '*limes impérial*'.

[34] Martin Thomas and Andrew Thompson, 'Empire and Globalisation: from "High Imperialism" to Decolonisation', *International History Review*, Vol. 36, No. 1 (2014), pp. 142–70. Related, there is a considerable literature on what some call 'imperial globality'. See e.g. Tony Ballantyne and Antoinette Burton, 'Empires and the Reach of the Global', in Emily Rosenberg (ed.), *A World Connecting, 1870–1945* (Cambridge, MA: Harvard University Press, 2012), pp. 285–431.

[35] Hämäläinen and Truett, 'Borderlands', p. 356.

[36] Jeremy Adelman, 'Mimesis and Rivalry: European Empires and Global Regimes', *Journal of Global History*, Vol. 19 (2015), pp. 77–98; 'Introduction: Encounters of Empires', in Volker Barth and Roland Cvetkovski (eds), *Imperial Co-operation and Transfer, 1870–1930* (London: Bloomsbury, 2015), pp. 3–33; Christoph Kamissek and Jonas Kreienbaum, 'An Imperial Cloud? Conceptualising Interimperial Connections and Transimperial Knowledge', *Journal of Modern European History*, Vol. 14, No. 2 (2016), pp. 164–82.

[37] Altuğ and White, 'Frontières,' p. 100; Gad Kroizer, 'From Dowbiggin to Tegart: Revolutionary Change in the Colonial Police in Palestine during the 1930s', *Journal of Imperial and Commonwealth History*, Vol. 32, No. 2 (2004), pp. 115–33.

# INDEX